Vanity
Karma

Vanity Karma

Ecclesiastes, the Bhagavad-gītā,
and the meaning of life

*A cross-cultural commentary
on the Book of Ecclesiastes*

JAYĀDVAITA SWAMI

THE BHAKTIVEDANTA BOOK TRUST
Los Angeles · Stockholm · Johannesburg · Sydney

Readers interested in the subject of this book
are invited to further pursue their interest here:
www.vanitykarma.com

Publisher's Cataloging-in-Publication

Swami, Jayādvaita.
    Vanity karma : Ecclesiastes, the Bhagavad-gītā and
the meaning of life : a cross-cultural commentary on
the book of Ecclesiastes / Jayādvaita Swami.
    pages cm
Includes bibliographical references and index.
LCCN 2014935896
ISBN-13: 978-0-89213-449-6
ISBN-10: 0-89213-449-6

    1. Bible. Ecclesiastes--Commentaries.
2. Bhagavadgītā--Relation to the Bible. 3. Meaning
(Philosophy)--Religious aspects.   I. Title.

BS1475.53.S93 2014
223'.807

                            QBI14-600074

This paper meets the requirements of
ANSI/NISO Z39.48-1992 (R 1997) (Permanence of Paper).

Text design by Govinda Cordua
Cover design by Raghu Consbruck

To a certain rabbi and a certain priest
and most especially to
His Divine Grace
A. C. Bhaktivedanta Swami Prabhupāda,
my spiritual master

prabhupāda-padaṁ vande
śāstra-sāra-prakāśakam
govinda-bhakti-yogena
jīvānanda-pradāyakam

I offer my respectful homage at the feet of Śrīla Prabhupāda,
who discloses the essence of the Vedic writings.
He gives in abundance the transcendent joy a living being
is meant for, through the yoga of devotional service to Govinda,
Krishna, the reservoir of pleasure.

tarko 'pratiṣṭhaḥ śrutayo vibhinnā
nāsāv ṛṣir yasya matam na bhinnam
dharmasya tattvam nihitam guhāyām
mahājano yena gataḥ sa panthāḥ

"Logical arguments are inconclusive, scriptures various,
and every sage has a different point of view.
The truth of dharma is kept a mystery.
So the way traversed by the great souls – that alone is the path."

— Mahābhārata (*Vana-parva* 313.117)

Contents

Chapter Two

Chapter Three

Chapter Eight

Chapter Ten

Chapter Eleven

Chapter Twelve

Appendices

Foreword

Vanity Karma invites us into an exploration of the meaning of life through deep philosophical reflections and a richly layered dialogue. To do this it places the book of Ecclesiastes (from the Hebrew Bible) in dialogue with the Bhagavad-gītā (from the Hindu epic poem the Mahābhārata), and we quickly find that this is not only an external dialogue but an inner one as well. It begins within the tormented mind and heart of Qohelet, the main speaker in Ecclesiastes, a man who "sees too much," or sees too well, who sees in the world a terrible emptiness, or, still worse, who sees contradictions and an ultimate disparity between what a sensible world should be and what the world in which we find ourselves finally is.

In exploring what it is that so troubles Qohelet and exploring how Qohelet's mind and heart respond, *Vanity Karma* draws upon rich and diverse commentaries, ancient and modern, Jewish and Christian, devout and critical (and many shades between).

The plot thickens. This dialogue also takes place within the author of *Vanity Karma*, whose sudden encounter as a young man with the existential issues thrown before him by Qohelet leads to a deep and far-ranging search for meaning. And finally the dialogue arises within ourselves, because we too, confronting the same issues, search within our own minds and hearts for a way to find harmony and meaning in our lives.

Jayādvaita Swami, recounting his own inner dialogue, tells how he himself responded to Qohelet's words. We learn how, as a young man born of Jewish parents and raised in New Jersey in their tradition, he heard Qohelet's disturbing message that all is vain and empty, a message that disrupted the course of his life. The inner tension this message created started him on a search that led, by a wandering route, to the Bhagavad-gītā, the sacred text most well known and honored within

Indic traditions (and the Indic text most read and known throughout
the world). For more than forty-five years the Swami studies the Gītā, in
which Krishna speaks as the supreme divinity, and pursues the practice
and vision of Krishna Bhakti, "a life dedicated to realizing Krishna, the
Absolute, and serving Krishna with all one's heart."

And now in *Vanity Karma* the Swami revisits Ecclesiastes. In doing
so, he shares with us what he found in Qohelet's words that so profoundly affected him, he reads Ecclesiastes again with a renewed, ma-
tured, and deepened regard, and – a unique contribution – he brings
the understandings he has gained from the Gītā into dialogue with
Ecclesiastes, juxtaposing the two texts, not by putting them side by side
on the page but by bringing their ideas together into a thoughtful, carefully considered work, where the two perspectives sometimes coincide,
sometimes diverge, and all the while engage and enrich us.

In this way, in our final level of dialogue, both Ecclesiastes and the
Gītā speak to us within our own minds and hearts, as they have within
the Swami's, and so each one of us comes into a dialogue with both
texts, a dialogue within each of us about the meaning of our own life.

To bring out for us these inner dialogues, Jayādvaita Swami crosses
cultures and invites us to do so as well. He juxtaposes the insights of
Jewish rabbis who have reflected on Qohelet with insights from the
Bhagavad-gītā. He draws upon Christian commentaries, pulls in a
thread from Buddhism, weaves in experiences from his suburban New
Jersey upbringing, the 1960s counterculture, and his travels in India and
elsewhere.

It is no surprise that Jayādvaita Swami would create such a thoughtful, multi-leveled dialogue. Within the Krishna Bhakti tradition out
of which he comes, we can find teachings and examples of dialogue
in many of the ancient texts. One need not look any further than the
earlier Upanishads, mystical writings that reveal wisdom on the nature
of reality and the self. This wisdom emerges through dialogues between
teachers and students.

Jayādvaita Swami, as both student and teacher, has been focusing
intensely for many years on the perennial wisdom of the Bhagavad-
gītā, which is revealed through dialogue. He thus participates in a tradition that sees dialogue as the very nexus of revelation. Indeed, it is
within this "sacred dialogue" (*dharmyaṁ saṁvādam*, Gītā 18.70) that

"the supreme secret of union with the divine" (*guhyam param yogam*, Gītā 18.75) is revealed.

The Swami's tradition promotes dialogue as a way to draw from the divine, share with others what one has drawn, and create an elevated state of community in which participants in dialogue reach a state of fullness as well as the greatest pleasure (see Gītā 10.9). Indeed, the very practice of Krishna Bhakti rests on the essential components of dialogue: the humility of receptive hearing (*śravaṇam*), the passion of authentic responsiveness and contribution (*kīrtanam*), and the grace that comes to speakers and hearers alike as they are collectively elevated to a new experience of community and a greater participation within the divine.

The kind of careful self-scrutiny, self-reflection, and self-honesty required for the level of inner dialogue found in *Vanity Karma* is an example for the rest of us. In this age, at this time, the world would be a better place if we, like the Swami, could delve deeply into ourselves to find out who we are and, further, engage in an interior dialogue that contributes to a greater sense of community, to a more heightened sense of humanity, and ultimately to an even greater dedication to divinity.

Graham M. Schweig, PhD
Professor of Philosophy and Religion
Christopher Newport University, Virginia

Preface

For me no book has asked more powerfully than Ecclesiastes what the meaning is for our life – or whether life has any meaning at all – and no book has responded as deeply as the Bhagavad-gītā. *Vanity Karma* therefore brings these two books together. It takes you through the full text of Ecclesiastes with the Bhagavad-gītā as your companion.

As wisdom meets wisdom, as found in these two books – one biblical, the other from spiritual India – we see the daily issues of our world in a different way as we rise above them to consider what life is for, what ultimate profit we can gain from it, what meaning, what happiness, what lasting value. And as we read, we grow in wisdom ourselves.

At the start, we need not know either book. As we go along we'll become familiar with both. And I presume from you no particular spiritual or philosophical commitments. The questions raised here are for everyone.

I begin by telling the story of how I first encountered Ecclesiastes, how it affected me, and how it led me eventually to the Bhagavad-gītā and the teachings of "Krishna consciousness." And then I dive into our study of Ecclesiastes itself.

You will find this a detailed study but not a heavily technical one. I use plain language, and I focus on what the text means to me, and what it might mean to you. Yet in so doing I draw upon the insights of biblical scholars, both traditional and academic. And I draw not only on the Bhagavad-gītā but also on other writings from the tradition to which it belongs.

Together, then, we may consider, you and I, what understandings we might gather about the most important question in human life – the question of what we best ought to do with it.

Acknowledgments

Many friends and well-wishers have helped me with this book. My thanks go first to Graham Schweig, professor, author, and lifelong friend. Having heard from me several decades ago of my interest in Ecclesiastes, he prodded me and finally insisted that I write this book, and he served as my advisor throughout. My gratitude to my lifelong friend Satsvarūpa dāsa Goswāmī for his guidance and encouragement and for his example in serving as a prolific Krishna conscious writer. My thanks to Edwin Bryant for putting at my disposal his excellent library.

Ūrmilā Devī Dāsī (Edith Best), with her brilliant Krishna conscious Jewish mind, read my manuscript and offered invaluable suggestions. Among other helpful readers were Draviḍa Dāsa, Nāgarāja Dāsa, Kaiśorī Devī Dāsī, Kenneth Valpey, David Wolf, Mahāsaumya Dāsa, Kālacandajī Dāsa, and Śraddhāñjalī Devī Dāsī. Nathan Katz, the pioneer in the field of Indo-Judaic studies, read a portion of the manuscript and offered helpful suggestions and criticisms, both equally welcome.

Apart from affection and encouragement, my mother, Gloria Shapiro, still sharp at 90, saved me from some wayward word choices and served as the go-to person for several details in my Introduction.

A fortunate outcome of my writing this book has been a friendly connection with Tremper Longman III, the author of the Ecclesiastes volume for the New International Commentary on the Old Testament. He was kind enough to read my manuscript and encourage me, as well as share with me some of his own writings. I am grateful to have benefited not only from his books but from his personal company.

For hearing portions of the manuscript and offering useful feedback, my thanks to students and faculty at Bhaktivedanta College in Belgium, the Krishna House at the University of Florida, Gainesville, and the Oxford Centre for Hindu Studies.

A group of friends deserve my thanks for reading the manuscript with me in Māyāpur, India: Sureśvara Dāsa, Gītā Nāgarī Dāsa, Murāri Gupta Dāsa, Omkar Chester, and my French friend Vāsudeva Dāsa.

For graciously affording me personal interviews, my thanks to the biblical scholars Michael A. Eaton, C. L. Seow, and Izak J. J. Spangenberg.

To the late Irwin M. Blank, in my childhood and youth the congenial rabbi of the temple to which my family belonged, a special note of thanks. He is not the rabbi I mention in my Dedication. But after I took up the path of a Krishna devotee he and I were sometimes in touch, and when I brought up my interest in Ecclesiastes it is he who recommended to me the work of the Jewish scholar Robert Gordis.

Another rabbi to whom I am indebted is Sheldon R. Isenberg, who guided me in choosing among various methods of Hebrew transliteration.

In 2007 I had the good fortune to attend a small gathering of young Krishna conscious scholars addressed by Francis X. Clooney, SJ. Among other topics, he spoke on how our background affects our reading of a text and how the text changes us. He is not the priest I mention in my Dedication. But his thoughts helped me in writing this book, and for this I am grateful to him as well.

Several Krishna devotees assisted me in locating and obtaining books: Keśīhanta Dāsa, Madhupati Dāsa, Śyāmānanda Dāsa, Pradyumna Miśra Dāsa, Vāsudeva Dāsa (from Holland), Ānanda Sevā Dāsa, and others. Ānanda Sevā also helped me with my reading of Ibn Ezra in Spanish.

Guṇāvatāra Dāsa (Gad Loven), from Israel, helped me with points of Hebrew, as did Hanan and Tsurit Schwefel (also from Israel) and Greg Schmidt Goering. Matsyāvatāra Dāsa helped me with points of Sanskrit.

Responsibility for whatever shortcomings the book still has lies not with those who gave their help but with me.

My thanks to Svavāsa Dāsa, my publisher at the Bhaktivedanta Book Trust, for his full-hearted encouragement and support and to Gauranga Kishore Rader and Yudhiṣṭhira Dāsa, who steered the book through to final publication. For help in publishing I am also grateful to Brahmatīrtha Dāsa and Nila Khurana, to Advaita Candra Dāsa of Torchlight Publishing, to John Kremer, and to Simon Warwick-Smith and Karen Misuraca of Warwick Associates.

For the design of the text my thanks to Govinda Cordua, and for the covers Raghu Consbruck. My thanks also to these longtime colleagues: for the layout, to Duḥkhahantrī Devī Dāsī and Yamarāja Dāsa, for proofreading to Nāgarāja Dāsa, and for adjusting the notes for the ebook version to Tattvavit Dāsa.

My thanks to Guru-prasāda Dāsa of Ottawa and to Dmitriy Yankauskas, Rustam Karimov, Madhupati Dāsa, and others for their donations to help produce the book.

Following tradition and following my heart, I offer my gratitude and humble respects to my spiritual master, His Divine Grace A.C. Bhaktivedanta Swami Prabhupāda. Once when Śrīla Prabhupāda went on a visit to teach in Honolulu, the local newspaper reported, "The swami is a small man, but he has a big message." It is that message that inspires this book. I offer my respects to his predecessors as well, who inspired him to inspire me and others. And I offer my respects to you, my reader, with gratitude for your picking up this book. May you find truth in the wisdom of Ecclesiastes and still further truth in the wisdom of the Vedic sages.

Introduction

A first encounter

I don't remember the year. I was about twelve or thirteen, and that would mean 1961 or '62. I was sitting in a classroom in Temple Sinai in Tenafly, New Jersey, on a Sunday morning for "religious school." We wouldn't call it Sunday School, because that's what the Christians had, but the idea seemed about the same. The temple was just over the border from Englewood, where I lived, and mothers and fathers from Englewood and Tenafly would drive their kids to the temple to endure a couple of hours of Jewish instruction.

This was a "Reform Jewish" temple, so the instruction was pretty light. We'd have maybe an hour of Hebrew class, where we'd learn the alphabet and some vocabulary and grammar. One year, I remember, our teacher was a woman from Israel, with a strong Israeli accent, and she'd teach us the kind of phrases we'd need to know to catch a bus in Tel Aviv. And later for another hour we'd hear some small portion of the scriptures.

For a while it was Genesis and Exodus. The Israelites had escaped Egypt and fled to the Red Sea, whose waters, by the grace of God, had parted to grant them passage and had then joined again, drowning the pursuing Pharaoh and his army. Modern scholars, our teacher explained, had found that the Hebrew term translated "Red Sea" could also mean "Sea of Reeds." And so what the Israelites had actually encountered was probably not a sea but a reed-filled swamp. They had reached it at low tide, when passage would be feasible, but when the high tide came the waters rose, and that's how the Pharaoh and his army perished. And so, you see, the story was reasonable; it could all be scientifically explained.

I kept my mouth shut, but I remember thinking, "Well, okay, I guess that makes sense. But then what was the need of God? He was superfluous. The story makes sense, but what's the point? Anyway, just as well."

Such was religious school: maybe thirty boys and girls sitting in a classroom on a Sunday morning, in a modern institutional room with cinder-block walls painted a light institutional color, and passing notes to one another and sometimes cutting jokes and throwing spitballs or looking out the aluminum-framed windows and waiting for class to be over so we could get out and go back home and get on with our weekend.

For a few weeks, though, we had a different teacher. Our regular teacher had gotten sick, or perhaps there was some other staffing problem, and we had a new fellow, a younger man who dressed in what impressed me as an intellectual fashion, casual and tweedy, and I think we were told he was actually a rabbi, a Conservative rabbi – that is, from the Conservative denomination of Judaism (which meant a little more traditional) – though in manner he came off just like a regular guy, except with this collegiate edge to him, like a cool young professor.

And the book he started to teach us was Ecclesiastes. "The words of Qohelet, the son of David, king in Jerusalem." That's how the book began. Our young professor explained to us that this must have been the famed King Solomon, great in wisdom and boundless in wealth, for no other son of David had ever been king in Jerusalem.

That was the intro, and now the book itself began. "Vanity of vanities, saith Qohelet, vanity of vanities; all is vanity." I knew what vanity was: It was a sort of pride, especially the kind that girls had when they thought they had good looks. Wasn't there something called a "vanity table," where a girl could sit and admire herself in the mirror and fuss over her makeup? When a girl in school was terribly stuck up, other girls would put her down as "vain."

I had it wrong. Here in Ecclesiastes, our teacher explained, *vanity* meant something else. *Vanity* meant that which was meaningless, pointless, empty, hollow. "Vanity of vanities" was a superlative, like "wonder of wonders," so it meant "superlative pointlessness." And "All is vanity" meant "Everything is pointless. Everything is meaningless."

Qohelet (pronounced "ko-*hell*-et") began to lay out his case. A man works his whole life, and what does he get for it? Generations come and go, the sun forever rises and sets, the wind blows about in circles, and the rivers endlessly pour into the sea. And for what? For nothing.

Whatever has happened before will happen again, whatever has been done before will be done again, "and there is nothing new under the sun." The people who lived before us have been forgotten, and we will be forgotten next. So whatever we do is vain, pointless, "a chasing after wind."

This was a far cry from the creation story of Genesis or the pious histories of the Jews struggling under the Pharaoh. I found myself focusing, paying attention.

King Solomon, already wise, undertakes to know still more clearly what is wisdom, and what is madness and what is folly. And he finds that this too is pointless, or worse, "For in much wisdom is much grief; and he that increaseth knowledge increaseth sorrow."

So the king, with his fabulous wealth, undertakes to try pleasure, but with a difference: He'll give himself to every kind of enjoyment, yet he'll keep his eyes in his head, watching himself enjoy, so that he can test the value of enjoyment itself. He'll have women and wine, he'll have houses, parks, gardens, orchards, vineyards, he'll have herds and flocks, gold and silver. He'll gather and enjoy more than anyone before him in Jerusalem. For any pleasure his heart might want, he won't hold back. Yet at the end he finds that this too is vain and pointless. And so he is left in despair.

By now I was absorbed in the story and its message. More than absorbed, more than struck, because I understood what Qohelet was saying – understood in a way that went beyond merely comprehending a lesson in a religious-school class. There I was in the classroom, amidst the kids sitting bored and restless through yet another lesson, and suddenly for me the great curtain was pulled back to reveal the meaning of life – and I saw that there wasn't any.

It's not that the heavens opened up and light burst forth and symphonic music thundered in crescendo. Instead, one little kid sat there in the classroom, dissociated, disconnected, out of sync, looking out the windows at a landscape that didn't mean anything, in a world that didn't mean anything, while the other kids joked and fidgeted and threw spitballs.

The world had become momentously trivial.

The lesson went on a bit, Qohelet making his case still stronger, and soon after the class ended my mother arrived and drove me home.

Home was a comfortable suburban house with grey shingles and white trim and a door (was it pink?) with a rose vine growing outside that in summer gave big red roses and sometimes needed to be cut back out of the way. My dad owned a paint-and-wallpaper store about a half an hour's drive away in Guttenberg, a commercial town that to me looked like old bricks and car exhaust. He worked hard every day, leaving home early, before my younger sister and I got up for school, and coming back tired for dinner at six or six thirty on the days when he didn't work late. After dinner he'd sink into a big well-padded navy-blue chair and watch television and snooze, or else he'd call painters for friendly chats aimed at asking when he could expect them to pay their long-outstanding debts: "So, Ernie my friend, . . ." He wouldn't read much, except when the Sunday newspaper would come and he'd read what he called "the educational page" – that is, the funnies. And after he started putting some money into stocks, he'd follow the prices of those he'd invested in, like IBM and Bausch & Lomb (which I always heard as "Bau Shalom").

My mom was busy at home (with a German maid to help her), and later she started a career as an interior designer, which she seemed to enjoy, except when it involved spending all day schlepping through big stores that sold fabrics and furniture in midtown New York. She was the one who'd been to college and majored in theater and had a cultivated vocabulary and would read the latest novels and sometimes use a phrase or two from Shakespeare.

She was the one, also, who as a child I'd plague with questions: "Why A?" "Because of B." "Then why B?" "Because of C." And so on, until she'd finally end the "why" chain by answering "Because Y is a crooked letter."

But this time, thanks to Solomon, I had no "why" questions. He'd answered them all. Why are we here? What is life for? For no reason. Reasoning about it would get you nowhere. Life is pointless – worse than pointless: absurd and unfair. And that was that.

I talked with close friends about what Solomon had said. They didn't get it. Though they could follow the logic, the message never registered.

But it registered with me, and I wouldn't let go of it. It defined a sad, lonely territory reserved for despairing souls condemned to see the world as it was, bleak and pointless, filled with artificial mirth and superficial meaning, deluding you into a life of hard work for nothing.

What was the use of cheering at football games or campaigning for president of your class? What was the use of good grades and the junk we learned at school? What was the use of anything?

But pulling out of the world wouldn't work. Even if the world was meaningless and if eating, for example, was pointless, you'd still have to eat, to go through that meaningless chomp chomp chomp, swallow swallow swallow – absurd and ridiculous as it was – or else you'd die. And death was meaningless too. Suicide, then, would also have been pointless (and, besides, I wasn't up to it). And so I went on living.

But the world had gone hollow.

I suppose that in later weeks our class read through the rest of Ecclesiastes, though I don't remember. The details of the book didn't seem to matter much. What mattered was the main theme, which Qohelet returned to again and again, the theme of the utter pointlessness of life. His argument was clear, powerful, undeniable, irrefutable. It hit the mark.

Still, the book did end with an answer. It came not from Qohelet but from the narrator of the book, who had introduced Qohelet at the start. After Qohelet speaks his final words, crying out just as he began – "Vanity of vanities, all is vanity" – the narrator briefly returns. He praises Qohelet as a man of wisdom, a speaker of truth, and then says, "Let us hear the conclusion of the whole matter." Indeed. And what is that conclusion? "Fear God, and keep his commandments: for this is the whole duty of man."

What kind of conclusion was that? It was an about-face, a repudiation of what Qohelet had said. It was the usual pious biblical line, the same old weary admonition: Tremble before the Almighty God and do whatever he says.

Oh, man! That just made things worse.

After Qohelet's argument that life has no ultimate meaning, an argument hammered in with examples from common experience that no one could deny, an argument I had powerfully felt, an argument as plain as death and injustice and hard work for no result, along comes our pious narrator and tells us that the gist of it all is just to be a faithful God-fearing Jew and be sure to play by God's rules. No reasons given, no supporting evidence, no nothing.

Well, sorry, Mr. Narrator, but I wasn't sold even on the very existence of God. God was a doubtful proposition, unproven and quite likely unprovable, a sacred myth, perhaps a crutch that man had invented for himself to lean on. The old man in the sky, sitting on a throne pushing buttons. Why should I believe it? And keeping his commandments – was that all there was to live for? Nothing more than that? Phooey! Better a life of bleak truth than comfortable self-delusion. Qohelet was right: Vanity of vanities, all is vanity!

For some weeks the theme obsessed me. I held on to, even savored, that dismal feeling of vacancy. But I couldn't sustain it. How long can you go on brooding over emptiness? The world was moving on, and I was moving with it. But the world kept a bitter edge to it, an absurdity, a drizzly grey cast of melancholia. One time, I remember, a friend dragged me out to Coney Island – a bus ride to New York and then a long, when-will-it-be-over subway ride. To Coney Island, where they had the greatest rides in the world, and Nathan's Famous hot-dog stand, and all sorts of fun things to do. And when I got there it was the saddest place I'd ever been in my life, full of dull-faced people *trying* to lift their spirits by screaming on a roller coaster, or shooting at a few metal ducks and maybe winning a teddy bear, or just wandering around in the crowds.

My parents had taken me to the circus once, and there'd been a clown named Emmett Kelly, whose persona was that of a sad sort of bum who pushed a broom around, getting involved in this or that but somehow always getting lost in the shuffle. Was this supposed to be funny? To me it *was* sad – not only sad but depressing. Like Far Rockaway, where every now and then, at great intervals, my parents would drive with my sister and me – another miserably long ride – to pay a kindly visit to our Aunt Reszi, who was some sort of retarded (the word we used back then) and who lived in a little room in an institution out there that faintly smelled of Lysol.

Such was the world.

I don't think this was all due to Ecclesiastes. I suppose I was destined to be moody and cynical anyway. But the words of Qohelet served to pull emptiness and sadness and absurdity into a heap and say, "That's finally what life amounts to." And his arguments proved it. So behind whatever might be going on in my life, whatever I might find fascinating or inspiring or amusing, in the background somewhere would be Qohelet with the bad news: Vanity of vanities, all is vanity.

At thirteen I had my bar mitzvah – by choice a less glitzy affair than the swanky ones of my friends but still a big deal. And then, the tradition said, I was a man.

A year later, in 1964, that little man went with his parents to New York – to Flushing Meadow in Queens, to be exact – to see the World's Fair. More than a square mile of marsh and dumping grounds had been converted into a colorful fairgrounds, where corporations like IBM, Coca-Cola, General Motors, and General Electric had erected futuristic pavilions to a vision of scientific progress and a better, more comfortable life. Countries like Spain, Finland, and Argentina had pavilions there too. And at the Vatican pavilion one could see – brought from Rome with every care and precaution – Michelangelo's Pietà, a priceless treasure, his sculpture of the Virgin Mary mourning over the body of Jesus Christ.

I drifted from place to place. At General Electric's Disney-designed Progressland, I sat with 250 other visitors in the Carousel of Progress, where animatronic versions of a man, his wife, and their dog sat in their living room back in the good old days of the 1880s and the man and wife talked about the comforts of their modern home and the dog barked. And then our entire gallery of seats moved sixteen degrees in orbit, and now we saw onstage before us the same man, wife, and dog forty years later, in the 1920s. And now they had electricity and electric appliances, and life was so much better! And then another sixteen degrees, the 1940s, and new electrical inventions, and, yup, modern life sure was nice. And soon there they were in the 1960s, with the latest washing machines and driers and televisions and frost-free refrigerators.

And after a while, after Progressland, and Ford's Futurama, and the Coca-Cola pavilion's twenty-minute tour of the world, where the ubiquitous Coke bottle turned up in a Hong Kong street, a Bavarian ski lodge, or a stream in a Cambodian forest, I drifted towards the Vatican.

As I neared the outskirts of the pavilion, the fair's walkways, filled with summertime tourists, became noticeably flecked with priests and nuns. And – I'm not sure how it started – I wound up standing there along the way doing something I'd never done before: talking about religion with a Roman Catholic priest. He was a young man, with short black hair, a bright face, wholesome yet intelligent (yes, for me that was a contradiction), and overall pleasant looks.

However we met, I soon pressed my own theme for the conversation: Give me a good reason why I should believe in your religion, your dogma, your story. I'm Jewish – and hardly even Jewish but more like an agnostic and frankly not that interested in temples and churches and prayers and ceremonies and holy pieties and thou-shalt-nots – and can you give me any decent reason why I should buy what you have to say about the Bible and Jesus and whatever it is?

I suppose I wasn't quite that rude. I must have tried to be a young gentleman about it. But that challenge was the gist of it.

I don't remember how the young priest answered. He said something, I countered it, he said something else, I countered it. And before long, I suppose, he knew what he had on his hands: a skeptical young Jewish kid who wasn't going to listen, for whom no answer would be enough, a persistent little smart aleck having a good time for himself that afternoon baiting an oh-so-holy Roman Catholic priest.

So, again I don't recall the blow by blow, but after it became clear he wasn't going to get anywhere he gracefully disengaged himself. But, he said, let me leave you with something:

"Seek, and you shall find; knock, and it shall be opened unto you."

Somehow I recognized instantly that he was right, that what he had said was true. Unexpectedly humbled, I accepted his words and thanked him, and that was that. We parted ways, and I never saw him again.

No, I didn't set off on a great quest to Jerusalem or the Himalayas, or consider becoming a Christian, or even a better Jew. But there it was, added to the mix: There is something to be found, and if you seek you can find it.

The next few years were a jumble. My later teenage years coincided almost precisely with that time of heady madness called the 1960s. What is usually remembered as "the 1960s" – an extraordinary time when hundreds of thousands, perhaps millions, of American young people turned their back in contempt on the culture they'd received and formed a counterculture energized by psychedelic drugs, a time of be-ins, flower power, acid trips, acid rock, free love, psychedelic mushrooms, and dropping out, of hippies off together in communes or wandering the streets adorned with beads, bells, and headbands, a time when tripped-out explorers gazed at the world through chemically distended pupils and "expanded minds" – that era flourished, if that's the word, essentially from 1966 through 1968. In 1966 two classmates turned me on to marijuana. By 1967 I had dropped out of high school, in my senior year.

Qohelet had something to do with my dropping out, though he is surely not to blame. From the time of my first encounter with him, I had increasingly felt that school was pointless, meaningless, that it was a place that prepared you for a life with no purpose, an empty life of hard work for nothing.

I was definitely college material, my teachers and guidance counselors had told me. Good chance I could even get into someplace like Princeton or Yale. But I was an "underachiever." If something interested me, I studied it. If it didn't, why bother? As my senior year began, instead of focusing on my classes I made my own list of books I wanted to read, an eclectic list, with Freud, Orwell, Bertrand Russell, Henry Miller, and others, and sat in the back of my classrooms reading. And then in the middle of the year I just dropped out.

In one of the books I'd read – *Compulsory Mis-education and the Community of Scholars* – the author had said, as I recall, that if you were serious about education you didn't need to enroll in college and be shuttled through the standard program meant to make you just another cog in the wheel. Instead you could make your own program – by auditing the classes that offered what you wanted – and that way have a *real* education.

So I did it. I had a friend in Pittsburgh attending what is now known as Carnegie-Mellon University – back then, Carnegie Institute of Technology. Without the knowledge of the administration I moved into his dorm, joined the university community, and with an okay from professors attended whichever courses I wanted. Psychology, film – whatever interested me.

But college was a disappointment. Why were young men there? Some to avoid the draft and stay out of Vietnam. Others to spend four years after high school living sheltered at their parents' expense in a big green park with girls and freedom and a little bit of study and in that way put off having to venture out into the job market. Then there were those – the jerks! I thought – who had their sights set on a career. They'd move up the job ladder, earning good money, and be well set up in life. And finally, some were in college because they were truly looking for knowledge. And they, I saw, were being cheated, because their professors didn't have it. My psychology professor could tell me about Skinner and rats and conditioning and response, but could he tell me anything about who I was or what the purpose was for my life? Or was I just another rat, avoiding shocks and pressing levers to be rewarded with food?

Meanwhile, marijuana, it seemed to me, helped you break free. When you "got high," you rose above the straight and trivial humdrum life of the world and the dry coursework of the university. The sacred cannabis, opening your mind, would let you directly experience reality in different and more illumined ways. You were on a voyage, off to discover new worlds and new meaning. And when a friend at Carnegie Tech turned me on to LSD, what the journey could offer seemed to get even better.

"Seek, and you shall find," the young priest had said. But I didn't know what I was seeking, and I found myself stoned and confused. In the name of "higher consciousness," I was sinking.

But along the way, in February of 1967, I had read an article about a swami who had recently come from India to New York to teach what he called "Krishna consciousness," and I heard his mantra:

> Hare Krishna, Hare Krishna,
> Krishna Krishna, Hare Hare
> Hare Rāma, Hare Rāma,
> Rāma Rāma, Hare Hare

From the article about the swami and his New York ashram, what he was teaching sounded authentic but forbiddingly austere. Perhaps I could find something else, equally authentic but less spartan.

I didn't. Instead, a year later, I became his student, his disciple. What happened was that sometime early in 1968, not from any wish of my own but because some other plans stopped working, I was pulled, as if caught in a tide, into living in New York City, in the very hub of the East Coast turned-on, dropped-out counterculture, the Lower East Side. And there, one day, I found myself wandering a little south of the center of the action, down to Second Avenue and Second Street, where the swami had set up his ashram in a small storefront, at 26 Second Avenue.

The swami wasn't there – he had gone back to India for a while – but his students were keeping things going. And, in short, I became attracted.

The austerities turned out a lot easier than I'd imagined, and his teachings, though surely authentic, were also much different from what I had expected. I won't elaborate on them here; you'll find out more about them in the course of this book.

But, for a start, he insisted on a life with no chemical or herbal intoxicants, not even coffee or tea (just by being in the material world, he said, we were already intoxicated enough) and no sex outside of marriage. (No gambling or meat-eating either, though for me these were less of an issue.)

I accepted the rules, and when the swami came back from India he was already my teacher.

From a sociological point of view, a narrative like this is a familiar story. A young person during a period of social change becomes unmoored from the religion and culture he was brought up with, drifts about in search of a new set of values, encounters something that seems to offer him answers, and re-anchors himself to whatever he has found. Exactly textbook.

And so it was. But there's more to life than sociology. Or is there? Perhaps there is nothing more to our lives than an acting out of already repeated patterns. What people have done before us, we do again. Nothing is new, and whatever we do has no meaning. So cries Qohelet. What to make of that cry is a central concern of *Vanity Karma.*

My teacher's name, with his full honorific titles, was His Divine Grace A. C. Bhaktivedanta Swami Prabhupāda. Scholars most often refer to him simply as "Bhaktivedanta Swami." His students and followers (and often scholars too, these days) usually refer to him as "Prabhupāda" or (adding one short honorific that literally means "eminent") "Śrīla Prabhupāda."

A crucial part of the work Śrīla Prabhupāda was doing was translating traditional Sanskrit spiritual texts into English, with commentary. I began helping type his manuscripts. After some time I began to assist in editing his books (an unlikely engagement for a high-school dropout) and after some years became his chief editor.

Those books formed the basis of an entire spiritual culture, a culture I adopted as my own, and it is largely from the perspective of that culture (though, as I'll explain, not entirely) that I write this book.

Crossing cultures

I intend this to be a cross-cultural commentary, in several ways. First, and most obvious, it is a commentary on a Jewish book from what might be called a Hindu perspective, and written by a born Jew who has crossed over to Hinduism.

Had I been a strictly observant Orthodox Jew, the contrast would have been more dramatic, but there's nothing I can do about that. The Judaism into which I was born is a particular strain – Reform Judaism – which, at least the way I grew up in it, sheds so much of tradition and blends so closely with modern values that it's nearly secular.

But then again, that helps us further define the culture from which I came. It was Jewish. It was secular. It was American. It was modern (or, if you like, postmodern). It was the culture (and counterculture) of those who came of age, white and middle class, in the cities and suburbs of the northeastern United States in the bizarrely neo-Romantic 1960s.

And what is the "Hinduism" to which I had crossed over? The term Hindu (never found in the traditional Sanskrit literature) is so broad that its meaning can be hard to pin down. "Hindu" can be an ethnic designation, so that, for example, one might be both Hindu and atheist. Alternatively, a Hindu might pursue oneness with an abstract all-encompassing Supreme Reality, or live a life of pious devotion to a pantheon of colorful gods and goddesses, or just not bother with any of that and focus on building a successful career in software, medicine, engineering, or popular films.

What Śrīla Prabhupāda taught was none of the above. As far as he was concerned, Krishna consciousness was not simply another brand of "Hinduism" and for that matter not even a "religion," a kind of faith or denomination one could switch to. Rather, he spoke of Krishna consciousness as being our eternal, natural spiritual consciousness, now covered but always intrinsic to every living being – not something from the world of religions to be adopted but something within oneself to be revived. Taking a straightforward approach to the Bhagavad-gītā, the foundational text of Vedic wisdom, he taught a path of spirituality in which one cultivates self-realization and a personal relationship with the Supreme, who is conceived as a distinct yet transcendent person, known by the Sanskrit name Krishna, "he who is all-attractive."

On this path, Śrīla Prabhupāda followed a long succession of teachers, a lineage that in the sixteenth century saw a flowering of devotion and scholarship under the guidance and inspiration of Śrī Caitanya Mahāprabhu. Because Śrī Caitanya Mahāprabhu began his devotional and philosophical movement in the region then known as Gauḍa (now, roughly, the Indian state of West Bengal) and because Krishna is identified with Viṣṇu ("the all-pervading Godhead"), the path of "Krishna consciousness" as taught by Śrī Caitanya is also called Gauḍīya Vaiṣṇavism.

My native Jewish culture, therefore, is that of Reform Judaism, and my "Hindu" culture Gauḍīya Vaiṣṇava.

Perhaps less obviously than with the cultural crossings I've mentioned, any later commentary on a much earlier work will be cross-cultural. The Jerusalem of today is a far cry from the Jerusalem of ancient times. Any commentator on a work from a distant past writes of words written from a distant culture.

Finally, each person is a culture unto himself, each of us seeing a different world. And yet some messages, like those of Qohelet and the Bhagavad-gītā, are not only cross-cultural but trans-cultural, in the sense that they go beyond times and places, beyond cultures and languages, to speak to our deepest issues. And so, whoever we are, we cross beyond our cultural boundaries to reach a deeper understanding of ourselves.

What right do I have?

I am a student of the Vedic teachings, not a biblical scholar, nor for that matter an academic of any sort. Then what right do I have to meddle with Ecclesiastes? I can only say: It has touched me. Ultimately Ecclesiastes, though deserving academic study, is not an academic book, nor an exclusive property of academia. And the issues it raises allow room for, even invite, a frankly non-academic response. One might finally say they even demand one, for what we do with our life is far more than an academic question.

Nonetheless, I have taken care to study and contemplate what thoughtful commentators before me have said. To my good fortune,

I've found works of great erudition, works of sensitivity and eloquence, works that squarely come to terms with the issues Qohelet raises. I've looked through old traditional Jewish commentaries, modern academic ones, Christian evangelical, a host of journal articles. In preparing to write *Vanity Karma*, I kept reading and reading, till most of what I read at the nontechnical level seemed like something I had read before, and then I figured I was ready to begin. If not a biblical scholar, at least I could call myself a well-informed layman.

On the other side, after forty-five years of study, practice, teaching, and editorial work in the Vaiṣṇava tradition, under the guidance of my spiritual master, I felt confident I could bring to a discussion of Qohelet an authentic representation of Vaiṣṇava tradition and thought.

But what right do I have, one might ask, to mess with a sacred *Jewish* book (a book that later, of course, became included in the Christian canon)? In a certain sense, a tradition's sacred literature *belongs* to that tradition, and outsiders are just that – outsiders. Since they don't belong to the tradition, how can they understand the tradition or its deeply felt message and values? Worse, they may try to appropriate the text for their own agendas, to "prove" some notion foreign to the book and its native worldview. These, I think, are objections worth taking seriously.

Of course, by birth and upbringing I can claim a marginal Jewish heritage, enough to say I'm not entirely an outsider. But that seems an awfully slim support, especially when it's a heritage I seem to have left behind.

In answer I can say that because the book played a transformative role in my own personal spiritual history, it's a book with which I can claim a special relationship.

Moreover, I can point to Ecclesiastes as a very strange book, one that barely seems to fit into the Bible. Far from arguing for conventional Jewish views, it often appears to argue against them. Qohelet is not a law-giver, bearing God's commandments, nor a prophet, urging God's chosen people to hold to God's ways, nor a hymnist, praising God's glories. He is a sage, a questioner, a skeptic, a soul anguished by the apparent clash between what we'd expect of divine wisdom and justice – or any sort of world that makes sense – and what our experience confronts us with. In this sense he is a biblical misfit, a maverick, as much a man of doubts and misgivings as of belief. And so, with his personal questioning, his skepticism, his going back and forth in a dialogue with his own heart, he seems closer to us, more a man whose thoughts we don't have to be Jewish (or Christian) to be moved by or to speak to. And so I have ventured to comment on the words of Qohelet. I don't think I'd try it with Moses, Isaiah, or Jeremiah.

Still, conscious of my weak claim to Jewishness, I have worked overtime to understand what Ecclesiastes means within the context of its own tradition and not regard it merely as global common property, "a classic of world literature," as if the book could easily be divorced from the religious community from which it grew, with whose language, culture, and religious life it is entwined, and by whom it is revered as a part of their sacred scripture.

That said, in commenting on the words of Qohelet (whom the scholar Tremper Longman calls "a confused wise man") I will be forthright in offering a Vedic point of view. But I think that's a fair way to engage in dialogue.

Scope

Now a few words about the scope of this book – what it deals with and what it does not.

As I mention in the Preface, what concerns me is the meaning of Ecclesiastes, its thoughts, its messages – what the text means to me, and what it might mean to you. "Meaning" in Ecclesiastes is more than a box to be weighed or a chemical solution to be analyzed. It's all tied up with Qohelet's *feelings*, with his cries, his laments, his expressions of outrage and despair, his cynicism and sarcasm, his sense of what is good, his need to search and to know. Meaning and feeling go together. So I care about both.

In the world of biblical scholarship, both ancient and modern, nearly everything about Ecclesiastes has inspired differences of opinion: When was it written? Where? In what language? To what extent might the author have been influenced by Stoicism? By Epicureanism? What should we make of parallels between Ecclesiastes and other ancient writings from the Middle East – the Gilgamesh epic, for example? To what genre should we assign the book, and what can we say about the book's literary structure? These and other such issues and controversies, important though they may be within their own domain, are not what here concern me. Of course, Ecclesiastes does have a history, a form, and a context. And if we want to do the book justice, they can't be so blithely ignored. But such topics, when I touch on them at all, I will only touch on, not dwell on.

Nor do I propose to make this an exercise in comparative religion, a great dialogue between Judaism and Hinduism. Judaism as a whole (let alone Christianity) is too vast for me, and, besides, Qohelet the maverick hardly represents it.

And if Qohelet isn't your ordinary Jew, he certainly isn't Hindu. So another thing you won't find me doing here is recasting Qohelet in a Hindu mold. It is not that he "must be" saying something that coincides with or validates the teachings of Krishna, that somewhere within his Jewish heart lives an aspiring Vedāntist, that Qohelet and Krishna are "really saying the same thing."

I've already mentioned, too, why I don't think of myself as a member of "the Hindu religion." So rather than anything as broad and catch-all as "Hinduism" you'll just have one person – me – and what I've learned from the more focused tradition of "Krishna consciousness," and I'll be engaged not with Judaism but with one sage, Qohelet, and what he has to say. I recognize that Qohelet speaks from within a tradition. So I won't try to wrench him out of it. And at some points comparing traditions will be natural. But a broad comparison between one religion and another, let alone a face-off between them, is not what I have in mind.

What I do have in mind is a deep exploration of the issues Qohelet raises, issues crucial to the life of every human being.

Common questions

Perhaps because of my own history with Ecclesiastes, I have been surprised at how many people are unacquainted with it. Is it in the Bible, they ask? Old Testament or New? Who wrote it? When was it written? And of course other people I talk with know the book, sometimes quite well.

But in any case, at the outset let's answer a few common questions.

Yes, it's in the Bible, in the Old Testament, or what Jews might prefer to call the Hebrew Scriptures. Among the three divisions of the Hebrew Scriptures – the Law (Torah), the Prophets, and the

Writings – Ecclesiastes belongs to the Writings (Ketuvim). And among the Writings it is sometimes known as one of the three "wisdom books," the other two being Job and Proverbs.

Who wrote the book? The simple answer is that we don't know. When was it written? We don't know that either. Precisely where? Again, we don't know.

The main speaker is someone called Qohelet, who is identified in the text as a wise man who taught people knowledge and who pondered and studied and arranged many proverbs. He "sought to find pleasing words" and "wrote words of truth plainly." This we are told by a narrator who with one line at the start of the book and a few lines at the end provides a frame for what Qohelet says. We know nothing more about this "frame narrator," and we know nothing more about Qohelet than we can glean from the book itself.

His name itself is enigmatic. Appearing nowhere else in the Bible, Qohelet shows signs of being an invented word, devised only for this one sage. It is usually traced to the Hebrew root qahal, which has to do with "assembling" or "gathering." And, unusually, it has a feminine ending, which seems to indicate a title. (Once or twice, the text even refers to our speaker as "Haqohelet," the Qohelet.) So Qohelet may be one who leads or gathers an assembly (or perhaps one of those gathered).

The King James Version of the Bible calls Qohelet "the Preacher," a poor title for such an unorthodox sage to be stuck with. The modern Revised Standard Version does better: "the Teacher." Other translators, drawing upon various possible Hebrew meanings, have called him "the Convoker," "the Arguer," "the Philosopher," "the Debater" – the list of translations is long. My preferred approach is that taken by the Jewish Publication Society in 1917. They simply kept the Hebrew: Qohelet.

In the first verse of the book, as I've mentioned, the narrator tells us that Qohelet was "the son of David" and "king in Jerusalem." Historically, this could only have been the wise and wealthy King Solomon. The rabbis accepted this nearly without question, fortunately so for us because without this acceptance a book so strange and full of self-contradictions might never have secured a place in the biblical canon and been preserved.

Later biblical scholars, beginning from the seventeenth century, raised doubts about the notion that the author must be Solomon, and today most scholars reject it. Various passages in the text suggest that the book wasn't written by a king at all, especially not *this* king. And then there's the language: The book is written in what most modern scholars say they at once recognize as a late form of biblical Hebrew, as different from the language of Solomon's time as Shakespeare's English from ours.

Today most commentators regard Qohelet's royal persona as a literary fiction, a device meant to dramatize the failure of efforts to find meaning in kingly pleasures and profound wisdom. (If indeed it is a device, at least for me the device worked.) In any case, the royal identity appears only briefly; after the second chapter we hear no more about Qohelet's being a king. For that matter, Qohelet may very well be an entirely fictional character, from beginning to end. We have no way to be sure.

In Hebrew, the name of the main speaker of the book is also the book's title: "Qohelet." The translators who rendered the book from Hebrew into Greek (at an uncertain date, perhaps in the third century BCE) came up with an apt Greek equivalent, *ekklēsiastēs*, similarly obscure, similar in meaning. The Latin translation of the Bible, the Vulgate, kept the same word – *ecclesiastes.* The word long precedes the time when *ecclesia* and *ecclesiastical* came to refer to a church. An *ecclesia* was simply a gathering or an assembly. (The word was chiefly applied to the general assembly of the citizens of ancient Athens.) *Ecclesiastes*, of course, has come down to us as the English title. Following a helpful scholarly convention, I use *Ecclesiastes* to refer to the book, *Qohelet* the speaker.

Where was the book written? Though Egypt and even Phoenicia have been proposed, somewhere in Palestine, perhaps Jerusalem, seems most likely. Finally, though, again we can't be sure.

As for the date, for those who hold to the tradition that the author was Solomon the date is roughly three thousand years ago, in the tenth century BCE. Most modern scholars would date the book to about the third century (again BCE). In biblical studies a variance of even fifty or a hundred years can make an immense historical difference. But in an early note to myself I wrote, "For my purposes, I don't care whether the book was written in ancient days by King Solomon in Jerusalem or two weeks ago by Sol Lefkowitz in Brooklyn." Well, that's cavalier. But there's still something to it. The issues Qohelet raises are timeless. And in the words of a leading scholar on Ecclesiastes, Robert Gordis, "the immortals are always our contemporaries."

I have already touched upon the question of how such a strange book as Ecclesiastes could have won acceptance into the biblical canon. The attribution to Solomon provides one answer. Another is that an epilogue wraps the book up with a pious and orthodox ending. A third answer given is that the forming of the Hebrew canon was determined not by a series of councils but by a historical process that stretched over centuries. Certain books that were a part of the literary heritage of the Hebrew people – in the words of one scholar, "a national literature upon a religious foundation" – gradually came to be thought of as scripture. And Ecclesiastes was a book of such searching thought and powerful expression that it had to be a book to keep. How it could be considered sacred was later debated, but by that time the book was already in.

Vedic sources

I have mentioned earlier that I will comment from a Vedic point of view. By *Vedic* I refer to a tradition of wisdom that has been preserved in the Sanskrit language for thousands of years. (The word *Vedic* comes from the Sanskrit root *vid*, meaning "to know, understand, perceive, learn," which is an ancestor of our English word *wisdom.*) Though scholars of Indology prefer to reserve the word *Vedic* for matters directly pertaining to the Vedas, the four vast and primordial "books of knowledge," practitioners use the term more broadly to include writings such as the Mahābhārata and the Purāṇas that make the Vedic message more accessible. And here I stick with the practitioners.

The two books I mainly rely on in this study are the Bhagavad-gītā and the Śrīmad-Bhāgavatam (which is also known as the Bhāgavata Purāṇa). The Bhagavad-gītā, which forms eighteen chapters in the epic Mahābhārata, presents the core of the Vedic philosophy in a relatively brief seven hundred verses. Celebrated and revered for its profound message, it is the one book turned to by philosophers, yogīs, and transcendentalists of nearly all paths of Vedic spirituality. In the West it early inspired, among others, the "American transcendentalists" Emerson and Thoreau and has been looked to ever since for its perennial wisdom. It is the essential Vedic text for spiritual realization. The

Śrīmad-Bhāgavatam, a much longer work – eighteen thousand verses –
is sometimes said to begin where the Gītā leaves off, since it goes even
further into the nature of reality and the relationship between all beings and the Absolute. The Vedic literature is sometimes said to be a
"desire tree," a tree that can yield whatever one might desire, and of that
tree the Śrīmad-Bhāgavatam is said to be the ripe and most relishable
fruit.

Representing Hebrew and Sanskrit

In the back of this book you'll find guides to Hebrew and Sanskrit
pronunciation. Since in English we're used to seeing *q* followed by *u*,
Qohelet may seem a strange-looking word. Though I first preferred *Koheleth* as looking more normal, I decided to go with a modern scholarly
standard.* The use of *q* for a *k* sound in Semitic languages has become
familiar ever since our newspapers became filled with news of Al Qaeda.
You can go ahead and pronounce the *q* as *k*. For the name Krishna I have
used the popular spelling found in English dictionaries. Transliterated
with precision it would be Kṛṣṇa.

The back of the book also includes a discussion of the original Hebrew text of Ecclesiastes and the English rendering you'll find in *Vanity
Karma*. At Temple Sinai I learned enough Hebrew to pass my bar mitzvah (which was hardly any) and then forgot whatever I'd learned. For
Vanity Karma, therefore, I have relied on the Hebrew expertise of others.

For the English translations of Sanskrit verses, I have followed the
explanations given by my spiritual master. Sometimes I have used his
translations verbatim, and sometimes for literary or contextual reasons
I have adjusted them or done a new translation, but for the meaning of
the verses I have always relied on him.

Gender neutrality

I have not revised Ecclesiastes for gender neutrality. Considering modern
sensibilities, I respect efforts to make biblical language more "inclusive,"
more linguistically universal. But Ecclesiastes is not a gender-neutral

---

* Apart from this standard, different ways of pronouncing Hebrew and different ways
  of putting Hebrew into roman letters have given us, among other spellings, *Kohelet*,
  Koheles, *Qoheleth*, and in older writings even *Coheleth*.

text. Though I trust the scholars who say that the Hebrew word for "man" can be generic, inclusive of people of both sexes, there's every sign that the author of Ecclesiastes uses the word with precisely the mentality that champions of gender-neutral language object to: He sees men as primary, women as secondary. Qohelet is speaking to men, to males. "Enjoy life with the woman you love" (9:9). That's clearly a message for men, not women, and Qohelet adds nothing for gender balance. And when the frame narrator says "Beware, my son" (12:12), he's not being gender inclusive. The author of Ecclesiastes did not grow up in a society that valued equal standing for both sexes. Quite the contrary. And by the time we hear Qohelet speak about women in chapter seven we can know for sure we're not dealing with a man who sees men and women as equal. Perhaps if the author of Ecclesiastes were with us today he would speak differently and think differently. But he's not. And I was not prepared to retrofit him to modern attitudes.

When paraphrasing Qohelet, also, for the most part I leave the gender of his language intact.

Vanity of vanities

The headline word in Ecclesiastes, of course, is *vanity.* "Vanity of vanities," says Qohelet. "Vanity of vanities. All is vanity." And at the end of the book he concludes with the same refrain. In all, Qohelet repeats the word *vanity* some thirty-eight times. But is *vanity* the right word? It's the word employed in the King James Version. But whether it's the right word, the most suitable translation for the original Hebrew term – and if not, what the best translation might be – is a question every translator of Ecclesiastes must grapple with.

The Hebrew term is *hevel,* and about its basic, concrete meaning there seems to be a consensus: The word means "breath" or "vapor," like the vapor we see when we breathe out on a cold morning. But when Qohelet uses the word, clearly he has something more than this basic sense in mind. When he says "All is *hevel,*" he surely doesn't mean that all is literally breath or vapor. He must have in mind some extended sense, an abstract, metaphorical one. What we understand that sense to be is central to our understanding of the book.

The Septuagint, the ancient rendering of the Hebrew scriptures into Greek, translated *hevel* as *mataios,* which generally means "vain," in the sense of "futile" or "meaningless." *Mataios*, scholars have said, "denotes the world of appearance as distinct from that of being," and it may imply "what is against the norm, unexpected, offending what ought to be." In the Latin version, the Vulgate, this became *vanitas* – "vanity" or "emptiness."*

Our English word *vanity*, in its older meaning, refers to something vain, futile, or worthless, something of no value or profit. This then is what the King James translators saw Qohelet's complaint to be, that all is vanity.

But not all translators are satisfied with this term. Some feel that the older meaning of *vanity* has now been overshadowed by the meaning "pride" or "self-conceit" – the sense I knew as a boy – and so they opt for close matches for that older sense like "meaningless," "useless," and "empty." Other translators believe that *vanity* and its near substitutes miss Qohelet's intended meaning, and so they favor other terms, such as "enigmatic," "mysterious," "incomprehensible," and "transient."

Especially powerful are the arguments given by Michael V. Fox in favor of "absurd." Qohelet's complaint, he says, is not that all things are enigmatic, mysterious, or incomprehensible, as though all would be fine if only we had a better understanding, nor that all things are transitory or fleeting (some of the evils Qohelet laments seem permanent, and we can only wish they might be fleeting). Nor is it even that all things are useless or meaningless, though this may come closer to what Qohelet intends. Rather, what so assaults and oppresses Qohelet is that the conditions of our existence are not merely senseless but contrary to sense, not merely meaningless but irrational. All things considered, what happens in the world is askew from what ought to happen. Life ought to make sense. Things ought to be consistent. And yet life appears senseless, and the workings of fate seem erratic. Where we should have order, harmony, and a consistent link between action and result, we have a deranged, disjointed reality, a reality that's absurd because, as Qohelet shows, it flies in the face of all reasonable expectations. (In Hebrew even today, *hevel* is used to mean "nonsense.")

The scholar Douglas Miller writes of *hevel* as a "multivalent symbol" – a word with multiple meanings and shades of meaning. Vapor

---

* *Vanitas vanitatum omnia vanitas.* "Vanity of vanities, all is vanity."

is transient, vapor is insubstantial, vapor is sometimes foul, and these varied qualities contribute to the power of the symbol.

Hevel is a heavily loaded term, says another scholar, William H. U. Anderson. It's a term that carries many nuances – "transitory," "empty," "meaningless" – "but ultimately with the loaded implication of absurdity." So the best course, Anderson suggests, might simply be to inform the reader of the depth and subtlety of the term and leave it in Hebrew – *hevel.*

All this considered, I have stuck with *vanity*, whose presence in Ecclesiastes is very much a part of our English literary and cultural inheritance. To me Ecclesiastes without "Vanity of vanities" would seem like Genesis without "In the beginning." Taking on board, however, the spirit of Anderson's suggestion, I might say: Where you see *vanity*, keep in mind *hevel.* In other words, I don't insist that *hevel* precisely means "vanity." Rather, let *vanity* stand for *hevel,* that multivalent symbol, that heavily loaded term. If I could insert into the dictionary a new definition for *vanity*, it might be "an intended equivalent for *hevel* as used in the book of Ecclesiastes." Moreover, I recall the sense of *mataios*, the Greek forerunner of *vanity*, as "offending what ought to be," which comes close to the very essence of absurd. When Sisyphus, again and forever, rolls his boulder up the hill only to have it roll down again, his labor is truly in vain.

The endless chore of Sisyphus brings us to the word *karma*, another short word with many meanings. Although *karma* sometimes refers to the path of good deeds, more generally it means "work" or "actions," whether good or bad – finally, all that we do. And *karma* also refers to what life gives us back for what we do. Then what is *vanity karma*? It can mean something we do that amounts to nothing, something meaningless or useless or absurd, with the implication that what life gives us in return is equally pointless and absurd. "All is vanity!" Qohelet cries out. Is there nothing more to our life than vanity karma? Let us see.

I

1:1–11: All is vanity

¹ The words of Qohelet, the son of David, king in Jerusalem.

² Vanity of vanities, says Qohelet. Vanity of vanities, all is vanity! ³ What profit does a man have from all his labor at which he labors under the sun? ⁴ One generation passes away, and another generation comes, and the earth abides forever. ⁵ The sun also rises, and the sun goes down, and hastens to his place where he arises. ⁶ The wind goes toward the south, and it circles to the north; round and round goes the wind, and on its circuits the wind returns. ⁷ All the rivers run into the sea, yet the sea is not full; to the place where the rivers go, there they go again. ⁸ All things toil to weariness, more than man can express; the eye is not satisfied with seeing, nor the ear filled with hearing. ⁹ That which has been is that which will be, and that which has been done is that which will be done, and there is nothing new under the sun. ¹⁰ Is there a thing of which it might

be said, "See, this is new"? It has already been, in the ages before us. [11] There is no remembrance of the people of former times; nor of the people of times yet to come will there be any remembrance among those who come after.

Introducing Qohelet

The opening words, introducing Qohelet, are those of the "frame narrator." He'll have but a parenthetical word or so within the text. We'll meet him again briefly at the end of the book.

Vanity

As I discuss in the Introduction, the word *hevel*, translated here as "vanity," has the root meaning "breath" or "vapor." And as we'll soon hear, it points to something as pointless as chasing after wind. Qohelet cries that all is vanity, and as he pours out his reasons we will see why.

"All is vanity," Qohelet says. But isn't there something worthwhile? The twelfth-century Jewish commentator Abraham Ibn Ezra writes that to drive from our hearts the notion that in the world there is vanity but also something of stable and enduring value, Qohelet concludes, "*Everything* is vanity."

What profit does a man have?

What is the use of life? Qohelet asks. What does one gain from it?

In my own childhood and youth, I saw my father working his life away. Every day he would drive early in the morning to his store, something over half an hour's drive. He'd spend the whole day there, keeping the business running, and then drive back, another half an hour, and get home exhausted. Before a time I can even remember, he'd suffered his first heart attack.

He'd bring his papers to work with him in a worn, bulging brown leather briefcase, which he'd bring back at night, full of work to do. One year on his birthday my mother and sister and I bought him a present: a new briefcase. He carried it to work with him every day until his second heart attack, from which he died at the age of fifty-four.

And what was the point?

The question may seem ungrateful: After all, he worked for his family – for my mother and sister and me. But if he hadn't, we'd have lived anyway, as we lived on after he left. And what good did all that work do him?

What profit is there? Qohelet asks. The word he uses is *yitron*. The word, we're told, is a commercial term. When we've summed up all the accounts, what's the surplus? What gain can we show? Qohelet leaves the obvious answer for us to supply.

"Under the sun"

We work, Qohelet says, "under the sun." In the Hebrew Bible it's a phrase unique to Qohelet, who uses it twenty-nine times, again and again and again. The phrase puts us in our place, for we live on earth, in our small spot on one planet within the machinery of the cosmos. We live beneath the sun, which marks out our life in finite units of time, in hours and days and years. With every rising and setting of the sun, the Śrīmad-Bhāgavatam says, another day is gone from our life. And each time the sun completes its full annual circuit, gone forever is another of our years.

And the sun not only marks the passing of time but dictates what happens to us within it. The days when we work and the nights when we sleep, the seasons when farmers plant and harvest, when merchants roll out their seasonal goods, when armies wait or move, when students and scholars have their semesters – all march by in regimen, in step with the commands of the sun.

In time with the ticking of the great solar clock, we journey from childhood to youth to old age, obeying the course charted out for us by the ever-moving sun, emblem and enforcer of time, the time that finally brings our journey to its end.

We work in slavery to time.

And in this we are no different from the rest of creation, for the trees and plants, the insects, birds, and animals, and the forces of nature herself – the snows, the summers, and the rains – all are fastened to the great wheel of time. And what more does the man gain for his labor than the beast?

It is the sun also that exposes to Qohelet the emptiness of the material world, a world of vanity, of endless toil for no profit.

Generation after generation

Generations come and go, Qohelet says, each following the same weary pattern. Here the Hebrew word for "generations" comes from a root that means "to move in a circle." Though we think we are making progress, we are going around in circles, each generation repeating what the previous ones have done: We eat, sleep, mate, and fend off enemies, and from the mating comes the next generation to do the same thing again. And what is the gain from all this?

Working and toiling our way through a life that lasts but an instant in eternity, we come and go, generations slipping by, yet the earth, our workshop, stands firm, its steady existence mocking our brief little lives.

And it's not only the earth that stands firm; it's the world of earth's people, of human society. The Hebrew word translated here as "the earth" can also mean "the world" in the sense of all humanity, "all the people of the world." Generations come and go, but the world stays the same.

We imagine that our lives make a difference. But what truly changes? Our human struggles – the great dramas of my small life and the great lives of Caesar and Einstein; the dramas of ancient Jerusalem and Rome and of modern Germany, America, and China; the dramas of families, dynasties, communities, nations, and peoples – are of no final consequence. As the sun rises and sets and rises again above the ocean of human society, that ocean never changes. Would you like to change the world? Qohelet implies: You can't.

All things are weary

As the sun travels its great arc in the sky, even that great sun pants as it rushes from east to west, only to arrive the next morning in the east where it began, to repeat the same relentless cycle. The Hebrew word for "hastens" (literally, "pants") implies not only vigorous movement but tiredness; like man below, the sun, going nowhere new, labors its way through a cycle of vigorous monotony.

The wind and water join the fiery sun in great movements of no ultimate consequence. Wind, water, fire, earth – these elemental ingredients of nature form the bleak habitat where man must endlessly labor for nothing. In the words of one commentator, George Barton, "The whole universe groans with man because of its useless and monotonous activity."

"All things are weary," Qohelet says. But here the Hebrew word for "things" may also mean "words." Words are more weary than words can express. And as the sea is never filled, neither are the senses. However much the eye and ear take in, they can never be satisfied in a pointless and meaningless world. All seems weary, stale, flat, and unprofitable.

Nothing is new

The world is full of new and exciting things, but nothing new ever happens. What has happened before will happen again, and what we have done before we will do again. The world offers nothing new to break the monotony. As the Śrīmad-Bhāgavatam puts it, "As the world is now, so it was in the past, and so it will be in the future."

As Michael Fox points out, new things and events do appear – "World War II, the book of Qohelet, the death of Lincoln" – but they are but another version of what we have seen before: another war, another book, another assassination.

Even the desire for something new is nothing new. It has been with us since before the time of Qohelet. And we can fulfill that desire only by fooling ourselves (as we have done before and as we will do again), because nothing new ever happens. In the words of the Bhāgavatam, we are "chewing the chewed" – chewing again what we and others have already chewed before. We tote around the latest computer and use it to do what people before us have done for thousands of years: write words, draw pictures, tally sums.

I recall my visit to the World's Fair and General Electric's "Progressland," where man, wife, and dog advanced through the decades: newer appliances, same old routine. As a T-shirt I once saw in Brooklyn crudely put it, "New day, same shit."

We meet one another and ask, "So, what's new?" Qohelet answers: Nothing. "There is nothing new under the sun." Under the relentlessly circling sun, fixed in its course, ticking off the hours and days and seasons and years of our lives, ticking off the lifetime of the ant and the rise and fall of human empires, nothing is new.

No remembrance

And not only is nothing new, but the old is forgotten. The past is soon lost to memory, and the present will be forgotten next. And "forgotten" may be too positive a word. Qohelet says, "There is no remembrance." There is nothing.

The Hebrew is ambiguous as to what is no longer remembered: people or things or times or events. What Qohelet says is true of them all. In school I resented having to memorize the names and dates of presidents and generals and wars. What was the point of it? I later learned that the Śrīmad-Bhāgavatam speaks of the entire world as "the world of names." Commenting on this phrase from the Bhāgavatam, my spiritual master said that such names are ultimately of no more significance than the babble of sea waves. "The great kings, leaders and soldiers fight with one another in order to perpetuate their names in history," he wrote. But "they are forgotten in due course of time, and they make a place for another era in history." The world's history and historical persons, he wrote, are "useless products of flickering time." They will not be remembered, nor shall we.

1:12–18: The pursuit of wisdom

¹² I, Qohelet, have been king over Israel in Jerusalem.
¹³ And I set my heart to seek and to search out by wisdom all that is done under heaven. It is a sore task that God has given to men* to be busy with. ¹⁴ I have seen all the works that are done under the sun, and – just see! – all is vanity and a chasing after wind. ¹⁵ That which is crooked cannot be made straight, and that which is wanting cannot be counted. ¹⁶ I spoke with my heart, saying, "Just see, I have gotten great wisdom,

---

* Here (and elsewhere) the Hebrew literally says "sons of men." This can be taken as a poetic idiom, meaning nothing more than "men" (or, if you will, people). But Ibn Ezra, commenting on 9:3, reminds us that the phrase can have a diminutive sense: "little men" or "mere men."

more also than all who were before me over Jerusalem."
Indeed, my heart had great experience of wisdom and
knowledge. [17] And I applied my heart to know wisdom,
and to know madness and folly. I perceived that this
also was a chasing after wind. [18] For in much wisdom
is much vexation, and he that increases knowledge
increases sorrow.

"I spoke with my heart"

Qohelet now introduces himself, telling us he has been "king over Israel
in Jerusalem." History has known only two such kings – Solomon and
David. And since the first verse of Ecclesiastes has already told us that
Qohelet was "the *son* of David," we are meant to identify Qohelet as
King Solomon.

Whether we take Qohelet's words here to be literally true (following
Jewish tradition) or regard his kingly persona as a literary device (following the consensus of modern scholars), going along with his royal
identity allows us to be open, intellectually and emotionally, to the full
strength of his arguments.

Qohelet says that he applied his heart to seeking a true understanding of the world. For the ancient Hebrews, the heart was the center of
the intellect. So the Hebrew word for "heart" may also mean "intellect"
or "mind" (just as in Sanskrit the word *citta* may mean "heart," "mind,"
"reason," and so on). Qohelet put his full self into the task.

Here we see Qohelet's method for gaining understanding. It is not
simply to receive and accept what tradition has told him, what elders
or sages or scriptures have said. He does not look to prophetic revelation, or the words of angels, or pronouncements held to have descended
from God. He relies on wisdom – his own faculty for wisdom – and so
undertakes his search.

Though the Hebrew words for "search" and "seek out" are essentially
synonyms, some scholars have commented that here "search" means "to
investigate the roots of a matter" and "seek" means "to explore a subject
on all sides." Together, the two words indicate that Qohelet set his mind
on gaining a thorough understanding.

But he found it a sore task. As the young Christian priest had advised me, "Seek, and you shall find." But seeking can be a confusing and frustrating enterprise, a business, as some translators would have it, "to be afflicted with,"* and what you find may be inconclusive or sorely distressing.

And this sorry task, this travail, Qohelet says, has been given to us by God. The first time in the book that God is mentioned, he is mentioned as a source of trouble.

The Hebrew name Qohelet uses for God, here and throughout the book, is Elohim. Among the forty times Qohelet mentions God, this is the word he always uses, and never the name Yahweh (Jehovah), the particular name for the deity of the Hebrew nation, the people of Israel. By using the name Elohim, some scholars suggest, Qohelet speaks of the God who is not limited to one nation or one people but is universal to all human beings. Another suggestion made is that Yahweh refers to a God conceived as more personal, the God who walks in the garden of Eden, who hears, who speaks, who shows emotions something like ours, who shows anger and jealousy, love and compassion, who has some sort of humanlike form, a more anthropomorphic sort of God, whereas Elohim denotes a more abstract entity, more distant, more diffuse, a God beyond name and form and qualities, a God seen "more philosophically." In short, some suggest, Yahweh implies a more personal God, Elohim more impersonal.

Either way, how does God even get into Qohelet's book? The matter is strange. Qohelet in his quest for understanding appears to rely on what he can see directly, what he can experience and verify, what he can empirically know to be out there in the world, or what he can reasonably deduce from what he has seen. But without recourse to dogma or revelation, why assume that God even exists?

Yet this is precisely what Qohelet seems to do. No reasons given, no arguments offered, no justification, no proof. Not even a sign of struggle or contemplation or discussion. God is just there, just assumed. (And giving man trouble.)

Qohelet and His Contradictions – that was Michael Fox's title for a

---

* With either translation –"busy with" or "afflicted with" – the upshot is the same. To be kept busy with a sorry task is to be afflicted.

book he wrote on Ecclesiastes. And a most apt title, because Qohelet is notoriously inconsistent. Qohelet looks at things one way, he looks at them another. He seems to conclude something, then turns around and refutes it, or accepts what he has earlier refuted. He contradicts himself so plainly and so often that many scholars have felt obliged to come up with different theories to explain why. Perhaps not everything Qohelet supposedly said is actually something he said; perhaps later scribes and glossators inserted their own interpolations, to balance his probing and impious thoughts with more conventional and pious ones. Or perhaps Qohelet was sometimes quoting conventional wisdom, only to over- turn it. Or perhaps we can sometimes assign inconsistencies to scribal errors, mistakes made in copying the book, and Qohelet wasn't really contradicting himself at all.

Or perhaps that's just the way people are: They mull things over, go back and forth, try out different solutions, hold to inconsistent points of view. To be human is to be a bit ragged.

Chasing after wind

Qohelet speaks of everything as "a chasing after wind." Depending on how one interprets the Hebrew, the phrase may also be translated as "shepherding the wind" or "feeding on wind," both also figures for utter futility. Reading the Hebrew yet another way, the King James Version says "vexation of spirit," which equally tells what Qohelet found.

We might hope that by gaining knowledge we might rise above fu- tility and vexation, but Qohelet says that his efforts to do this failed and that wisdom only makes matters worse, for the more wisdom one gains the more sorrowful one becomes to see a world where everything, even the very pursuit of wisdom, is but a chasing after wind.

2

2:1–11: The experiment with pleasure

[1] I said in my heart, "Come now, let me make you try
pleasure. Enjoy what is good!" And – just see! – this
also was vanity. [2] I said of laughter "It is mad" and of
pleasure "What does it accomplish?" [3] I searched in my
heart how to ply my body with wine – my heart still
guiding me with wisdom – and how to lay hold on folly,
till I might see what is best for men to do under heaven
the few days of their life.

[4] I made great works: I built myself houses; I planted
myself vineyards. [5] I made myself gardens and parks,
and I planted trees in them of all kinds of fruit. [6] I
made myself pools from which to water the forests
springing up with trees. [7] I bought men and women as
servants, and had servants born in my house. I also
had great possessions of herds and flocks, more than
all who were before me in Jerusalem. [8] I also gathered
myself silver and gold, and the treasures of kings and

provinces. I got myself singers, both men and women,
and many concubines, the delights of men.

[9] So I became great and flourished more than all who
were before me in Jerusalem. And also my wisdom
stood with me. [10] Nothing that my eyes desired did I
keep from them, nor did I withhold my heart from any
joy, for my heart had joy in all my labor and this was
my portion from all my labor. [11] Then I turned to look
upon all the works that my hands had done, and on
the labor I had labored to do. And – just see! – all was
vanity and a chasing after wind, and there was no profit
under the sun.

"Come now, let me make you try pleasure"

As the second chapter begins, we find Qohelet again in dialogue with
himself, with his heart, seeking meaning and purpose in life. He has
told us (in 1:17) that he tried not only wisdom but also madness and folly.
Wisdom only made matters worse, he has said, and now he tells us of his
experiment with folly – that is, with the pursuit of pleasure.

In the third verse he lays out the essence of the plan: to abandon
himself to pleasure yet at the same time watch himself do it, to enjoy
freely yet monitor and guide the whole process with wisdom.

It is a bold and risky undertaking – what if pleasure were to overwhelm wisdom, if the experiment in madness were to turn into true
madness, with no door by which to escape? I think of Odysseus yearning to hear the lovely singing of the Sirens, the sea nymphs whose ir-
resistibly beautiful voices would enchant the mind of every sailor, drive
him mad with passion for the sound, and beckon him to pursue it till he
destroyed himself amidst the waves and rocks.

Odysseus, you might recall, ordered his men to tie him to the mast,
stop their ears with wax so they would hear neither him nor the singing, and keep him tightly bound, however he might plead and cry and
bellow to be released, until the dangerous region of the Sirens was far
behind.

Qohelet's plan was more dangerous. To which mast could his mind be tied, and where were the deafened sailors to ensure him a safe passage? He might have wound up terminally, irretrievably foolish or mad, his experiment ruined, his life wrecked, his book never to be written.

Or – the hell with Odysseus – what about the 1960s?

In the 1960s the use of mind-altering herbs and chemicals, mild or potent, was sometimes a deliberate strategy for the simultaneous pursuit of both pleasure and spiritual enlightenment. With marijuana, the thinking went, one could free oneself from ordinary, socially conditioned modes of perception and could experience reality in new and deeper ways. And besides, as the poet Allen Ginsberg had announced, "Pot is fun."

In the mid 1960s Timothy Leary, Harvard psychology professor turned psychedelic apostle, spread the good word that LSD, a chemical more wondrously potent, could open the way to cosmic consciousness and realization of God. (And besides, LSD was even more fun.)

So we searched how to cheer ourselves not with Qohelet's favored wine (alcohol, the writer William Burroughs had observed, is the American "national drug") but with "weed" and "acid." And in this way, through insights and realizations gleaned on inner voyages, we hoped to discover true meaning in our lives.

For our minds to still guide us with wisdom under those circumstances was problematic because our minds were what we were messing with, even deliberately seeking to "blow." Since our pitifully conditioned minds, the idea went, were what was holding us back (the idea owed much to popularized notions of Hinduism and Buddhism), by "blowing our minds" – knocking them for a loop, short-circuiting them (with the aid of those sacred herbs and chemicals) – we could go beyond our minds and see reality with new and clearer eyes. As a slogan of the times put it, you had to "go out of your mind to use your head."

For a while, "going out of our minds" seemed to open new vistas, lead to wellsprings of creativity, offer genuine communion with God and the universe. Or else it was just enormous fun. But "going out of your mind" sometimes led to "going out of your head" permanently, or going on to still other types of herbs and chemicals, not even arguably sacred, which could make "the few days of one's life" still fewer.

That aside, by the time the sixties ended, most of us who had "turned on, tuned in, and dropped out" had given up on the experiment, frustrated and disappointed, realizing that it was futile, that it led nowhere, that this too was vanity and a chasing after wind. Still left with no clear picture of what was good for us mortals to do under heaven during the few skimpy days of our lives, we went back to school or went looking for jobs.* (Or, in my case, in 1968, though not yet disillusioned with the prospects of psychedelia for opening the way to inner growth, I encountered the Hare Krishna people, who persuaded me that I had not "laid hold on folly" till I could see what was good; rather, folly had laid hold on me. In the Sanskrit parlance, I was in *māyā* – illusion – and no amount of "alternative māyā," no amount of herbal or chemical mind-bending, could get me out. Māyā would recede only in the presence of truth – Absolute Truth – as darkness would recede only in the presence of light.)

In any case, the māyā to which Qohelet gave himself was more sensible, more conservative, more respectable – and more solid and tangible. He didn't just pop a pill or eat a mushroom and hallucinate palaces and women and a royal domain – he actually had them. As he tells us, he built houses, planted vineyards, made parks and orchards, amassed treasures, employed men and women singers – in general, built up an enormous estate, greater, he tells us, than anyone's in Jerusalem before.

And the enjoyments Qohelet gathered for himself sprang mainly from gifts of the earth: the vineyards, gardens, parks, and orchards, the pools of water, the trees, the herds and flocks, the silver and gold of his treasures. These gifts of nature he pulled together for himself for his own enjoyment. And people too, children of the earth – these he employed for his own pleasure, as singers and slaves and most notably as partners in sex.

Some commentators offer alternative translations for the Hebrew

---

* A brand of meditation popular at the close of the 1960s as a means of enlightenment – to live in transcendence, all you had to do was meditate for fifteen minutes twice a day – performed a useful function: It allowed young people who had turned their back on a fruitless, empty materialistic way of life to glide back to it (yet still be transcendental!) without having to admit to themselves or others that this was what they were doing. And this for only $35 (back in those days, the price for your own personal mantra).

words rendered here as "many concubines, the delights of men." The Hebrew passage, they say, need not have sexual connotations. But most agree that it does. They note that Solomon is elsewhere said to have had seven hundred wives and three hundred concubines. So in the list he gives of fine enjoyments, how could he leave out sex? Rather, he places it as the final item, the ultimate, the summit of all earthly pleasures.

The path of karma

From Qohelet's description of his endeavors, it seems he followed what the Vedic literature refers to as the path of karma, or acts performed for one's own enjoyment.

The word *karma* sometimes refers to whatever acts one does, especially for one's own pleasure. But, more precisely, karma refers to such acts that are right or proper, meritorious acts, acts that conform to religious principles or higher law and are therefore materially uplifting. The path of karma, then, is the path by which one strives for material enjoyment but does so rightly, even nobly.

Enjoyment pursued recklessly, irresponsibly, is another story altogether. We might still call it karma – action – but more precisely it's *vikarma*, "wrongful action," action that is lawless or harmful, and ultimately self-destructive.

When Qohelet built his houses and planted his vineyards, when he made his gardens and parks and orchards, when he fashioned his pools of water and gathered his herds and flocks, he exercised his rightful prerogatives as king. Even the keeping of slaves was seen as rightful, for the king was duty-bound not only to benefit from their service but to maintain them well. In the days of ancient monarchy, the king bore the heavy charge of guarding the safety of the state, cultivating its natural wealth, and caring generously for the welfare of its citizens, and with these royal duties came the royal pleasures reserved for his supreme station. The treasures, the songs, the feasts, and ultimately the intimate gratifications yielded him by his wives and mistresses – all these were rightfully his to enjoy.

Such indeed is the picture we have of King Solomon: wise, judicious, noble, strong, religious, and endowed with every sort of luxury one might desire. Qohelet, presenting himself in that role, says that he gave his eyes – and so, he implies, all his senses – whatever they might desire.

The Hebrew word used here for "desire" can also mean "demand." The senses don't just politely ask; they press, they urge, they demand. And Qohelet says that whatever they demanded he gave them, holding nothing back. Gratifying his senses, he followed the path of karma to its heights, enjoying "the right way" on a grand scale. And Qohelet tells us he found pleasure in his work. He undertook great endeavors, for which he could be justly proud, and he received great rewards.

Giving one's heart to such feelings, says the Bhagavad-gītā, is characteristic of the "mode of passion." In the Gītā's analysis, what we do with our life, and what we think and feel, reflects a mixture of three modes, or qualities: goodness, passion, and ignorance. Goodness is marked by purity, calmness, and knowledge, passion by intense endeavor and desire, and ignorance by darkness, inertia, madness, and illusion. In the human heart these qualities mix in various proportions, yielding a palette of subtly differing temperaments, much as the three primary colors yellow, blue, and red blend to form countless colors, tints, and shades. Sometimes one main quality – one primary color – prevails in the mix, sometimes another.

When we see great material aspirations and desires, strong endeavors, and attachment to what one has gained or achieved, the main color in the picture is passion. It is passion that moves one along on the path of karma, in which one's pleasure is to work and achieve and to enjoy what one has gained.

On this path of karma, Qohelet says that what he enjoyed as a reward for all his work was but his due, his allotment or portion. The Hebrew word is *ḥeleq*, a keyword in the text, a word Qohelet uses several times. Our *ḥeleq* is what we have been given, what destiny or God has assigned to us, be it meager or abundant, pleasing or displeasing. It is what we are meant to get, our lot. The possessions measured out to us and what pleasure we may hope to derive from them are our *ḥeleq*. We will not receive less, and we cannot expect more.

Such a portion is also mentioned in the first mantra of the Īśopaniṣad, a straightforwardly theistic text among the Upaniṣads, the essential philosophical writings of the Vedic tradition. The Īśopaniṣad advises:

īśāvāsyam idaṁ sarvaṁ   yat kiñca jagatyāṁ jagat
tena tyaktena bhuñjīthā   mā gṛdhaḥ kasya svid dhanam

"Whether alive or dull, all within this universe belongs to its controller, the Lord. What you may enjoy is only what he has set aside for you as your portion. One should not strive for other things, knowing well to whom they belong." It is in that which has been given us – our allotment, our portion – that we may hope to find our rightful pleasure.

But Qohelet, at the height of his achievements and summit of his enjoyments, says he found everything hollow. Worse than hollow, it was absurd, irrational, not merely senseless but contrary to sense. With all his possessions and all that his eye might want, he ought to have been delighted, not depressed; fulfilled, not empty. And yet he found he had nothing, and for this nothingness – was it not absurd? – he had worked and toiled. Not only had he gained nothing, but – worse – the world offered nothing to gain.

2:12–16: Wisdom, folly, and fate

¹²And I turned to look upon wisdom, and madness and folly. For what can the man do who comes after the king? Just that which has already been done. ¹³Then I saw that wisdom excels folly as much as light excels darkness. ¹⁴The wise man's eyes are in his head, but the fool walks in darkness. And I also perceived that one event happens to them all. ¹⁵Then I said in my heart, "As it happens to the fool, so will it happen even to me. And why then have I become so very wise?" Then I said in my heart that this also is vanity. ¹⁶For there is no lasting remembrance of the wise man any more than of the fool; in the days to come, all will have long been forgotten. And how must the wise man die just like the fool!

For the fool and the wise, the same fate

Qohelet now considers wisdom and folly and even madness. We assume that wisdom is better, that it gives us an advantage. But does it?

The question "For what can the man do who comes after the king?" is puzzling. Why is it here? In fact, the Hebrew text itself is grammatically obscure, to the point of being nearly unintelligible. The scholar Wesley Fuerst comments that the text literally reads something like "What (of) the man who comes after the king? that which already have done?" Translators and commentators have simply had to do their best to give us something that makes sense. One possible meaning: Once even the king himself has tried the experiment (under the most promising conditions) and the experiment has failed, what can lesser men do who follow?

In any case, we still have Qohelet's argument: How is wisdom better than folly? And he answers that the wise man, relatively speaking, is better off. At least the wise man has eyes in his head. He can see where he's going. But this is but a *relative* advantage because, though fools walk in darkness and the wise in light, at last they all walk to the same place: they all die.

What then is the use of so much wisdom? As Qohelet has said before, "In much wisdom is much vexation." The wise will anguish over existential problems the fool doesn't worry about or even see. Isn't the fool then better off? As the commentator E. H. Plumptre puts it, "The very wisdom of the seeker might lead him to see that he has not only been wiser than others, but wiser than it was wise to be."

So again, vanity: The way things are is absurd. The wise man ought to be more fortunate than the fool, more at peace with himself, more contented, and ought to achieve a higher destination. And what does he get? Greater vexation and the same damn grave.

2:17–23: Working for nothing

¹⁷ So I hated life because the work that is done under the sun was grievous to me; for all is vanity and a

chasing after wind. [18]And I hated the fruit of all my labor at which I had labored under the sun, because I must leave it to the man who will be after me. [19]And who knows whether he will be a wise man or a fool? Yet he will have power over all for which I have labored, and in which I have shown myself wise under the sun. This also is vanity.

[20]Therefore I turned my heart to despair over all the labor at which I had labored under the sun. [21]For there is a man whose labor is with wisdom, and with knowledge, and with skill, yet to a man who has not labored at it he must leave his portion. This also is vanity and a great evil. [22]For what does a man have from all his labor, and from the striving of his heart, at which he labors under the sun? [23]For all his days are painful, and his occupation vexing; even at night his heart has no rest. This also is vanity.

Pleasure turns bitter

Now it comes to this. Qohelet's pleasures have turned to gall.

The Bhagavad-gītā says that this is what we can expect. "From the union of the senses with the objects of desire comes a happiness at first like nectar but at the end like poison. Such is happiness in the mode of passion."

And happiness in ignorance, with which passion is so often mixed, is still more dismal: "Delusion from beginning to end, arising from sleep, indolence, and madness – such is happiness in the mode of ignorance."

Happiness in goodness, the Gītā says, is superior. Though for that happiness one might have to undergo the trouble of self-discipline, of self-restraint, of forgoing what might seem like enjoyment, one eventually finds tranquility, serenity, and joy. "At first like poison but at the end like nectar – such is happiness in the mode of goodness, born of the satisfaction of knowing oneself."

But happiness through goodness, through knowledge, is what Qohelet has already tried and found vexatious, and now, he finds, happiness in passion has turned bitter. And so, though wisdom excels folly as light excels darkness, finally "all is vanity and a chasing after wind."

And his work, too, in which before he said his heart found pleasure, he now has come to hate. The Hebrew word for "labor" has a dual meaning: it can refer either to work – to wearisome, burdensome toil – or to the fruit of that work, its payoff, its enjoyable reward. But now Qohelet has found hateful even that fruit of his work because he knows that after all the labor he has gone through to get it, with so much care and thought and skill, he must leave it to someone else, who may well turn out a fool. One builds up a fortune, only to have sons and grandsons squander it, builds up a business, only to have descendants run it into the ground, builds up a kingdom or empire, only to have future generations throw it to the dogs.

What is left but despair?

The path of knowledge and the path of work for one's own enjoyment have both proven useless, empty, absurd, so what is left but despair? Our English word *despair* comes from the Latin meaning "loss of hope." The Hebrew word used can literally mean "to give up for lost." Qohelet gives up his heart to despair as he sees that all for which he has worked with such diligence and skill will be left to someone else, someone who did nothing to earn it. Qohelet calls this a "great evil," using what the commentator Moses Stuart calls "an intensity of expression not before employed."

So again Qohelet asks a rhetorical question: What does a human being gain out of all his work? The answer is clear: nothing.

In the same question, Qohelet employs another phrase, which can be literally translated "the desire of his heart." What does one get from "the desire of his heart" with which he works? Fox translates this as "his heart's thoughts." "Heart," we might recall, indicates what we sometimes call the mind, the center of our thoughts: "I had my heart set on it."

The Bhagavad-gītā too observes that such desires are "coming forth from the mind" and "born of some notion in the heart." Elsewhere the Gītā even speaks of "one who desires to desire." That is, we get some notion in our mind, some thought of enjoyment, and we start ruminating on it, thinking about it, picturing it, letting our imagination run with it, pumping it up, and so the notion grows. My spiritual teacher called this process "agitating the mind for sense gratification," stimulating the mind with thoughts of what we imagine our senses might enjoy. The Gītā says this can never lead to peace.

Our minds agitated with thoughts of enjoyment, we work hard to fulfill our desires – and wind up with nothing. Our only reward is the pain of work and a mind so troubled that even at night we cannot rest. Again Qohelet laments, despairs, that this is all vain, empty, pointless, absurd.

2:24–26: Nothing better than enjoyment?

> [24] There is nothing better for a man than that he should eat and drink and let himself enjoy pleasure for his labor. This also, I saw, is from the hand of God. [25] For who will eat, or who will enjoy, apart from him? [26] For to the man who pleases him God gives wisdom and knowledge and joy, but to the one who is offensive he gives the task of gathering and heaping up, only to give to one who pleases God. This also is vanity and a chasing after wind.

Eat, drink, and enjoy

Changing directions, perhaps even seeming to reverse himself, Qohelet now commends enjoyment, or at least offers that this is the most we can expect. "There is nothing better," he says, and this is a theme to which he will return several times.

Some commentators see this theme as Qohelet's essential conclusion, his answer, his "joyous message" about life. I don't read it that way. The solution is too easy, offering a joyous outlook by discounting the book's tension between enjoyment and inanity – but I leave the matter for you to decide.

45

At any rate, here Qohelet says there's nothing better than to eat, drink, and enjoy through one's work. And he has a rationale: "This is from the hand of God." If God has given us some work to do and the pleasures the work may yield, the reasoning would go, why should we not accept them?

This, precisely, is the Vedic "path of karma," on which one works honestly for the sake of the resulting pleasures one hopes the God one worships will grant one to enjoy.

The Śrīmad-Bhāgavatam, however, suggests that living merely to eat, drink, and enjoy is a waste of one's human life because human life has a higher purpose. The Bhāgavatam says:

> kāmasya nendriya-prītir   lābho jīveta yāvatā
> jīvasya tattva-jijñāsā   nārtho yaś ceha karmabhiḥ

"Not for pleasing of the senses should one's desires be aimed but only for gaining what one needs to live, because human life is meant for inquiry about the ultimate truth. Nothing else should be the goal of one's work."

Qohelet, surely, is engaged, even obsessed, with such inquiry. But here, at least, he seems to have come full circle, offering that there's nothing better than working and enjoying material pleasure, even though such pleasure, on a grand scale, is what he has already tried and left.

Work, eat, drink, and enjoy. How bright is the outlook? The Bhāgavatam tells of a king who late in life, about to hand over his kingdom, instructs his sons,

> nāyaṁ deho deha-bhājāṁ nṛ-loke
> kaṣṭān kāmān arhate viḍ-bhujāṁ ye

"Of all the living beings granted bodies in this world, one given this human form should not work hard day and night simply for sense gratification, which can be had even by the hogs that eat stool."

In the rural villages of India one commonly sees the sort of hog here referred to, who enjoys eating feces. The local people, using old-time natural bathroom arrangements, will defecate somewhere out in the fields, and soon a hog will show up, having sniffed out what the man or woman has left, and eagerly chow it down.

The king's point is that the pleasure the hog gets from such eating is no less than the pleasure of eating enjoyed by a human being. Though the human and the hog may differ in their choice of food, the pleasure they derive is the same. So why should a human being work so hard just to get the same pleasure as a hog?

Qohelet himself seems far from content with such a project. But now he seems resigned: "There is nothing better." Or perhaps he is trying to be upbeat. Anyway, he says, this all comes from the hand of God.

God now appears for the second time in the text. The first time, in 1:13, he was introduced as he who had given men "an unhappy business to be busy with." Now he appears more benevolently, as the supplier of our enjoyments. "For who will eat, or who will enjoy, apart from him?" That is, without his assent.

But how benevolent is a God who merely supplies enjoyments for a pleasure-seeking project that is doomed? Could he have given "nothing better"? From what Qohelet seems to say, apparently not. (Or else this doomed "nothing better" is the most God chose to give.)

Strange notions, but so what?

"Who will eat, or who will enjoy?" Examining the meaning of a particular Hebrew verb, Michael Fox suggests the translation "For who will eat, or who will fret, except as he determines?" In that case, from the hand of God come both enjoyment and anxiety.

This fits well with the verse that follows, in which Qohelet says that God rewards the person who pleases him and gives trouble to one who offends. Coming from Qohelet, though, such a statement is strange. Now God justly gives whatever one deserves, whereas only a few verses back the rewards of work might descend upon a person who did nothing to deserve them, or even upon a fool. Stranger still is the notion that God neatly arranges for the offender to gather possessions, heap them up, only to forfeit them to one by whom God has been pleased. Nowhere else does Qohelet come out with such an idea, and how could his sharp eye have failed to notice offenders holding on lifelong to their heaps of stuff and good men getting nothing?

Perhaps, as some scholars suggest, this verse is a pious interpolation. Or is Qohelet gently mocking a pious view that conflicts so badly with the way we see things go? Or perhaps, for the moment, Qohelet is actually adopting that conventional view. In any case it hardly matters, because Qohelet sums things up with his usual big "So what?" Ultimately, this too – this heaping up or losing, this joy or anxiety, this eating and drinking and finding pleasure through one's work – all is useless, pointless, meaningless, absurd, nothing more than a chasing after wind.

Qohelet in the modern world

I pause here to take note of extraordinary comments made on this verse by Moses Stuart, whose work on Ecclesiastes was published in 1851. A learned scholar who had served as a Congregationalist pastor, Stuart for nearly forty years chaired the department of sacred literature at Andover Seminary. His commentary on Ecclesiastes appeared the year before his death.

Apart from offering a thoroughgoing treatment of the linguistic particulars of the text ("I have endeavored to leave not a single grammatical difficulty ... untouched"), his book gives deeply considered insights into what Qohelet has expressed, as seen from a viewpoint of devout Christian piety. For Stuart, Ecclesiastes is a fully canonical, divinely inspired work, portraying "a struggling mind, which comes off triumphantly at last, and settles down on 'fearing God, and keeping his commandments,' as the way to happiness and as the sum of human duty."

Though I don't share Stuart's view of Qohelet's final triumphant answer (that joyous wrap-up, if that's what it is, comes not from the dour Qohelet but from the narrator), here that's not my topic. What interests me is far more curious. It's Stuart's thoughts on how impressed our man Qohelet would be by modern intellectual progress.

Qohelet has brought us to conclude, Stuart writes, that no material pursuits or possessions can yield us the ultimate good we seek, that the most they can afford us is the enjoyment we get from satisfying "the wants and cravings of our physical nature," and that even for this we must depend not merely on our own efforts but on "the special favour of God." A fair summary.

"Such is the conclusion," Stuart says, "of a most acute observer, a man endowed with high intellectual powers, and who sought for wisdom and knowledge, in all the various ways practicable at the time when he lived."

Stuart then asks:

> But what was science or philosophy then, and specially
> what were they among the Hebrews, who never set up
> any academies or colleges for the study of science and phi-
> losophy? How different, we may well believe, would be
> the conclusions of the same investigator, in some respects,
> and to a certain extent, were he now to reappear and come
> among us, and again make his experiments!

Were Qohelet to reappear now, he would see a world full of academies
and colleges and scientific institutes. And that would make so much of
a difference!

> In his day, all that science could offer of satisfaction, in the
> pursuit of it, was meagre indeed, and very unsatisfactory to
> an active and inquisitive mind. In a little time [such a man
> as Qohelet] would come, by diligent study, to the *ne plus
> ultra* [the highest point one could attain] and well might
> he call it *vanity* and an *empty pursuit.*[*]

That, of course, was in Qohelet's day.

> But at the present time, the same inquirer might turn, in
> scores of directions, and find enough busily to engage his
> whole life and much more, in any one of the numerous sci-
> ences. He would find, too, that there was much to instruct
> and to gratify the mind, in each or any one of them.

So many sciences. So much to instruct and gratify the mind. Enough to
engage one's whole life and more!

> Put such a man as Coheleth, at the present time, in the
> position of a Newton, Laplace, Liebig, Cuvier, Owen,
> Linnaeus, Davy, Hamilton, Humboldt, and multitudes of
> other men in Europe, and in America, …

You don't recognize all these names? Only some? Not surprising.

---

[*] The italics, here and below, are all Stuart's.

As Qohelet said, "The people of long ago are not remembered." But anyway, put Qohelet in the position of one of these great men,

> and he would find enough in the pursuit of *wisdom and knowledge*, to fill his soul with the deepest interest, and to afford high gratification. "To eat, and drink, and enjoy the good of one's toil," while it is always a grateful blessing, would not even be named in comparison with pursuits like theirs.

Forget eating and drinking. Now we have literature, philosophy, and science!

> How would every true votary of science now look down on mere sensual gratifications, (important and even necessary as they might be in their proper place, and in their appropriate measure), compared with the delights which he would experience in his literary and scientific pursuits!

Stuart has a point there. Though I suspect that even true votaries of science might sometimes take time out for an *extra* measure of "mere sensual gratifications," literary and scientific pursuits certainly offer grand and profound delights.

The Vedic sages say that we each have, as it were, two bodies: a gross body (the physical one we see) and a subtle body (the "body" of mind and intelligence). And just as the gross physical body has senses that crave gratification – the eyes, ears, nose, tongue, and sense of touch – so the mind and intellect are "senses" for the subtle body, and they too crave to be gratified. Just as on the grosser level one might delight in physical pleasures, on the more subtle level one may delight in the higher, more rarefied pleasures of the intellect and mind.

And so, Stuart suggests, if Qohelet were to reappear in the modern world – which for Stuart meant the 1840s – instead of declaring that all is vanity he might have reveled in the pleasures of modern philosophy, literature, and science.

In fairness to Stuart: Though he says "In our day, the pleasure or good that towers high above all other mere worldly enjoyments and pursuits … is the *pursuit of knowledge*," he makes clear that he is speaking only in terms of the present world and its worldly, temporal happiness.

If we look to the soul, he says, and compare worldly happiness with the happiness of "the world to come" (a world, by the way, that Qohelet doesn't believe in), "then all the delights of even science and philosophy, ardently pursued, dwindle down to insignificance" – especially, for Stuart, "in comparison with hope animated by a living faith" in God and Jesus Christ.

Nonetheless, Stuart clearly does seem to think that modern philosophy, literature, and science, in comparison to those of Qohelet's time, are so dazzling they would likely have turned Qohelet's mind. In Qohelet's day, the pleasures offered by science and philosophy were so limited, especially since the Hebrews "never set up any academies or colleges for the study of science and philosophy." But now, like so many modern Jews, Qohelet could go to college and then grad school. He might become a great scientist and work for a multinational corporation or the United States Defense Department. Or he could become a professor at Berkeley or MIT or Carnegie-Mellon, or perhaps Brandeis. And if Qohelet, as Stuart suggests, might have been so enchanted by philosophy, literature, and science in the 1840s, just imagine the delights that would await him now! Surely he would not declare that all is vanity and a chasing after wind; "nay, one cannot help the feeling that, in regard to the pursuit of *wisdom and knowledge* his conclusions would have been very different."

But I suspect that if Qohelet were to reappear today he would be in even greater despair. He would see our great and marvelous progress and see it all leading nowhere, except perhaps to greater destructiveness, confusion, and angst. He would observe that even the greatest writer, the greatest philosopher, and the greatest scientist dies just like the fool. And he would cry, "The more knowledge, the more grief!"

3

3:1–8: A time for every purpose

¹To every thing there is a season,
   and a time to every purpose under heaven:
²A time to be born, and a time to die;
   a time to plant, and a time to pluck up what is planted;
³A time to kill, and a time to heal;
   a time to break down, and a time to build up;
⁴A time to weep, and a time to laugh;
   a time to mourn, and a time to dance;
⁵A time to cast away stones,
   and a time to gather stones together;
a time to embrace,
   and a time to refrain from embracing;
⁶A time to seek, and a time to lose;
   a time to keep, and a time to cast away;
⁷A time to rend, and a time to sew;
   a time to keep silence, and a time to speak;
⁸A time to love, and a time to hate;
   a time for war, and a time for peace.

Qohelet's song

In 1959 the American folk singer Pete Seeger put this passage to music. He moved the words around a bit, he pulled them together with the refrain "Turn! Turn! Turn!" and to even out a verse he added to "a time of peace" the line "I swear it's not too late." Having written the song, he "sang it around," as he put it, other singers in the folk-music scene picked it up, and I suppose I first heard it sometime soon after 1962, when he first put it out on a record. In the winter of 1965 a folk rock group, the Byrds, came out with a version that for three weeks was the number-one song in America.

It was a beautiful song, simple and profound. Though I'd read Ecclesiastes, or soon would, I thought of the song separately from Qohelet's gloomy despair over a world in which he could discern no sensible meaning. The song, it seemed, had a different mood, in which time imparted to all things a timeless and graceful balance.

Why is there time at all?

To me now, Qohelet's song brings questions to mind, of which this is the first: Why is there time at all?

I should at once note that the Hebrew word used here for "time" doesn't refer to time in the abstract, time as that continuous force that moves all events through the sequences of past, present, and future. For that, Hebrew has other words. Here "time" refers, rather, to a "suitable time," or a time when something is meant to happen, whether once (like the day in your childhood when you first set off to school) or repeatedly (like the time each day to start work). But these occasions could not occur were it not for that silent, unceasing, all-powerful force under whose control all events unfold. Without that force of time, things could be but could never become. All would be static, frozen, and nothing could ever develop or change. A pot of water could sit on a fire, but it could never come to a boil. There could be no moments, hours, or days, no occasions, no seasons at all.

We take time for granted. It just is, always. And always has been. But why? From where could time have arisen? And how? And when? The very questions send our minds in circles. How can there be any "when" without time? And how could time have arisen without time in which to do so?

We find ourselves stuck with having to regard time as irreducible and inconceivable, beyond our power to fully understand. It always was and always will be. It was here before we were and will still be here once we are gone. Ruling the life of every atom, every star and galaxy, every microbe and king, it is all-powerful. Every philosopher and every scientist must stand within the limits of time. It objectively exists – we see its effects everywhere – and yet we can't quite put our finger on it, can't quite figure out what it is. Everything has its origin within time, yet time, limitless and all-pervading, seems to have no origin beyond itself.

And so time is God.

For those of us who are agnostic as to the existence of God, of a supreme being, a supreme controller, a supreme absolute, a God beginningless and endless, all-powerful and all-pervading, here is that God, undeniably evident, undeniably real.

Granted, this is not the personal God of biblical history or faith, the God who speaks to Moses or sits in heaven on a lofty throne. Yet time fully qualifies as the supreme entity, the supreme mover, to whose power even the greatest of us must willingly or unwillingly submit.

In the eleventh chapter of the Bhagavad-gītā Śrī Krishna, who throughout has served as personal teacher and guide for his friend and disciple Arjuna, grants Arjuna the spiritual eyes to see him in a cosmic "universal form," in which Arjuna can see, as if in one place, all that exists in the universe. That wondrous form, having limitless arms and legs and faces, dazzling like thousands of suns, and filling earth and sky in all directions – encompassing all rivers and mountains and seas, all people and all planets, all creatures and all creations – inspires in Arjuna an overwhelming awe.

Yet soon that form assumes a fierce aspect, all-devouring, cataclysmic, into whose blazing mouths Arjuna sees all beings, wave upon wave, rushing to destruction, like moths into a fire.

"Who are you?" Arjuna manages to ask, trembling, as his awe cascades into chaotic bewilderment and fear. "And why have you come?"

"I am time," the dreadful form responds. "And I have come to destroy all."

Krishna soon withdraws the vision and resumes his congenial human form. But now Arjuna has seen God in the form of time, the supreme controlling force and ultimately the destroyer of all. It was a vision he could scarcely bear to see, a vision that had to be withdrawn, yet a vision of which readers of the Gītā may remain ever mindful.

The Vedic literature speaks of God as having different aspects, beginning with an aspect that is all-pervading, silent, invisible, and impersonal. That impersonal feature of God as time exquisitely governs every moment of existence. And it both creates and destroys, builds up and tears down.

How much is predetermined, and how much are we free?

Qohelet's poetic verses also suggest another question: To what extent are the events of our lives predestined, predetermined?

Here the Hebrew word for *season*, writes the scholar C. L. Seow, "is ordinarily used of predetermined or appointed time." This view is generally accepted, and therefore scholars are of two minds about this passage. Some agree with Seow, who says, "The text is not about moments that people choose. It concerns events that people encounter in life, those that just happen whether one is ready or not." After all, what power do we have over the time of birth or the time of death? And yet other scholars point out that, for example, when to embrace and when to refrain from embracing is a matter of free choice – it's up to us.

So what is Qohelet's view? Is he saying that the time for everything is fixed, or is he speaking of times we can choose, or where at least we have some wriggle room?

I can't presume to know Qohelet's mind. Precisely what he intended in words recorded thousands of years ago is beyond my power to nail down. So let us consider the issues his words suggest to us now.

Qohelet begins by saying there is a time to be born and a time to die. Surely the time of our birth is beyond our control; we have no say in the matter. And the time of death? Perhaps we would like to think we have some control over it. By healthy living, by suitable medical care, by availing ourselves of the gifts of modern science, we can extend our lives.

Yet death freely exercises the privilege of disregarding our precautions, confounding our science, overstepping our plans, and arbitrarily showing up whenever it very well pleases.

As the Śrīmad-Bhāgavatam points out, despite caring and attentive parents a child may die, despite an expert physician a patient may succumb to disease, and despite a strong boat a voyager may drown. (Or else a homeless child may live, the sickest patient survive without a doctor, or a voyager make it to shore even on a makeshift raft.)

We may hasten our death, or at least try, but even if we opt for suicide we may lose courage or botch the job or be improbably and unaccountably rescued; death still has the final say. We may "die before our time," but even then the revised time for our death is decided by forces beyond our control.

So all the times and occasions in our lives lie bracketed between these two fixed boundaries, chosen for us, not by us – a time to be born and a time to die.

Now, what of the times in between?

Again, nature rules, and we are but her subjects. Nature has her own rhythms, her own seasons, her own times, her own way of doing things, and we can either cooperate or else be foolish enough to go against her and imagine we can get away with it.

And even that foolishness is part of the workings of nature. The Bhagavad-gītā says,

> *prakṛteḥ kriyamāṇāni guṇaiḥ karmāṇi sarvaśaḥ*
> *ahaṅkāra-vimūḍhātmā kartāham iti manyate*

"All acts are carried out by dint of the qualities of nature. Yet a soul bewildered by false ego thinks, 'I am the doer.' "

Here the idea is that just as the laws of nature control the movements of the celestial bodies – the planets, the stars – those laws also control the movements of the bodies of even the smallest living being. Living beings too follow their ordained course – taking birth, growing, staying for a while, multiplying, dwindling, and dying. And all this lies beyond our control. We can no more halt or reverse this course than revise the grand cycles of the cosmos, for the bodies of living beings, including mine and yours, are as much a part of the machinery of nature as the planets and stars. As in any machine, the great wheel turns and the small wheel spins according to the clockwork. A boy cannot make himself old, nor can an old man make himself young. This we know.

Yet the Bhagavad-gītā takes this further. Even the things we take for granted *we* are doing, the Gītā says, are in fact carried out by the machinery of nature. Though we believe we act because we want to, in fact we act because we are compelled to. We eat, we sleep, we love, we defend ourselves because the bodies we live in tell us we must and give us no choice but to obey. We are strapped to the machinery. And so the acts we think *we* perform are in fact carried out by the force of the modes of nature.

The "modes" mentioned here are the three modes, or qualities, I talked about earlier in relation to karma: goodness, passion, and ignorance. A person at peace in goodness acts calmly and thoughtfully, a person charged with passion strives and endeavors, driven by ambitions and yearnings, and a person steeped in ignorance declines into lethargy, foolishness, and delusions. The Vedic literature says that a living being, though by nature pure, becomes colored by these three qualities, as pure water might be colored by minerals with which it comes in touch.

What then of free choice? In ignorance one is so dull or mad that the ability to make choices is practically obliterated. In passion one seems to have more freedom, but one can hardly break free from acting in service to one's impulses and desires. In goodness, yes, one can make choices with a calm and thoughtful mind. But even goodness predisposes one to choose in certain ways. So however free we imagine we are, the Gītā says, the particular modes we're colored by lock us in to a certain karmic trajectory, a certain destiny, a certain fate.

One can go beyond that destiny, the Gītā says, only by going beyond even the mode of goodness, and this one can do by true knowledge, for by such knowledge one sees everything in its natural relationship with the supreme truth, or God, and so one gets free from false ego and sees oneself as a spiritual being, beyond material qualities, sharing instead in the qualities of God, as a part shares the qualities of the whole. There is nothing so sublime and pure as transcendental knowledge, the Gītā says, and one can realize and enjoy that knowledge within oneself in due time when one is mature in devotion to the truth, or mature in God consciousness.

But if the material modes determine all we do, if we have no freedom to act except as they compel us, how can we develop the knowledge to go beyond them? The Vedic literature answers that if we are fortunate (and I'll discuss what that means later) then by following the guidance of those who know more than we do we may gradually elevate ourselves from ignorance to passion, from passion to goodness, and from goodness to transcendence. Or else, if still more fortunate, we may take a direct path toward transcendence, much as one might skip the stairs and take the elevator.

An important Vedānta-sūtras commentary written in the eighteenth century by Śrīla Baladeva Vidyābhūṣaṇa, a teacher in the Gauḍīya Vaiṣṇava tradition, gives a fine argument supporting the idea that we at least have the freedom to follow such advice. The Vedic literature, he says, offers directions or guidance on how we should act, and these directions would be pointless if we had no freedom to follow them. And so, despite the statement in the Gītā that *all* acts are carried out by the modes of nature, nature at least allows us this much tiny freedom: if we so choose, we can follow higher guidance, the guidance given by sages who know more than we.

Qohelet too, it seems, must have thought we have at least that much freedom, since in chapter eleven he gives direct advice for a young man – and what is the use of giving advice unless we believe that the person we're advising has the freedom to follow it?

In any case, here Qohelet advises us that the creation is so made that all things have their season, their suitable time. Implied is that to be in harmony we should recognize what those seasons are and tune our acts accordingly. We should swim with nature's currents, not against them. The Vedic sages would say that a first step toward elevation to goodness is to place oneself in harmony with nature's laws, or God's laws, and this implies knowing what to do at what times. The Hebrew sages, too, placed great importance on understanding the suitable times for what we do, though this can be tricky because we may be unsure what those times are. Hence the need for sages – and sometimes even sages may be unsure.

Suitable times
Now, on to the times and occasions Qohelet mentions.

There are times to plant and times to pluck up what has been planted, times to kill and break down, times to heal and build up.

There is a time to weep and a time to laugh. By nature's arrangements, sorrow comes in its own time, uninvited. And so joy will also come, of its own accord. The Śrīmad-Bhāgavatam therefore advises that we not waste our life trying to stave off sorrow and boost our joy, but rather accept them both as they come and stay focused on the real purpose of life: spiritual realization.

And since everything has its suitable time, we should suit our acts to the time as well. As Fox observes, a funeral is not the time to laugh.

A time to cast away stones and a time to gather them can be taken straightforwardly. The Ecclesiastes Targum, an ancient Aramaic paraphrase of the book, offers that there is a time to demolish a building and a time to gather stones to prepare to rebuild. Or, some scholars say, "casting stones" might refer to strewing rocks about a field to render it unfit for an enemy to cultivate, and one might "gather stones" to clear the field to make it useful once again.

Other commentators, both modern and medieval, have said that "cast away stones" may be an idiom for having sexual intercourse (in modern vulgar slang, "getting one's rocks off") and "gathering stones" refers to sexual abstinence.

For people who see no higher goal in life than the gratification of the senses, what is the time for sexual intercourse? Whenever one feels like it and gets an attractive opportunity. The Śrīmad-Bhāgavatam bluntly compares that sort of sex to the sexual congress of monkeys, who follow a similar principle. I spend about a month every year in Govardhana, a sacred place in the northern Indian countryside where Krishna frolicked as a child and which today, as in ages past, is also home to literally hundreds, even thousands, of monkeys. And there one can't help but notice that the monkeys, apart from being rambunctious, often to the point of tearing things to pieces, are also exceptionally active in sex. Scrambling about and scurrying together with one partner after another, they seem always ready to "hump and pump." The Bhāgavatam asks, When human beings have no higher interest than to gratify their senses, how is their sex life any better?

According to the Bhāgavatam, and the entire tradition of Vedic civilization, sex, like all human activity, is meant to be divinely purposeful. In the Bhagavad-gītā Lord Krishna says that he himself, the ultimate divinity, is represented in all that is beautiful or powerful in the universe, including "sex not contrary to dharma" – to right action, to responsibility, to spiritual principles for advancement in human life.

This implies that sex has its own right time and context, fitting to a divine purpose. For sure, it gives us pleasure. But is that the whole story? Okay, it expresses love. But is "hump and pump" whenever we are moved by the urges of passion really such a great expression of love?

The problem is one of time and context. Take Fox's example of laughter: There's a time to laugh, certainly – but a funeral is the wrong time and context. Though even at a funeral something might strike us as funny, the time and context tell us to hold that laughter and save it for some other occasion. Or take eating: However hungry a surgeon might be, we wouldn't expect him to chomp into a sandwich in the midst of doing surgery. That's "the time to heal." Again, he needs to put his hunger aside until after the operation is over.

What then is the right time and context for sex? The Vedic tradition plainly says, Within marriage.

Prudish? Repressive? Absurdly moralistic and antique? Consider: Marriage is the context within which a man and woman profess long-term mutual commitment and responsibility. The girl is not just hungry for affection, the guy not just looking to score. Presumably it's not a tryout, a quick fix, or a torrid but passing affair. They're in it for the long haul. Marriage, therefore, is also the context that provides a home for children. After all, if we don't do something to stop the outcome of sex (and sometimes even if we do), the natural result is pregnancy and in due course the birth of a child. And children deserve stable parents and homes.

Yes, we can try to circumvent nature with pills and condoms so that we can have sex with the partner of the moment and enjoy the process without the natural result. That makes us better than monkeys, doesn't it? Should the girl get pregnant we have another pill to dissolve the little whatever-it-is, and should that fail we have salts and needles and forceps and other such tools for terminating pregnancy ("A time to kill"?). Now I ask you, what monkey could pull off that?

The Bhāgavatam says that the human lifetime is the time for spiritual realization and that sex out of context doesn't help. Rather than enabling us to express love in a manner superior to beasts, it drags us down from goodness to passion and ignorance and even to a brutality few beasts would have the heart for.

In contrast, the Vedic traditions of spirituality place great value on self-mastery and self-restraint, on being able to control the urges of one's senses instead of being forced to do whatever the senses demand. By following this ideal, so foreign to modern Western notions, one "conquers the lower self by the higher self" and gains the freedom needed for steady advancement in spiritual realization. Within this context of freedom, sex assumes its rightful place within marriage. And even in marriage, the focus of life is not on sex but on spirituality.

As for "a time to embrace," it may refer to friendly embracing or the embracing of parents and children. Or perhaps here (rather than in Qohelet's previous line) we may include embraces between man and woman (and, by implication, further sexual activity).

And here too, when we come to embraces between man and woman, in modern Western society the sense of suitable times appears to be slipping away. What are the time and place for warm, intimate sexual embraces? Well, anytime, and anywhere. On the street, in the library, the mall, the bus station, the train station, the airport, the airplane. Will a couple standing in front of a monk on an airplane express their deep feelings for one another by a chest-to-chest, waist-to-waist, hip-rolling, butt-clutching embrace? That was on one of my recent flights.

Restraint? Self-control? "A time to refrain"? The monkeys have nothing like that. Why should we? Again, it's because human life is meant for higher purposes – for spiritual inquiry and spiritual realization – and these purposes are poorly served by a mode of life in which anytime is the time to embrace and there's never a time to refrain. When the time for embracing is whenever we feel like it, then the mode of goodness fades, passion and ignorance prevail, and the search for higher understanding takes a serious hit.

Cultures not yet obliterated by television, the box office, and the American flag may still retain the antiquated sense that everything has its time and place. Such a cultural sense is conducive to spiritual advancement.

A time to seek and a time to lose

As for a time to seek, the Vedānta-sūtras say that the time to seek spiritual understanding is now. The first sūtra says, *athāto brahma jijñāsā:* "Now is the time for inquiry about the Absolute."

Why now? Commentators on this sūtra have given various reasons.

Now can mean "Now that we've come to the human form of life." According to the Vedic writings, within the body of every living being is the ātmā, the soul, the spark of consciousness – our real self – which travels from lifetime to lifetime, each time taking on a new body the way a person puts on a new set of clothes. In this journey from life to life, the ātmā, the conscious force, when dwelling in the body of a lower species – animal, fish, insect, plant, or whatever – automatically makes its way to the next form higher, until it gradually reaches the human form, a process that may take millions of lifetimes.

In the lower species the body limits one's freedom, so that one may eat, sleep, mate, and defend oneself but one is simply not equipped to reflect upon one's own existence, to ask questions about it, or to inquire about spiritual realization. That freedom, that ability, is granted in the human form. So now that we have come to the human form, we should use this opportunity for spiritual reflection and spiritual inquiry. We don't know when such a time and opportunity will come to us again.

Suppose I don't buy into the idea of multiple lifetimes. Even then, even if I think that my life on earth now is the only one I shall ever have, now that I have it I should use it for spiritual realization. Otherwise, if I use my life to strive for little more than better food, more comfortable sleep, more satisfying sex, or greater security for my self, my family, or my community, how am I better than an animal? More polished at it? At least I must inquire whether there's something greater.

Or *now* may mean "Now that the question has arisen." Now that I still have my wits about me and I see the importance of the question, I should not neglect it.

Or else *now* can be taken to mean "Now that other paths to self-fulfillment have failed." Like Qohelet, I have tried my best to do good work, to build up something for myself, to find pleasaure and enjoy, but even when I have succeeded I have failed because whatever I have achieved is absurdly vain, as fleeting and meaningless as vapor. (And how often do I even succeed?)

Even the project of acquiring knowledge and wisdom may seem doomed to failure. What is the use of it? What does it get us but greater frustration and anxiety? What is the use of being smart, educated, and skillful, of being well read and well informed, even of being logical, discriminating, and wise? The wise man and the fool end up in the same graveyard. So what is the use? I must seek for something that goes beyond this. That is the meaning of "inquiry about the Absolute."

Of course, the materialist seeks not for spiritual realization but for material profit, comfort, security, and enjoyment. For the avid materialist, any time is the time to seek material gains, and modern society increasingly reflects this. And we hardly consider that every material gain must eventually be lost and the "time to lose" may come at any moment. As I write, major American banks have collapsed, stock markets around the world are plunging, and the national economies of the leading nations are cascading in enormous losses. Indeed, a time to lose.

Some biblical commentators offer that a time to lose may also be volitional – for example, when a captain voluntarily throws merchandise overboard to save a ship. By recognizing a time to lose and accepting it, one may save oneself from still greater losses.

Of course, we may keep things for some time, but the Vedic tradition advises that we not become excessively attached to what we have nor accumulate more than we need. When we have more than needed we should distribute it, give it away, and not let it burden us down. And we should keep in mind that the ultimate time to lose is the time of death, when one is forced to lose everything.

A time to rend and a time to sew

Commentators have generally glossed the "time to rend" as a time of mourning, when in Jewish tradition one tears one's garments in sadness, and later comes the "time to sew," when the sadness is past and the garments are repaired.

Likewise, mourning could be a time for silence, with speaking resumed when the time for mourning is over. More generally, however, there are apt times to keep silent and apt times to speak. When we have nothing to say of spiritual value, there is much to be said for keeping silent.

A time for war and a time for peace

War and peace are the times for love and hate. It is here that Mr. Seeger, with a voice of determined hope, added to "a time of peace" the line "I swear it's not too late."

Yet in the years since Mr. Seeger came out with his song, or the millennia since Qohelet, peace has come but rarely. Could it be that the fitting times for peace have come but we have failed to recognize them? Or is it that we are helpless, that the machinery of nature works in such a way as to ration out times of peace only in small and scattered portions and there is nothing we can do about it? Or is it that while we are thick in ignorance and hot in passion we cannot expect the calm and peace that quietly grow from goodness?

The Bhagavad-gītā says that so long as we try to exploit and enjoy the resources of the world as though they were ours to do with as we like, we can never have peace, individually or collectively. Only when a sincere search for truth brings us to acknowledge the higher owner of all the planets of the universe, the higher enjoyer of all that the world provides, the higher friend of all living beings – only then can we have a time of peace, within the world or at least within our own selves. Perhaps for you and me, if we're serious and sincere, the time is not too late.

3:9–11: Working for God knows what

> [9] What profit has he who works in that in which he labors? [10] I have seen the travail that God has given man to be busy with. [11] He has made everything fitting for its time. He has also set the world in their hearts, yet they cannot find out the work that God has done from the beginning to the end.

"Times" in context. Alas!

Standing alone, Qohelet's "catalogue of times" may seem a lovely poem, celebrating the way all things come and go, each taking its suitable turn within the cycle of nature's divine arrangement. "God's in His heaven, all's right with the world."

With Qohelet, we can't get off so easy.* George Barton aptly sums up what Qohelet has to say: "Human activities are limited to certain times and seasons in which man goes his little round doing only what other men have done before. His nature cries out for complete knowledge of the works of God, but God has doomed him to ignorance, so that the best he can do is to eat and drink and ignorantly get what little enjoyment he can within these limitations."

"What gain have the workers from their toil?" Qohelet asks. And his answer is plain: None at all. Under the sun, which pants in the futile labor of its vast and endless cosmic rounds, little men labor for nothing, time forcing them to plod through their routines within the prison walls of days and seasons, year after meaningless year.

"I have seen the business God has given everyone to be busy with," Qohelet says. And he has already told us (in 1:13) what kind of business that is – "an unhappy business," all amounting to nothing more than "vanity and a chasing after wind." We are busy in useless labor. And why? Because God has stuck it on us.

God has made every one of our engagements "suitable for its time" and made them all absurdly meaningless and pointless. Worse still, he has tantalized, vexed, and frustrated us by putting into our hearts something crucial we'll never get to the end of.

The Hebrew word for what that is has been variously translated and argued over. God has put "the world" in our hearts, or put "eternity" there, or "the course of the world," or "a sense of past and future." Or he has put "ignorance" there. Or if (as several commentators have suggested) scribes have inadvertently switched two Hebrew letters, what God has put there is "toil" – mental labor.

However you take it, God has made us in such a way that we long to

---

* And like Qohelet's poem, the lovely expression of contentment in the line above from Robert Browning has an ironic context. It's from a song Browning puts in the mouth of an exploited Italian orphan girl who had to work long wearisome hours at a silk mill, with only one day off in a year. The girl innocently sings the song while passing by the mill owner's wife and her lover, who have murdered the mill owner. "All's right with the world" indeed!

understand what's going on – what the meaning of our life is, why the world was made the way it is, what its purpose is, and what our place in it might be. We want to know how our small lives fit into the great picture of endless time, why time exists at all, and what the "right" times might be for the things we have to do. God has made us hungry to know what is ever concealed from us, and yet he keeps it concealed, and keeps us ignorant and frustrated.

"I have seen"

Here Qohelet seems forced to contend with the consequences of the way he has chosen to gain understanding. How will we understand what is what? By direct experience – by gathering evidence with our senses, especially by the powerful sense of sight. "I have seen … ," Qohelet says. And he will say it several times more: "I saw … I saw … I turned and saw …" And if we follow Qohelet's method, after seeing we will sift and weigh what we have seen – ponder it, analyze it, dwell on it, theorize about it, try somehow to make sense of it.

And ultimately we will fail. We will run up against the limitations of our senses: There's only so much we can see, and there's so much we can't. Put a thin piece of paper in front of my eyes, and I can't see beyond it. Put too much distance or too much haze, and my vision starts to blur. If something's too small I can't see it, or even if too big. I can't see my own eyelid, the closest thing to the eye. And at night if you turn off the lights I can't see anything at all. With my mighty power of sight, I can't see sounds. I can't see the wind. I can't see anything that's hidden. And all my other senses bump into the same sort of limitations.

I can extend my senses with various devices – spectacles, microscopes, telescopes, amplifiers, sensors for heat and movement – but shortly I'll come to an extended set of limits. There's no way around this. However many rings I burst through, I will always find the next. However much I can see, there's always so much I can't. My vision will always be boxed in.

And when I try to make sense of what I see, I run into the shortcomings of my mind. I see a rope and think it's a snake. I see a woman and mistake her for a man. I see someone smile at me and don't realize the smile is meant for someone else. I see a stray toy on the road when in fact it's an improvised bomb.

And these are just basic errors in the mind's work of recognizing patterns, of turning sight into perception. Now extend such mental failings to the work of understanding life as a whole. When I try to make ultimate sense of what I see, when I try to find ultimate meaning, my mind will inevitably take wrong turns, or drive about in circles, or get stuck in mental traffic and finally just give out.

According to the Vedic teachings, we are all shot through with four defects: imperfect senses, a tendency to make mistakes, a tendency to get carried away by illusion, and a tendency to cheat. (Despite our imperfect senses and our proneness to make mistakes and get bewildered, we come on like we've figured it all out. Cheating, no?)

In short: Direct experience and inductive reasoning may be fine within limits, but when we come to ultimate questions these methods fail, and so we "cannot find out what God has done from the beginning to the end."

Even if we think that there's no God, that nature just runs on its own, we can't be sure of that either. Nor figure out how or why existence pops into existence, nor where it's finally headed or why. Finally, whatever we think and however much we think, the secret remains secret. As we find in the epic Mahābhārata, *acintyā khalu ye bhāvā na tāṁs tarkeṇa yojayet:* "That which lies beyond the power of thought cannot be understood by logic."

3:12–13: Eat, drink, and have a good time toiling away

> [12] I know that there is nothing better for them than to
> rejoice and to get pleasure so long as they live. [13] And
> also for any man to eat and drink and enjoy pleasure in
> all his labor – this is a gift of God.

Nothing better?

When Qohelet says "I know that there is nothing better" we might well ask him, "How do you know?" All he can reliably tell us is what lies within his experience, not "all that is." So perhaps he could more defensibly say, "I know of nothing better."

But let's not argue with him, because in any case his conclusion doesn't seem one he's delighted with. "I know that there is nothing better," he says, and we might envision him saying it with a disappointed sigh. Again: Is this all? Nothing more than this?

Qohelet has come again to the same place where we found him in 2:24: Having failed at his experiment with pleasure (and that too on a royal level), he now commends as the best there is the very pleasure he has found meaningless and empty.

This is what the Bhāgavatam refers to as "chewing the chewed again and again." In tropical countries people often enjoy chewing fresh sugarcane, which yields a sweet and tasty juice. You chew the cane, relish the juice, and then leave the woody fiber aside. And that's it. If you try to chew the same cane again – okay, you might get a bit more juice, but not much, hardly enough to be worth it, and if after putting it aside the second time you pick it up and try again, what can you expect?

Such, the Bhāgavatam says, is the nature of material enjoyment. We try something and extract a little joy, and then try the same thing again, with diminished results, and then try it yet again. Soon whatever we're trying becomes dry, tasteless, and frustrating, but for lack of anything better we keep trying, "chewing the chewed," imagining there's still more joy to be had from it.

I could talk about kids and how quickly they tire of old toys, but let's go for the top: the pleasure of sex. Qohelet had it to the highest extent – "many concubines, the delights of men" – and at the end he told us what it came to: "vanity, and a chasing after wind." And now should we try it again? Our senses cry out for it, and our mind can picture how satisfying it will be *this time*, and at the end – disappointment.

The pleasure a human being gets out of eating, drinking, or sex is in essence the same as what a hog gets, or a dog, or a mosquito. Finally, eating is eating, sex is sex. And yet, Qohelet says, "there is nothing better."

In fact, he says there is "nothing better as long as they live." Even in old age, it seems, people still pursue the same pleasure. And so a study published in 2007[*] found that of American men between the ages of 65

---

[*] S. T. Lindau et al., "A Study of Sexuality and Health among Older Adults in the United States," *New England Journal of Medicine* 357, no. 8 (2007): 762–74.

and 74, nearly seven out of ten were "sexually active," and for men 75 through 85, nearly four out of ten. For more than half the men in the older group, this meant two or three times a month, and for one out of four, at least once a week. (For women in the same age groups the numbers were lower, in part because of not having a man: Men, on average, marry younger women, and men die somewhat earlier.) As the study's authors tell us, "The prevalence of sexual activity declines with age, yet a substantial number of men and women engage in vaginal intercourse, oral sex, and masturbation even in the eighth and ninth decades of life." And this despite arthritis, diabetes, heart disease, hypertension, and an array of troublesome physical ailments directly related to sexual performance. Amidst all this, Qohelet says, "I know that there is nothing better for them than to be happy and enjoy themselves as long as they live."

For those done with sex and too old to enjoy working, there's still the pleasure of eating and drinking and schmoozing with what's left of their friends and families. Nothing better? As long as they live? Alas!

And what's this about "taking pleasure in all their labor" – as many translations have it, "all their toil"? Toil, by definition, is not pleasurable but troublesome, wearisome, miserable. And toil is what Qohelet says. The Hebrew word – 'amal – carries the same strongly negative sense. As we hear from Seow, in the Bible the word is closely linked with "extremely negative terms" – trouble, grief, evil, falsehood, vexation, lies, destruction, violence, affliction, poverty, deceit. 'Amal – labor or toil – is not just work or effort but struggle, sweat, drudgery, travail. Is that what we're supposed to take pleasure in?

As I've mentioned before, the word does have a dual meaning. It can refer either to wearisome labor or to its results, what we earn by such labor – or it can refer to both. The two, after all, go together. More than going together, they are bound together. What we earn is a result of our toil, but in one sense our toil is the result of what we earn because it is for the sake of those earnings that we undergo the toil. Work brings us money, but money – the need or desire for it – makes us work. We work for happiness, but since the work itself is misery, the very pursuit of happiness makes us miserable.

That is why the Vedic sages advise that one not work for happiness at all. Happiness, they say, will come of its own accord. After all, no one seeks misery – no one works for it or stands in line for it – yet misery comes anyway, on its own. Then why not happiness as well? By nature's way, each time a living being is born his physical embodiment brings along with it a certain quota of happiness and distress. Both will find us, in whatever measure we are destined to receive. The Śrīmad-Bhāgavatam therefore advises that one work only to keep body and soul together, for the sake of the true human project of spiritual inquiry. That alone should be the purpose of one's work.

This, the Bhāgavatam says, is the actual gift given by God for a human being: the ability to inquire about our purpose for existing, about ultimate meaning. But if that's not the gift we want, God (or nature, if you will) has others to offer – in essence, the same gifts offered to other creatures: some food, something to drink, some sex. And for such rewards a life of hard work.

Here to enjoy

Now, let's look at things another way. We all want to eat and drink and enjoy, and seeing the enjoyments we receive as a gift from God reflects a sense of gratitude toward the divinity, and a sense of humbleness. "So entirely dependent are we on the divine Being, that even the little which we enjoy, is not secured by our own plans and efforts, but by God's own arrangements." So writes Moses Stuart, with his usual thoughtful piety.

This fits well with what we've already heard from the Īśopaniṣad: "Whether alive or dull, all within this universe belongs to its controller, the Lord. What you may enjoy is only what he has set aside for you as your portion. One should not strive for other things, knowing well to whom they belong."

Without reference to God the nonreligious person may think, "I am here to enjoy, and by good luck or hard work I'll do it." And with reference to God the religious believer may think, "I am here to enjoy, and by God's grace I can hope to do so." For both, the central concern is their own enjoyment. And both, therefore, are "chasing after wind."

In the Bhagavad-gītā Krishna says, "Enjoyments born of stimulation for the senses are themselves the very sources of misery. They have a beginning and an end, and one who is wise does not delight in them."

Yet it is those enjoyments, those "gifts of God," that religious believers are often keen to receive. By prayers, by rituals, by following commandments, by "being good," they hope that God will grant them the gifts of good fortune, of peace and prosperity, of a bountiful life in which they can eat and drink and take pleasure in all the results of their work.

In the Vedic literature the part called *karma-kānda*, "the part concerning karma," deals with precisely such goals: How can we best act to reap the best material rewards? From the point of view of the follower of karma-kānda, a virtuous or religious life is worthwhile because it will bring us prosperity, which will enable us to enjoy (or after death gain us a welcome into a heavenly realm where we can enjoy still more).

Yet the Śrīmad-Bhāgavatam, in its opening stanzas, rejects such religious life as being materially motivated and as therefore a kind of spiritual fraud. In the name of religion or spirituality or dharma we seek pleasure for the tongue and the stomach and the little organ down below. Spiritual? The Bhāgavatam rejects such "fraudulent dharma" and invites us to discriminate between reality and illusion for the sake of our ultimate welfare and the attainment of the highest truth.

3:14–15: Nothing added, nothing subtracted, nothing new

¹⁴ I know that whatever God does will be forever; nothing can be added to it, nor anything taken from it. And God has so made it so that men should fear him. ¹⁵ That which is has been long ago, and that which is to be has already been; and God seeks that which is pursued.

Keeping us in fear

Qohelet once again says "I know," though he doesn't tell us how he gains his certainty. Let us examine what he knows.

First, he says, he knows that what God does lasts forever. If God sets things up in such a way that everything has its time, if he implants in our hearts a yearning to discover the true nature of the world or eternity, and if he nonetheless plays his cards so close to his chest that understanding what he's up to is impossible, that's just the way it is, for all time, and there's nothing we can do to change it. The formula "nothing can be added to it, nor anything taken from it" – reminiscent of words for a legal decree – certifies a seal on what God has arranged. We're utterly stuck with it.

Assuming that behind everything moves the hand of God (again, an assumption for which Qohelet gives no evidence), it seems plain that God's arrangements are fixed and cannot be tampered with. The laws governing the cosmos will work as they will, ruling even our own tiny lives, and nothing we can do can change that.

But Qohelet says he knows something more: He knows God's motive. He knows *why* God has done all this: "so that men should fear before him."

Here the Hebrew word for *fear* has been taken two ways. One way – and this is how the NRSV translates it – is "stand in reverential awe." God acts not to frighten people but to arouse in them a pious admiration of his might and grandeur. The other way – and this is the view of commentators like Fox and Longman – is that Qohelet really means *fear*. The God who runs the universe in such an arbitrary and oppressive fashion, subjecting his finest creatures to ignorance, toil, and death, is a dangerous deity, an all-powerful and unpredictable despot, in Longman's words a "cosmic bully," truly deserving to be feared.

Whichever way we take it, how does Qohelet know? Certainly Qohelet's distant God didn't appear before him and tell him. Nor does Qohelet mention receiving this knowledge from tradition, whose wisdom he always seems to question, never merely accept.

What we're left with is that either Qohelet must be relying on an intuitive conviction (he just *knows* it) or else he must be expressing a conclusion he has become sure of by thinking about it, by speculating. I don't see how either way of knowing could make Qohelet sure, but he says "I know," and let's leave it at that, adding only that what he knows does not make us know.

What is and what will be: no more than what has already been

Finally, Qohelet reasserts that the world offers nothing new but only monotonous repetition, in which the present and the future endlessly redo the past. God does again what he has already done, filling the future with routines pulled back from the past, bringing events around in a circle, in which what happens now is nothing more than what has already happened before.

"God seeks that which is pursued," a puzzling line, has been variously interpreted. The commentator A. H. McNeile paraphrases it this way: "God seeks out and brings again onto the scene of the present that which has been driven into the past by the lapse of time."

3:16–22: One fate for all

[16] And moreover I saw under the sun: There in the place of justice, wickedness! In the place of righteousness, wickedness there! [17] I said in my heart, "The righteous and the wicked, God will judge, for there is a time there for every purpose and for every work." [18] I said in my heart in regard to men, God is testing them so they may see that they are but beasts. [19] For what happens to men and what happens to beasts are the same. As the one dies, so dies the other; they all have one breath, and man has no advantage above the beast, for all is vanity. [20] All go to one place; all are from the dust, and to dust all return. [21] Who knows whether the spirit of man goes upward and the spirit of the beast goes downward to the earth? [22] And so I perceived that there is nothing better than that a man should rejoice in his works, for that is his portion. For who will bring him to see what will be after him?

Justice where and justice when?

Moving on to a new topic, Qohelet hurls before us his report of what he has seen in the place of justice and the place of righteousness. These two, Fox suggests, are in fact the same place, for which Qohelet uses a figure of speech that in effect says "the place of righteous judgment." What is that place? The court of law. And what has he seen there? Wickedness. The syntax of the Hebrew is abrupt, as if to telegraph Qohelet's outrage. In the very place where a man should find justice – wickedness! Will the guilty be declared guilty; the innocent, innocent; and both receive what they deserve? Bah! They will get the judgment of evil courts, bribed, fooled, played with, corrupted.

But justice, Qohelet says to himself, will come to everyone in due time because everyone will receive judgment from God. Really? Coming from Qohelet, the thought is odd. He has seen for himself that the courts award injustice and, as he has said before, "What is crooked cannot be made straight." Later too, he will give vivid examples of how fate deals unfairly, examples we could easily multiply with our own: A child is crippled by a bomb blast. A Gestapo officer who helped plan the torture and extermination of hordes of captive Jews slips away to Argentina and lives respectably into his nineties in quiet wealth and comfort. Justice? When and where?

In fact, verse 17 includes a puzzling instance of the word *there*: "The righteous and the wicked, God will judge; for there is a time *there* for every purpose and for every work." A time where? Qohelet hasn't mentioned any place for *there* to refer to. The Hebrew word used could also be translated *then*. But that doesn't help. Where is *there*, and when is *then*? A way out (used by the NRSV) is to count the word an error and replace it with a word that means *appointed*: "There is an appointed time ..." But that doesn't solve the underlying problem: When will that appointed time come?

At death, we may say. We will be judged at death. But Qohelet doesn't accept that. As he says next, man shares the same fate as the beast: They both die and go to dust. And what justice then? We might propose that at death the spirit of man ascends to some higher realm. But the most Qohelet will grant that notion is a dismissive "Who knows?" Putting off justice to some unseen post-mortem court that no one can be sure even exists – what is the use of that?

So much for the notion that God, in due time, will judge the righteous and the wicked. If it's not, as some commentators suggest, a pious interpolation, we can chalk it up as yet another of Qohelet's many contradictory thoughts. He says to himself, "Sometime or other, God will judge," and then leaves the thought behind to turn from absurd injustice to blind and meaningless death, a death by which, as far as anyone knows, any further chance for justice is forever extinguished.

All have the same breath

Until we die, what does God do with us? Qohelet says to himself, God tests us to show that we are nothing more than animals. Why God should do this, Qohelet does not say. To instruct us? To humble us? To humiliate us? In any case, we are meant to see that as the animals die, so do we. And therefore, Qohelet says, life as a human being confers no final advantage over life as an animal.

Both humans and animals, Qohelet says, "all have the same breath." Here the Hebrew word for "breath" is *ruah*. The same word is used in Genesis in the fuller phrase "the breath of life." Several commentators make clear that this "breath of life," especially in the context of Ecclesiastes, is not an "immortal spirit" or "immortal soul." It's closer to a "vital breath," a "vital force," the force of life.

A similar term in Sanskrit is *prāṇa*. Of course, in drawing one-to-one correspondences between subtle terms from two different languages and two different cultures we are bound to oversimplify, and we need to be careful not to assume too much. Still, within our present context the two terms do seem a close match.

The word *prāṇa* comes from a verbal root that means "to breathe in, inhale" and so "to live," and it is often defined (like *ruah*) as "the breath of life," "the vital force," "the living force," and so on. Sometimes the prāṇa is called "the life air." As with ruah, prāṇa is a force common to all living beings. And prāṇa is something other than an immortal spirit or soul.

Prāṇa is related with respiration, and yet it is different from mere air. It is more subtle. According to the Upaniṣads, the tiny ātmā, or spark of consciousness, rests on five kinds of prāṇa, or the air of life moving in five subtle ways – moving upward and downward, shrinking and expanding, and so on.

In following the ancient methods of yoga, the yogī practiced prāṇā-yāma ("breathing exercises"), which were not mere drills in the way one breathes but a more subtle technique meant to control the movements of the inner prāṇa in such a way as to liberate one's consciousness from all material contact. The rigors of this technique, described in brief in the sixth chapter of the Bhagavad-gītā, render it virtually impossible to perform in the modern age. Although the sort of prāṇāyāma and other yogic exercises taught today may help one look better and feel better, that's a far cry from the liberation of consciousness the ancient yogīs sought to achieve.

In any case, at death one's prāṇa, the subtle "air of life," leaves the body, and so the body dies. The Īśopaniṣad says that at death the air of life merges with "the totality of air" (just as the "dust" of which Qohelet speaks, the coarser stuff of which our physical body is made, returns to dust – that is, to "the totality of dust"). Both for the human being and for the beast, at death the breath of life leaves the body, and the dust of the body returns to dust.

The Vedic teachers make the point that death is not the only feature that animals and human beings share. Even in life, how different are they? According to a Sanskrit proverb, "Eating, sleeping, defending, and sex – these the animals and human beings hold in common." That a man may eat in a restaurant while a dog eats in an alley doesn't make the man fundamentally better than the dog. It only means the man is more polished at doing the same thing. So too for sleeping, fighting, and sex. Instead of nests and lairs we have bedrooms; instead of teeth and claws we have rifles and bombs; instead of "hump and pump" we have "making love." That the man does these things in a more polished way only makes him a more polished animal. When the life of a man hardly goes beyond these four engagements he has in common with the animals – eating, sleeping, fighting, and sex – the Vedic teachers refer to him by the disparaging term *dvi-pāda paśu*, "two-legged animal."

The proverb continues, "The special feature of human beings is dharma, spirituality. Without this, the human being and the animal are the same."

There's that word *dharma* again, a rich word that can mean "spirituality," "religion," "higher principles," "spiritual laws," and much more. That human beings can follow principles of dharma is what distinguishes them from beasts; a human being devoid of dharma is no better than a beast.

But what's the advantage of cultivating spirituality or following spiri-tual principles if ultimately man and beast share the same fate, if both die and return to dust? We're back to vanity, something meaningless.

Qohelet does seem to briefly entertain the possibility that the human spirit "goes upward" and the spirit of animals down. But again the word here for "spirit" is *ruah* – "life-breath," not "soul." Does the ruah go up or down? Qohelet says, "Who knows?" And what would it matter? Nor does Qohelet talk about whether there might be something *other* than the ruah, or something more *to* the ruah, nor what that something might be. "Who knows?" he says, and that's that.

The nature of the self

Let us pause, then, to consider these issues that Qohelet does not.

For the Vedic tradition, practically the first topic of inquiry – a topic Qohelet never raises – is the nature of the self: Who am I?

As I've mentioned, the Upaniṣads say that resting on the prāṇa, the physical "air of life," is the ātmā, or spark of consciousness. The Muṇḍaka Upaniṣad says, *eṣo 'ṇur ātmā cetasā veditavya:* "This tiny ātmā can be known by intelligence." That is, by sharp discrimination.

In the Bhagavad-gītā Krishna begins his spiritual instruction to his friend and disciple Arjuna by speaking about the nature of the ātmā. The knowers of truth, he says, have studied two kinds of entities – the nonexistent and the existent. Krishna uses these words with a particular meaning. By *nonexistent*, he at once makes clear, he means that which doesn't endure; by *existent*, that which endures permanently, without change. The knowers of truth, he says, have distinguished between these two by observing the ultimate nature of both.

What is it that endures? It is the very consciousness that pervades one's entire body. That consciousness, Krishna says, is indestructible and imperishable. One's physical body is sure to come to an end. But not so the conscious self, the ātmā, within the body. For that conscious self, Krishna says, there is never birth or death. It never "comes into being"; it always exists, birthless, deathless, permanent.

The notion that consciousness develops from complex interactions of matter was known at the time Krishna spoke, but he rejected it as worthless, and though in modern times that notion is often assumed true, it has never been *shown* true. No scientist has been able to mix and energize chemicals and come up with consciousness, or even detail how one could do it, nor point to any instance where nature has been seen to do it. The notion that consciousness spontaneously arises from matter remains just that – a notion, sketchy and unproven.*

I was taught that notion at Dwight Morrow High School by one of my teachers, Dr. Casper Hill, in an advanced course in biology. Dr. Hill, as I recall, was the only teacher in the school with a doctorate. (In the early days of the civil rights movement, the school authorities had scored double by bringing in a teacher who was both black and a Ph.D.) Over several weeks – in the school's newly built auditorium, if I remember right – he took us through the story of evolution, starting from modern human beings and working his way all the way down to the simplest one-celled creatures. And then – one more step – he told how those simplest of beings had arisen from complex biochemicals.

That's where I got stuck. I considered myself pretty smart, but this time I just didn't get it. Through the whole evolutionary chain, he'd shown us one form of life evolving from another, life from life, but this time we were supposed to be seeing life evolving from *stuff*, from chemicals, from matter. Perhaps matter, bombarded into vitality on the primordial earth by some sort of cosmic rays, somehow "became alive."

No alarm bells went off. I didn't stand up and say that something about this idea seemed weird. I just figured Dr. Hill was trying to get across to us something I was too dense to understand. And I can tell you, feeling dense was something hard for me to admit to. So I just kept mum and hoped that nothing about that little bridge between chemicals and one-celled beings would turn up as a question on an exam.

As things turned out, I passed the course fine. And it wasn't till years later, when I read the Bhagavad-gītā, that I remembered Dr. Hill and that gap between matter and one-celled living beings and started to suspect that the reason the story of complex matter springing to life hadn't quite made sense to me was that it didn't make sense.

---

* It also has severe internal problems. In 1977 one of my friends, Dr. Richard L. Thompson, a mathematician, published a monograph entitled *Demonstration by Information Theory that Life Cannot Arise from Matter*, showing that life-from-matter theories seem mathematically unrealistic. Other internal objections have also been raised.

In the Bhagavad-gītā Krishna presented an alternative that seemed a lot more sensible: Life and matter are just two different things, one conscious, the other not, one permanent, the other temporary.

The conscious self, Krishna pointed out, endures throughout all the changes through which the body goes. I remember when I was a short and skinny child, and I remember when I grew to be a tall and skinny young man. And now, still tall, still skinny, but with youth well behind me, I still feel myself the same person. Even though my mind has changed too, the person whose mind it is – me – perceives himself to be the same conscious being.

And so the basic teaching my spiritual master repeated so often it began to sound like a slogan: "You are not that body." The self and the body are different.

In the Bhagavad-gītā Krishna says that just as the spark of consciousness persists from the body of childhood through the body of youth and on to the body of one's old age, at death this conscious spark still persists, but it moves on to yet another body, in another birth, another lifetime. As one might put aside old clothes for new, the spark of consciousness leaves behind one body, the old, useless one, to live in the next, a new one.

The ātmā, the conscious spark, cannot be pierced by weapons, or burned by fire, or moistened by water, or withered by the wind. Krishna says, "Some see it as amazing, some speak of it as amazing, some hear of it as amazing, and some, despite having heard of it, just do not know what it is."

For Qohelet, as I said, the issue barely seems to come up. Though preoccupied – obsessed – with questioning the meaning of life, he never raises questions about the nature of the living being itself. All living beings have the same breath, they all turn to the same dust, and who knows anything more than that? Human being and animal share the same fate, they go to the same death, so "all is vanity."

The "cheery gospel of work"

No one can bring us to see what will come after us – that is, after we die. And so again that leaves us with "nothing better" than to enjoy our work while we're here, chewing the chewed again and again. How splendidly miserable!

Yet one commentator, John Franklin Genung, writes this up (in 1906) as Qohelet's "cheery gospel of work." Genung's comment is worth quoting at length:

> It is marvellous how slow the students of this book have been to discover this cardinal feature of it; this cheery gospel of work, promulgated so long before Carlyle, by an old Hebrew sage, who saw that the work in which we can rejoice, or at least the rejoicing in it, is the true reward of living. "Blessed is the man that has found his work; let him seek no other blessedness," the modern sage [Carlyle] says; but long before him the ancient sage had drawn out of the turmoils and occasions of life this conclusion: "Wherefore I saw that there is nothing better than that man should rejoice in his own works; for that is his portion. For who shall bring him to see what shall be after him?"*
>
> Nor is this given as a last resort, as the only thing man can make of a bad job. It is in itself a blessedness to sweeten not only the ills but the good fortunes of life, adding the saving ingredient, the coefficient without which riches and boundless plenty were vain.

Amidst all of life's turmoils, blessed are we to cheerily toil away.

---

* Elsewhere, Genung calls this "a verse fairly representative of the whole book." Huh?

4

4:1–3: The tears of the oppressed

¹Then I turned and considered all the oppressions
that are done under the sun. And oh, the tears of the
oppressed, and they had no one to comfort them! And
on the side of their oppressors there was power – and
no one to comfort them. ²So I declared that the dead,
since already dead, are better off than the living who
are still alive. ³But better than both is he who has not
yet been, who has not seen the evil work that is done
under the sun.

"No one to comfort them!"
Turning away from the bleak thought that we are no better than the
animals, with whom we share the same death, and turning away from
the thin consolation that we can enjoy our work, Qohelet now tells us
of another evil he saw, that of oppression.

The Vedic literature, when speaking of the miseries we suffer in
this world ("under the sun"), groups them as three. First come those
caused by the great forces of nature: droughts, floods, typhoons, snow-
storms, earthquakes, volcanic eruptions, scorching heat, freezing cold,

and similar natural afflictions and disasters. Then there are the miseries caused by our own bodies and minds: our myriad of physical troubles and diseases and the countless doubts, burdens, distresses, upheavals, embarrassments, confusions, and agonies the mind forces us to endure. And finally there are the miseries caused by other living beings: flies, rats, mosquitoes, viruses, poisonous plants, howling dogs, and worst of all our fellow human beings – in the words of Jonathan Swift, "the most pernicious race of little odious vermin that nature ever suffered to crawl upon the face of the earth."

The world knows no creature as vicious and cruel as an uncontrolled human being. Oppressors with power: the fist, the whip, the blade, the gun; the fear, the threats, the curfews and barbed wire, the boot in your face; the tanks, cruise missiles, and supersonic bombers; and when things are just quietly humming along, the governmental bleed-you-dry suction machine of tax.

On the side of the oppressors there is power; on the side of the oppressed, tears – and no one to give comfort. The oppressors and oppressed are many (Qohelet uses the plural); the comforter, not even one.

Qohelet twice cries out, "No one to comfort them!" Grievous enough that the oppressed should be pushed down and crushed, but that they should have no one at all to give them even sympathy or solace – this is overwhelmingly painful.

The Bhagavad-gītā says that a person in godly consciousness will naturally feel sympathy and compassion for others. The sufferings of others he will feel to be like his own. The Gītā, however, extends this ideal of compassion to one's feelings not only for one's fellow humans but for all living beings. According to the Gītā, the person in true spiritual consciousness sees all living beings with equal vision. Although seeing the outward differences between the physical forms of men, women, animals, fish, insects, trees, and so on, the self-realized person sees that within each dwells an eternal ātmā, or spiritual spark of consciousness, and that the ātmā within all living beings is of the same nature. Not that there is one kind of ātmā within the butterfly, another within the horse, a third within the human being. The bodies, of course, are entirely different, but the ātmā – the spark of consciousness – is the same.

In the previous chapter Qohelet observed that both men and beasts all have "the same breath" and all are of the same dust, to which they all alike return. We have fellowship, therefore, with all living beings. All of us are conscious, sentient, alive. Though human beings may have greater intelligence, lower creatures less, we all have our own way of thinking, we all have desires, and we all have feelings.

Once at a farm where I was staying, many years ago, my Krishna friends had recently purchased a cow, but the cow was bellowing and crying because she had been pulled away from her calf, which my friends had not been able to buy. The poor cow was literally weeping, big tears gliding from her eyes, and she even ran under an electric fence (the charged wire scraping her spine from head to tail) in a hopeless search for her calf.

So when Qohelet says he considered "all the oppressions," did he take these into account, the oppressions wrought by man upon the animals? In Qohelet's time, of course, the oppressions would have been small-scale and primitive. Today, more advanced, we have electric prods, "packing plants," crowded pens and stalls and cages, force-feeding, drugs, and the production-line machinery for slaughter.

"The tears of the oppressed" – millions and millions of poor helpless creatures, cruelly subjugated, tortured, and killed – and no one to comfort them.

Qohelet, I suppose, didn't consider the animals. He was thinking of his fellow human beings. But even then, "all" the oppressions human beings are made to suffer would have been more than he could have conceived, except in the abstract. Clearly, then, Qohelet is generalizing from what he has actually seen. And what he has seen is enough to move him to lament, "No one to comfort them! No one to comfort them!" So painful is this that he praises the already dead as better off than those still condemned to live, and those not yet born as still better.

Here Qohelet sorrows not only for the plight of the oppressed but for his own, the plight of the sensitive soul tortured by having to see all this. Death would be better, or never having been!

Qohelet ended the previous chapter by saying there is nothing better for a man than to rejoice in his works. Where is that rejoicing now? One can hardly rejoice while crying under oppression, and even having to witness the tears of the oppressed is so painful that now Qohelet despairs that it would be better to have never even lived. And ironically, though this is the better option, it is not an option one can choose.

Qohelet and the Buddha
In the despairing thought that never having lived would be better than having to live and see the evils of this world, E. H. Plumptre sees a sentiment akin to Buddhist nihilism: "The same feeling lies at the root of Buddhism and its search after *Nirvana* (annihilation or unconsciousness) as the one refuge from the burden of existence."

Qohelet, of course, was far from being a Buddhist. And Plumptre perhaps oversimplifies the idea of nirvāṇa. But here Qohelet and the Buddha do seem to share some common ground, enough to warrant our here taking a short excursion from Palestine to Nepal, where Gautama Buddha was born, roughly 2500 years ago.

Siddhārtha Gautama, as he was first known, was a prince who lived a life of royal privilege and indulgence within the palace grounds, where his parents sheltered him from the harsh realities of the outside world, a world to which they never allowed him to stray. But one day he ventured out and encountered, for the first time, a man who was diseased, and a man who was old, and the corpse of a man, and a wandering ascetic. Inquiring from his servants, he came to know of the miseries of disease, old age, and death, and came to know that these were the common fate of everyone, and that he himself, therefore, would inevitably suffer disease and finally grow old and die.

Profoundly understanding that these miseries rendered meaningless his life of royal enjoyment, he soon abandoned the palace to wander as an ascetic himself, in search of ultimate enlightenment. After years of fasting and self-denial seemed to have brought him nowhere, he sat beneath a tree, determined not to rise again until he had attained perfection. And it was there that in his meditation he at last became the Buddha, "the enlightened one."

From Bodh Gayā, the place of his enlightenment, in what is now the Indian state of Bihar, he traveled west to Sārnāth, near Vārāṇasī (Benares), and there in a place called the Deer Park gave his first sermon, in which he set forth what came to be called the Four Noble Truths.

The first of these was the Truth of Suffering: Life is full of miseries – the miseries inevitably imposed upon us by birth, disease, old age, and death; the miseries of pain, grief, sorrow, despair, and lamentation; the miseries of having thrust upon us what we would wish to avoid and having wrenched away what we wish to keep; the miseries we must endure when what we strive for eludes our grasp.

The second was the Truth of the Cause: Suffering is caused by desire and by ignorance, which ultimately depend on one another in a sort of "interdependent origination." (Ignorance, he said, causes false impressions. These in turn – I won't go into how – give rise to consciousness, which causes the mind and body. The mind-body causes the sense organs, which cause contact with the objects of the senses. This contact gives rise to experience, which leads to desire, and then to clinging. Clinging leads to the will to be born, which then causes rebirth. Rebirth leads to suffering, which in turn causes ignorance. And so we are back where we started.)

Third was the Truth of Cessation: Our suffering will cease when we are free from desire and ignorance.

Fourth was the Truth of the Way: To reach this freedom from suffering, one should follow an eightfold path, consisting of right vision, right resolve, right speech, right conduct, right livelihood, right effort, right mindfulness, and right meditation.

Such are the four noble truths and the righteous eightfold path said to have been taught by the Buddha. The first of the noble truths is what Qohelet so acutely feels: We live in a world of suffering. Beyond this, however, the Buddha and Qohelet go their own ways, two sages, each facing the problem of suffering in his own way, with his own thoughts, his own way of looking at the world.

The Buddha and the Gītā

The Buddha draws a connection that Qohelet does not, a causal connection between desire and suffering. In this, the Buddha shares in the Vedic worldview, which sees the same connection. Our desires send us running after enjoyment; whatever enjoyment we find, we become attached to; and our attachments pull us forward into another round of birth and death. The Bhagavad-gītā (13.22) says:

> *puruṣaḥ prakṛti-stho hi   bhuṅkte prakṛti-jān guṇān*
> *kāraṇaṁ guṇa-saṅgo 'sya   sad-asad-yoni-janmasu*

"When a living being standing in the world of matter tries to enjoy the qualities to which matter gives rise, this quest becomes the cause of his clinging to those qualities in birth after birth, higher or lower."

And so (Bhagavad-gītā 5.22):

ye hi saṁsparśa-jā bhogā   duḥkha-yonaya eva te

"Enjoyments born of the contact of our senses with their objects are themselves the very sources of distress." Not knowing this – being in ignorance – we try to enjoy and so bring suffering upon ourselves.

We hear, therefore, both from the teachings of the Buddha and from those of the Bhagavad-gītā, that to become free from miseries we must become free from desires and ignorance. But now the Buddha and the Bhagavad-gītā part company, the Gītā pointing toward purification of self, the Buddha toward repudiation of self.

According to the Gītā, I am covered by ignorance and afflicted by material desires, but by self-purification I can attain spiritual knowledge and transform my desires from material to spiritual. According to the Buddha, however, the very sense of "I" is illusory. There is no "I," no self. From moment to moment, what I suppose to be my "self" is but an ever-changing assemblage of physical and mental forces: the body, sensation, perception, mental formations, and consciousness.

And so, in this view, the attainment of nirvāṇa (literally, "blowing out" or "extinguishing") involves the cessation not only of desire and ignorance but of one's own supposed existence, of one's very sense of self, one's own individual being. When "I" no longer exist, neither does my ignorance, nor do my false impressions, my consciousness, my mind and body, my senses and the objects with which they come in touch, nor my experience, nor desires and clinging, nor the will to be born, nor rebirth.

This, then, solves the problem of suffering: When "I" no longer exist, neither can my suffering.

And so we can see why, when Qohelet cries out that it is better to have "not yet been," Plumptre says, "The same feeling lies at the root of Buddhism and its search after *Nirvana* (annihilation or unconsciousness) as the one refuge from the burden of existence."

To style *nirvāṇa* as "annihilation or unconsciousness" is imprecise, for there never was any "something" to turn to nothing, never any conscious self to become unconscious. "I" never existed to begin with. And so we have a solution to the problem of suffering, a final refuge from the burden of existence: A self that doesn't exist can feel no pain.

Now, I don't know about you, but I personally find this solution, this supposed refuge, exceedingly cold, bleak, and unsatisfying. To get free from pain by getting free from one's very self-existence seems like getting cured of a disease by committing suicide. When you're no longer living or breathing you'll no longer have the disease – but is that really the way to solve the problem?

And I find the Buddhist solution unsatisfying not only emotionally but philosophically as well. It leaves too many questions unanswered. To insist that an answer lies "beyond intellectual conception" might work once or twice, but when every fundamental question leads back to silence, we have to ask what kind of philosophy we have.

On origins, what does Buddha tell us? Nothing exists independently. The existence of everything depends on the existence of everything else. Fine. But why should that be so? If that's some sort of law, some sort of universal principle, where does the law itself come from? Instead of an answer, we find silence.

Concerning rebirth, again we wind up in perplexity. Since there's no soul, no "I," no individual me, "I" never transmigrate from one birth to the next. Rather, at death the last moment's assemblage of physical and mental forces – the body-mind, perceptions, consciousness, and so on – bubbles up into the birth of a new such assemblage, in the next moment. But why then should the new "I" have to suffer for the karma of the old one? And, again, if there's some law, some universal principle, that makes this happen (and how else could it happen?), where does that law or principle come from? Again no answer, only silence.

Why even should the noble path of right vision, right resolve, right speech and other "rights" lead us to freedom from suffering unless there's some universal law, some universal principle, that makes it so? Without such a universal law, the "right path" might lead to nirvāṇa on Tuesday and away from it on Thursday, or nirvāṇa at 9 AM but near miss at noontime. And again: If there's some law that makes the noble path reliably lead to nirvāṇa, must some ultimate cause not lie in the background to make it so? Silence is no answer. Over the centuries, of course,

Buddhism has developed refined and intricate systems of metaphysics. But still these questions remain.

The oppressed and the Vedic way

Let us return, then, from our excursion to Nepal, Bodh Gayā, and Vārā-ṇasī and make our way back to Palestine, there to rejoin Qohelet.

When we left him, he was grieving for the tears of the oppressed, who were trodden down by power – "And no one to comfort them!" Elsewhere the Bible speaks of a great comforter, but here Qohelet laments that no comforter is to be found. God seems absent or indifferent.

And though Qohelet cries out at the suffering of the oppressed, he urges no action to help them. Why not?

Some have suggested he was bound by the traits of his class: Wealthy, well educated, he could afford to go about observing the woes of the world and philosophizing but could never get up the revolutionary zeal that can come only from the desperate and oppressed themselves.

Or perhaps any thought of action he might have had was overcome by a hopeless sense of futility. Beneath the endless rising and setting of the sun, with nature taking its relentless course, nothing new ever happens, nothing ever changes, so what would be the use of standing up for the oppressed, of taking their side, of trying to plead with the oppressors or hold them back or overthrow them? People will always be oppressed, and that will never change. Since "what is crooked cannot be made straight," social action will be ultimately useless.

Could it be, then, that Qohelet is the sort of philosopher who just observes but never recommends a course of action? No, because he several times urges that we "seize the day" and enjoy while we can.

But for those crying under the weight of oppressive power, that advice would be worse than useless and absurd; it would be callous and cruel, because for them there is no enjoyment to seize. And what else can Qohelet do for them? He has no advice that can help them. He can't lift their oppression. He could extend sympathy, but to how many, and for how long, and how much good would it do? He has nothing to offer. All he can do is lament.

Can the sages of the Vedic tradition offer anything better?

According to the Vedic social system, sages and intellectuals cannot be expected to combat the forces of oppression. The people to do that are the people with military and executive power. The intellectuals (*brāhmaṇas*, in the Vedic terminology) are to guide and advise those with power as to what is fair and right, and those with power (in the Vedic language, the *kṣatriyas*) are to use their strength and courage to protect and relieve the innocent and oppressed. When we have strong kṣatriyas guided by wise brāhmaṇas, the oppressed can expect relief.

But unless we're going to be naively utopian, we have to recognize that even under the best social system we will always find oppression. Brāhmaṇas will sometimes fail to give good advice, and kṣatriyas will sometimes become oppressors themselves. And finally everyone is oppressed – oppressed by the miseries of material existence. And only by gaining freedom from material existence can the oppressed be free of their tears.

As Buddha saw, there must be a process, a way, to bring about cessation of suffering, and that way must enable us to get free from ignorance and the material desires that bind us to material existence. But, again, the Vedic approach to freedom from ignorance and material desires is not to negate or cancel out or obliterate the self or to suppose that it never existed but rather to enlighten and purify the self. As long as I – the self – wrongly identify myself with my material body, as long as I think "I am American" or "I am Indian" or I am rich or poor, thin or fat, old or young or whatever, I am ignoring my spiritual nature, and so I will drift about in material desires. But when I realize my eternal nature as a spiritual being, and especially when I realize my relationship with the supreme living being, or Krishna, my thoughts and desires become spiritual.

It is to reach this spiritual realization that the Vedic literature especially recommends the chanting of mantras, spiritual sounds that redirect and purify the mind, especially the mahā-mantra, or great mantra: Hare Krishna, Hare Krishna, Krishna Krishna, Hare Hare / Hare Rāma, Hare Rāma, Rāma Rāma, Hare Hare.

4:4–6: Toil and envy

⁴ Again, I saw that all labor and all excelling in work
arise from a man's rivalry with his neighbor. This also

is vanity and a chasing after wind. [5] The fool folds his hands and eats his own flesh. [6] Better is a handful of quietness than both hands full of labor and a chasing after wind.

Excelling for nothing. Or doing nothing. Or a handful of quietness.
"Again," Qohelet says, signaling a new topic: Men work hard to succeed and excel, and why? Just out of rivalry, out of envy of their neighbors. The great accomplishments, the great monuments of human achievement – the great buildings and cities, business enterprises and works of philosophy and music and art – all testify to a timeless urge to beat out the guy next door. For the meanest of motives, men scramble and strive, absurdly competing for trophies of plastic or gold and the inner satisfaction of having invented a new kind of toothpick. "I did it!" So what?

Yet the idle man is a fool. He folds his hands together – that is, does nothing – and what does he get? Too dull and lazy to work, he winds up starving and miserable. "He eats his own flesh," devouring himself, ruining himself, destroying himself. He can only "eat his heart out" – that is, grieve bitterly or be jealous. As Krishna says in the Bhagavad-gītā, "One cannot even maintain one's own body without work."

The Bhagavad-gītā provides us a useful perspective from which to view the different kinds of workers Qohelet here talks about. Applying once again the idea of three qualities of material nature – three material "modes" that govern human behavior – one can view these workers as those in ignorance, those in passion, and those in goodness.

The worker who folds his hands and does nothing is the worker in ignorance. Such a worker (if that's the right word) has no spiritual vision, and his work is empty of any spiritual direction or purpose. He is materialistic and stubborn, a dull, deceitful blockhead, expert only in insulting others. He puts work off, always morose, procrastinating, getting hardly anything done. Such, Krishna says, is the worker steeped in ignorance.

The worker who strives and toils out of envy of others is the worker in passion. Spurred on by love of family and home and comforts, by attachment to what he has and visions of what he hopes to achieve, he earnestly, obsessively, pursues the fruits of work. He is greedy, and for the sake of getting ahead he is ready to push, shove, scratch, bite, or kick. Dirty dealings come natural to him. When things go well for him he floats in delight, and when things go badly he is immersed in pain and distress. Such, Krishna says, is the worker aflame with passion.

And the worker content with a handful of quietness is the worker in goodness. Though he works with determination and enthusiasm, he is free from attachment to the results of his work, and he works without false ego, understanding that he alone cannot determine the outcome of his work, that everything ultimately depends on higher arrangements, on the will of the divine. And so neither success nor failure can affect him; he works unchanged amidst both. Such, Krishna says, is the worker poised in goodness.

From the mode of goodness, Krishna says, knowledge develops; from the mode of passion develops greed; and from the mode of ignorance develop foolishness, madness, and illusion. One is best advised, therefore, to work in the mode of goodness.

4:7–8: The lone miser

> [7] Then I turned and saw another vanity under the sun.
> [8] There is one who is alone, and he has no one else; he
> has neither son nor brother. Yet there is no end to all
> his labor, nor is his eye satisfied with riches: "And for
> whom then do I labor and deprive myself of pleasure?"
> This also is vanity – a grievous business.

"For whom do I labor?"

Now Qohelet observes yet another instance of vanity. A man is alone, with no friends or relatives, no brother to serve as partner, no son to stand as heir, and yet working endlessly, piling up money, and ever dissatisfied, however much he gets. That his eye – the organ of desire, as several commentators say – is never satisfied means that none of his senses are satisfied. Of course, the senses will never be satisfied, however much we give them. Such is the opinion of the Vedic sages. Yet here we find that this miser, rather than even trying to please his senses, denies them anything good. He is working, it seems, for the money itself. And yet he has no one to share it with, no one to give it to. All he can do is look at it, and how much pleasure can there be in that?

"For whom then do I labor and deprive myself of pleasure?" While narrating the story, Qohelet slips into the first person. He may be taking a shortcut, quoting the miser without bothering to say so. Or, as many commentators suggest, Qohelet may slip into the first person because in that lonely miser he sees himself, doomed to vanity, trapped in the grievous business of working for no one and nothing.

4:9–12: Strength in numbers

[9] Two are better than one because they have a good reward for their labor. [10] For if they fall, the one will lift up his fellow; but woe to him who is alone when he falls, and has no one to lift him up. [11] Again, if two lie together, then they have warmth; but how can one be warm alone? [12] And though an attacker might prevail against one man alone, two will withstand him. And a threefold cord is not quickly broken.

Joint efforts

The meaning here is straightforward. To work with another in partnership offers advantages. It can be profitable – two can accomplish not only twice as much but more – and should one partner fall into difficulty the other can help. Several commentators discern here the context of a journey, in which being alone would be more perilous and companionship offers greater safety, greater protection against attack, and even, at night, greater physical warmth (the desert nights of a place like Palestine can be shivering). Michael Fox comments that although

Qohelet recognizes these benefits, they are "rather cheerless." As Fox says, "Qohelet does not mention the emotional blessings of fellowship."

A threefold cord

"A threefold cord is not quickly broken," Qohelet says. Two men are better than one, and three still better. Apart from this obviously intended point, some Christian commentators have suggested a veiled reference to the Trinity. And a Vedic commentator may naturally be reminded, though surely this is not what Qohelet had in mind, of the three qualities, or "modes," of material nature: goodness, passion, and ignorance. In Sanskrit these three modes are called *guṇas*, a term also used more broadly for qualities in general and used in the more plain and tangible sense to mean "ropes."

The three material qualities are likened to a triple cord that binds a living being to the world of lifeless matter. The quality of goodness, Krishna says, binds one to happiness, the quality of passion binds one to work, and the quality of darkness, covering one's knowledge, binds one to madness.

From goodness, knowledge develops, illuminating all one's senses. Purified by knowledge, one perceives more clearly what is what, and this imparts a natural feeling of happiness. Yet with this happiness can come a satisfaction that can act against us, making us content with the material world. One is content to be a scholar, a philosopher, a scientist, involved in profound and fascinating intellectual pursuits, doing research and publishing one's thoughts, yet subtly tricked into losing sight of the urgent need for freedom from material existence.

In the mode of passion, one doesn't get that far. One is overwhelmed by desires and longings, by the demands of the senses to be gratified. One wants honor and one wants things. One wants love, and one wants the pleasures of sex. Spurred on by passion, one wants and wants and wants. And for what one wants one has to run the race, fight the battle, do the deal, spend and acquire, woo and win. A man wants a woman, a woman a man; and when they unite, their feelings for one another grow, forming a knot of attachment in the heart. If that knot stays tight they want to live together, to have a home, to live in comfort and raise a family, and hobnob with friends and relatives, and all of this takes money, hence work. And so one spends most of one's life working to earn a living, toiling to enjoy a happy life.

But in the third mode, the mode of darkness or ignorance, one is too dull or foolish to strive, too thick, lazy, or deluded. In ignorance one plods along, mopes about, or takes refuge in sleep or madness. Why work so hard when it's just as easy to be happy with a bottle, some tablets, or a syringe? The fog takes over, blanketing the world with a dense covering of stupidity. Or the mind is warped, one's inner world fractured, perverted, distorted, bizarre. The quality of ignorance gives us dullards and madmen.

And what makes these qualities so powerfully binding is that they act not alone but together. The person in goodness slips also into bursts of passion and falls into spells of ignorance, the passionate person descends into ignorance and rises into interludes of goodness, and the ignorant person sometimes surfaces to passion and even shows flashes of goodness, as these qualities endlessly mix and intertwine. We are sometimes reflective and good, sometimes impulsive and passionate, sometimes stupid and foolish. Acting together, then, these threefold qualities bind spirit to matter, strap spiritual living beings to material minds and bodies, enforcing the illusion that these are the self, and imprison us so tightly we have no way to escape.

"By the states of being brought on by these three modes," Krishna says, "the whole world is bewildered." Illusioned by these three, we don't know who we are, we can't make heads or tails of the world in which we live, let aside understanding God. Krishna continues, speaking as God himself, "And so the world fails to understand me, who stand above these three modes as supreme and inexhaustible."

According to the Bhagavad-gītā, these three modes are supernaturally powerful because they are energies of the divine, of God. For souls who turn their gaze from reality to illusion, from spirit to matter, from the eternal to that which comes and goes, these three modes of māyā – the bewildering force that rules the material world – are practically insurmountable. Like the heavy lines made of three ropes together that moor a ship to a dock, they tie us with triple strength to material life. "But one who surrenders to me," Krishna says, again speaking as God himself, "can easily cross beyond them." The various methods of yoga are ultimately meant, therefore, to bring one to the point of surrender to Krishna, or the Supreme.

Again, none of this is what Qohelet is talking about – his topic is simply that two or three men are better than one – but for readers of the Bhagavad-gītā these themes will naturally suggest themselves.

4:13–16: The coming and going of kings

[13] Better a poor but wise youth than an old but foolish king who no longer knows how to receive advice. [14] For out of prison he [the youth] came forth to be king, though in his reign too a poor man was born. [15] I saw that all the living who walk under the sun were with the second youth, who was to succeed him. [16] There was no end to all the people, all those whom he led; yet those who come later will not rejoice in him. Surely this also is vanity and a chasing after wind.

Taking advice

According to the Vedic civilization, it is essential for a king to be guided by learned and saintly advisers. The king provides executive power, and the advisers provide clear vision, both spiritual and practical. Power and vision – both are needed. Power without vision will be aimless, confused, misdirected, and dangerous, and vision without power will be ineffective and merely theoretical. The right combination: strong power, with pure and intelligent guidance.

In Indian medieval history, the emperor Candragupta was guided by his renowned adviser Cāṇakya, who is said to have aptly observed: "Trees on a riverbank, a loving woman in another man's house, and kings without counselors go undoubtedly to swift destruction." And just as bad off as a king with no counselors is one who has them but can't heed them.

Qohelet here offers an anecdote in which a king, no longer wary, finds himself supplanted by a poor youth emerged from prison (into which the king, perhaps, had thrown him). That youth too is replaced by another, who wins popular acclaim (hyperbolically, the support of endless numbers of people, "all who walk under the sun"). Yet he too will lose popular favor and be replaced by yet another. So despite the truism that it is better to be wise than foolish, each king in succession, whether foolish or wise, will be reduced to a nonentity. King, kingdom, followers, acclaim – the whole picture turns into meaningless vapor.*

---

* In the Hebrew the pronouns and syntax of this passage are so cloudy we can't be sure whether the story speaks of one youth or two or even three. Crenshaw, Longman, and Whybray observe the ambiguity but opt for two, and our English rendering here follows that choice. Whichever the reading, the vapor will be the same.

5

5:1–7: Watch your step when you deal with God

[1] Watch your step when you go to the house of God.
Drawing near to listen is better than offering the
sacrifice of fools, for they do not know that they do evil.
[2] Don't be rash with your mouth, and let your heart
not be hasty to utter a word before God, for God is in
heaven and you are on earth. Therefore let your words
be few. [3] For dreams come with many doings, and a
fool's voice with many words. [4] When you make a vow
to God, do not be slack to pay it, for he has no pleasure
in fools. Pay what you vow. [5] Better for you not to vow
than to vow and not pay. [6] Do not let your mouth bring
you into sin, and do not say before the messenger that
it was an error. Why should God be angry at your voice
and destroy the work of your hands? [7] For through a
multitude of dreams and vanities there are also many
words; but fear God.

The superiority of hearing

When you go to the house of God, be careful, Qohelet says. Barton gives the meaning this way: "Do not run to the place of worship thoughtlessly, or because it is the fashion to go frequently, but consider the nature of the place and thy purpose in going."

Every religion has its rituals, and at the time of Qohelet the rituals of the Jewish cult apparently involved the sacrificing of animals on the temple altar as a means of atoning for sins, giving gratitude to God, or seeking God's blessings. Other forms of sacrifice were also possible. According to the commentator Michael Eaton, in the particular type of sacrifice mentioned here an animal would be killed and then the offering used for a meal.

More than two millennia later, we can't know for sure whether Qohelet took a dim view of such ritualistic sacrifices generally (in which case the priests and worshipers generally would be the fools) or only when the worship was foolishly performed by worshipers with ulterior motives. The fools, in any case, are so dull they don't know they are doing evil. Or else (an alternative translation) they don't know how to do anything *but* evil. Or else, fools that they are, they don't even know how to do evil.

Whichever way we read it, Qohelet clearly says that the better thing to do is listen. The Vedic tradition, too, has so many sacrifices and rituals, but more important by far is to listen, to hear. A student gains knowledge by carefully hearing from the qualified teacher, and this is true both in ordinary education and on the spiritual path. The Vedānta-sūtras say (with repetition for emphasis), *anavṛttiḥ śabdāt anavṛttiḥ śabdāt*: "By sound one becomes liberated. By sound one becomes liberated." One can become free from illusion by hearing from a self-realized soul. One then acts in compliance not with the binding force of material motives but with the liberating wisdom of spiritual sound.

Do not be rash

Having told us to watch our step, Qohelet next advises that we keep a rein on our tongue. We should listen, not chatter. Some commentators see the context as prayer. As Plumptre says, we should not turn into a prayer our every hasty wish. Others see the context as vows, a topic Qohelet takes up in verse 4: One should not make rash vows.

By pointing out that God is in heaven and we are on earth, Qohelet reminds us that God is distant and that he is great whereas we are small.

"For dreams come with many doings, and a fool's voice with many words." The text has a proverbial form to it, and, as Longman suggests, Qohelet is here perhaps quoting a proverb. Since the point about dreams and doings seems out of context, it may have slipped in only because it had been paired with a relevant comment about talking too much.

Seow offers that *dreams* can be taken in the sense of "illusions," those pictures of the world that seem real but are as ephemeral as vapor. With such dreams come much travail and many anxieties. From that point of view, the many words of a person praying to God to fulfill his dreams are the words of a fool asking for trouble.

Pay what you vow

Though Qohelet often questions or even challenges the accepted wisdom of the biblical tradition, sometimes the advice he offers is conventional. Such is the case here. One should not, he admonishes, make a vow to God and then lightly slough it off. As Plumptre comments, Qohelet's words "point here to a time when vows ... entered largely into men's personal religion." Having made a vow to God, one would feel compelled to honor it. Or at least one was supposed to. One might always be tempted to renege on one's promise or at least put it off. Therefore, better to watch what we say and not let our mouth get us in trouble.

And if we do make a vow to God, we shouldn't make excuses when his messenger – his angel, his priest, or the man from his temple – shows up to collect. You don't want to get in trouble with God and have him smash whatever you've done or repossess your property.

Beyond fear of God

Scholars have a hard time with the Hebrew for verse 7. Longman says, "This verse is difficult to translate and understand." He offers the translation "For when dreams multiply, so do meaningless words. Instead, fear God." Crenshaw gives "Yes, in a multitude of dreams and futility and many words – still, fear God." Zlotowitz: "In spite of all dreams, futility and idle chatter, rather: Fear God!" All that's certain about the verse is its conclusion, "Fear God."

In Proverbs (1:7) we find "The fear of God is the beginning of knowledge." We can take that fear literally (recalling the view of God as a dangerous "cosmic bully"), or else, putting terror aside, we can take "fear" to mean a sense of awe and reverence.

Either way, if "The fear of God is the beginning of knowledge" I suppose I never got started. I can't recall growing up afraid of God. I had all sorts of fears, but fear of God wasn't one of them. And as for awe and reverence, I might sometimes have been awed by the powers of nature, but I don't recall being awed by God. What did he have to do with anything? Far from having pious reverence, I was irreverent, about God as much as anything else (in fact more).

As far as I can tell, instead of getting started with knowledge by fearing God, I went the other way: Encounters with knowledge, without "fear of God," led me slowly and gradually toward some attraction toward God. And God's most attractive feature was not his power but his sweetness. For Krishna was neither a cosmic bully nor a kind and majestic cosmic regent but, astonishingly, a young and innocent rural cowherd.

In Gauḍīya Vaiṣṇava theology, God has a majestic feature, a majestic persona, in which he is every inch a king, replete with crown, throne, attendants, kingdom, limitless opulence, cosmic powers, and the like. And in this role he satisfies those who devote themselves to him with reverential awe.

But for those who wish to see him in less formal, more spontaneous moods, he sheds the royal persona and reveals a free, intimate, and loving person who is just as much God but not constrained to act the part of the divine version of an earthly king. In the role of Krishna, he adopts the sport of playing as if an ordinary human being, dropping all formality and majesty to show instead a divine beauty and sweetness beyond imagination, a beauty and sweetness blended with eternally limitless knowledge and joy, embodied in his own transcendent personal form. The charming role of pastoral cowherd affords him the luxury of abandoning himself to loving relationships in which his pure devotees express their dedication to him by taking on roles as his friends, parents, and innocent rural sweethearts.

That God can express his divinity in more than one role at once, that he can simultaneously rule as a king and play as a cowherd (or teach as a sage, or meditate as an ascetic, or even adopt extraordinary guises in forms other than those of a human being) or, moreover, that he can appear diffuse as an all-pervading presence while at the same time dwelling within everyone's heart and yet all the while live personally beyond the universe in a specific and definite locale – all this is part of the Vedic understanding of God.

Understanding? I couldn't understand it. When I first came in touch with these ideas, they seemed strange, certainly – perhaps more like weird – yet strangely attractive also. My vague idea of God as cosmic button-pusher, a faceless eminence seated in glory and expressing his pleasure or displeasure by lavishing blessings or visiting curses upon the heads of men – to me that sort of God seemed an awkward and unlikely proposition, unattractive, unsatisfying, unpersuasive, if not to say ridiculous. Did he sit on that throne all day? Didn't he ever get bored? Yet that seemed the standard picture.

Against such a picture a diffuse, impersonal, all-pervading truth seemed much more plausible. That impersonal "something," that underlying reality, the unifying ground of existence, the oneness always hidden from us but always there – in the popular terms of the 1960s "the One" or "the Great White Light" – made better sense to me.

That this impersonal ground of all being could be identical with a Personality of Godhead was a thought that never occurred to me. It's not the sort of idea I would have come up with. Yet this was the teaching I came to know and value. The Śrīmad-Bhāgavatam said:

> *vadanti tat tattva-vidas   tattvaṁ yaj jñānam advayam*
> *brahmeti paramātmeti   bhagavān iti śabdyate*

"Those who know that Absolute Truth say that it is nondual knowledge, expressed as the impersonal ultimate reality, as the supreme guide within the heart of all beings, and finally as the Personality of Godhead."

According to this idea, the one supreme truth could be seen in three different ways, according to the level of one's realization. In the beginning (was this only the beginning?) one could realize the all-pervading impersonal aspect of the Supreme. With further progress one could realize the presence of the Supreme within one's own heart as one's inner guide, the guide that offers intuition, hints, reminders, knowledge. And with still further progress one could realize that same Absolute as the Supreme Personality of Godhead, a person made not of bones and blood and muscles like us but of "nondual knowledge," the very stuff of transcendence. And Krishna, the Bhāgavatam declared, was that Personality of Godhead himself.

My spiritual master gave several examples to explain this – most often, that of the sun. The sun is seen first as the brightness all around us, the sunshine. But by looking up in the sky one comes to see that the sunshine radiates from one place, from the orb we call the sun. And according to many traditions that orb lies under the control of a presiding deity, a sun god, and if one were to go there one could meet him face to face. All three of these – the sunshine, the sun as orb, and the sun god – can equally be called "the sun." One sees the sun by seeing any one of the three. And moreover, the example continues, each aspect of the sun is more inclusive than the one before it. One who sees nothing more than the sunshine sees only one aspect of the sun, one who sees the shining solar orb sees the sunshine included as well, and if one were to see the sun god one would naturally see both his sunshine and his sunny orb, in this way seeing all three aspects of the sun. In the same way, when we realize the Supreme as an all-pervasive oneness we realize one aspect of the Supreme, when we realize the presence of God within the heart we realize his second aspect and his first as well, his all-pervading nature, and when we realize the Personality of Godhead we realize all three aspects of the Supreme – all-pervasive, dwelling within, and transcendent in a personal form. This, then, was Krishna, the all-inclusive Absolute.

This same Krishna, the Śrīmad-Bhāgavatam says, appears on earth from time to time to reveal the spiritual activities – the "pastimes," as they are called – that he enjoys in his own transcendent world, where his unlimited powers enable his pure devotees to express their love for him in roles such as parents, neighbors, and friends. The last such occasion, the Bhāgavatam says, occurred five thousand years ago.

While playing on earth his joyful pastimes as a cowherd child, Krishna lived in a simple rural village, and he and his friends sometimes stole the newly churned butter his mother and the neighboring women kept stored in clay pots in their homes. (Eating butter was a lot of fun, and stealing it made the butter still more tasty.) On one occasion Krishna's mother found him out and chased after him to punish him, and Krishna ran away in fear, until his mother finally caught him in the chase. Then Krishna, perfectly playing the role of child, broke into tears, invoking his mother's sympathy. The Bhāgavatam marvels that the Supreme Absolute, the all-powerful God, feared by fear itself, could play in this manner, as if afraid of being punished by his mother.

If the fear of God – whether literal fear or awe and reverence – is the beginning of knowledge, where can knowledge finally bring us? The Bhāgavatam says that when knowledge finds its devotional perfection it can bring us here, into personal loving dealings with God in which God puts aside his supremacy to enjoy sweet and spontaneous pastimes with his devotees. Though God is distant – "in heaven" – and we are upon earth, after many lifetimes on the path from fear to love one can traverse the distance and enter his personal company. And so we might say, after all, "The fear of God is the beginning of knowledge." But not its end.

Why is God here at all?

I'd thought that for this section of Ecclesiastes, a section so uncharacteristically conventional, I'd have less to say. But I find I have more, because this seems the place to deal with a question suggested not only here but in earlier chapters of Ecclesiastes too: Why does Qohelet assume the existence of God at all? As several commentators have noted, Qohelet seems to take what for the Bible is a radically empiric approach to understanding what is true. He doesn't say, "This is what is written in the sacred texts" or "These are the teachings of our forefathers" or "This I have heard from previous sages." Rather, again and again, "This is what I saw." He speaks from personal experience, on which he ponders and ruminates, in inner dialogue with his heart.

So why should God be in this picture at all? Surely Qohelet had no empiric proof of God – Qohelet didn't see him or touch him or hear him speak, any more than we do. We might suppose that Qohelet might have hypothesized that God must exist, but we see no sign of such speculation. Qohelet brings forth no evidence for God, no arguments, no pros and cons. He never says to his heart, "How do I know this?" He just seems to assume it.

There's so much else, routinely accepted by those around him, that he questions and doubts – that life has meaning, that work or wisdom will make one happy – so why should he so easily accept, unexamined, unquestioned, the empirically untestable assumption that behind our absurd, miserable, contradictory world is the hand of an all-powerful God?

Qohelet doesn't even say, "Well, we can't prove it, but let's just assume it." There's no "for the sake of argument" or "Let's just take it on faith." For Qohelet – the doubter, the debater, the despairingly realistic independent thinker in a universe where everything seems empty and vain – God just is. How strange!

Robert Gordis offers this comment: "The modern reader might expect that Koheleth would be led by his views to deny the existence of God, but that was impossible to an ancient mind, and especially to a Jew.... Koheleth, a son of Israel, reared on the words of the Torah, the Prophets and the Sages, could not doubt the reality of God for an instant. For him, the existence of the world was tantamount to the existence of God."

Perhaps. Or perhaps not. Since Qohelet was able to doubt virtually everything else, would his upbringing alone have been enough to prevent him from questioning such a major assumption as the existence of God?

Of course, we don't know. We might suspect that even Qohelet's ancient Jewish mind might have questioned whether God exists. But even suppose we go along with Gordis and say that for Qohelet, with his orthodox upbringing, such a question was out of the question. That still leaves a question for us: Why was Qohelet born into such a circumstance?

Perhaps this question may seem odd. People are just born wherever they happen to be born. So, yes, by putting the question this way I'm presupposing something. I'm assuming that the circumstances of his present life grew from antecedent circumstances, from his life or lives in the past. In other words, I'm presuming reincarnation. But what alternative do we have? We can say he was born who he was by chance, but that tells us nothing. It's not "by chance" that World War II arose or Lincoln or Kennedy was assassinated or Beethoven wrote his symphonies or apples fall from trees. We may not fully understand the reasons for such events, but we're sure the events do have reasons. And "chance" is a non-reason, a non-explanation: "It happened because it *could* happen." Even if we say "It happened because the odds favored it," we still have to ask why.

We can say a person is born who he or she is because of genetics, because of biochemistry, or – simply – because two people had sex. But even then we still have to look for earlier causes: Why was a particular person born to inherit a particular biochemical genetic makeup? Or if that question seems too biased (because it quietly assumes that a person differs from the body into which he or she is born), we can even ask, Why is it that two particular parents came together to have sex? Yes, we know about love and physical attraction. But if we take that attraction and trace the causal chain as far back as we can – for generations, for eons – do we finally wind up with nothing more than chemicals coming into existence for no reason and (again for no reason) rubbing against one another and pushing and pulling, attracted to one another in a spontaneous prebiotic sexual heat?

We can go with that conclusion if we wish: Things happen because of reasons but ultimately because of no reason. In that case someone might well say to us (adjusting the comment above from Gordis), "Perhaps to accept the idea of an ultimate cause is impossible for a modern mind, and especially for you. Perhaps you're a child of 'Nothing is real,' reared on words of cold, reductionistic mechanism, in a world of profit and wages, unable to doubt the finality of chance and randomness for an instant. For you, perhaps, the existence of the world is tantamount to the existence of odds."

A skeptic could go either way: doubt the existence of God or doubt the adequacy of undirected material forces. Or, uncritically, one could either just assume the existence of God or assume that matter is everything.

I accept, of course, the role played in our lives by genes and chemicals or, at the level of sociology, by human "social chemistry." But I choose to look for deeper causes. If we don't, if we assume that matter is everything and that it just automatically does what it does, then that's that; there's nothing deeper to understand. But if we do look for deeper causes for the events in our lives, then the idea of reincarnation, the idea that what happens to us in this life grows from what we did in a life before – that the law of cause and effect doesn't stop at the border but extends for more than one lifetime – provides a sensible way for us to interpret what we see.

If we accept this idea, then Qohelet was predisposed to assume the existence of God – or was born into a culture where that assumption was so powerful he couldn't possibly doubt it – because of who he had been in his previous life, that is, because of the tenor of his previous lifetime's thoughts.

Viewed with reincarnation in mind, who we are and what we're like, even at birth and in our earliest years, grow out of who we were and what we were like in the life before.

To take an extraordinary example, let's consider Mozart, who began creating his own worthy musical compositions at the age of five. Precocious genes? Exceptional environment? His father was a deputy Kapellmeister and a minor composer, and his older sister (his only sibling) took up keyboard lessons from her father at the age of seven and was talented, but the young boy soon surpassed not only his sister but his father. By the age of sixteen he had written three operas and twenty-five symphonies. Mozart's exceptional genius, difficult to account for by genetic inheritance and a musical environment, makes sense when seen as carried over from a previous life.

Mozart, of course, was extraordinary. But we all have innate abilities and weaknesses, innate likes and dislikes, our own natural temperaments, evident from early on. And for that matter we're each born with our own set of physical characteristics – yes, our own genes – and in our own unique set of circumstances.

The Vedic worldview explains such qualities and circumstances by ascribing them not to chance but to continuity. In particular, the Vedic view is that from lifetime to lifetime we can spiritually progress, accruing a kind of "spiritual credit" that never diminishes but we can always add to. Or, at the least, we can cultivate a mentality and way of life conducive to spirituality, living in "the mode of goodness," the mode in which spiritual credit can most suitably be accrued. When we stop grossly violating the laws of nature to try to squeeze from her an enjoyment we cannot have, and when we act instead in harmony with nature's laws, purifying our life so that we act beneficially, uplifting ourselves and others, then, the Bhagavad-gītā says, we can be freed from duality and illusion and so progress with determination in reviving our relationship with the Supreme.

What impelled Qohelet to raise questions about the ultimate meaning of life? Why couldn't he just settle down and teach traditional lessons like an ordinary sage? Why did he have to see so clearly the futility of piling up wealth and cultivating mundane wisdom? If we take the view of reincarnation, it was his spiritual credit, accrued in previous lives. While others trudged about or dashed about under the spell of their illusions, Qohelet, disillusioned, sought to make sense of an apparently senseless world. And the same spiritual credit that compelled him to this task also implanted within him, whether by culture or by inner guidance, the certainty that God exists, at the same time that he despaired over the bleak, dismal, absurdly vaporous existence to which God seemed to have consigned his creatures.

"Both the lowest of fools and the person transcendental to all intelligence enjoy happiness," says the Bhāgavatam, "whereas persons between them suffer the material pangs."

Until we go beyond material intelligence and attain a direct experience of the Supreme, an experience that now seems beyond our reach, we will still have to contend with the troubles and perplexities of the material world.

5:8–9: For oppression, high officials; for prosperity, simple fields

> [8] If you see in the state the oppression of the poor and
> the perversion of justice and right, do not be astonished
> at the matter, for the high official is watched by one
> higher and there are still higher ones over them. [9] But
> the profit for a land in every way is a king who makes
> himself a servant to the field.

Hands of oppression and injustice

Qohelet here returns to the themes of oppression of the poor (lamented earlier in 4:1–3) and the perversion of justice (observed in 3:16). Given the workings of officialdom, he says, such oppression and injustice are not astonishing.

In the corrupt state – and where will we find a government not corrupt? – officials abound, feeding off the life of the citizens. Anyone who has lived in the East will be familiar with the abundance of great and petty officials one needs to satisfy to get things done, even to carry on with the normal affairs of life.

And why the East alone? In Africa, in Latin America, in Eastern Europe … And the West is not immune. Even in America, in New Jersey, my father had his store on a large commercial avenue that ran through several towns in quick succession, and he used to say that the only reason for so many towns was so that each (like the town his store was in) could have its own government officials to collect salaries and bribes.

In the network of officialdom, the higher officials feed off the lower ones. At each level of the hierarchy, each squeezes what he can from those below and yields what he must to those above. The superior watches over the subordinates to make sure those underlings send up the rightful share of wrongful profit and don't get too big, and he also watches over them protectively to keep the game going. In all of this, the unfortunate citizens are the losers because they are the ones from whom everything must ultimately be squeezed.

In the modern Western context, the officials busy squeezing are not only the political ones but also the military and corporate ones, all bound together in networks of mutual interest. And even the highest elected officials may owe their political existence to yet higher material powers, who watch over them and prosper.

When Qohelet speaks of officials with "still higher ones over them," Barton suggests that this may be an oblique reference to the king. And indeed the Śrīmad-Bhāgavatam says that in the present age the heads of state will be hardly better than plunderers. By taxes, bribes, embezzlement, and fraud, by collusive manipulation of banks and markets, and ultimately by armed force, networks of politicians will loot, and the head politician will be but a leader of thieves. In this age, the Bhāgavatam says, law and justice will stand only with those who wield power.

A plowed field

In translation, verse 9 seems clear enough, but the Hebrew words and syntax are such that Crenshaw comments "The meaning of this verse is totally obscure" and other scholars concur. Longman tells us the verse may be interpreted either positively or negatively. Reading positively, one might say that a land benefits by the presence of a king who sees to having the fields well tilled. Even in a land oppressed by greedy bureaucrats, a sensible king will make sure that farming goes on well, to the benefit of all. Reading negatively, Longman translates, "The profit of the land is taken by all; even the king benefits from the field." That is, the profit of the land is sucked up by greedy authorities all along the line, from the most petty official all the way up to the monarch.

Granting either reading (or any other), prosperity comes finally from the field, from the earth. In the Bhagavad-gītā Lord Krishna says, "All living beings live on food grains." Not on nuts or bolts or silicon chips, not on things invented by human beings or banged out from factories, not on notes run off on a press and declared money. Finally, it all comes down to food. With food you can live, without it you die – simple as that. And so the plowed field is the basic unit of prosperity. An economy dependent on producing and selling needless necessities is an artificial economy; natural wealth comes from the land.

By an arrangement higher than ours, from the land we can gain everything we need. From the earth – from mere dirt – emerge the trees and plants that sustain our lives. You put a seed in the ground, you add some water and sunshine, and up come trees and plants.

Of course, nature provides the basics – the seeds, the water, the sunshine – and trees and plants can grow on their own. But to receive in abundance the rice and wheat and corn we need, the apples, oranges, and lemons, the beets and spinach and pumpkins and potatoes and yams, we need farmers. If society needs deep thinkers of pure character to give it vision, and brave, strong, noble leaders to defend it and keep it well managed, it equally needs industrious farmers to cultivate the land and draw from it the food nature is ready to supply. If the thinkers are the head, and the political and military leaders the arms, then the farmers are the stomach, supplying the strength of food to the entire social body.

It's farmers who care for and cultivate the land, farmers who plow it, farmers who give us the food on which we all live. And so it is farmers who give us true prosperity, drawing on the gifts of nature.

And by nature's arrangement, farmers can do this with the help of animals. Man was not endowed with the strength to plow on his own, but the animal has it, and man and animal can work together. Before the modern tractor, it was the animal that provided traction, sometimes the horse but more often and more effectively the ox. This we can see even today where agriculture still retains its old simplicity. In the fields of the villages of India, man and ox still work the field, the man guiding and directing, the ox providing power. The ox, with splendid economy, lives on mere grass and grain, which grow from the very land the ox plows. And (talk of economy!) even the ox's dung is useful. Forget factory-made chemical fertilizers; the ox's dung provides a perfect balance of nitrogen, potassium, and other nutrients for the soil, mixed together as a natural fertilizer, collected, valued, and used by generations of farmers who never heard of "organic farming" but just did it, and still do. And that valuable dung is a multipurpose commodity. Pressed into cakes and dried in the sun, it burns as a natural, efficient fuel for cooking. And so the ox plows the field, fertilizes the soil, and even provides the fuel with which to cook.

The ox, of course, is the son of that very symbol of abundant productivity the cow. As far back as we go in history we'll find humanity depending on and cherishing the cow for her milk. In exchange for mere grass, the cow yields that miraculous liquid on which nearly all of us have grown up. The child goes from the milk of the mother to the milk of the cow, and so the cow is like the second mother of the human being.

From milk, too, come cheese, cream, yogurt, butter, all sources of vitality and health. Yes, I know. Some say that milk – in derogatory terms, "cow juice" – is bad for you. But their wisdom runs contrary to the wisdom of virtually every ancient culture of the world, and most modern ones. In ancient times the sages of India would often live happily just on milk, provided by a cow at their hermitage or at whatever village they might wander through at the time of milking. And the Bible itself speaks several times of the promised land as a land flowing with honey and with milk.

In the Vedic society, therefore, the duty of the farmer was to care for the land and for such valuable domestic animals as the cows and bulls. Even Krishna himself, when he appeared on earth, chose to spend his childhood in a pastoral village of cowherds, where he enjoyed the pastime of tending to calves and cows, whom he all knew by name and who would respond with affection to the call of his celebrated flute. And so Krishna is known by names such as Govinda ("source of pleasure for the cows") and Gopāla ("the cows' protector").

A greedy and grossly ignorant society poisons with chemicals the land of mother earth and mauls and slaughters the mother cow. How can such a society ever expect happiness and peace?

5:10–12: Vainly watch your money grow

> [10] He who loves silver will not be satisfied with silver,
> nor he who loves wealth, with gain. This also is vanity.
> [11] When goods increase, those who eat them increase,
> and what advantage has their owner but to see those
> goods with his eyes? [12] Sweet is the sleep of a laboring
> man, whether he eats little or much; but the overfull-
> ness of the rich man will not allow him to sleep.

The love of wealth

The wisdom here is proverbial and universal. As the Śrīmad-Bhāgavatam agrees, "The miser is never satisfied."

Since coins in ancient Palestine were of silver, the word *silver* also by extension means "money." The Hebrew word used here for *wealth* indicates possessions of all kinds, and the word for *gain*, meaning "fruit, yield, harvest, produce," comes from agriculture but can stand for any sort of gain. And so, as Crenshaw notes, Qohelet's language here covers a wide range of stuff a miser might hold on to (and be dissatisfied with).

Paradoxically, money held on to has no use. We gain from it only when we spend it, thereby losing it. And whatever we gain will also eventually be lost. The whole business is vain and absurd.

Regarding the supposed pleasure of heaping up wealth, Barton quotes from the Greek historian Xenophon: "Do you think, Sacian, that I live with more pleasure the more I possess? Do you not know that I neither eat, nor drink, nor sleep, with a particle more pleasure than when I was poor? But by having this abundance I gain merely this, that I have to guard more, to distribute more to others, and to have the trouble of taking care of more."

Among those to whom the "more" must be distributed are of course the tax man. The more you gain, the more will be eaten by whatever tax authorities have made you their unwilling partner. And also among the eaters will be the members of one's own family, traditionally known for their expertise in spending whatever one might earn.

Meanwhile, if we pile money up, all we get to do is look at it. If we keep silver, we can look at our silver. Or since today, lucky us, our coins are of base metal and our bills of paper or plastic (yes, in Australia and Canada they use plastic), we can feast our eyes on piles of notes that are "money" only by fiat and whose value could at any time dribble away. In any case, assuming we keep our precious money in the bank, all our eyes get to look at is a number on a bank statement – a few marks on paper, a few dots on a computer screen.

The rich can't sleep

And if my number is high – that is, if I become rich – then along with the empty joy of looking at my smudges, dots, or silver coins comes greater trouble and anxiety. The rich have a hard time sleeping, either because of indigestion (they eat too much) or because of anxiety (they have too much to worry about).

In the words of the Śrīmad-Bhāgavatam, "Ever thoroughly disturbed are the thoughts of those who grasp at the unreal." The word the Bhāgavatam uses for "unreal" is *asat*, which also means "false," "nonexistent," or "temporary." In the view of the Bhāgavatam, that which exists only temporarily, only for the moment, has no substantial existence. What doesn't exist forever doesn't "exist." It is "unreal," like a dream, which "exists" for the few brief moments we're inside it but then vanishes into nonexistence and "was only a dream."

As with what we dream of while sleeping, so with the dreams we have while awake. Home, family, job, bank balance, even my very body itself – all appear as real as anything and yet disappear into nonexistence within a moment of cosmic time. Meanwhile, within that moment, from body, bank balance, job, family, home we seek security, love, satisfaction – and from these we seek meaning. Grasping in this way at what doesn't exist and trying to hold on to it, how can we not be disturbed? To use Qohelet's word, what we are grasping at is *hevel*, vapor, the dissipating fog of a breath. And the more we grasp for, the greater our anxiety.

From that point of view, the rich man is worse off than the ordinary worker. Once a few years ago when I was staying in Mumbai, I was called into a dispute between two families, one a friend's sister and her husband, the other a couple I somewhat knew. They were at each other's throats, my friend said, and he asked whether I could try to intercede. And so I visited both families. They lived in adjacent condominium apartments in a well-to-do Mumbai suburb, half an hour from where I was staying. I'd take a motor ricksha in the early evening and find myself in a pleasant "colony," as they're called there (what in America we might call a community), with modern pale-colored apartment buildings of not more than two or three stories, the buildings interspersed amidst a campus walled off from the street, graced by hedges and shade-giving trees, with spacious grounds where children in bright blue shorts and clean white shirts played here and there. In this colony stood a newly constructed building of three connected units, called Satyam ("Truth"), Shivam ("Good Fortune"), and Sundaram ("Beauty"), the last two being the dwellings of the two families concerned.

The family known to me were well established in business and active in religious activities, and the fellow my friend's sister had married was an up-and-coming young man, bright, sensible, university educated, and exceedingly pleasant. Both families were well set up and comfortable in their new homes.

The problem, as I recall, had to do with the use of a stairway and access to a water tank, a typical fixture on the roofs of Indian buildings. The stairs and tank were shared in common by the two units, or lay between them, and that was the problem. Whose were they? Or who had the right to *control* them? A small issue, surely, but it had grown into a point of contention, a dispute, a battle, a feud, a war. Shouting matches had broken out between the wives: "You blocked me from getting to my water tank!" "How can you say that! I've never blocked you. And what do you mean, *your* water tank!" Each family had gone to the neighbors to tell a tale of woe, badmouth the opposition, and seek an ally in the fight. The children had been duly politicized, told to shun this child or that. The Sundarams complained their phone rang at odd hours of the night, with no one answering when it was picked up, though it had to be the Shivams, and the Shivams had similar stories. At some point the police were called in, and the lawyers, and soon there were suits filed and counter-suits. "We thought it would be so nice here," Mrs. Sundaram told me, "and now our life has become hell." Over a stairway and a water tank.

Though I came out and shuttled between the families on a few occasions, on little missions for peace, to tell you the truth I failed to accomplish anything. (The Sundarams later ended the war by moving elsewhere.) But the last night I visited, after hours of listening to complaints, arguments, and appeals, with tears from the women and angry protestations from the men – "Why can't those people just leave us alone?" – on the way out I saw by the gate, in what by then was the cold and darkness, a small hut that was the station of the colony's hired watchman, who had lit a small fire, as such watchmen at night typically do, and was probably half dozing (also typical), unruffled, I thought, by the saga of Shivam and Sundaram that was raging in another world, with its angry face-offs, trumped-up lawsuits, bribed police, divided neighbors, politicized children, and disputed stairway and water tank. While the Shivams and Sundarams roiled in their passions, the watchman sat peacefully by his fire, quietly dozing now and then.

Earlier Qohelet has said, "In much wisdom is much vexation," and now we can turn that around: In little wisdom, little worry. A person of wisdom, of sensitivity, will recognize the perplexities of human existence and seek, perhaps despairingly, for some way to resolve them. Such a person will ask, "Why am I here? What is the purpose of my life? Why the miseries and absurdities of this world?" One step lower, the "lovers of silver" or "lovers of wealth," those in passion, always striving, will enjoy, they think, by profit, by possessions, by finding pleasure for the senses, by doing more and having more. But, still lower, those who are slow and dull won't even go that far. They work, they get paid, they have a few good beers and watch a ball game. Life goes on.

The watchman, of course, was a simple worker, not a sage or intellectual. If the intellectuals are like the head of the social body, providing thought and vision, and if the military and political leaders are the arms, providing protection and making sure the state is properly run, and if the farmers are the stomach, supplying the strength of food, then the ordinary workers are the legs, on whose labor the whole body stands.

In literature we can read stories romanticizing the simple life of the worker, the laborer, the peasant. And though even workers, of course, have their problems, there's much to be said for the simplicity of such a life, or even for its dullness. As Qohelet observes, "The sleep of the worker is sweet." But it's not that everyone can become a worker.

I recall a time during my days as a quasi-student at Carnegie Tech. What I saw at the university had disappointed me, getting high as a way of life wasn't much of a way of life, and my mind was plaguing me: I thought too much. The Christmas break was coming, all my friends would be going home, and, having turned my back on home, I would be left there on campus, looking at the Pennsylvania snow.

So I picked up a newspaper and looked for a temporary job, something physical, something that would wear me out and take my mind off my mind. That's how I wound up working at the massive Kaufmann's department store, in the candy department, lugging heavy boxes of candy canes, lemon drops, and Russell Stover chocolates from 9 to 5. I was a worker, and it worked, for a while. But it was boring, it was meaningless, and I knew it, and when Christmas was over and they moved me to the clothing department, where the boxes were light and there wasn't much to do, I quit, thus ending forever my life as a worker. "Sweet is the sleep of the laborer," but I wasn't one, and I couldn't fake it.

Shortly after, I left Carnegie Tech as well and went to New York, where I was soon to meet the Hare Krishna people.

5:13–17: Working for nothing, eating in the dark

[13] There is a grievous evil I have seen under the sun:
riches are kept by their owner to his hurt, [14] and those
riches perish by a bad venture; and though he has
begotten a son, there is nothing in his hand. [15] As he

came forth of his mother's womb, so again will he go, naked as he came, and will take nothing for his labor that he may carry away in his hand. [16]And this also is a grievous evil, that just as he came, so will he go; and what profit does he have that he should labor for the wind? [17]All his days also he eats in darkness, and he has much vexation and sickness and wrath.

Lost wealth

The evil here is painful rather than moral. And it is literally a "sickening evil." A man tries to keep his money, but he loses it by misfortune. That he kept it "to his hurt" may mean that he had to go through all the trouble and worry that keeping money entails, or, reading the clause differently, the man kept it *against* hurt – that is, he was saving it for an emergency or trying to protect himself from any hurtful financial loss. Either way, he tried to keep it but lost it.

And now we run into more of Qohelet's ambiguous pronouns. When the rich man has a son, he has nothing in his hand. Is the *he* the father or the son? And who comes and goes naked – father or son (or, as some interpreters would have it, everyone)? And is it the father or son who eats in darkness? As usual, scholars are divided.

By any interpretation, the father lost his money, so both father and son were left empty-handed, a cruel circumstance for both. Both (like all of us) came naked into this world and after a lifetime of work would have to leave the same way, nothing in hand. We toil "for the wind," for something we can grasp for but never hold on to – that is, for nothing. A grievous evil.

If we assume verse 17 speaks of the once-wealthy father who worked hard but lost all to misfortune, Qohelet says the empty-handed man, nothing left to give his son, spent the rest of his days sick and bitter, "eating in darkness." A literal interpretation, though prosaic, is possible (he was so poor or so miserly he had no money to spend for lamp oil, or he had to work such long hours he could have his meals only at night). Or we can read "he eats in darkness" as a figurative way to depict the ruined man's gloomy mind, a mind so depressed and afflicted that, extending the figure further, his days verged on the darkness of death.

The man eating in darkness could be the son, but only if terribly bitter over not receiving the inheritance he had expected. If the son was bitter it was because he was spoiled; if the father, because devastated.

5:18–20: Eat, drink, and enjoy

> [18] This is what I have seen to be good: It is fitting for one to eat and to drink and to enjoy pleasure for all his labor at which he labors under the sun all the few days of the life God has given him, for this is his portion.
> [19] Every man also to whom God has given riches and property and the power to enjoy them, and to take his portion and rejoice in his labor – this is a gift of God.
> [20] For he will scarcely mark the days of his life, for God keeps him occupied with the joy of his heart.

What's good? Not much.

Moving away from the "sickening misfortune" of the previous verses, Qohelet now turns again to what he has seen to be good, and again it isn't much.

What is good is to be able to eat, drink, and enjoy the result of all the hard work one has toiled at in the material world, in the limited world whose days are marked by the relentless rising and setting of the sun. God gives us a life, whatever it is, only for a few days – literally, in the Hebrew, days that are "numbered" – the sun subtracting one of our small number of days every time it rises and sets. And what is good for us in those few days, Qohelet says, is to eat, drink, and enjoy what we can, for that is our portion, our lot, our little ration.

If God gives us wealth and possessions and lets us enjoy them and be happy, then we can count it as a gift of God. But that's a formidable series of *ifs*: *if* he gives us wealth, *if* he gives us possessions, and *if* he gives us the power to enjoy them. Which implies he may not. I might be poor, and my possessions few, or like the man in the previous passage

I might lose whatever I have. Or I might have all the wealth and possessions I might want and hold on to them but be too sick or old or troubled at heart to get any taste from them. So *if* I get wealth and possessions and the power to enjoy them – a matter not up to me – well then it's a gift from God.

And what is the value of that gift? It will keep me busy, diverted, pacified, entertained. I won't notice how short are the days of my life. I'll forget the past, not think about the future, and for the present enjoy what I have received.

For some commentators, again, this is Qohelet's central message, his gospel of joy. For some it is even God's answer, the way to find true communion with God, for God is present through his divine gift of material enjoyment.

Does that work for you? It didn't work for me. As an adolescent Jewish kid growing up in New Jersey, I wasn't a king, but we were prosperous enough, we had more than we needed, and I did plenty to enjoy. But I was dissatisfied, discontent, weighed down by the sense that what I had was not what mattered and that what I was doing was of no consequence. Of course, I was far from laboring hard for what I had, but my father did that, and what kind of happiness did he have? How happy was it to come home exhausted after a long day at work, have dinner, and fall asleep in a big blue chair in front of the TV?

I had classmates who seemed to be enjoying – they were big in sports or lively at parties and popular with girls – but in my eyes they were fools. "Better to be Socrates dissatisfied than a fool satisfied." Of course, I wasn't Socrates, but even though I sometimes might have wanted to, I couldn't quite bring myself to be that kind of fool.

Nor, clearly, could Qohelet. He could advise that one eat, drink, be merry, and not brood over the few days of one's life, but this was not advice he could follow. God, it seems, never gave him that gift.

From the Vedic point of view, that gift is the gift of māyā, of illusion, of bewilderment, the gift awarded to one who wants to enjoy at the cost of losing the power to see what is what. Māyā – literally "that which is not" – is the energy divinely empowered by God to give us what we may want but what doesn't exist: a kind of small-time godhood of our own, a life in which instead of being integral parts of the supreme reality, the source of all existence, and therefore meant to serve that Supreme, as parts serve a whole, on the contrary we can each be independent, fully whole on our own, and stake our own claim to controllership and enjoyment of a piece of the world, big or small, and each play at being our own "center of existence." The deceptively "real" world in which māyā enables this to happen is the world in which we now live, what the Vedic literature calls the material world. Because the material world is only a semblance, a distorted reflection of reality, not reality itself, it can never be what we want it to be. The material world, the Gītā says, is in fact a world full of miseries and a world where nothing lasts. How can we enjoy in such a place? We can enjoy only under the spell of illusion, by which we can live in a dream of happiness and imagine it will go on and on. Māyā has the power to cloud and cover our vision so that even though we see, we don't see.

Māyā accomplishes this through the three modes, or qualities, of material nature I've discussed earlier: goodness, passion, and ignorance. Though these qualities mix and blend in the heart in different propor- tions, so that we are sometimes more in one mode, sometimes another, it is especially in passion that one works hard for wealth and posses- sions and one's heart becomes filled with the supposed joy these bring.

There is a story about Indra, the Vedic "king of the gods," the very picture of lordly enjoyment. Once while he was in his grand assem- bly, entertaining himself in various ways, into his court came the great sage Bṛhaspati, his own spiritual teacher. Yet Indra was so absorbed in diversions – perhaps it was the celestial dancing girls – that he failed to welcome his teacher with respect or even notice his presence. And so Bṛhaspati, displeased, and more than a bit disgusted, cursed his student Indra to fall from the heavenly kingdom and descend to earth, there to become a pig.

By the power of the sage the curse at once took effect, and now the great Indra found himself in a pigpen on a farm on earth, a lowly pig, fat and grunting. But he was well cared for, it seemed, and life wasn't so bad at all. He was sumptuously fed – the farmer regularly provided him large buckets of excrement, which, yes, pigs really do enjoy – and he had good mud to wallow in, and after eating he could sleep as long as he wished. Apart from this – how much better could life get? – he was soon able to couple up with a truly splendid young sow and became father to a whole litter of charming little piglets.

Meanwhile, back in Indra's celestial kingdom, things weren't going very well. In the absence of Indra, lord of the realm, disorder was setting in, and life was starting to get disrupted. And so Lord Brahmā himself, Indra's superior in the universe, came down to earth to retrieve Indra and restore him to his heavenly post.

"All right, Indra, blessings upon you. The curse may now end, and now you may return."

"Return? Return where?"

"To the kingdom of heaven, your rightful abode."

"Heaven? This is heaven. What better life could I want? I have my home, my comforts, my good food. And what about my wife and children? I have responsibilities here."

Brahmā did all he could to persuade Indra to return to heaven, but Indra, determined, obstinate, one might even say pig-headed, refused to go anywhere.

Finally, seeing that reason and argument would be of no avail, Brahmā killed the sow and piglets, to Indra's squealing dismay, and showed Indra that the farmer who had been so generously providing Indra's fine buckets of food was in fact sharpening a knife for Indra himself. It was only then that Indra came to his senses and agreed to return to his heavenly realm.

Those whose hearts are occupied with the joys of wealth and possessions have received a gift from God through his power of illusion. When this illusion is peeled away one is more fortunate.

6

6:1–6: Better born dead

[1] There is an evil I have seen under the sun, and it lies heavy upon men: [2] a man to whom God gives riches, property, and honor, so that he lacks nothing for himself of all he may desire, yet God gives him no power to enjoy it, but a stranger enjoys it. This is vanity, and it is an evil disease. [3] If a man begets a hundred children and lives many years, so that the days of his years are many, but his desire to enjoy good things is not fulfilled and moreover he has no burial, I say that a stillborn child is better than he. [4] For it comes in vanity and departs into darkness and its name is covered with darkness; [5] moreover, it has not seen the sun nor known anything; yet it has more rest than he. [6] Indeed, though he live a thousand years twice told, if he enjoys no good – do not all go to one place?

Back to what's bad

After the skimpy offer of what he has seen to be good, Qohelet returns to what he has seen to be evil. It is an evil which, depending on how one translates, is either "heavy" or "frequent" – or, of course, both. And in fact it is the same fortune he has just seen to be good, now cruelly turned on its head. In verse 19 of the previous chapter God gives at least some people wealth and possessions and the ability to enjoy them and be contented. Now, again God gives the same wealth and possessions in abundance, as much as one might want, and adds honor besides – but without the power to enjoy. He gives tasty food to a man who can't eat, or a beautiful young wife to a man old and impotent. Worse, what the man has but can't enjoy, someone else devours – some outsider, some stranger. Qohelet calls this an "evil disease" or a "sickening evil."

And who is responsible for this evil? It is God. It is God who tantalizes and tortures his hardworking creature. It is God who showers upon this man everything the man might desire yet deprives him of the ability to enjoy it. And why? For no apparent reason. Again, it is vanity, a circumstance not merely pointless but perverse – offensive to justice and contrary to sense.

Longman writes, "The attempts to mitigate divine responsibility here have been numerous and may be illustrated by the Targum, which adds the foreign idea of the rich person's sins: 'But the Lord has not given him power, on account of his sins, to enjoy it.' "

Clearly, the Targum's fix doesn't fix much. A man vicious and sinful may be well endowed with power to enjoy, and a virtuous man may suffer wretchedly. Or consider those born into prosperity but born terribly diseased or deformed, thus deprived of the power to enjoy before they even have the option to do anything nasty or sinful. Where's the divine justice there?

Here the Vedic literature answers with the idea of karma. Earlier I wrote of "the path of karma" as the path of acts performed for one's own enjoyment, especially the path of noble, meritorious, uplifting acts. But apart from having the general meaning of "acts" and the more particular sense of "meritorious acts," karma also has the extended meaning, now common in English, of the results our acts bring upon us, the consequences, whether good or bad. We speak of a person "getting his karma." (Yes, usually bad.)

That acts have consequences is no great revelation. Causes have effects. That's understood. The Vedic view, however, adds the idea that the chain of causes and effects extends throughout not only one life-time but many. As in one lifetime an embodied living being, in the body in which it lives, passes from childhood to youth to old age, so at the time of death, the Bhagavad-gītā says, the living being passes on to another lifetime, in another body altogether. And by the law of cause and effect, what we do in the present life brings on what happens to us in the next. And so our present life, too, is a consequence of what we did in our previous lives. Our physical features, our health, the country and family into which we are born, the traits of what we call our per-sonality, and so much more, including events that befall us – all these follow as natural results of our previous lives. The karma – the actions – we performed in past lives become the karma – the results – that come to us in the life we have now.

Over a myriad of lifetimes, the ins and outs of our karma become endlessly complex. In the course of a day, every time I buy or sell some-thing, every time I sit down to eat, every time I smile or frown or say a word or swat a bug or sign my name, every action must later have some result, perhaps immediate, perhaps deferred, perhaps great or perhaps imperceptibly small. And those results too have their results. And so it goes, throughout the weeks and months and years that make up my life. And when we multiply those actions and results by lifetimes and lifetimes, the patterns of karmic actions and reactions that form the tapestry of even one person's life are intricate beyond knowing.

Suppose a man gets wealth, possessions, and honor. Why? Is it just a result of chance? Again, "chance" explains nothing. When we don't know why something has happened, we say it happened "by chance." "By chance it rained that day" means we don't know why on that par-ticular day it rained. There were reasons, certainly; we just don't know them. A weatherman could show us a map of warm fronts, cold fronts, and the like and start to replace "chance" with specific reasons. And if "by chance it rained that day" meant that soggy ground retarded an attack by Napoleon's army, holding him back just long enough to cost him the battle at Waterloo and change the course of European history, then this too – this apparently random happenstance of rain – hap-pened not just "by chance" but because of specific reasons, although we may not know them. Deep in the tapestry of karma – that of Napoleon, of Wellington, of France, of England, of Europe – lay causes poised to yield that result.*

According to the Vedic literature, the results of one's karma are arranged not directly by God but by nature's laws, both the obvious and the subtle. If we touch a hot skillet we'll get burned, not because God has decided to burn us but because of the laws of nature, acting through cause and effect. Instant karma, if you will. Or a karmic result may be delayed. We may smoke cigarettes for years and only late in life develop cancer of the lung. Again, it's not that God has decided to give smokers long-fuse karma but that laws of nature, in this case biological ones, inexorably respond to a destructive pattern of action by giving a destructive result. More subtly, when we cause pain to other human beings, or any other creatures, nature's laws will respond, sooner or later, by revisiting that pain upon us. Of course, this too can happen in quick and obvious ways: You punch someone, and he punches you back. But it can happen in ways so distant and subtle we don't even see the connection. The man who slips on ice and falls wouldn't imagine it had anything to do with the time when he was a kid and he tripped another kid on the playground. And of course there's no way to trace a cause-and-effect connection. But the Vedic literature says that the laws of nature, subtle and unseen, act in such ways, giving each act, each cause, its eventual results.

And this can extend over lifetimes. So the person given wealth and possessions and honor but denied the power to enjoy inherits this fate as a result of his karma, of what he has done in the past. We may not see a specific karmic connection – we may not see a specific cause for this result – but everything that happens has a reason why it happens; "chance" only means we don't know what the reason is.

In the Vedic view, God is the remote cause, the ultimate cause, the cause of all causes. When "God gives a man wealth and possessions and honor," it's not that God must deliver these personally or even that he

---

* I take this bit of history about the rain and Napoleon from Victor Hugo's vivid account of the Battle of Waterloo, given in *Les Misérables*, an account I happened to read when, by chance, the book was lying about in a room where as a guest I recently happened to stay.

must personally make a decision in the matter. But the forces of nature are ultimately his energies, and the laws by which they act are ultimately his.

As the sun has various energies, such as heat and light, so, in the Vedic view, God too has various energies, working in various ways, and among these energies are all the powers of nature. These powers are ultimately under his control – he provides the intelligence and direction behind them – and yet by his will they act automatically, each in its own way, just as the workers in a factory do their work as a matter of course, fitting in with the will and plan of the factory's owner.

In this view, then, God need not run the world by pushing buttons or pulling strings, nor by getting involved in every minute aspect of how things go. Rather, the Vedic literature says, God "has nothing he needs to do," since he delegates all the work to his energies, which automatically do whatever needs to be done. This is not to say that God cannot get involved, cannot directly intervene, but only that as a general rule he does not. Our lives go on, therefore, under the laws of nature, with God deep in the background.

A particular difficulty, however, is that we unduly try to exploit nature and so we become entangled in negative karmic results. Not even understanding what the laws of nature are, we imagine we can bend nature to our will. And that doesn't work. Rather, nature retaliates.

By nature's law I can eat only a certain amount, and if I go beyond that, nature is likely to strike back by giving me indigestion or disease. Collectively, too, when a society "overeats" – that is, when it tries to overexploit the resources of the world, battling over them, devouring them, economically sucking the world dry – nature will inevitably strike back. And so, sooner or later, on my own or with others, I may find that though I have wealth and honor and lack nothing I might desire, I have no power to enjoy. Worse, I may have to look on as some stranger enjoys for himself what is "mine." Meanwhile some sensitive onlooker like Qohelet, sensitive but seeing only within the borders of one lifetime, may cry out that what has befallen me, what God has inflicted on me, is a cruel absurdity, a sickening evil, a circumstance not only pointless but perverse.

Better a moment of full awareness

In ancient Hebrew society, to have many children was regarded as a great blessing, much to be desired, and so also to live a long life. The image of a grand old patriarch, surrounded by his generations – his children, grandchildren, and great-grandchildren – was the very emblem of good fortune. But what is the use of having many children, Qohelet says, or of living a long life, if you don't or can't enjoy life's pleasures? To follow the Hebrew text more precisely, what is the use if one's appetite (the King James Version says "his soul") is not filled to satisfaction with good things? What if God gives a man many children and a long life but deprives him of the power to enjoy? Qohelet declares that a man so blessed but cursed is worse off than a child born dead.

And so too a man who has no burial. To the ancient Hebrews, it seems, as to the ancient Greeks, to die and go unburied was horrid. "For a man to know that 'he should be buried with the burial of an ass,'" comments Plumptre, quoting the book of Jeremiah, "or, in Homeric phrase, that his body should be 'cast out to dogs and vultures'" was "the direst of woes."

The stillborn child comes for nothing and goes to the darkness of the grave, and "its name is covered with darkness," meaning it has no name at all. The stillborn sees nothing, experiences nothing – it never has any consciousness whatever – and so it is better off. Rather than live and die only to be thrown to dogs or drowned beneath the ocean, or live a long life as a tormented he or she, the stillborn child, nothing more than an "it," from the start "finds rest" in its nothingness.

Again Qohelet's despairing view of a meaningless life, a life of frustration and pain, of dashed hopes for enjoyment, or a life at whose end one can't even be shoveled into oblivion with the common rites that honor a pauper, brings him close to a Buddhist outlook, in which the best thing one could do with one's existence as a conscious personal self would be to snuff it out, extinguish it, obliterate it, erase it, so that one will no longer suffer because one will no longer exist. And better than that would be never to have existed at all.

Even if you were to live for two thousand years, Qohelet says – more than twice the age of Methuselah, the Bible's oldest man – if you are not able to enjoy … And here Qohelet just breaks off, throws away the rest of the thought, and asks again, "Do not all go to the same place?"

We are meant to enjoy, Qohelet thinks. To enjoy at least a little. As we trudge about under the sun, going about our dreary toil, as we grunt and sweat under a weary life, the only good thing in our few miserable days is that God allots us some portion of enjoyment. But the evil is that so often what he grants us is negligible, paltry, a drop of water in the desert, or else he showers upon us all the pleasures we could want but refuses to let us enjoy them.

What are we to make of this?
What the Vedic sages might say (and I have so much regard for Qohelet that I almost hold back from writing this) is that Qohelet, for all his abundant wisdom, is bewildered, illusioned, because he doesn't know who he is – or, rather, because he thinks he is something he is not.

Five hundred years ago in what is now the Indian state of West Bengal, when Sanātana Gosvāmī, a powerful and wealthy government minister (and a scholar besides), gave up all he had to become a disciple of Śrī Caitanya Mahāprabhu, he asked Śrī Caitanya, "Who am I? And why do the threefold miseries always afflict me?" The threefold miseries, you might recall, are those inflicted by nature (through heat, cold, floods, droughts, tornados, earthquakes, and the like), those inflicted by other living entities (like gnats, mosquitoes, viruses, mad dogs, and our fellow human beings), and those inflicted by our own bodies and minds.

Qohelet too, though not counting categories, asks the same question: Why is life in this world so miserable? But the question he never asks is "Who am I?" This very question, so crucial for the sages of India, seems outside his frame of reference. It never nags him, never puzzles him, never intrigues him, never torments him. It simply never comes up.

Who am I? "I am Qohelet," he says at the outset. And that is that. Am I the body? The soul? A combination of both? For Qohelet this just doesn't seem an issue to examine. In verses two and three he uses the word *nefesh*, which some versions translate as *soul* – "he wants nothing for his soul of all that he may desire," "If a man begets a hundred children ... but his soul is not filled with good" – but *nefesh*, scholars tell us, doesn't refer to an "eternal soul." It can sometimes mean "appetite," or the seat of desire, or it can simply mean "person" and be translated by "he" or "she" (or "himself" or "herself"). But it by no means refers to an eternal part of oneself. (Indeed, it's entirely possible to speak of a "dead *nefesh*" – that is, someone dead.)

For the Vedic sages, however, the question of who we are is a question we have to ask. It is fundamental.

As Krishna says early in the Bhagavad-gītā, "seers of the truth" who have turned their minds to this question have seen two categories in existence – that which changes and that which endures. That which changes comes and goes, and that which endures stays ever the same. Considering this, those seers have observed that as we move through our lives, from birth and growth toward old age and death, our bodies constantly change, whereas our consciousness – not the content of our consciousness but the fact of our consciousness – remains the same. Whether I see a fire truck or a flamingo, whether I'm thinking of philosophy or how to hit a nail, I the conscious person am the same. My body changes, my mind changes, but the same "I," the same conscious self, keeps living on. And therefore, the sages conclude, I am not my body, not my mind, but the conscious self within.

This self, the Vedic sages tell us, is joyful by its very nature. It need not seek joy outside itself, because it is practically made of joy, and not joy that comes and goes like vapor but joy that endures, the way sunlight stays forever with the sun.

One who realizes this self, who identifies with the "self within himself," at once becomes joyful, the Bhagavad-gītā says. And so such a person has nothing to desire and nothing over which to lament. He is equal in all circumstances, and so he dedicates himself not to pursuing material enjoyment but to reviving his relationship with the Supreme Self, or God, the complete eternal whole of whom he realizes himself to be a small eternal part. Thus he enters the world of *bhakti*, the world of eternal happiness and knowledge in the service of the Supreme.

But for Qohelet material enjoyment and the material body itself seem very much at the center of things. When God gives wealth, possessions, and honor – *and* lets us enjoy them – then all is good. And when he holds back and won't let us enjoy, then all is vain and evil, grievously evil.

The center of that enjoyment is the physical body. The wealth, the possessions, the honor, the enjoyment – all pertain to my body. But I think of them as pertaining to *me* – *my* wealth, *my* possessions, *my* honor, *my* enjoyment. And so I think of the body as "I" and of the bodily core, crust, ecosystem, and satellites as "mine." My wife, my home, my children, my country. To lament "Not to be able to enjoy them!" is to lament over the cosmos of which the center is my body; and to cry out at the prospect of having no burial is to cry out that the cosmos explodes without a ritual to celebrate the blown-apart dust.

But if my actual core is spiritual, not material, if it exists forever and is not destroyed when the body is destroyed, then why should I lament? Suppose the body gets no burial. So what? What does that dead body have to do with me? If they dress it in fine clothes, or carry it in a stately procession, or build for it a great tomb, what good does that do me? And if, on the other hand, the body is hacked to bits, thrown to the dogs and vultures, drowned beneath the sea, or "buried with the burial of an ass," why should I care about a body I once called mine? As Krishna says in the Bhagavad-gītā, one who laments over the body, whether it be alive or dead, "grieves for what is not worthy of grief."

Yet so grieves Qohelet, for the unburied body and for the failure of the hope to enjoy through the body, and through the offspring of the body, and through the good things for which the body has an appetite.

Of course, Qohelet, early on, has already rejected material enjoyment as vain and useless ("I said of laughter, 'It is mad,' and of pleasure, 'What use is it?' "), but he keeps coming back to it – "This is what I have seen to be good." It may not be *very* good, but there seems to be nothing else. And when that good is denied us, Qohelet says, then even the longest life, for its emptiness and frustration, is worse than useless, and he declares we would be better off born dead.

And so we have two poles: To enjoy would be good, and if enjoyment is denied us, then better (were it possible) would be nullity, a dark and restful nonexistence, void of having to see or to know, void of all the pain of life, void of everything.

Yet as pointed out before, Qohelet himself can't seem to enjoy. Knowing how vain the enjoyment is takes the fun out of it. (How heartily can you enjoy while seeing your enjoyment as petty, superficial, fleeting, mad, and vain?) And nullity is not possible, except perhaps by suicide, a ghastly option Qohelet never considers (or, if he considers it, never sees fit to voice).

From the Vedic point of view, by the way, suicide only makes things worse. According to the Bhagavad-gītā, the self is too subtle to be cut to pieces by any weapon, or burned by fire, or wetted by water, or withered by wind. And so by suicide, instead of "putting an end to oneself" (for that which is eternal can never be killed), one plunges oneself into karmic consequences still worse than those one hoped to escape. Having tried to put an end to one's life, but instead having destroyed only one's physical body, one finds oneself a ghost, full of all the desires one had before yet deprived of a physical body with which to fulfill them. Instead of becoming a no-self, the suicide becomes a miserable, tormented slip of himself, bodiless, anguished, and deranged.

And so – back to the option of life – "Even though he should live a thousand years twice over, yet enjoy no good . . ." Commenting on "twice over," one eighteenth-century commentary interprets: "And if he lived a thousand years *and then relived his life*, starting over as a youth and living another thousand years." Surely reincarnation is not what either Qohelet or the commentary intended. But the idea of living multiple useless lives is a familiar theme in Vedic literature. In any case, whether one life or many, the Śrīmad-Bhāgavatam says, "Of what use is a long life that is wasted, with years in this world but no power to understand what one sees? Better a moment of full awareness, because that gives one a start in searching for one's supreme interest."

The Vedic king Parīkṣit was cursed in his youth to die within seven days. Seven days left in which to enjoy? Instead, the king gave up his throne and went off to the bank of the Ganges to inquire from great sages about what he should do in the seven days left of his life. The discourse between the king and the sage Śukadeva provides the text of the Śrīmad-Bhāgavatam.

Qohelet laments, "Even though one should live a thousand years twice over, yet enjoy no good – do not all go to one place?" For that matter, even if one *does* enjoy good, does he not go to that same place? Of what use, then, is the enjoyment? Better, the Bhāgavatam says, is even a moment of full awareness.

6:7–9: Vain desires

[7]All a man's labor is for his mouth, and yet his appetite
is not satisfied. [8]For what advantage does the wise
have over the fool? Or what advantage the poor man
in knowing how to conduct himself before the living?
[9]Better is the seeing of the eyes than the wandering of
desire. This also is vanity and a chasing after wind.

Working for the mouth

As with the mouth, so with the other senses. However much we work
to feed them, they always want more. As Qohelet earlier said, "The eye
is not satisfied with seeing, or the ear filled with hearing." Or the sexual
organs with what they get from sex.

In material life, the highest enjoyment is sex. But though sex has its
moment, it's quickly over; and soon, appetite not satisfied, we hunger
for more. The more we try to satisfy that hunger, the greater and more
persistent it becomes. So we have to hunt around for a partner for sex
(or else resort to "self-pleasuring"), or rather than go it alone or have
to forage and scrounge every time we get hungry, we sometimes "enter
a relationship" or enter a contract of marriage to have (among other
boons) a steady partner in our passionate exertions to satisfy a hunger
that is never satisfied. The Śrīmad-Bhāgavatam says,

> *yan maithunādi-gṛhamedhi-sukhaṁ hi tuccham*
> *kaṇḍūyanena karayor iva duḥkha-duḥkham*
> *tṛpyanti neha kṛpaṇā bahu-duḥkha-bhājaḥ*
> *kaṇḍūtivan manasijaṁ viṣāheta dhīraḥ*

"Meager is the happiness of those who hope to enjoy a happy life at
home through pleasures of which the leading one is sex. Worse than
meager, such happiness is like that of scratching an itch, in which the
more one scratches the more the itch grows and the more the trouble.
Instead of becoming satisfied, the miserable soul just multiplies his
miseries. And so the thoughtful, serious person, having learned what
itching is, tolerates the itch, knowing that the supposed happiness of
scratching is merely a figment of the mind."

The more we feed our desires, the more they grow. And the more they grow, the harder we have to work – literally, work – to satisfy them. The Bhagavad-gītā therefore advises that rather than work hard our whole lives to satisfy ever-growing desires that can never be fulfilled, better to treat the demands of the senses with thoughtful indifference and be content with whatever comes to us by nature's own way. The Gītā says, "A person undisturbed by the incessant flow of desires – that enter like rivers into the ocean, which is ever being filled but always still – can alone achieve peace, and not one who strives to satisfy such desires."

The Gītā's word for "one who strives to satisfy desires" is *kāma-kāmī* – literally, "one who desires desires," who longs for greater longings, who wishes to wish for more. This is the alternative to being content with whatever comes: instead to agitate our minds with dissatisfaction over what we don't have and imagine what having it would be like, to dream, to fantasize, and at last feel frustrated when achieving our dreams lies beyond us and all we can do is imagine. Or else to achieve what we imagine, only to find out it's not what we thought and so we have to cook up something more, something new. This road has no end.

And that is why the Bhagavad-gītā recommends that one be satisfied with whatever moderate happiness comes of its own accord. Sense gratification, my spiritual master said, is like salt: too little and you can't eat, and too much and you can't eat. Sense gratification is natural, but there's no point in knocking oneself out to push for more.

From this point of view, married life is meant not as a never-ending sexual quest but as a way to meet the natural demands for sexual company and go beyond them by always remembering that life has a higher purpose. This is possible, the Gītā says, when one experiences a higher taste in relationship with the Supreme. The Bhagavad-gītā, therefore, does not recommend that one pursue material enjoyment but advises instead that one pursue spiritual realization, by which one can find unlimited enjoyment, in touch with the Supreme.

No advantage

"For what advantage does the wise have over the fool?" Qohelet asks. But why does he ask the question here? (That is, why the connective *For?*) Perhaps the verse is a proverb, parenthetically inserted. Longman suggests that according to conventional teachings wisdom should lead to wealth; but if the appetite can never be satisfied, then what is the use? The wise and wealthy will be as dissatisfied as the foolish and poor. And the poor, too, have nothing to gain from knowing "how to conduct themselves before the living" – that is, how to get ahead in the world or get along with others. The endeavor is pointless.

The wandering of desire

"Better is the sight of the eyes than the wandering of desire." That is, better to be content with what one has than to let one's mind wander here and there, longing for what it *could* have and becoming ever more discontent.

In the view of the Italian Jewish commentator Obadiah Sforno (1475–1550), "Man may long for certain goals, but the quest is in vain; he will achieve only what was predestined for him at birth."

The Bhāgavatam agrees and therefore says:

> *yasya yad daiva-vihitaṁ   sa tena sukha-duḥkhayoḥ*
> *ātmānaṁ toṣayan dehī   tamasaḥ pāram ṛcchati*

"One who is satisfied with that which comes by destiny, by the will of the Divine, whether it be happiness or distress, can cross beyond the darkness of nescience."

Though Qohelet says that the sight of the eyes is better than the wandering of desire, he finally says, "This also is vanity." And once again he is vague with his pronoun. What is *this*? The wandering of desire? The sight of the eyes? We might say both – and the whole circumstance. To chase what we don't have is vain, but so too is to try to squeeze enjoyment from what we do have. We can have "better vanity" or "worse vanity." But finally *all* is vanity and a chasing after wind.

6:10–12: Who can know? Who can tell?

[10] Whatever has come to be, its name was already given;
and what man is, is foreknown; nor can man contend
with him who is mightier than he. [11] The more words,

the more vanity. How then is man the better? [12] For
who knows what is good for man in his life, all the days
of his vain life, which he spends like a shadow? For who
can tell a man what will be after him under the sun?

Halfway

Here the medieval Jewish scholars who preserved and transmitted
Ecclesiastes include a marginal note that we have now come midway
through the book. The first half ended with "vanity and a chasing
after wind." Now we begin the second half, which Seow comments "is
marked by a repeated emphasis on what people cannot know, cannot
tell, and cannot discover."

Known long before, determined long ago

What does it mean to say that whatever has come to be has had its name
"already given"? If something has already been named, commentators
say, it has been defined; it is something known: tree, rock, battle, birthday party. So if *everything* has already been named, there is nothing new
under the sun.

We can read "what has come to be" as "what has happened." And if
whatever has happened was already named, then it was already defined,
already known – that is to say, destined to happen, predetermined.

"For one who has been born," Krishna says, "death is certain." With
this conclusion one can hardly argue. But why is death certain? Because
of the mechanics of nature's laws. Nature works in such a way that for
one who is born, death is sure; that one must die is predetermined. But
between birth and death, is the body free from the mechanical workings of nature? Obviously not. In accordance with nature's laws, the
body will grow and develop, stay for some time, and gradually dwindle and die. Throughout life it will need food, of which a portion it
will assimilate and a portion be compelled to excrete. The lungs will
breathe, the heart will pump, the blood will course through the veins,
hormones will appear at appointed times and circulate, the mind will
be busy, and millions of other things, great and small, that are supposed
to happen with the body will happen, "automatically" we say, meaning
they happen in obedience to nature's laws.

And not everything happens the same way for everyone. According to the body with which one is born, nature will work differently. The child born a boy will not grow up to be a girl or become a mother. The child born black will not grow up white, nor the white child grow up black. This too is predetermined.

The house into which we are born is assigned to us. We are plopped into the house of a beggar or an aristocrat, of a professor, a salesman, a gardener, a scientist or a pickpocket, in New York or New Delhi or New Guinea. And that determines what language we'll speak, what food we'll eat, what sort of friends and relatives we'll have, and much more. All predetermined.

And so we grow up differently, with different circumstances, different opportunities, different limitations – different destinies. How much, then, as we look more closely into details, actually remains an open question, an open choice, free and clear, with nothing in the background to determine which way we'll choose? How much freedom do we have?

What we hear from the Bhagavad-gītā is that practically everything in our life, great and small, is controlled by the workings of nature, although we egotistically think, "I am the one who makes it happen." Whatever we may think, we are not in control but under control, pushed and pulled this way and that by powerful natural forces along a course long ago defined which we imagine we chart out for ourselves.

Our independence, my spiritual master taught, is tiny. The Śrīmad-Bhāgavatam begins by asserting that the Supreme, or the ultimate origin of everything, is absolutely independent. This must be so, or else what do we mean by supreme? The Supreme, the ultimate, cannot be subject to any higher power or law, and therefore must be supremely independent. Further, according to Vedic teachings, all living beings are tiny parts of the Supreme, as sparks are part of a fire. Whatever the Supreme may be, we are small parts of it. And as sparks share the qualities of a blazing fire, we share in the qualities of the Supreme. As a spark, then, has its own small share of heat and light, we have our own small share of what the Supreme has, including independence.

But whereas the independence of the Supreme is infinite, ours is infinitesimal. And what does our tiny, minute independence consist of? It consists of the freedom to turn toward the Supreme or away from the

Supreme, toward the Divinity or away, toward spirit or toward matter, toward reality or toward illusion.

As soon as we turn away from reality we turn at once toward illusion, just as when we turn away from light we turn toward shadow. Turning away from our connection with the Supreme, we place ourselves in the illusion that we are free and independent, that we can do whatever we set our minds on, that we can control and enjoy what the world has to offer. And in this way we become bewildered. The Bhagavad-gītā says, "When standing in the world of matter, the living being tries to enjoy what is brought forth by material nature's three modes – goodness, passion, and ignorance. And coming together with those modes is the cause of birth in higher and lower forms of life."

Trying to control and enjoy – that is, to exploit – the resources of nature, we become stuck. To control matter, to enjoy matter, the stuff of this material world, we have to come in touch with matter, to get involved with matter and preoccupied with it. And in this way we forget our spiritual nature and become entangled in matter, overwhelmed by matter, and subject to material conditions, to the conditions of birth and death and all that lies between. Seeking independence from a higher reality, in fact we lose our independence. Seeking to master nature, we become enslaved by nature's conditions. This is the essence of what the Bhagavad-gītā refers to as māyā, or illusion.

It is only by turning away from the illusion of enjoying matter and toward our original connection with the Supreme that we can be restored to our natural condition and free from māyā's power. Speaking as the Personality of the Supreme, the Personality of Godhead, Krishna says that the forces of nature, the very laws of nature, work under his control, that they are his and therefore, being divinely empowered, they are insurmountable. But one who surrenders to him, Krishna says, crosses beyond them.

The freedom to turn toward the Supreme or not is what our tiny independence consists of. When we misuse that independence by trying to exploit the resources of material nature, we become entangled in nature's complexities and bound by the laws of destiny. But by turning toward the Supreme, surrendering to the Supreme, we use our independence rightly and become free.

It is known what we are

Scholars differ about how to understand and translate the second clause in verse 10. "And it is foreknown what man is" gives one way of reading it. Perhaps even more to the point, Zlotowitz offers "And it is known that he is but a man." (The *but*, he says, is not in the Hebrew but is implied according to most traditional commentators.)

Here the Hebrew word for "man" is *'adam*, the name of the original human being. And this man is born of *'adamah*, "the ground." How then can this mere man, his fate already known, dispute with one stronger than he?

For some commentators, that stronger one is God himself, for others the angel of death.* If God alone knows beforehand what will happen and what man is, what power does man have to argue with him? And if we're agnostic about God, all right then: What power do we have to argue with the angel of – okay, leave aside the pious "angel." What power do we have to argue with death?

We can argue if we like, but "The more words, the more vanity." Arguing with death is pointless, and arguing more still more pointless. Death always wins. Here Fox's word for *hevel* hits the mark precisely: "The more words, the more absurdity."

In the Bhagavad-gītā Krishna speaks of himself as the true well-wisher of all living beings, but he also identifies himself with time and with death. "I come as time and destroy all the worlds." "As death, I take away all."

As I write, a British scientist has written a book railing against the foolishness of belief in God and campaigning to disabuse people of "the God delusion." But though the scientist may fill a book with taunts, pejoratives, put-downs, and arguments, eventually Krishna in the form

---

* The New Revised Standard Version, a finely edited translation, here sacrifices meaning on the altar of gender-neutral language. Changing a singular pronoun to plural often works as a supple way to avoid the dreaded *he*. But here that strategy yields "they are not able to dispute with those who are stronger," losing both God and his angel in a gender-neutral haze. The NRSV editors, I suppose, were aware of the loss and regretted it but saw no way out.

of time, of death, will come and silence him. Even for those who don't believe in "a higher power," death always has the last word.

How then is one the better – what advantage does one gain – from arguing against God's existence? If death is final, what was the use of our words? And if death is not final – if after death there's a next life – our words, first of all, were wrong, and second can be expected to get us into karmic trouble.

Applying what Qohelet says more broadly: What – in any context – is the use of words and words and words? We fill books with words, we send students to school and barrage them with words, we publish newspapers and magazines and put out broadcasts on television and radio to add to the sea of words. We talk and talk. All day long, it's words words words. And how are we the better?

Here Fox detects in Qohelet a "self-directed irony" because Qohelet too is adding to the sea of words. (Adding to the irony, Qohelet adorns his aphorism on the vanity of words with fine alliteration: *devarim harbeh marbim havel.*)

The Vedānta-sūtras begin by saying that amidst all these words real talking begins when we inquire about the Absolute, or the source of everything. As I've mentioned before, the Śrīmad-Bhāgavatam says that this one Absolute is realized in three phases – by the beginning transcendentalist as the impersonal all-pervading reality, by the intermediate transcendentalist as the Supersoul, the indwelling presence of God within one's own heart, and by the advanced transcendentalist as the Personality of Godhead, the supreme reality in a divine personal form.

Building on this understanding, the Bhāgavatam, in two verses, distinguishes between words that are empty and useless and those that have substantial value.

The Bhāgavatam says:

> *na yad vacaś citra-padaṁ harer yaśo*
> *jagat-pavitraṁ pragṛṇīta karhicit*
> *tad vāyasam tīrtham uśanti mānasā*
> *na yatra haṁsā niramanty uśik-kṣayāḥ*

"The profusion of words that do not describe the splendor of the Personality of Godhead, who alone can sanctify the atmosphere of the universe, are considered by saintly persons to be like a place of pilgrimage for crows. The swanlike perfected souls take no pleasure there, for they dwell in the transcendent abode."

> *tad-vāg-visargo janatāgha-viplavo*
> *yasmin prati-ślokam abaddhavaty api*
> *nāmāny anantasya yaśo 'ṅkitāni yat*
> *śṛṇvanti gāyanti gṛṇanti sādhavaḥ*

"But the words that tell the glories of the unlimited, the Personality of Godhead – that tell of his names, his forms, his pastimes – is a different creation, meant to bring about a revolution in a misdirected world. Such transcendental words, even though imperfectly composed, are heard, sung, and accepted by purified people who are thoroughly honest."

Who knows what is good?

Who knows what is good for a man during his life, during all the vain days of his life? Here the Hebrew word for *all* ambiguously expresses an indeterminate number, either large ("all the many days") or small ("those few days"). If we read "all the many," then we are looking at an absurdity: all those days in vain. And if we read "all the few," again an absurdity: We hardly get any days, and even the few we get are in vain. Though our days are as ambiguously indeterminate as the word itself – will they be many or will they be few? – Qohelet flatly says they will be vain.

If we think of life as long, the shadow of our life slowly moves toward darkness, lengthening until lost in twilight. And if we think of life as short, the shadow flits by. Either way, it is but a shadow. "The effect is particularly touching," Crenshaw says, "for the celebrated life under the sun is relegated to the shadows." Plumptre quotes Sophocles:

> In this I see that we, all we that live,
> Are but vain shadows, unsubstantial dreams.

And we don't know what will be after us. "Man's ignorance of the future, of what may become of children or estate," Plumptre says, is "another element in the 'vanity' of human life." Even if a man's life is long and prosperous to the end, "still the man is vexed or harassed with the thought that his work may be all undone, his treasures wasted, his plans frustrated."

What then should man do? As Barton notes, "power, possessions, sensual enjoyment, and wisdom have been shown to be vanity." What then would be good for me? What should I do with my life?

In response to this essential question – *the* essential question – the sage Qohelet throws up his hands and says, "Who knows?" Your life is meaningless, it has no more substance than a shadow, and no one can tell you what will happen here after you're gone. So who knows.

The same question – What should I do with my life? – defines the central issue in the Śrīmad-Bhāgavatam. From the Bhāgavatam we hear that the young king Parīkṣit, suddenly cursed to die within seven days, was a man of vast wealth and power (much as Qohelet described himself) yet upon learning of the curse he left everything aside – wealth, queen, palace, kingdom, royal attire, everything – and went to the bank of the Ganges, to sit there till death, not even eating or drinking but only absorbing his mind in meditation on the Supreme in the form of Krishna.

At that time, providentially, great kings and sages gathered there from all directions, on the plea of traveling on pilgrimage. After honoring them all, the king placed before them this question: "What is it that a man should do in this life, and especially a man about to die?"

Just at that moment the great sage Śukadeva Gosvāmī arrived, merely sixteen years old but extraordinarily learned, free from all material concerns, and deep in spiritual realization. The gathered kings and sages all rose to acknowledge his preeminence, and after they were all again seated King Parīkṣit placed before Śukadeva the same question: "What is it that a man should do in this life, and especially a man about to die?"

In reply the sage congratulated the king, saying, "Your question is glorious, of benefit to all, as every knower of the self will agree. Of all topics of which to hear, this is the most important."

The Sanskrit commentators note that although the king had been cursed to die in seven days, everyone is in fact "about to die." It is only a question of time. The king, at least, knew that for seven days more he would live, whereas for our life we cannot be sure. And therefore the question of what our life is meant for, what we should ultimately do, is not only essential but urgent.

Yet for most people, the sage said, the question doesn't even occur. "Those who stay at home materially engrossed, blind to the truth of the self, have thousands of useless topics of which to hear. Such people spend the nights of their lifetime sleeping or having sex and their days looking for money or spending it to maintain their family." Where then do they have the time or thought for spiritual realization?

"Madly relying on fallible soldiers, such as body, children, and marriage partner, such people can't see their own impending destruction. Though they see, they do not see." The body, children, spouse, friends, relatives, career, and home are called "fallible soldiers" because although we depend upon them for strength, for security, for driving away our cares and troubles, all of them must perish.

"Therefore, O King," the sage said, "one who wants to be free of all fear" (for who is not afraid of death?) "should hear about, speak about, and remember the Personality of Godhead, the Supersoul, who takes all illusions and miseries away.

"Whether by understanding of matter and spirit, by practice of mystic yoga, or by doing whatever one is meant to do, the highest perfection to be gained in human life is to remember the Personality of Godhead at the end."

Again, when Śukadeva speaks here of the Personality of Godhead, he refers to the Absolute, the Supreme, as a supremely attractive divine and transcendent person who includes within himself all other realities and yet is beyond them. The Supreme realized as an impersonal all-pervading truth and the Supreme realized as the ultimate intelligence and guide that dwells within everyone's heart – these other two aspects of the Supreme, Śukadeva says, are included within the Supreme realized as the Personality of Godhead.

The Bhāgavatam relates, in fact, that Śukadeva himself had been more attracted to the Supreme as impersonal. Having attained freedom from all material attractions and attachments, he had absorbed his mind in the all-pervading supreme spiritual truth, and so he had achieved complete satisfaction within himself. Yet when he heard about the transcendental activities of the Personality of Godhead in the form of Krishna, he became attracted and so came to see Krishna as the same supreme spiritual truth, more deeply understood.

He therefore told the king that by thinking of Krishna during one's life one absorbs one's mind in thinking of the highest form of the supreme reality and by thinking of Krishna at the time of death one enters the realm of that reality, thus becoming free from birth and death and restored to one's eternal nature in a loving relationship with that reality, with Krishna himself. The Bhagavad-gītā is the beginning study in these topics, and the Śrīmad-Bhāgavatam explores them in detail.

Though none of us can know every act, every scene, every word of what will exist after us under the sun, Śukadeva knows in essence what there will be, and so does Qohelet, for he has already told us: nothing of consequence, nothing of meaning, nothing worthwhile, nothing new, only the same weary and relentless pattern of birth and death and toil.

What then is good? Śukadeva and the Vedic tradition say that what is good is to turn from the unreal to the real, from darkness to light, from death to immortality.

7

7:1–6: Much wisdom in a few words

¹A good name is better than precious oil, and the day of
death than the day of one's birth. ² Better to go to the
house of mourning than to go to the house of feasting,
for that is the end of all men, and the living should take
it to heart. ³ Vexation is better than laughter, for with
a bad face the heart is made better. ⁴ The heart of the
wise is in the house of mourning but the heart of fools
in the house of mirth. ⁵ Better to hear the rebuke of
a wise man than to hear the song of fools. ⁶ For as the
crackling of thorns under a pot, so is the laughter of the
fool. This also is vanity.

Better is the day of death

Having denied that anyone knows what is good for the days of a man's
vain life under the sun, Qohelet now proceeds to tell us what is good, or
at least what is relatively better. He writes here in proverbs, aphorisms –
in Hebrew called *mashals* – compressing much thought into few words,
to be contemplated, remembered, or probed and puzzled over.

"A good name is better than precious oil." In Hebrew the wordplay is exquisite: *tov shem mishemen tov.* A good name (*shem*) is better than fine oil (*shemen*). The message seems simple and traditional enough: A good reputation is more valuable than fine oil. It is more precious, it travels farther than an oil's fine scent, and it lasts longer, even beyond one's life, for one lives on by one's reputation. Oil was used in ancient times to preserve a dead body from disintegrating, but compared with that oil, says one traditional commentary, a good reputation will more effectively preserve the dead.

So much for the first part of the verse. But the second part seems odd, even backwards. Why should the grim day of death be better than the joyous occasion of birth?

Some commentators offer that at birth a man literally has no name and his future is uncertain but by the time of death he has earned and secured his reputation, which is then full and complete. The body having perished, as will even the most expensive oil, his good name lives on.

But this comfortable and conventional view seems contrary to the brooding and melancholy spirit of Qohelet. Far from proclaiming that the dead live on through eternal repute, he earlier said (in 2:16) that whether they have been wise or foolish all memory of them soon disappears.

Qohelet, therefore, may count the day of death superior because at death the miserable, laborious, meaningless life which birth hurls a person into is over. People celebrate a child's birth – a birth into a vain life – with a nearly giddy, intoxicated joy. Qohelet may prefer the more sober occasion of death. Indeed, in the next verse he directly says, "It is better to go to the house of mourning than to go to the house of feasting." A person who wants to party and enjoy, a person bewildered and intoxicated – what will such a person understand?

The Vedic literature commends the way of serious, thoughtful life. The Śrīmad-Bhāgavatam says, "After many, many births one achieves the rare human form, and though not permanent it can enable one to attain the highest perfection. Therefore as long as the body, always subject to death, has not fallen down and died, a sober human being should strive at once for the ultimate perfection, and not be diverted by sense gratification, which can be had in any species."

Death is the end of everyone, and yet, in the Vedic view, not the end, because death marks the occasion when a living being moves from one lifetime to the next. In the words of the Bhagavad-gītā, "Just as the embodied soul continuously passes, in the present body, from childhood to youth to old age, the soul passes into another body at death. A sober person is not bewildered by such a change." Again, a sober, serious person. Such a person will not ignore death but will take to heart the need to understand what it is and what to do about it, because each of us is moving toward it. As Michael Eaton comments, "Every funeral anticipates our own."

Better than laughter and song

Vexation is better than laughter because the heart troubled by the problems of life feels acutely the need to resolve them whereas the laughing man can float in shallow joy and ignore them. The sad or troubled face of the philosopher, therefore, is the face of a person making progress in his heart. Alternatively, as Fox suggests, the scowling face of a person who rebukes and instructs us helps us more than the hollow laughter of the merry.

Commenting on verse 4, Ibn Ezra says that even when the wise don't physically enter a house of mourning, the house of mourning is always within them.

Verse 5 is straightforward: "Better to hear the rebuke of a wise man than to hear the song of fools." Noting Qohelet's use here of the singular and the plural, the scholar Graham Ogden says that a rebuke given by a single wise man is better than a song sung by many fools. Instead of the word *song*, some translations say *praise*. Better to be rebuked by someone wise than praised by fools.

The themes of the troubled heart and the rebuke by the wise find perfect expression in the Bhagavad-gītā, which deals with a heart not merely troubled but plunged into hopeless dejection. As the Gītā opens, a battle for justice is about to begin, and the warrior Arjuna has asked Krishna, who has taken the role of his friend and charioteer, to draw their splendid chariot between the two opposing armies. This is to be a dynastic war between royal brothers, so as Arjuna surveys the field he sees on both sides his friends and relatives, all arrayed and ready to fight to the death.

Suddenly overwhelmed by compassion, his skin in fever, his mouth drying up, his limbs trembling, his bow slipping from his hand, Arjuna loses his resolve and becomes bewildered. What should he do – charge ahead into a war of heroic fratricidal slaughter? The outcome seems at once so horrific and so utterly pointless that now he thinks he would rather flee the field and slip off somewhere to live as a beggar, or else just stand and let the enemy slay him. He argues for detachment, for selflessness, for morality, he recoils against condemning himself to sin, he asks what profit or pleasure, in such a ghastly war, he could possibly hope to gain. And yet he knows that to fight for a just cause is a duty he must perform no matter how painful, that to fail would be to heap shame upon himself and the noble kings from whom he has descended. Distraught beyond distraught, torn beyond torn, he finally casts aside his bow and sinks down onto the seat of the chariot, his mind overcome with grief.

Thus dejected and despairing, Arjuna turns to Krishna, his divine charioteer, and surrenders to him for decisive guidance, for instruction, for enlightenment, as a disciple surrendering.

It is then that Krishna steps out of the role of charioteer and friend and accepts the role of spiritual master. Gently smiling in the field between the two armies, he begins to speak to the grief-stricken Arjuna. And the first words from his mouth are a rebuke. "While speaking learned words," Krishna says, "you are mourning for what is not worthy of grief." That is: "You have been speaking like a learned man, but no learned man would speak like you." Or in plain terms: "You are speaking like a fool."

As my own spiritual master once said, "Strong words are sometimes needed to awaken a sleeping man." The duty of the spiritual master, the spiritual teacher, is to awaken the person sleeping in illusions, and for this the master may employ sharp words. The sharp words of the master are like the knife of the surgeon, which cuts for the patient's cure.

The Śrīmad-Bhāgavatam, too, is full of encounters in which wise teachers, instead of speaking honeyed words, tell bitter and unwelcome truth. There is no use approaching a wise man to hear what we want to hear, what we think we already know, to get a spiritual stamp of approval for our illusions.

It was to dispel Arjuna's illusions that Krishna spoke to Arjuna, and at the end of the Bhagavad-gītā Arjuna affirmed that by the grace of Krishna his illusions had indeed been dispelled.

All the Vedic literature therefore advises that we avoid the jolly company of fools and instead try to hear from the wise, the self-realized, for even by the briefest association with such a person one can achieve the highest perfection.

The word *gītā* refers to a poem or song, and so the Bhagavad-gītā may be called the song of *Bhagavān*, which means the person supreme in beauty, fame, strength, wealth, detachment, and wisdom – that is, Krishna. It is infinitely better to hear the divine song of Krishna than the songs of fools.

Qohelet compares the merriment of the fool to the crackling of thorns under a pot. The common fuel in the Middle East was charcoal, which burns with slow and steady heat. In contrast, thorns burn quickly, giving little heat but lots of noise. Qohelet plays with sound to his advantage, writing the noise into his verse. *Ki keqol hassirim taḥat hassir ken seḥoq hakkesil.* His *s*'s hiss, his *k*'s and *q*'s crackle. And he has other games going on. In the last words of the previous verse – *shir kesilim* (the *shir*, "song," of *kesilim*, "fools") – his *s* sings, his *k* cackles, and now the *shir* (song) of that verse turns into the *sirim* (thorns) of this one. And *sir* is "pot," so he has *sirim* under the *sir* – as Barton translates it, "nettles under kettles."

But finally this also is vanity.

As usual, Qohelet is ambiguous with his pronoun. What does *this* refer to? It could refer to the laughter of fools. But the futility of that laughter, as Fox points out, is so obvious it is hardly worth mentioning. Alternatively, *this* could refer to the rebuke given by the wise, with Qohelet denying that in the ultimate issue such a rebuke has any value. Or *this* could refer to all the wise aphorisms Qohelet has just recited, in which case he would be mocking traditional wisdom – or "wisdom" altogether – setting it up only to knock it down, denying, as Seow offers, that "the wise who know 'better' . . . can really be relied on more than fools." (After all, "Who knows what is good?") Or, as Leslie Fuerst comments, Qohelet, again in self-directed irony, may be speaking about his own thought process, "as a man might mutter or muse to himself 'what's the matter with me?' " Wise sayings, splendid word games, but if all is vanity, so too are the words of Qohelet.

7:7–10: More proverbs

> [7] Surely oppression turns a wise man into a fool, and a bribe corrupts the heart. [8] Better is the end of a thing than its beginning, and better the patient in spirit than the proud. [9] Do not be hasty in your spirit to be angry, for anger rests in the bosom of fools. [10] Do not say, "How was it that the former days were better than these?" for it is not out of wisdom that you ask this.

Better patience than pride

Duress or largesse may turn the heart of even a wise man. And so, again, even wisdom may fail. A good thing is better at the end than at the beginning because its outcome, at first uncertain, has now been fulfilled. And a bad thing is better at the end because it's over. We recall that in 7:1 Qohelet praised the day of death as better than the day of birth.

Since we don't know at the beginning how any endeavor will turn out, better to be patient than proud. Crenshaw quotes the biblical proverb "Let not the person putting on armor brag like the one taking it off."

The Hebrew for *thing* ("Better is the end of a thing") can also mean *word*. In that case: We can't know the full value of what someone has begun to say until that person has finished speaking. So rather than proudly cut people off as soon as they begin to speak (a terrible habit of mine), better to hear patiently till the end.

The literal Hebrew here for *patience* and *pride* is the more colorful "length of spirit" and "height of spirit." Longman brings out the spatial metaphor by saying "Better long patience than soaring pride."

The Bhagavad-gītā says that from anger, bewilderment arises. It follows, then, that a person who lets the heart becomes a lodging place for anger will have a heart bewildered by illusion and so will be a fool.

"Why were former days better than these?" Qohelet says that this is not a wise question. As the Śrīmad-Bhāgavatam says, "As the world is now, so it was in the past, and so it will be in the future." We imagine that days past were better than the days of the present, or that the future will be better than now. But from a broader point of view they're all the same. Against a backdrop of birth, death, disease, and old age, all creatures struggle their way through their tiny lives. When has this been different? And when will it not be the same?

From the Vedic perspective, we are all spiritual beings trapped in material existence, and true wisdom is directed to getting out of material existence altogether and returning to freedom, to our natural spiritual state.

7:11–12: The advantage of wisdom

[11] Wisdom is good with an inheritance – indeed, a profit to those who see the sun. [12] For wisdom is a refuge, even as money is a refuge; but the advantage of knowledge is that wisdom preserves the life of him who has it.

The ultimate refuge

"Wisdom is good with an inheritance." The Hebrew can be translated several different ways and yield several different meanings.

If we read "Wisdom is good with an inheritance," with the emphasis on *inheritance*, then Qohelet is being cynical – or practical: Wisdom is especially good when you've been handed down a good financial cushion to sit on. Then you don't need to scramble for money, and you can spend your days in intellectual pursuits.

If we take the same reading with the emphasis on *wisdom*, then Qohelet is being practical in a different way: He is suggesting (as Rashbam comments) that your inheritance won't last unless you have the wisdom to look after it.

Alternatively, we can read "Wisdom is *as good as* an inheritance." In that case, an inheritance may be good, but equally good is wisdom, though such honor for wisdom – it's as good as money, not better – falls short of the high praise wisdom usually receives. If again we think Qohelet is just speaking practically, what he might have in mind is that wisdom is as good as an inheritance because with wisdom we can make money. Wisdom, then, is "like money in the bank." Or else, more profoundly, as Seow comments, by putting wisdom on the same level as money Qohelet intends to undermine our confidence in wisdom; ultimately our wisdom, like whatever possessions we might inherit, will prove unreliable and perishable.

Then again, the Midrash, an ancient collection of commentaries by esteemed rabbis, offers a third possible reading: "Wisdom is good *as* an inheritance." With the emphasis on *wisdom*, this would mean that wisdom is indeed a good legacy to inherit. With the stress on *inheritance*, wisdom is especially good when passed on from father to son, or teacher to student.

Indeed, the Vedic literature recommends that one gain wisdom in this way – as an inheritance passed down from previous generations, from teacher to student, from master to disciple. The Bhagavad-gītā says, "Just try to learn the truth by approaching a genuine, self-realized spiritual master. Inquire from him submissively and render service unto him. The self-realized soul can impart knowledge unto you because he has seen the truth." In the Vedic tradition, the self-realized soul is one who has submissively heard from another self-realized soul who has received spiritual understanding the same way, passed down from generation to generation. As Krishna tells Arjuna, "I originally spoke this imperishable science of yoga [one's relationship with the Supreme] to Vivasvān [lord of the sun], who in turn imparted it to Manu, who in turn imparted it to Ikṣvāku. Thus the knowledge of yoga was received in a line of succession, and the sagacious kings understood it in this way."

When Qohelet says that wisdom is a profit to "those who see the sun," he refers to all who live on earth, who all benefit from wisdom received. According to the Vedic tradition, knowledge received should be distributed for the benefit of others.

In verse 12 Qohelet likens wisdom to money, since both offer refuge – literally "shade," with its welcome protection in hot climates. If one is in the shade of wisdom, says the eminent medieval commentator Rashi, one is in the shade of wealth, since wisdom brings wealth. But wisdom is better, Qohelet says, because wisdom preserves one's life. The Midrash gives several examples of how people, by their smarts, have saved their lives.

But there's another angle to this, as Seow points out. Shade, or "shadow" (an equally good translation), may provide refuge, but shadows are shadowy: brief and insubstantial. So too, then, is the refuge provided by money. Can our money really protect us? And if our wisdom does nothing better than bring money, can our wisdom protect us? Of course, by shrewdness or cleverness we may save our life, or simply by living wisely we may preserve it – but for how long? Death takes no bribes. And what is the use of prolonging a vain life?

The Śrīmad-Bhāgavatam asks, "Don't the trees also live?" They do, and sometimes for thousands of years. How then is a human being's long lifetime better than that of a tree? We may answer, "Well, a tree doesn't breathe, the way we do." The Bhāgavatam replies, "Doesn't the bellows in the blacksmith's shop also breathe?" We may say, "Yes, the bellows may breathe, but it can't enjoy like us by eating or having sex." And the Bhāgavatam answers, "Don't the other animals all around us also eat and have sex?"

By speaking of "other animals" the Bhāgavatam implies that human beings who simply live to prolong their lives, to go on breathing, to eat and have sex, are hardly better than animals – "polished animals," one may say, because they do with refinement what other animals do crudely, but animals nonetheless. Better than even the longest life, the Bhāgavatam says, is even one moment of full consciousness because that gives one a start in searching after one's ultimate benefit, or one's ultimate shelter.

For the Bhāgavatam, "wisdom" must aim at more than making money or keeping oneself alive. Wisdom aimed at those things is hardly worthy of the name. One must try to understand the ultimate source of everything, or the ultimate refuge of everything.

The Bhāgavatam speaks of the Supreme as that ultimate refuge, in the sense that everything else proceeds from the Supreme and therefore depends on the Supreme for its very existence, the way sunlight depends on the sun. The source of everything is by definition not dependent on anything else – it needs no other source – whereas everything else, for its very existence, depends on the Supreme. We may therefore take shelter of money, or of our home and family and job and country, or of our wisdom or skill or whatever, but ultimately each of these depends on something else, which in turn depends on something else, and so on, all the way up to the level of the cosmos, and beyond, until we finally come to the supreme source, or the Absolute, the ultimate refuge of everything.

The Vedic literature looks at everything as being energy of the Supreme, the way sunlight is the energy of the sun, or as heat and light are energies of fire. As a fire, though in one place, spreads itself throughout a room by heat and light, so the Supreme, by its energies, pervades the entire world. Whatever material phenomena may exist – earth, water, fire, air, sky, and even mind, intelligence, and our very sense of who we are – all emerge, issue forth, radiate, from the Supreme. Finally, life itself issues forth from the Supreme.

In this scheme of things, all beings, material and spiritual (or non-living and alive), are seen as energy, and the Supreme is regarded as their energetic source, as we might picture rays of sunlight and their origin, the shining orb we call the sun. And these two – energy and energetic – constitute all that is, the totality of all existence.

In this picture, the question "If everything has a source, where does the source come from?" hardly even arises. Existence simply has two distinct components: limitless energies and their limitless energetic source. As the idea "sunlight" cannot be complete without "sun," the idea of "energies" cannot be complete without "ultimate energetic source."

It is this ultimate source of all energies that the Bhāgavatam describes as being realized first as an all-pervading spiritual reality, then as the Supersoul within one's heart, and finally as the Supreme Personality of Godhead. The Bhāgavatam, therefore, regards the Personality of Godhead as the refuge of all existence and regards knowledge of that ultimate refuge, and of one's relationship with that refuge, as the ultimate goal of all wisdom.

7:13–14: Crooked, joyful, adverse, and bewildering

[13] Consider the work of God, for who can make straight
what he has made crooked? [14] In the day of prosperity
be joyful, and in the day of adversity consider: God has
made the one as well as the other, so that man should
find out nothing that will come after him.

The crooked world

When considering the work of God, Qohelet doesn't rhapsodize over
how lovely it is; he sees what's wrong with it – it's crooked. We may say
it's partly straight and partly crooked, but that still amounts to crooked.
And there's nothing we can do about it, because that's the way God
made it.

The Vedic literature shares Qohelet's view that we live in a crooked
world and agrees that we can't make it straight. From the Vedic point
of view, the entire material world is crooked, bent, twisted, warped,
because it's an imperfect reflection of the spiritual world. In the Vedic
conception, the spiritual world is that place where every living being
lives in a perfect relationship with the Absolute Truth, the Personality
of Godhead, and where everything therefore exists in truth, in perfection, in harmony – in that sense, "straight." But those living beings who
turn away from the Absolute Truth find themselves in absolute illusion
– that is, in the crooked reflection of truth, the material world.

The Bhagavad-gītā speaks of this world metaphorically as a great and
expansive banyan tree, standing upside down, its branches below, its
roots above. No one, the Gītā says, can see where that tree begins, where
it ends, or where its foundation lies.

Trees, of course, don't grow upside down, but by gazing at the quiet
surface of a river or lake one can see such trees: upside down, backwards, shimmering, and diffracted, reflecting the trees on the bank.
The crooked trees in the reflection can never be made steady or straight.

God has made the spiritual world straight, the Vedic teachers say, but
we turn away from the spiritual world to the material world and then are
perplexed to find that the world we're in is crooked. It's crooked, they
say, because our consciousness is crooked. The Bhagavad-gītā therefore

advises that with determination we cut ourselves free from this upside-down tree, from illusion, by the weapon of detachment and turn toward the reality, the world of truth, the spiritual world of Krishna, of which the material world is but a crooked reflection.

Prosperity and adversity

Where our text has "the day of prosperity" and "the day of adversity," Qohelet speaks literally of "the day of good" and "the day of bad." On the good days, he says, "be in good." This is usually taken to mean "enjoy the good," and that is consistent with what Qohelet says elsewhere. Rashi, however, says that on the good days one should "be among the good" – that is, among those who do good. And Sforno comments that one should "seek to acquire eternal perfection, which is the greatest good."

On this point Sforno accords with the Vedic view. The Bhagavad-gītā advises that one not rejoice when one obtains what is pleasing nor be disturbed when things go the other way. Rather, with steady intelligence one should remember one's identity as an eternal part of the Supreme and not be bewildered by falsely identifying oneself with the temporary material body. Those who in this way see themselves in relationship with the Supreme are already situated in transcendence. Detached from outward happiness and distress, they enjoy happiness from within, and because they connect themselves with the Supreme the happiness they enjoy is without limits.

Rather than be philosophical only in adversity and at other times enjoy, the Bhagavad-gītā advises that we keep our philosophical wits about us on both the "good days" and the bad ones.

Good days and bad days are flip sides of the same material coin. We seek to enjoy the good and avoid the bad, but they go together. So by pursuing one, we inevitably bring upon ourselves the other. The Bhagavad-gītā therefore advises us to go beyond both good and bad by seeking happiness from within, in relationship to the Supreme, and in this way attain the perfection of human life.

Qohelet asks us to consider that God has made both the good times and the bad, both prosperity and adversity. (Fox offers a valuable nuance by translating, "God has made the one to happen *next to* the other.") God does this, Qohelet says, to hide from us the future, making us unable to know it. As Qohelet has said before, God makes us want to understand what is what but makes us incapable of doing so.

As the sagacious warrior Bhīṣma says in the Śrīmad-Bhāgavatam, "O King, no one can know the plan of the Lord. Even though great philosophers inquire exhaustively, they are bewildered."

7:15–22: "I have seen everything"

[15] Both I have seen in the vain days of my life: there is a righteous man who perishes in his righteousness, and there is a wicked man who prolongs his life in his evildoing.

[16] Do not be righteous overmuch, nor make yourself overwise; why should you ruin yourself? [17] Do not be overly wicked, nor be foolish; why should you die before your time? [18] It is good that you should take hold of the one while not letting go of the other, for he that fears God will succeed with both. [19] Wisdom gives strength to the wise more than ten mighty men who are in a city. [20] Surely there is not a righteous man on earth who does good and does not sin. [21] And do not give heed to all words that are spoken, lest you hear your servant revile you; [22] for your own heart knows that you yourself have likewise many times reviled others.

Justice violated again

From practical observation, Qohelet disputes the pious notion that the righteous will live long and the wicked soon perish. Sometimes just the opposite occurs. For a person who thinks one lifetime all there is, such violations of the traditionally expected norm would certainly seem to fly in the face of justice.

Virtue and wisdom

In verse 16, Qohelet advises against excess in either righteousness or wisdom. This has been interpreted variously. Here is one way to read it. Scriptures and religious traditions prescribe all sorts of rules meant to keep one on the straight path, the path of ethical and spiritual conduct. These rules can help us live a pure life and spiritually advance. We should not, however, follow such rules so zealously that we thwart their ultimate purpose. The rules are meant to help us reach the goal; they are not the goal itself.

Śrīla Rūpa Gosvāmī, who in the sixteenth century took a leading role in codifying the teachings of Lord Caitanya, advises that we avoid what in Sanskrit he calls *niyamāgraha*. By an elegant feature of Sanskrit grammar, the word has a double meaning, indicating both "neglect of the rules" and "obstinate insistence on the rules." By neglect of the rules one loses their benefit and strays from the spiritual path. But by overdoing the rules one becomes a fanatic or a prig, again losing the benefit of the rules and straying from the path another way. One should not, therefore, become too righteous. Śrīla Rūpa Gosvāmī says that by doing so one can ruin one's spiritual life.

How do we know when we are too righteous? We have to be wise. But if we become *too* wise we may overestimate how well we can follow or adjust the rules. Because *we* know the spiritual path, because *we* know the spiritual goal, we think *we* know when to follow the rules and when to adjust them. And so our wisdom can become a tool for *niyamāgraha* – overzealously following the rules or overconfidently setting them aside. In this way, we can become too wise, what my spiritual master called "overintelligent."

In particular, one should not think oneself more wise than one's own spiritual teacher, imagining one knows better than he. Before one's teacher, it is always wise to think oneself a fool. But one should not *be* a fool.

For a higher purpose, one may sometimes violate the rules, doing something ordinarily considered unrighteous, even wicked. To use a classic example: Although a principle of righteousness is to be truthful – it's wicked to lie – the Christian in Nazi-occupied Europe whose home hides a family of Jews serves a higher purpose when he tells a Nazi officer there are no Jews in the house. But such prudent lying should not become an excuse for lying wholesale. One should not become actually wicked – or at least not *too* wicked. We are already wicked enough.

We might also read Qohelet's advice as a lesson in worldly pragmatism. To get along in the world, we shouldn't become too righteous. In the words of the Hindu moralist Cāṇakya, "Do not be too upright in your dealings, for by going to the forest you would see that straight trees are cut down, crooked ones left standing." In mundane dealings, one can also ruin oneself by acting too wise (either outsmarting oneself or putting others off by being a know-it-all), and by being too wicked or foolish one can even invite early death.

When Qohelet says we should "take hold of one while not letting go of the other," again he perplexes us with his ambiguity. What do "the one" and "the other" refer to? Again, scholars differ. A sensible interpretation is given by Yosef Qara, a commentator from the late eleventh century and early twelfth, who interprets these terms as referring to righteousness and wisdom. Although we should not become hyper-righteous or act excessively wise, we should not go to the opposite poles by becoming hyper-wicked or entirely foolish. Rather, we should hold on to both virtue and wisdom, in suitable balance.

Proverbial truths

Though Qohelet sometimes doubts or disparages the value of wisdom, in verse 19 he acknowledges its proverbial ability to give strength. That no one is perfectly good is also proverbial.

But although (or because) no one is perfectly good, nearly everyone is good at talking about the faults in others. So if we listen to everything people say we'll only vex and irritate ourselves because we're likely to hear others, even our underlings, badmouth us. We know this is so because we know – at least our heart, our conscience, knows – that we badmouth others the same way, and often.

Śrīla Rūpa Gosvāmī says that a heart free from the tendency to speak ill of others is found in persons who have attained the highest level of God consciousness.

7:23–24: I said, "I will be wise."

²³All this I have tested by wisdom. I said, "I shall be wise," but it was far from me. ²⁴ Far away is that which is, and deep, very deep. Who can find it out?

Wisdom: deep and distant

"All this I have tested," Qohelet says. And we don't know whether what he's referring to is what he has just spoken of, what he will speak of next, or both, or more. In any case, since the first chapter we have seen that "testing by wisdom" is how Qohelet seeks to understand what is what.

But he recognizes here the inadequacy of this approach. "I shall be wise," he had resolved, but however wise he became, wisdom always seemed far away. Paraphrasing Qohelet, the commentator Ibn Yaḥya says, "I could not master the kind of wisdom that would enable me to solve the deeper perplexities of life."

The Vedic literature says that the speculative approach, the path of "trying to figure things out," will always fall short of enabling one to unravel such perplexities. The recommended Vedic path, therefore, is not the "ascending method," the method of intellectually trying to work one's way up to the truth, but the "descending method," the method of receiving truth in a line of spiritual heritage, of spiritual descent, understanding it by hearing from self-realized souls who have heard from other self-realized souls before them.

This involves more than mere reception of dogma. According to the Śrīmad-Bhāgavatam, when one hears from self-realized souls in a humble, submissive way, this process of hearing awakens one's own self-realization. The process is not merely mechanical. From within one's own heart, the truth itself – Krishna himself – gradually reveals himself. The person who sincerely hears from the right source receives guidance from within by which to gain true understanding.

Qohelet seeks to understand "that which is" – in other words, the nature of existence: what is what, and why things are the way they are. According to George Barton, " 'That which exists' [that which is] seems here to refer to the true inwardness of things, the reality below all changing phenomena." In Vedic terminology this underlying reality is called Brahman, the Absolute.

According to the Bhagavad-gītā, "That Supreme Truth exists outside and inside of all living beings, the moving and the nonmoving." Diffusely pervading everything, subtly present in the hearts of all as the superior inner guide, that Supreme Truth is ultimately realized as the Personality of Godhead. Yet "Because he is subtle, he is beyond the power of the material senses to see or to know." Nonetheless, "Although far, far away, he is also near to all." And deep, very deep.

In the Upaniṣads it is said,

> nāyam ātmā pravacanena labyo
> na medhayā na bahunā śrutena
> yam evaiṣa vṛṇute tena labhyas
> tasyaiṣa ātmā vivṛṇute tanūṁ svām

"The Personality of Godhead is not obtained by expert explanations, by vast intelligence, or even by much hearing. He is obtained only by one whom he himself chooses. To such a person, he manifests his own form."

Understanding of the truth is obtained by the grace of the truth, not by one's own intellectual or academic power or by attendance at erudite lectures. In the Bhagavad-gītā Krishna says, "The Supreme, the Personality of Godhead, within whom all exists and who exists within all, is attainable only by unalloyed devotional service." Because the Supreme chooses to favor his unalloyed devotees, one finds the Supreme by serving the Supreme.

7:25: To know, to search out, and to seek

[25] I turned, I and my heart, to know and to search out and to seek wisdom and the sum of things, and to know the wickedness of folly and the foolishness of madness.

To seek wisdom and to know folly

Here Qohelet tells us he turned his mind, his heart, his inner self, toward a quest for wisdom and "the sum of things" – the bottom line, what everything comes down to. And as at the start of the book, he seeks to know not only what is wisdom but what are folly and madness. Though wisdom is far off and difficult to arrive at, folly and madness are near at hand and readily found and embraced, as Qohelet relates in the coming verses.

7:26–29: "This is what I found"

> [26] And more bitter than death I found woman, whose heart is snares and nets, whose hands are chains. He with whom God is pleased will escape her, but he who goes wrong will be taken by her. [27] Just see, says Qohelet, this I have found, adding one thing to another to find the sum, [28] which my soul sought again and again but I have not found. One man among a thousand I have found, but a woman among all those I have not found. [29] Only, see this that I have found, that God made man upright but they have sought out many inventions.

More bitter than death

Qohelet's despairing judgment that life is empty, meaningless, or absurd seems easier for many commentators to digest than the direct meaning of what he says here about women. Such commentators would restrict his judgment to a subset of women – the loose, lusty, seductive ones – or they'd have him speaking of an allegorical woman, perhaps representing heresy or folly. Or they'd offer some other way to lighten his remarks.

I see no persuasive reason to think Qohelet doesn't mean what he says. Can we then simply write him off as a woman-hater and dismiss what he concludes? I'd rather not. Instead, I'd say he's on to something, and I'd like to examine that more closely, from the Vedic point of view.

From the Vedic perspective we are all spiritual living beings who misidentify our selves with our bodies, thereby losing sight of the one inner spiritual nature we all share, and so we sort and grade one another by bodily categories of country, race, class, and gender, forgetting our higher identity. The bewilderment by which we turn in this way from spirit to matter, from who we spiritually are to what our outward bodies are, is what is known as māyā, or illusion.

And where does this illusion most powerfully concentrate its force? In the attraction of sex.

In the words of the Śrīmad-Bhāgavatam, "The attraction between male and female is the basic principle of material existence. When this attraction brings a male and female together and ties together their hearts, both become caught up with body, home, property, children, relatives, and wealth. In this way life's illusions multiply, and one thinks in terms of 'I and mine.'"

When a man and a woman are drawn to one another, spiritual thoughts recede to the wayside as thoughts of material enjoyment rush and tumble to the fore. When the couple embrace and sexually unite, nature seals a strong knot of attachment in their hearts. And as the body becomes the cherished object of affection, the tender fount of pleasure, deeper and stronger becomes the illusion that body and self are one and that whatever most pleases the bodily self is intrinsic to one's very life. The man thinks, "I am hers, and she is mine," and she thinks the same way about him.

As their affection expands, they want to be together, to share their life, to have their own apartment or home, and they want their home to be homey, to have comforts and conveniences and things to make life more happy – if possible a garden, if possible an estate. In course of time, from the couple's sexual union come children, *their* children, uniquely part of them, dependent on them, extending life for them into the future, genes wondrously melded into offspring, full of possibilities, children to be cared for and cherished, to give joy and receive love, to grow up and be trained and educated, and to extend the branches of the family tree, a tree full of relatives and friends. And so: *my* children, *my* home, *my* family, *my* friends.

And all of this needs money. What do people gain from all the toil at which they labor under the sun? They gain money. And earning it and spending it takes up most of their life.

Caught up in this way, with a false sense of "I," forgetting the inner self, and falsely thinking family and possessions "mine," people hoping for a happy life through family and home become trapped in a life devoid of meaning, a life of hard work for nothing, a life of superficiality, of illusion, a life of vanity and a chasing after wind.

And, again, the bait for this trap, the nets and snares of this trap, the chains of this trap, are disguised in the alluring form that offers the enjoyment of sex – for a man, the form of woman.

Woman raises a man's dreams and passions and the urge to enjoy, but she's a trap because happiness in passion, as the Gītā says, is like nectar in the beginning but poison at the end. It starts out so lovely – the jasmines bloom, the nightingales sing, the moon sends down beams of love. And the woman is so fascinating, so mysterious, so endowed with beauty and grace. Her voice, her hair, her smile, her scent, the very movements of her eyebrows, all pull the man toward her for enjoyment. But her heart ensnares him, her hands lock him in, and soon, caught both by her mind and emotions (her heart) and by her physical features (her hands), he finds himself trapped in a life of hard work, of domestic servitude and inconsequence, of struggle, of anxiety, frustration, and disappointment, of so much endeavor for so little return.

Do you know the old Indian way to trap an elephant? You can't catch it with ropes or nets. You dig a pit, and on one side of it, across from where you expect the elephant to be, you chain a female elephant. When the male elephant lumbers out and charges forward to enjoy, he falls into the pit, and so the mighty elephant becomes a slave for the rest of his life. Such a trap may indeed be called more bitter than death.

The forcefulness of Qohelet's expression – "more bitter than death" – suggests he speaks from experience, telling what he personally found: nectar in the beginning, poison at the end. If he sought "the sum of things" in a relationship with a woman – if he there hoped to find true happiness or divine meaning in life – his hope was bitterly frustrated.

Alternatively, as Dominic Rudman suggests, Qohelet may have discovered that when a man sets out to seek the truth, to probe the purpose of his existence, to understand the sum of things, woman serves to divert him and thwart his search. Enchanted and excited by a woman, a man turns from the spiritual to the worldly, from the ultimate to the immediate, from the meaning of life to the cost of shoes and curtains. For a sage like Qohelet, this would be more bitter than death.

We find in the Śrīmad-Bhāgavatam, "There is no stronger obstruction to one's self-interest than to think something else more pleasing than one's self-realization." And what could seem to a man more pleasing than a woman? As the Bhāgavatam says elsewhere, "The infatuation and bondage that come upon a man from attachment to any other object is not as complete as that which results from attachment to a woman or [since such attachment is so easily communicable] to the fellowship of men attached to women." And so in the Bhāgavatam the Lord himself declares, "Just try to understand the mighty strength of my energy of illusion in the shape of woman, who by the mere movement of her eyebrows can keep even the greatest conquerors of the world under her grip."

And for women the same holds true in reverse. Since "man" and "woman" are but outward forms the soul assumes when it takes on a material body, as the soul travels from one lifetime to the next it may sometimes be born a woman, sometimes a man. And so: "As a result of attachment to a woman in one's previous life, one may next be born in the form of a woman, who then, by the influence of my energy of illusion, foolishly looks upon a man, her husband, as the provider of money, children, home, and other material assets. A woman, therefore, should consider her husband, her house, and her children the divine arrangement for her death, just as the sweet singing of the hunter [meant to attract a curious deer] is death for the deer."

So from the viewpoint of the Bhāgavatam it works both ways: Men are bewildered by attachment to women, and women by attachment to men. As my spiritual master sometimes jokingly said, "Man is good, and woman is good. But man and woman together are not good."

Such a radical put-down of the natural attraction between man and woman may seem grossly unfair. Or, on the other hand, it might seem right on target.

Because the material, physical attraction between man and woman powerfully distracts us from spiritual realization, the Vedic culture advises that if you can live celibate, that's better. You'll save yourself a lot of expense and trouble – to use the Yiddish, a lot of *tsuris* – and free yourself for full-time focus on spiritual advancement. You'll be free as a bird. Alternatively, there's spiritually progressive marriage, meaning marriage in which the higher purpose of life – spiritual realization – is always kept in mind. In such a marriage, husband and wife both master their own senses, look beyond the temporary body and temporary things – beyond "I" and "mine" – and direct their energy toward spiritual realization, or God consciousness.

Bhakti-yoga (the yoga of devotional service), as recommended in the Bhagavad-gītā, provides a way of life in which married couples can do this, together serving Krishna, or the Supreme. By hearing about Krishna, chanting Hare Krishna, thinking of Krishna, and serving Krishna, husband and wife (and their children) can mold their lives in such a way that their consciousness is always connected with Krishna. In this way, material attachment slackens as spiritual attachment – attachment to Krishna – becomes more and more strong. As Krishna says in the Bhagavad-gītā, "My material energy is difficult to overcome. But those who have surrendered to me can easily cross beyond it."

Here, however, Qohelet says nothing to encourage either unmarried partnership or marriage. When a woman, he says, comes on the scene, all snares, nets, and chains, one with whom God is pleased will escape her, but one who goes wrong, who trips up, will be captured.

The word rendered here as "one who goes wrong" is often translated "sinner" or "offender." But "one who goes wrong" is closer to the root meaning, "one who misses the mark." Seow writes that the word refers to what one might call a "bungler" or a "loser."

For the loser, however, there is a consolation prize – the woman herself. He gets her companionship and the pleasures and comforts she has to offer, but at the cost of his freedom. This is not what Qohelet is seeking.

Finding and not finding

In verses 27 and 28 Qohelet in his search for the sum of things continues to tell of finding and not finding. He sought in earnest – not merely "I sought" but "my soul sought, again and again." As mentioned before, the word for "soul" can also mean "mind" or "heart." Heart, mind, and soul, Qohelet tried again and again to find the sum of things. And finally:

"See, this I have found." His *this* is ambiguous but may presumably refer to what he will speak of next. In any case, he found something, but not what he was seeking. He sought the sum of things, the conclusion, the bottom line. "One to one to find the sum" – that trim formula is what the Hebrew literally says. But the numbers refused to add up. "I will be wise," but with all the wisdom he had, he couldn't get life to tally.

Instead we have the unhappy account of what he did find: one man among a thousand, and no woman at all. Qohelet leaves it to us to fill in the blank: What kind of man? What kind of woman? We can fill it in with "upright," "worthy," "decent," or whatever. Whichever good word we supply, such men are rare, Qohelet implies, and such women nonexistent.

When Qohelet says "one among a thousand," this may simply be a round number, or it may play on the tradition that Solomon had seven hundred wives and three hundred mistresses. In that case, counting each of them one by one, he found not one of them worthwhile. And among a thousand men, hardly one man worthy of the name.

Many inventions

In verse 13 Qohelet asked, "Who can make straight what God has made crooked?" The implied answer, of course, was no one. But here, turning the issue around, Qohelet says that although God has made man straight, men have come up with all sorts of crooked schemes and intrigues. As Fox says, "Man may not be able to straighten what God has twisted, but it seems that he can twist what God has made straight."

Earlier, Qohelet has used the word *heshbon*, meaning "sum," and now he uses the word *hishebonot*, meaning "inventions." Both Hebrew words come from the same root, meaning "to think, to calculate." Crenshaw says, "Qohelet's search for the sum (*heshbon*) has failed, but human-kind's search for many devices or intrigues (*hishebonot*) has succeeded admirably." And yet that success is our greatest failure. We have made a great civilization, filled with anxiety, globally destructive, and ultimately lacking in purpose. God has made us upright, but we by our calculations have hacked ourselves down.

We dream we can be happy by artfully using and enjoying the resources of this world. But inevitably our dreams fail. The schemes for happiness don't work, or they work only for a while and then fail, or they seem to work but lead us into more problems than we started with. In the words of the Bhāgavatam, "A man carrying a heavy burden on his head may seek relief by shifting the burden to his shoulder. Just like this are all our devices for counteracting distress." Shifting a burden from head to shoulder, or from one shoulder to another, or from shoulder back to head, doesn't get rid of the burden. The solutions we invent only shift our miseries around.

Elsewhere in the Bhāgavatam a seeker inquires, "Though everyone in the world works to become happy, people by their efforts achieve neither happiness nor relief from distress. On the contrary, they simply bring themselves misery. Therefore, O sage, please enlighten us about the right course."

The right course, the Bhāgavatam says, is to abandon the hopeless pursuit of material happiness and reawaken to our spiritual nature and our relationship with the Divine, with Krishna. Any other course we invent, any other device, any scheme we come up with, is sure to fail.

8

8:1: Who is like the wise man?

> [1] Who is like the wise man? and who knows the inter-
> pretation of a thing? Wisdom makes a man's face shine,
> and the hardness of his face is changed.

Known by his words of wisdom

Like so many verses of Ecclesiastes, this one can be read more than one way.

First: Qohelet may be praising the wise man. Who else is like the wise man? he asks rhetorically, the obvious answer being "no one." In the paraphrase by Rashbam, "Who is as important in the world as the wise man, and who knows the explanation of a matter as he does?"

But the verse can also be read another way, as expressed in the translation by Fox: "Who is so wise? And who knows the meaning of anything?" Again, the answer both times would be "no one." Even the supposedly wise are finally baffled and bewildered.

The commentator Roland Murphy says that this ambiguity – are the wise being praised or deprecated? – may be intentional, that Qohelet may mean to "suggest the exalted task of the sage at the same time as the impossibility of that task." Who indeed, then, knows the interpretation of a thing (and who the interpretation of Qohelet)?

Depending on how we read the first part of the verse, we have two ways to read the second. Straightforwardly, a man's wisdom brightens his face and softens it with joy, purity, compassion. Alternatively, perhaps Qohelet, having questioned how much anyone really knows, is speaking cynically: When dealing with a king (who appears in the next verses) a man wise enough to know what's good for himself puts on a content and congenial face.

Taking the straightforward meaning, wisdom *does* illuminate one's face. According to the Bhagavad-gītā, wisdom arises when one lives in "the mode of goodness." In comparison to the modes of ignorance and passion, goodness is pure, healthy, joyful, and illuminating. And since "the face is the index of the mind," the person in goodness will have a naturally shining face. The face of my spiritual master was notably effulgent.

Of course, one cannot judge wisdom simply by facial luminosity. Ultimately, a person of wisdom has to be known not by how he looks but by what he says. According to a proverb from the Hitopadeśa, a popular Sanskrit book of fables and moral precepts, "A smartly dressed fool can dazzle us – until he speaks." And a wise man will be known by his words of wisdom.

The Vedic direction, therefore, is that one should seek a person of genuine wisdom, approach him in a humble and submissive mood, inquire from him, hear from him, and serve him. The wise, self-realized person can give us knowledge because he has seen the truth.

The Bhagavad-gītā says, "There is nothing so sublime and pure as transcendental knowledge. And one who has attained perfection by being connected with the Supreme enjoys this knowledge within himself in due course of time." Who else could be like such a wise man? And who else could know what things actually mean?

Knowing the future

Considering the way the Hebrew word for *interpretation* is used elsewhere, Scott C. Jones suggests that in this verse it refers to prognostication: Who can know what a sign portends? (Does the wise man? Or no one?) From the Bible and other sources we find that kings in ancient courts called upon seers, astrologers, and the like to read signs and omens and foretell what was to be. In the following verses, Qohelet speaks of the king.

8:2-4: The king does what he pleases

> [2] Keep the king's command, in the manner of an oath
> to God. [3] Do not be hasty to go out of his presence, and
> do not persist in an evil thing, for he does whatsoever
> pleases him. [4] For the king's word has power, and who
> may say to him, "What are you doing?"

The power of the king

Qohelet here advises prudent dealings in relation to a king. A traditional role of a sage was to give advice in practical dealings, and here Qohelet's pragmatic advice would seem especially meant for young courtiers.

For verse 3 especially, several alternative translations are possible, but none change the essential theme of judicious conformity to the orders and wishes of the king. According to the English rendering here: Whatever the king might say, one should not rashly bolt from the court, nor should one persist in a bad idea (especially, as some commentators have it, not in rebellious conspiracy against him).

Various traditional commentaries read *king* in this passage as referring to God, the supreme king. Whatever one might think of the way God does things, one would be foolhardy to challenge him.

Plumptre sees divine power ironically attributed to the earthly ruler: "The despot stands, or thinks he stands, as much above the questionings and complaints of his subjects, as the Supreme Ruler of the Universe does above those of men in general."

8:5-9: When one man has power over another

> [5] Whoever obeys the command will come to no harm,
> and a wise man's heart discerns the time and way. [6] For
> to every matter there is a time and a way. Truly the
> troubles of man are heavy upon him, [7] For he does not
> know what is to be, for who can tell him when it will
> be? [8] There is no man who has power over the wind to

restrain the wind, nor power over the day of death, and there is no discharge from war, nor can wickedness save the one who has it. [9]All this I saw as I applied my heart to all that is done under the sun, when one man has power over another to the other's hurt.

Knowing the time and way

The astute attendant at the court, knowing what's good for himself, will carefully obey the king's command, knowing how and when to speak and act. Problematically, however, no one can know for sure what the future will bring. And so "the time and way" to speak and act are also hazy and obscure. And as we stumble amidst the haze, we are sure to come in for all sorts of troubles. Our diligent service to a king may earn us his favor, yet in the future he may be deposed, and those who served him best may be most cruelly purged.

The man for whom troubles are great may indeed be the king himself, for he has no way to be sure of the future. No one is so wise as to be able to tell him (and were there someone that wise, the king himself might lack the wisdom to listen).

And what's true for the king is true for us all. Each of us, or the king, may know that eventually we must give up what we have, that the king must cede his throne, that empires must pass, that death must come – but we do not know when. And if we do not know when, we are in the dark. The wise man, or the astrologer, may know the future vaguely, but can he know precisely? And if not, what is the use?

The limits of power

Whatever powers we may think we have, finally we are powerless. The powers of nature, such as that of the wind, rage beyond our power to rule. None of us can stop a hurricane or a tornado. Alternatively the word given as *wind* may be read as "spirit," the "air of life." In that case, no one has the power to hold that life force within the body past its destined time. As Qohelet says, none of us can overcome the power of death. In an ordinary war one might hope to prevail, one might hope for an exemption or discharge, or in ancient times one might arrange for a proxy to fight in one's stead. But in the war with death, no one can either win or slide out. By foul means – by wickedness – one might win an ordinary war, but no extent of foulness can save one from death. My spiritual master once quoted a Bengali proverb to the effect that one can't escape the lord of death by smearing oneself with excrement. However bad one might smell, death will take him anyway.

Again, this applies even to kings. Where our translated text denies "power over the day of death," Rashi and Ibn Ezra read the text as saying "Royalty is of no avail on the day of death." Death grants no exemption to presidents or kings. Rashi notes that the Bible always speaks of the great "King David" except when it finally speaks of his impending death. Then he is only "David": "And the days of David drew near that he should die." Kingship ignored.

Indeed, one might even say that death descends upon the king to settle scores. Where our text reads "a time and a way," an alternative reading is "a time and judgment." And so one might read the entire passage as a subtle critique of royal oppression. Beneath an arbitrary despot, one should act with obedience to stay out of harm's way and smartly let time deal with him. For the ruler and all his whims are subject to time – and judgment.

Rogues in command

One must obey the king's command as one would honor an oath to God, for the king has power. Indeed, in days gone by the king was thought to have received his place on the throne by the divine will, his power was quasi-divine, and the earthly regent was meant to serve as an agent of the divine regent. In the Vedic tradition, as in various others, biblical included, the king was seen as God's representative, meant to protect, guide, and regulate his subjects for their welfare on God's behalf. If justice and law come ultimately from God, so too, in this worldview, does the king who dispenses them.

In fact, the Śrīmad-Bhāgavatam says that in previous ages kings were so wise, strong, noble, and generous that the word of the king would indeed deserve honor like the word of God. But the Bhāgavatam predicted five thousand years ago that in the Age of Kali, the present age of degradation, quarrel, and hypocrisy, which was then just beginning, kings and heads of state would sink to the level of arrogant plunderers.

The Bhāgavatam foresaw: They will do whatever they please, and no one will be able to tell them anything. Devoid of spiritual power, and devoted instead to all that is contrary to decent life, these rogues and liars – furious barbarians in the guise of presidents, prime ministers, and kings – will give hardly even trifling benefits to the citizens. Instead, the rogues in command will loot and plunder, either through taxes and trickery or by outright brute force. They and their minions will slaughter cows, murder intellectuals, and wage wars, turning men, women, and children into corpses. The moody, arbitrary, degraded rulers, ruled by their own passion and ignorance, will grab money, land, and resources, use other men's wives for sex, and in short virtually devour their own citizens. In this Age of Quarrel and Hypocrisy, such are the divine agents of God.

One need not be as wise as Qohelet to observe such oppressions already happening under the sun, and the Bhāgavatam says that eventually governments will become so oppressive that people will flee to the mountains and forests rather than endure torment at the vicious hands of those in power.

To his hurt

Though our English rendering speaks of the time when one man has power over another "to the other's hurt," the Hebrew ambiguously says "to his hurt." Though "to the other's hurt" seems the most likely meaning intended, an alternative reading is that the abuse of power brings harm not only to the oppressed but also, finally, to the oppressor.

8:10: I saw the wicked buried

> [10] Then I saw the wicked buried, and they entered into
> their rest; but they who had done right went away from
> the holy place and were forgotten in the city. This also
> is vanity.

A problematic text

Here Qohelet yet again observes something vain, meaningless, or absurd. But we can't be sure what it is, because the Hebrew text, open to various possible readings and interpretations, has puzzled and perplexed the best of scholars since ancient times. Were the wicked buried in the holy place, or did they approach it, or go in and out of it? Were they praised in the city, or were the righteous forgotten there? To delve into the textual issues that here vex scholars lies beyond my purposes and abilities. Qohelet saw yet another vanity. I leave it at that.

8:11-14: The righteous and the wicked in an unjust world

> [11] Because a sentence against an evil deed is not
> executed speedily, the heart of man is fully set to do evil.
> [12] For a sinner does evil a hundred times and prolongs
> his days. And I also know that it will be well with those
> who fear God, who fear before him, [13] but it will not be
> well with the wicked man, nor will he prolong his days,
> which are like a shadow, because he does not fear before
> God.
>
> [14] There is a vanity which takes place upon the earth:
> that there are righteous men to whom things happen
> that are fit for the acts of the wicked; again, there are
> wicked men to whom things happen that are fit for the
> acts of the righteous. I said that this also is vanity.

Justice delayed . . .

The world is ruled by a just and all-powerful God, is it? Then where is the justice? If justice is to be worthy of the name, it ought to be consistent, and it ought to be quick. The cruel and vicious should be punished, the gentle and innocent protected and rewarded – not only sometimes but always, and not in some vague, distant future but right away.

Of what use is divine justice if it's endlessly deferred? If sentence and its execution, act and consequence, stretch so far apart that they seem to lose all connection, justice becomes meaningless, and who will care for it? In particular, if a wicked and oppressive despot sees in view no punishment for himself, if it looks like he can "get away with murder," then he can murder wholesale, with full-hearted brashness and determination. Why not?

Now, in the midst of such thoughts as these, why should Qohelet, halfway through verse 12, slip into pious confessions, saying he knows that all will turn out well for the God-fearing but not well for the wicked? Perhaps, some commentators say, these words don't come from Qohelet at all but have been put into his mouth by some pious glossator (who, strangely, did a patchwork job, leaving most of the dark thoughts in). Or else perhaps these pious thoughts belong to Qohelet after all, though he is unable to square them with what he sees. Or perhaps Qohelet is acknowledging the conventional dogma with a "Yeah, I know ...", only to mentally consign that dogma to the vanity bin. In any case, what he finally says is that once again vanity prevails.

In verse 13, with its pious view, the days of the wicked man are "like a shadow" because they pass quickly or lack substance, or else the wicked person himself is like a flitting shadow. As the day grows longer, a shadow lengthens, but the life of the sinner will be cut short.

But again Qohelet has observed that for the sinner this doesn't always happen. And the sinner himself knows that it doesn't, and so he fills his heart with evil plans.

On earth, our absurd and meaningless earth, Qohelet says, not only is justice often delayed, but it is often perversely misapplied, with the good people getting what the wicked deserve, the wicked what's deserving for the good. Evil men should have their lives cut short, the good be blessed with lives long and happy. Things should not end up the way they so often do: the good people beaten down, the evil people triumphant.

And this, Qohelet says, is yet another vain absurdity.

In essence, Qohelet expects that there ought to be a divinely administered "law of karma," a law by which for all that we do we get what we deserve. And he doesn't see it. Or else he sees it but sees it randomly violated.

From a Vedic perspective, at least this part of the problem is not a problem. From a one-life-only viewpoint, Qohelet certainly seems right: Justice seems to lurch from side to side, senselessly, unpredictably, heedless of civilized rules. But when we consider our present life only one snippet from an endless sequence of millions upon millions of lives, the problem resolves itself, for in each of our lives in the past we have performed actions whose results (if they have not already caught up with us in the present life or a lifetime gone by) may come upon us at any time now or in any of our lifetimes in the future. So when the seemingly innocent suffer or when the evil enjoy, it is not without reason but because of acts they did in lifetimes past. The law of karma works.

But still, Why the delay? Why should I suffer in this life for things I did in a previous life I don't even remember? What is the use? Of what sense could it be? Of what instructive value? The gap observed by Qohelet between sentence and punishment, deed and consequence, becomes even greater, now extending not only for years but for lifetimes.

To consider more deeply what's going on here, we need to broaden our understanding of what the world in which we live is all about. According to the Vedic sages, this world is neither a place of enjoyment nor merely a place where we get rewarded, punished, and thereby instructed. Rather, it is the world of māyā, of illusion, of "that which is not." It is the world in which we choose to imagine that we are entirely independent, that our existence is not contingent on an ultimate existence greater than our own, that we are not part of the supreme reality, or Krishna.

To accommodate that choice, Krishna has a potency, an energy, "the energy of illusion," which enables "that which is not" to seem real. Through that energy, called māyā, Krishna provides for us a bewilderment we ourselves choose to have.

This "illusory energy" masks from us the real nature of this world so that we can think it's a place where we can control and enjoy. If you'll recall the incident in which the king of heaven was reduced to a pig, you'll recognize this energy at work. Even when degraded to the filthy life of a pig, the king of heaven thought he was enjoying: "This is the life."

The pig, the lion, the mosquito, the fish, the bird – all are so thoroughly covered by māyā that they can't even question whether their life makes sense. They just go on with their lives of eating, sleeping, having sex, and defending their turf, and that's about it. Only in the human life does māyā slightly ease up so that one has the opportunity to raise the kind of questions asked by Qohelet: Why does the world seem so frustrating, so empty, so painful, so absurd? Why its contradictions? Why its injustices?

And now coming back to the point: Why the delay between sentence and execution, between deed and consequence, a delay, as Qohelet sees, that emboldens men to do evil?

One answer is that this delay is māyā's deliberate contribution to our bewilderment. We want to have a good time and not pay for it, cheat and not get caught, grab the world's honey and not get stung, and māyā so deceives us that we imagine we can pull it off. When we turn away from Krishna, illusion is what we want, so illusion is what we get.

And even when a sentence *is* swiftly executed, we tell ourselves that it happened to *him* but won't happen to us, or that it caught us this time but next time we'll be smarter and not get caught. Such is the power of māyā, and delays between sentence and execution only enhance the effect, most exquisitely when we're allowed to keep our winnings and are smashed for how we got them only in a future life.

And there's yet another angle to this. The world is set up in such a way that we serve as agents for one another's karma. For example, if by your karma you're meant to get a hundred thousand dollars, I as your uncle may decide to leave you a hundred thousand dollars in my will. So, without knowing it, I act as the delivery boy for your karma. Similarly, if you're meant to lose a hundred thousand dollars, I as a thief may steal it from you, again acting as your karma's delivery boy. So when delays in justice embolden men to do evil, those delays serve a greater plan by engaging men to deliver "bad karma" to those meant to receive it. (A catch for the delivery boys, however, is that even though they serve a greater plan, they do so unwittingly, with their own purposes in mind, and so incur their own karmic reactions.)

And this brings us to one point more. Qohelet seems to expect the laws of justice, ordinary and cosmic, to be simple: When you do something evil and get sentenced, you should speedily get punished. But from the Vedic viewpoint the intricacies of karma – of action and reaction – are unlimitedly complex. Yes, I may have done an evil deed, and so I may deserve to get punished. But then again, I may have done some good deed sometime before, and on that account my punishment may be reduced or deferred. Even from what I do in this one lifetime, my karmic credits and debits may form a complex account, and when we view that account as extending over an infinite number of lifetimes, how complex does it get? Beyond that, when we consider that we not only have our own individual karmic bank accounts but are interacting with one another, the karmic complexity, already inconceivably intricate, explodes into complexity still greater. No one can figure it out.

And this too is part of what it means to be under the influence of māyā. In the realm of illusion, we may hope to tap the resources of nature and enjoy. But the workings of māyā are so densely complex that they lie beyond our ability to fathom. So even if our efforts for happy independence in the world of "that which is not" may appear for a while to succeed, at last they end in failure, in frustration, in defeat.

In the Bhagavad-gītā, therefore, Krishna advises that the only solution is to move from "that which is not" to "that which is," from falsely acting as though absolutely independent to acknowledging that we are dependent on the Supreme, on him. "This divinely empowered māyā," he says, "is my energy and is insurmountable. But one who surrenders to me can easily cross beyond it." The process of surrendering to Krishna, known as bhakti-yoga, is therefore the means the Gītā most recommends for crossing beyond infininite lifetimes of karma and getting free from the vain struggle for happiness in the world of "that which is not."

8:15: Eat, drink, and be merry

[15] So I commended enjoyment, for a man has no better thing under the sun than to eat and to drink and to be

merry, for this should accompany him in his labor all the days of the life that God has given him under the sun.

Recommending what doesn't work

Baffled by life's apparently absurd injustices, Qohelet once again recommends a life of toil and enjoyment that from the very start of his book he has so effectively shown vain. Fox comments, "Qohelet is recommending pleasure as a distraction from the painful awareness of realities such as he has just described." Avoiding such awareness is contrary to the Vedic approach.

8:16–17: Seek and you shall not find

[16] When I applied my heart to know wisdom, and to see the business that is done upon the earth – for neither day nor night do men's eyes see sleep – [17] then I saw all the work of God, that man cannot find out the work that is done under the sun. Though a man labor to seek it out, he will not find it. And even though a wise man claims to know, he will not be able to find it out.

No one can understand it

When Qohelet applied his heart – that is, his mind, his thoughts – to know wisdom and to know what is done on earth – that is, what happens – he saw that it is all God's work but that no one can figure it out. The Vedic literature agrees with this conclusion. We may understand this world to a certain small extent, or think we understand it, but the complex workings of the "illusory energy" by which God controls this world are, by design, beyond our ability to penetrate.

In the Hebrew, Qohelet's reference to eyes that sleep neither day nor night is grammatically ambiguous; one cannot be sure whose eyes it is that do not sleep. The eyes may be everyone's (as rendered here, "men's eyes"). In that case, people are so busy working that they hardly have a proper chance to sleep. Alternatively, Fox offers (with a slight adjustment to the Hebrew text) that what's intended is "my eyes" – that is, the eyes of Qohelet himself. Though trying day and night, forgoing sleep, Qohelet has not been able to understand the perplexing ways in which God makes the world work. Coming to the same conclusion by another route, Rashbam says that the eyes are those of the personified heart itself. The heart – the mind – has taken up the work of trying to understand the world, has lost sleep trying to understand, but has failed.

In the first verse of this chapter, Qohelet asked who knows the interpretation of a thing. Who knows what things mean, what's behind them? Does the wise man? Now Qohelet concludes that God has made the world in such a way that what's going on here is incomprehensible. No one can understand it.

The attempt to make sense of the world by exhaustive (and exhausting) speculation will never succeed. Our modern wise men – our scientists – may claim to understand what's behind the workings of the world, but they too are ultimately bewildered. They too are under the spell of māyā, and no amount of research or speculation will get them out of it.

9

9:1–3: Finally, to the dead!

> ¹ Indeed, all this I laid to my heart, and I examined all
> this: that the righteous and the wise and their works
> are in the hand of God. Whether it be love or hatred,
> man does not know; all is before them. ² All things
> come alike to all; there is one event to the righteous
> and to the wicked, to the clean and to the unclean, to
> him who sacrifices and to him who does not; as it is
> for the good, so it is for the sinner, and for him who
> swears as for him who fears to swear. ³ This is an evil in
> all that is done under the sun, that there is one event
> for all. Moreover, the hearts of men are full of evil, and
> madness is in their hearts while they live, and after
> that – to the dead!

In the hand of God?

Here again, Qohelet dedicates his heart to trying to understand what he
sees. The righteous and the wise and all that they do are supposed to be
in the hand of God. So too of course are everyone and everything else,

but we might expect that for the righteous and the wise God's hand would furnish special care and favor. Yet Qohelet sees that finally this is not so. Rather, of the supposedly benevolent treatment God gives the wise and righteous, Qohelet says, "Whether it be love or hatred, man does not know." Sometimes, as Qohelet has observed before (in 8:14), what hits the righteous seems like what God ought to inflict upon his enemies. Where's the special care?

But though "all things come alike to all," the Vedic teachers say that trouble visited upon the wise and righteous may indeed be a favor to them. Even those who have spiritual understanding may still cling to material attachments, perhaps even against their better judgment. "This attachment will hold me back," they may think, but they hold on to it nonetheless. For such persons, aspiring to get free from māyā's grip but still holding on to māyā (the grip their own), Krishna may show special favor by smashing them.

In the Śrīmad-Bhāgavatam Krishna says, "If I especially favor someone, I gradually deprive him of his money. In his poverty his relatives and friends abandon him, and he suffers one distress after another. When he grows frustrated in his attempts to make money and instead makes friends with my devotees, I bestow my special mercy upon him. One who has thus become sober fully realizes the Absolute as the highest truth, the most subtle and perfect manifestation of spirit, the transcendental existence without end. Realizing in this way that the Supreme Truth is the foundation of his own existence, he is freed from the entanglement of material life." Sometimes, therefore, apparent calamities befalling the wise and righteous may be a sign of the greatest favor.

Of course, loss of money isn't the only way trouble descends. It may come in the form of accident, disease, persecution ... But the Vedic teachers say that for the person on the spiritual path these troubles are but tokens of what would otherwise be karmic troubles still greater, brought on by past deeds, and that by accepting this "token karma" one becomes progressively free. The person advanced in spiritual realization therefore sees good fortune and misfortune with an equal eye.

In the Śrīmad-Bhāgavatam, therefore, a devotee offers this prayer: "My dear Lord, one who earnestly waits for you to bestow upon him your causeless mercy, all the while patiently tolerating the reactions of his past misdeeds and offering homage to you with body, words, and heart, is surely eligible for liberation, for it has become his rightful claim."

None of this, however, is available for empiric examination – it is not on the surface, to be seen by the mundane eye. By ordinary intellectual analysis, one can't fully understand what is going on in this world, and so one may not know whether what happens to the wise and righteous reflects divine favor or divine disfavor. Or again, able to go no further than the empiric approach will allow, one may conclude that no divine control even exists to treat people one way or the other. Such are the limitations of the empiric approach.

"All is before them"

All, Qohelet says, is before them. We may take this enigmatic phrase to mean that everything (at least everything yet to come) lies in the future. And who can be sure of the future? Alternatively, we may take *before* in a spatial sense, meaning that we don't understand even what is spread out before our very eyes. That is, we don't understand even the present.

And there is yet a third alternative: Some traditional commentators, such as Ibn Ezra, interpret the text to mean that all *precedes* us, that our lives unfold according to a fate decided even before we are born. In the Vedic view, this would mean that we journey on a course set out for us by our infinitely complex karma, by the acts we have taken over millions of lifetimes. And so our fate lies beyond our ability to know because it proceeds from an infinitely complicated past.

However wise we may be (or may think we are) we are largely in the dark about the past, about the future, and even about the present. The Bhagavad-gītā says that all can be known only to the person we do not know – that is, to God, or Krishna. As Krishna says in the Gītā, "I know all that has happened in the past, all that is happening at present, and all things yet to come. I also know all living beings; but hardly anyone knows me."

The same fate for all

The wise and righteous whom Qohelet mentions in verse 2 may not be great, highly realized souls but merely those who conform to a pre-scribed path of religious laws, perhaps even with an eye toward earthly rewards. In any case, Qohelet's tradition would say that those who followed a righteous path could expect a better fate. Not so, Qohelet says: Fate treats every person, good and bad, the same way. Finally all meet the same event: death. Whatever people may do, evil and madness are in their minds while they live, and finally – the sentence ends, as one commentator says, with a clause that "breaks off like life itself" – finally, to the dead!

9:4–6: Better a living dog than a dead lion

> [4] For him who is joined to all the living there is hope, for a living dog is better off than a dead lion. [5] For the living know that they will die, but the dead do not know anything, nor do they any longer have any reward, and even the memory of them is forgotten. [6] Their love, their hatred, and their envy have already perished; nor do they have a portion any longer in anything done under the sun.

Death snuffs out everything

In the previous verse, when Qohelet says that death is "an evil in all," many scholars take this as a way of expressing the superlative – "the worst evil." And here Qohelet speaks of death as bringing a superlative nothingness.

At least the living have some meager hope – "While there's life there's hope" – though there finally seems nothing to hope for. Alternatively, some scholars, instead of "hope," offer the translation "certitude." The dead know nothing, but the living, still endowed with the faculty of knowledge, can at least have one thing to be sure of – that they will die. For the man who is dead, as Plumptre says, "There is no longer even death to look forward to as the wages of his life." Even the idea that one will live on in someone's memory is a delusion. At death our love, our hatred, our envy are extinguished. Plumptre says, "Even these are all hushed in the calm of the grave. There are no passions there, and the deadliest foes, rival statesmen and rival controversialists, rest side by side together." The drama is over.

If the body is the self, this is the end. Whatever may happen in the world, one no longer has a share in it. But the Bhagavad-gītā says that the very passions that move us in our present life force us at death to take on another body, in which love, hatred, and envy again move us – and again move us along. From Qohelet's one-life point of view, we have only this one meaningless life, ending in death. From the viewpoint of the Bhagavad-gītā, we go through an endless succession of meaningless lives, in an endlessly repeated cycle of birth and death, in which we die and are born again and again, and not only into human bodies but into a chain of millions of different species. In each life we have our loves, our hatreds, our envy as well, all urgently important, all of no ultimate consequence.

In this endless cycle of birth and death, the human life affords the opportunity for self-realization. And so the Śrīmad-Bhāgavatam says that if a human being neglects this opportunity his life is a failure. As long as one fails to inquire about the truth of the self, the Bhāgavatam says, ignorance brings about one's defeat, for one's mind remains absorbed in the life of the body – in one's life as a woman or a man, as a statesman or a street sweeper, the life of another one of nature's insignificant little puppets, working hard on the way to the grave, and not even to the grave, because that's only the pit for the body, but on the way to another life that is no life because one has forgotten one's actual self. In such forgetfulness, one tries to be happy in what seems to offer enjoyment, but one is forced again and again to lose whatever one thinks one has gained.

There's a story about a man who throughout his life worked hard and saved diligently, depositing his money in the local bank and looking forward to his retirement. When the time came for him to retire he went to the bank to withdraw his savings. There the teller said, "I'm sorry, sir, but your account is empty."

"But I've been saving for my whole life, putting money in the bank every week!"

"I'm sorry, sir, but our records show …"

"What do you mean, your records show!"

When the two of them got to the bottom of the matter, they found that the old man had throughout his life been depositing his money in someone else's account. And now, therefore, his own account had nothing.

And so, one who never inquires about spiritual realization and instead stays preoccupied with working hard for the enjoyment of a body meant for death is putting all the money in the wrong account. In the words of the Bhagavad-gītā, "One who lives to satisfy his senses lives in vain."

But according to the Bhagavad-gītā, in the pursuit of spiritual realization there is never any loss, because even though one might not attain perfection in one lifetime one's spiritual credit carries over into the next, so that one will automatically be attracted to spiritual inquiry and begin from where one left off. But if one lives only to satisfy the senses of the body one lives for nothing because the satisfaction is paltry and at death the very senses one hoped to satisfy disintegrate into nothingness.

9:7–10: Enjoy your useless life

> [7] Go your way, eat your bread with joy, and drink your wine with a merry heart, for God has already approved what you do. [8] Let your garments be always white, and let oil not be lacking for your head. [9] Live joyfully with the woman you love all the days of your life of vanity, which he has given you under the sun, all the days of your vanity; for that is your portion in life, and in your toil at which you labor under the sun. [10] Whatever your hand finds to do, do with your strength, for there is no work, nor thought, nor knowledge, nor wisdom in Sheol, to which you are going.

Enjoyment already approved
Amidst bleak contemplations of death, Qohelet turns again to tell us to eat, drink, and be merry. Earlier he said that whatever enjoyment we receive comes from the hand of God, and now again he says that when

we accept this gift whatever we do has already received God's approval. If God has already approved, why hold back? Enjoy!

How much of what we might do to enjoy has already received divine approval, Qohelet doesn't say. And how are we to know? Many commentators say that the sagacious Qohelet would not urge hedonistic abandon. But if all ends in death and till then we're meant to celebrate while we can, why should we limit our merriment and joy, especially if it has all been divinely pre-approved?

From one point of view, of course, our divinely pre-approved enjoyment has built-in limits because we can't get more than what our destiny will allow. We get our portion, nothing less but nothing more. For some people, as Qohelet himself has lamented, that portion is to live oppressed, in tears, with no one to give comfort. For others the portion – worse than death, and even worse than never having lived – is to have to witness such evils under the sun. But even when Qohelet, at the start of his book, told of a life of wealth and privilege, of land and servants, flocks and vineyards, and great works and many women, he said that he found it all *hevel* – vain, useless, and absurd. And now he urges us to eat, drink, and be merry. What is the use of this?

I am reminded here of a Sanskrit term, *bhoga-tyāga*. *Bhoga* denotes material enjoyment, and *tyāga* means renunciation. *Bhoga-tyāga*, therefore, is a bouncing back and forth between, on one hand, trying to enjoy material happiness and, on the other, giving up or renouncing it. We try to live a life of enjoyment, and when the effort brings us to emptiness or frustration we give it up as useless or false. But after a while, when shunning false happiness proves a dry, unrewarding alternative, and difficult to sustain, we go back to trying to enjoy, until enjoyment once again seems superficial, pointless, unattainable, or stale.

Go your way with a merry heart, then give up the merriment as meaningless and absurd, then go back to it again and give it another try, and then – what sort of life is that?

The Vedic point of view takes into account both the path of enjoyment and the path of renunciation and says that both have been approved by God. The path of enjoyment, however, it regards as inferior, the path of renunciation superior.

As I have mentioned in earlier chapters, the Vedic literature sometimes recommends "the path of karma," the path of suitable work, of worthy deeds, of "good karma" for the sake of fulfilling one's desires in this world. If we act according to good karma, we will enjoy the good results. Such work is divinely approved, and one is entitled to whatever happiness it may bring.

But such happiness is limited and temporary. It's the kind of happiness we get through our material, physical bodies and subtle material minds. Because such happiness has a beginning and an end, the Bhagavad-gītā says, it is not the kind of happiness in which a wise person takes delight. Moreover, such happiness, being material, must inevitably be mixed with distress. In this material world, that is simply the way things are.

The Vedic literature therefore recommends this path only so that our karma can be good rather than bad or terrible. If we try to enjoy unrestrictedly, willy-nilly, however we might like, we will inevitably run afoul of nature's laws and suffer unrestrictedly – and, more important, make little or no spiritual progress. But by following the path of karma under Vedic guidance, we agree to a more moderate, more balanced life, in which we may eat only a few candies instead of the whole box – or we may enjoy with our wife or husband rather than a succession of lovers – but we wind up more healthy, more in control of ourselves, and more peaceful, satisfied, and happy. And on this path, because we recognize that we must function within a greater scheme of things, within a higher law, under a higher power, we slowly, gradually, also make spiritual progress.

But this is the slow path because it is the path of material desire, the path on which, though we might acknowledge higher laws in the background – and we might even acknowledge that everything "comes from the hand of God" – we still keep material enjoyment in the forefront. And this keeps us still materially entangled. Because material happiness depends on the material body and material things, it binds us to the material world and the cycle of birth and death; to continue enjoying these things, we have to keep coming back for another birth in this world, lifetime after lifetime.

The faster path, the one more recommended, is the path of detachment, of renunciation, in which we put dreams of material happiness aside and strive for the greater happiness of spiritual realization.

According to the teachings of bhakti (devotional service), "renunciation" doesn't mean merely giving things up. It means recognizing that nothing is ours to begin with. It's not that I toss aside my wallet or abandon my car, declaring them material, but that I come to understand that both wallet and car – and whatever else I may have – belong not to me but to God, to Krishna. Whatever I may have can be in my hand only for a few days, and then it goes elsewhere. So how is it mine? Even I myself come and go. In a greater sense, therefore, whatever I have belongs to the world, to the cosmos, and the cosmos belongs finally to the Supreme, to Krishna. Trying to enjoy Krishna's property as if it were my own finally brings about only frustration. Instead, on the path of bhakti one comes to recognize that since everything belongs to Krishna, everything should be used for the service of Krishna. My wallet, my car – whatever I may call mine – I can dedicate to Krishna and use in Krishna's service. And learning how to do this, in a spirit of genuine detachment, is part of the path of bhakti. On this path, one leaves aside the petty and hopeless project of trying to enjoy for oneself and finds enjoyment in serving Krishna. "Eat your bread with joy, and drink your wine with a merry heart" is one path, but higher by far is the path of serving Krishna.

On this path, the Gītā says, we are happy within, we enjoy within, and our aim is inward. We realize our spiritual identity, understanding "I am not my material body but the conscious self within," and we walk on the path of liberation by rediscovering our eternal relationship with the Absolute, the Supreme Self, the Personality of Godhead. The Padma Purāṇa says, "The transcendentalists derive true and unlimited pleasure from the Absolute Truth, and therefore the Supreme Absolute Truth, the Personality of Godhead, is also known as Rāma."

One begins on this path by the process of "transcendental hearing" – that is, of hearing about the Personality of Godhead, known by such names as Rāma and Krishna, from books like the Bhagavad-gītā and the Śrīmad-Bhāgavatam. The Vedānta-sūtra says, repeating itself for emphasis, "By sound one becomes liberated. By sound one becomes liberated." As one hears about the Personality of Godhead from his pure devotees one's heart becomes free from material misconceptions, one becomes free from passion and ignorance, and in the state of pure goodness one engages in the Personality of Godhead's service. Engaged in this way, one becomes joyful within, one develops an ever deepening understanding of the Personality of Godhead and one's relationship with him, and so one automatically becomes detached from illusions of material enjoyment.

Though the slow path of enjoyment through "good karma" is also approved, the path recommended – and ultimately the path of greater enjoyment – is that of detachment and devotional service, bhakti-yoga.

White garments, fine oil

Let your garments be always white, Qohelet says, and let oil not be lacking for your head. In Qohelet's world, white was a color of festivity, and cooling, fragrant oil a pleasure for a happy and well-appointed head.

Enjoy with the woman you love

When Qohelet says to live your whole life with "the woman you love," in his world that woman would be your wife. But what could have been a tender and happy picture of lifelong married love, Qohelet spoils with his persistent melancholy reminder that the life we may hope to share with the woman we love is but a wisp of vapor. Enjoy! he says. Enjoy with the woman you love, all the days of your fleeting, empty, absurd, and meaningless life. And then he repeats it: all the days of your vain life, the life that you live for nothing.

That's what God has given you. That (and nothing more) is your allotment, your portion in life, your reward for your toil under the sun. I could hardly find one man out of a thousand, Qohelet has said, and not even one woman at all. But you have found her. Her heart is snares and nets, her hands are chains, he with whom God is pleased will escape her, one who goes wrong will be taken by her – and you love her. So now enjoy with her all the vain and useless days of your life.

If we put Qohelet's thoughts together – those in chapter seven and those here – that's what we come up with. "Qohelet and his contradictions" indeed. On one hand, Qohelet sees woman as a trap, and on the other he urges us to jump in. After all, as he has said before, there is "nothing better."

In the Vedic view, there is something better, and that is found through the higher path, the path of detachment, of renunciation. "All living beings are attracted toward the path of enjoyment," the Manu-saṁhitā says, "but in detachment lies the greater reward."

Suppose a man has no wife or girlfriend, no children, no house, no job, no obligations – and no desire for them. To that extent he is free. He can go where he likes, do what he likes, and not worry. And he is free to dedicate his full energy to spiritual realization.

In the Bhagavad-gītā Lord Krishna says, "Those who are free from anger and material desires, who are self-realized, self-disciplined, and constantly endeavoring for perfection, are assured of liberation in the Supreme in the very near future."

Great. But can we do that? Can we go through life without attraction to the comforts of home, the enjoyment of good things, the pleasure of sex (and without anger or frustration at not having them)? To deny oneself everything for the sake of an abstract "spiritual perfection" – for the sake of "attaining the Supreme" – how long can that last? Perhaps a few rare souls with the calling to live as hermits and sages can do it. By wisdom, by philosophical understanding, by inner strength and determination, they may escape worldly attractions and stay focused on spiritual goals. But even those rare souls may find this a struggle. Then what hope is there for us?

Vedic writings like the Bhagavad-gītā and Śrīmad-Bhāgavatam therefore say that the best path for renunciation is the path of bhakti-yoga, or devotional service to Krishna, meaning God in his supreme personal form. The Śrīmad-Bhāgavatam says, "By rendering devotional service to the Personality of Godhead, Śrī Krishna, one quickly acquires causeless knowledge and detachment from the world."

Because Krishna, the Bhāgavatam says, is the origin of everything, the source of everything, he is also the source of all pleasure. In his abstract, impersonal feature he may be a source of abstract pleasure, but in his form as the Personality of Godhead he is full of tangible, specific transcendental qualities that attract even souls already liberated and satisfied with impersonal realization of God as an abstract all-pervading truth. The pleasure found even in impersonal spiritual realization far exceeds the temporary pleasure found in material things and material relationships, but the literature of bhakti says that the pleasure one finds in realization of the Personality of Godhead is like an ocean that makes the pleasure of impersonal realization seem like the small puddle of water that might collect in the hoofprint of a calf.

That ocean of pleasure is realized in Krishna's name, form, qualities, pastimes, and everything else about him. When one hears about these in the association of realized souls and renders service in a humble mood, such realization takes place. This is the method of bhakti-yoga.

Because Krishna the person has a spiritual form of delicate and fascinating beauty, his feet are called "lotus feet," their beauty compared to that of the most surpassingly beautiful flower. Service to Krishna in a humble mood is therefore spoken of as service to his lotus feet. The Śrīmad-Bhāgavatam says, "By the enjoyment found in devotional service, transcendentalists always engaged in service to the lotus-petal feet of Krishna can easily get free from the hard knots of desires for material enjoyment. Without devotional service, even great sages, though they may try, cannot so effectively control the waves of desire to gratify their senses. Engage, therefore, in devotional service to Krishna."

So on the path of bhakti-yoga one doesn't exactly give up enjoyment. One gives up *material* enjoyment because one has found more satisfying enjoyment in relationship with Krishna. The more one advances in Krishna consciousness, the more one experiences this higher taste and so becomes detached from the demands of the senses for material enjoyment.

Those who are advanced in detachment can happily forget about the much-acclaimed happiness of family life. That happiness is brief, they will think, and that life is troublesome: small in its rewards and great in its entanglements – a trap to stay away from.

But for those less inclined toward detachment, the bhakti-yoga process recommends marriage. Marriage involves natural attachments – between husband and wife and for home, children, and comforts. But in bhakti-yoga one molds one's life in such a way as to keep Krishna at the center of one's family life. By regularly chanting the name of Krishna, hearing about Krishna, remembering Krishna, keeping company with devotees of Krishna, and serving Krishna in various ways, husband and wife cultivate a spiritual consciousness that helps them stay detached, above material entanglements, even while involved in the ordinary activities of this world.

Enjoy! Qohelet says. But the married person on the path of spiritual detachment takes a different approach. The purpose of human life, such a person thinks, is not to pursue small-time enjoyments but to pursue spiritual realization. By nature's arrangement a certain portion of enjoyment will come on its own, just as distress does. Therefore, no need to try to throw oneself into a mood of enjoyment. What that really amounts to is throwing oneself, ultimately, into disappointment, frustration, conflict, suffering, and the terrible emptiness of a life in which spiritual realization is meager or nil.

On the contrary, therefore, married people on the path of bhakti-yoga, cultivating spiritual realization, control their senses and – shall we get to the nub of it? – dedicate themselves to something higher than sex.

For a common person in married life (or unmarried too, for that matter), sex lies at the very height of enjoyment. *This* is what there is to look forward to. It's glorified as "love," and how could there be anything higher? The greatest fulfillment in life is found in bed.

But for the married person on the path of detachment, not so. Married life, of course, involves sex – it's a civilized arrangement for sex, we might even say – but it's an arrangement for limiting sex rather than getting caught up in it. Unless limited by self-control, the drive for sex can send a man from woman to woman. And while he imagines he is conquering, in fact he is being vanquished, because he is tied up and dragged about by his own desires, and by those of the women he pursues. He becomes a stud, and a fool, a dancing dog in the hands of women. And where then is the hope of spiritual realization? And what spiritual hope can a woman have when she is trapped by her own desires and the desires of the men who pursue her?

And so, marriage places sex within a context. And here too it is not a context for a hopeless dream of "unlimited sex." The wife is not a machine for sense gratification. Rather, for the man on the path of detachment a wife is a partner in spiritual practice, in spiritual realization, in spiritual service. Together, they cultivate detachment from matter, attachment to spirit, in order to find the deepest love where it is actually to be found – not in passion but in goodness, not in a physical act of a few moments but in the eternal relationship with the Supreme, with Krishna, the reservoir of all enjoyment, the source of unlimited love.

Not all the days of your life

Enjoy with the woman you love all the days of your life, Qohelet says. Of course, there's no guarantee you can do that. She might die before you, perhaps long before. Or, as with the wife of one of my friends, she might turn chronically ill, not a companion for joy but a bedridden patient to worry over and attend to. Or, as so often happens these days, she might leave you for someone else.*

But even if all goes well, enjoying with your wife till the end of your days is contrary to what the Vedic writings advise. Rather, you should enjoy with her for some days of your life, a span of many years, but not till the end. Why? Again, because the Vedic culture, the culture of bhakti-yoga, aims at detachment, at freedom, from material existence. And attachment between male and female, husband and wife, is the strongest material attachment there is.†

Because the attraction between man and woman is so strong, the Vedic culture makes an affirmative place for it in the form of married life and then seeks to mold that life in such a way that even while married one makes spiritual progress. But within your whole lifetime, the Vedic culture makes your years of marriage only a part. Whereas Qohelet here advises that you enjoy with your wife all your days, "for that is your portion in life," the Vedic writings advise that you enjoy with your wife only some of your days, only a portion, some years of your life, not all.

Suppose you live a hundred years. Here's how the Vedic culture would divide it: twenty-five years for education, twenty-five for family

---

* Here I follow Qohelet in framing the words for men. Just tweak the words, and for women the same problems hold true.

† To give just a small image, a cameo, of how deep this goes: In 1990, at the age of 78, Jacques Ellul, a French philosopher, law professor, sociologist, and lay theologian, published a book-length "Meditation on Ecclesiastes" entitled *Reason for Being*. Having written more than fifty books and nearly a thousand articles, he envisioned this book as serving as the conclusion, "the last word," to his life's work. He gave the book this touching dedication:

> I dedicate these final words
> to the one who all my life
> has been the imperative
> and the hope
> of the Reason for being:
> my wife.

His wife, by the way, died the following year, and he died three years after her.

life, twenty-five for retirement, and twenty-five for complete detachment. This makes sense both spiritually and biologically.

The beginning of life is meant for learning – not merely learning academic subjects but learning spiritual and cultural values, such as cleanliness, fearlessness, simplicity, tolerance, humility, self-control, and a sense of responsibility. Childhood and youth, when the mind is so open for learning, are the time for this. Therefore young boys would be sent to live at the school of a spiritual master, where they would learn these values by practical experience, as well as gain an understanding of the difference between matter and spirit, between themselves and their physical bodies, between acting to gratify the senses and acting for spiritual advancement. At this school too they would learn the needed skills for whatever occupation in life seemed most to suit their leanings. (Girls and young women would receive their spiritual and cultural training at home.)

During this time for education, there was no scope for sex. Unlike modern schools and universities, the school was not a place where people in their teens and twenties would experiment with sexual encounters and relationships. Rather, young people would learn how to master sexual impulses, how to keep the senses under rein rather than let unbridled senses drag them helplessly about. Boys and girls, men and women, were therefore educated separately. If we throw pubescent boys and girls, budding young men and women, together into a classroom, what do we suppose they'll have their minds on? Their studies? The Vedic culture was not so naive.

In the Vedic culture, also, boys and young men were trained to regard women with respect, as they would their own mothers, not as targets to be hit, goals to be scored, rides to be tried out, or toys to be used and disposed of. And girls and young women were trained to value their worth and integrity and not be fooled into serving as playthings.

After the first stage in life, the time of education, a young man would have a choice: stay on at the teacher's school or enter family life. If strong in detachment and not interested in family life he would stay on. Otherwise, with the permission of his teacher, he would marry, and with the strength of his spiritual training he would live in family life with a spiritual focus. This time in life, this second quarter, is most suitable for family engagements: earning a living, supporting a wife, having and raising children. This is the time, also, when longings for female companionship most strongly demand to be satisfied, and marriage provides the suitable context.

All right, now we're in family life. We have a home, a family, and we're busy in the labor to support them. And we have whatever enjoyment comes with the package. For Qohelet, it seems, this is it. You stick with this till the end of your days. Perhaps at some point in your old age you retire from work, but you stick with your wife and enjoy with her till the end.

In the Vedic culture, however, there is more to retirement, and it has a higher purpose. The purpose of the entire Vedic culture is to free the soul, the spiritual spark of consciousness, from material attachments and revive its eternal relationship with the supreme source of all consciousness, Krishna. Retirement, therefore, is meant to serve this ultimate purpose. It is a stage of life at which one seeks to loosen one's material attachments for the sake of regaining one's spiritual freedom.

Suppose a man has married by twenty-five. After twenty-five years in family life – that is, by the age of fifty – he should be ready to retire. If we look at a man's physical life as a bell curve, in youth he is moving up the curve – growing, developing, moving up in the world – and by the time he is fifty he has passed the halfway point, the top of the curve, and is moving down, his body and senses diminishing in strength. By endeavor or good fortune he may prosper a while longer, but the downward side of the curve is a slope he must inevitably descend.

At this stage of his life, what should he do? Enjoy? The Vedic wisdom says no. In one sense, the spirit of enjoyment lies at the root of all our problems. We are all trying to enjoy whatever the world has to offer, but the more we try, the more this world tricks us, bewilders us, snaps back on us, and makes us suffer. Because we are spiritual beings, enjoying this material world is simply not what we're meant to do – and it's not even possible, though by illusion we persist in believing it is.

Because the urge for enjoyment is so strong, the twenty-five years of married life provide a way to accommodate it, to give it some scope, within the larger context of spiritual growth. But now, by the age of fifty, "enjoyment" is an illusion from which one should seriously endeavor to get free.

And from this age onward, anyway, how much can we expect to enjoy? The body gets weaker. We tire. Bones and muscles ache. Eyes and ears start losing power. Any number of diseases can afflict us. And sex? Ha! What young man would trade youthful sex for the sex to be had at the age of fifty or sixty? Geriatric sex? Old goat, what can you expect to enjoy?

Still, we can enjoy some "finer pleasures" – some cultivated tastes in art, music, or literature, some intellectual pursuits. We can enjoy mature companionship and the affections of children and grandchildren. We can read the newspaper, spend time with crossword puzzles, sit by the side of the water and wait for some poor fish to bite our bait. We can waste the remaining years of our life and then die.

But the Vedic literature urges us instead to use our remaining years for detachment and spiritual realization. How? In eras past, a man, perhaps with his wife, would leave home for the forest, there to practice austerity and meditation. They would live on fruits, roots, and whatever other simple foods the forest might provide, they would bathe in a nearby river, and they would live under the trees or in a simple hut. In this way they would detach themselves from the material buildup of their family life and revive the realization that they can get everything they need by depending on what God provides.

Today we can no longer expect to do that. We're no longer fit for that sort of austerity, the change from town or city to the forest would be too much for us – and, besides, if we managed to find a good forest and start to live there, some park ranger would probably kick us out.

So we need a more modest program, and several options are available. Instead of the forest, husband and wife might choose to live in a sacred place, a place of pilgrimage. In India there are hundreds of such places, dedicated to spiritual progress, such as Māyāpur, Vrindāvan, and Purī, where one can live a simple life in a spiritual atmosphere and take pleasure in hearing regularly from the self-realized souls whose presence is the most valuable feature of such a place. Alternatively, husband and wife might travel as pilgrims from one such place to another, in each place gaining deeper spiritual understanding. These days, even in the West there are spiritual communities where people retiring from family life can render service to Krishna and cultivate spiritual life. As yet another alternative, the husband might periodically travel out, letting his wife stay at home with their grown children, then periodically come back for a while, and then again go out.

Among my middle-aged married friends who are dedicated to bhakti-yoga, several have taken up one or another of these options. And it has given their life a freshness, a regained vitality and freedom, a renewed spirit of inspiration and adventure.

In retired life, also, husband and wife completely give up sex. As mentioned before, after fifty it's not what it used to be, and it's a poor thing to cling to for the rest of your life. If at this stage we are to cultivate detachment, free ourselves from falsely identifying with that aging material body, and revive our natural spirituality, sex can only get in the way and hold us back. If we want to put out to sea, we have to pull up the anchor.

Finally, after not more than twenty-five years of cultivating detachment in retired life, husband and wife would separate completely. The wife would return home to spend her last years in spiritual dedication with the support of her grown children, and the husband would travel alone, with the same purpose. The wife (now a "former wife") would serve as a source of spiritual guidance and inspiration in the home, and the former husband would offer spiritual guidance and inspiration to those he would meet in his travels. Thus they would end their lives not pathetically trying to enjoy some scant remnants of pleasure together till their last day, but instead finding pleasure in the Supreme, in Krishna, and sharing that pleasure with others.

My own spiritual master set this example in his life. After many years of marriage he retired from family affairs at the age of fifty-four to live in the sacred town of Vrindāvan, where he mainly wrote and studied, and nine years later he formally accepted the order of complete renunciation. At nearly seventy he traveled alone from India to America, in 1965, to teach consciousness of Krishna as taught in the Vedic literature, and so it was that three years later, in New York City, I had the good fortune to meet him and place my life under his guidance. Had he so chosen, he could have stayed at home in Calcutta to enjoy with his wife (and his children and grandchildren) all the days of his life. What then would have happened to me?

Where you are going

"Whatever your hand finds to do" is an idiom that means "whatever you're able to do." Do that, Qohelet says, according to your strength. Work hard, enjoy well, and do it now, because where you're headed to, all is extinguished.

In the King James Version, where you're headed is "the grave." The Hebrew, however, says *Sheol*. Sheol (pronounced she-*ol*) is a sort of dark, shadowy underworld, a cavernous, permanent, and dismal repository of huddled-together departed beings where no one enjoys, no one suffers, no one even thinks, and nothing ever happens at all. Go your way, eat your bread with joy, and drink your wine with a merry heart, Qohelet says, for soon you will die like a beast and be consigned forever to that insensible oblivion.

The notion of Sheol, scholars tell us, belongs to the ancient traditional Semitic view. With one's final gasp one gives up the "breath of life" (*ruah*), which returns to God; the physical dust of which the body is made returns to the earth; and whatever shadow is left goes to Sheol.

If Qohelet accepts nothing more than he can empirically verify, that obviously leaves out Sheol. So either he just accepts the existence of that dreary place by tradition, or else, as the King James translators seem to have thought, he uses the word as a figurative reference to the grave.

The difference hardly matters. After death, either we go to a shadowy, inert semblance of existence, a near nothingness, devoid of action, thought, knowledge, and wisdom – empty, that is, of all the features that make one a person – or else we go to the absolute nothingness of the grave.

Even the nothingness of the grave, though, is empirically not verifiable. That the body goes to the grave is what we can see. What else might happen is beyond the power of our senses to either confirm or deny.

By analysis, however, the Vedic sages arrive at a conclusion different from that of nothingness or Sheol. They distinguish between the physical body and the consciousness that knows it and moves it. They observe that this consciousness persists throughout all the bodily changes we go through in our life, that as we move from childhood to youth to old age the same conscious observer, the same self, continues to exist. And they conclude that even after the body is entirely destroyed, that conscious self continues on, this time to another body entirely. They give the example that just as a person may move from one mental state to another – from happiness to sadness or pensiveness or anger – yet still be the same person, the self moves from one physical body to another. And as our thoughts might lead us down one road or another, what next body we go to depends on our thoughts at the time of death – which in turn depend on the thoughts we have cultivated throughout our life. And so, rather than try to enjoy materially to the very end, one is advised to live in such a way as to finally detach oneself from matter, attain liberation from birth and death, and go not to Sheol, some bleak place of no activity, no thought, no knowledge, no wisdom, but to the spiritual realm where all activity, all thought, all knowledge, all wisdom exist in joyful relation to the ultimate source of all enjoyment, Krishna, the Supreme, the Personality of Godhead.

9:11–12: Time and chance

> [11] I turned and saw under the sun that the race is not to
> the swift, nor the battle to the strong, nor yet bread to
> the wise, nor yet riches to men of understanding, nor
> yet favor to men of skill; but time and chance happen
> to them all. [12] Indeed, man does not know his time; like
> fish taken in an evil net, and like birds caught in a snare,
> even so are men snared in an evil time, when it falls
> suddenly upon them.

Not to the swift

The swift may win the race, the strong the battle, but not always. The swift may stumble. The strong may get stuck in the mud. All of us, Qohelet says, are subject to time and chance. From the Vedic viewpoint, however, this "chance" would not be random "luck," good or bad, but the result of one's karma. When the swift lose the race, the strong the battle, they lose because they must, because of deeds they have done before, either in the present life or in a lifetime gone by. Because of karma one is swift or strong, and because of karma, too, despite swiftness or strongness one may lose.

In the Bhagavad-gītā Lord Krishna says that success in any undertaking depends on five factors: the place; the doer; one's various senses, like the eye and ear; the different kinds of endeavor; and finally *daiva*. *Daiva* may be taken to mean destiny or fate, which is another way of saying one's karma. And finally it refers to the hand of the Supreme, the divine controller of all time and events. The ignorant person who imagines "Success depends only on me" cannot, Krishna says, see things as they are. The race cannot always be to the swift, the battle always to the strong, because time and events lie beyond our control. Behind all events are the workings of karma, of destiny, and behind the workings of destiny, behind time itself, is the original cause of everything, the divine will of the Supreme.

The evil time

The catastrophe, the "evil time," that suddenly falls upon men is the same as that which falls upon fishes taken in a net and birds caught in a snare. And we do not know when that time of death may suddenly fall upon us. For some people – fools, the Vedic literature would say – this argues for enjoying now, while we can, before death comes and the opportunity is gone. For others it argues for urgently inquiring about the ultimate purpose of life.

9:13-16: The poor man's wisdom

¹³ This also have I seen as an example of wisdom under the sun, and it seemed great to me: ¹⁴ There was a little city, and few men within it; and there came a great king against it, and surrounded it, and built great siegeworks against it. ¹⁵ Now there was found in it a man poor but wise, and he by his wisdom delivered the city. Yet no one remembered that poor man. ¹⁶ Then I said,

"Wisdom is better than strength; but the poor man's wisdom is despised, and his words are not heard."

How wisdom is treated, what wisdom may accomplish
Wisdom saved the city, and its people lived on as fools.

9:17–18: Wisdom among fools

¹⁷ The quiet words of the wise are more to be heeded than the shouts of a ruler among fools. ¹⁸ Wisdom is better than weapons of war, but one bungler destroys much good.

Quiet words of wisdom; shouting words among fools
For wisdom to work, we need both a speaker with a wise tongue and a listener with an open ear. The wise man need not shout; his wisdom has a force of its own. But that force brightens the mind only of a person willing to hear, humbly and submissively. The Vedic teachers say that as the joining of a potent man with a fertile woman will bring about conception, the meeting of a wise speaker and a humble, attentive listener will give rise to understanding.

In the Bhagavad-gītā, Krishna and Arjuna were speaking as friends, each giving his own arguments, but Arjuna was unable to benefit from Krishna's friendly advice. Only when Arjuna admitted his own confusion and accepted the role of a student, a disciple, did Krishna take the role of spiritual master and impart the teachings that led to Arjuna's enlightenment.

The Gītā itself therefore counsels that to understand spiritual truth one should submissively approach a spiritual master, inquire from him, and serve him. The wise man, the person in knowledge, will impart knowledge to you, the Gītā says, because he has seen the truth.

In contrast to the quiet words of the wise, the shouting of a ruler among fools is of little use. Even if he shouts the fools cannot hear, because they are fools. And as one commentary says, "Very often the ruler of fools is a fool himself."

Wisdom undone

As illustrated by the story of the wise man who saved the city, wisdom can be more powerful than weapons of war. But one bungler ... All it takes is one. And bunglers are abundant.

But the wisdom that can be undone is the wisdom that seeks to save the city – that is, to bring about some desired results in the material world. The truly wise know that everything here in the material world, good or bad, will finally be undone. So if the material world is all there is, worldly wisdom is ultimately useless. This understanding can serve as the starting point for spiritual inquiry.

IO

10:1-3: The weight of folly

> [1] A dead fly makes the perfumer's ointment stink; so does a little folly outweigh wisdom and honor. [2] A wise man's heart is at his right hand, but a fool's heart at his left. [3] And even when a fool walks by the way, he lacks sense, and he says to everyone that he is a fool.

The way of the fool

The first verse is the origin of the common phrase "a fly in the ointment." The meaning is clear. In verse 2, as Barton comments, the word *heart* can be used for "intelligence," "moral perception," or "will" – and could include all three. As in many cultures, right and left can stand for good and bad, right and wrong, and so on. Crenshaw says that in ancient Israel the right hand indicated power and deliverance, the left hand ineptness and perversity.

In the third verse, the fool's brainlessness announces itself to all. Alternatively (in the Hebrew as in the English the last *he* is ambiguous), the fool could say to everyone else, "You are a fool!"

10:4–7: Folly in high places

> ⁴ If the anger of the ruler rises up against you, do not
> leave your place, for gentleness allays great offenses.
> ⁵ There is an evil I have seen under the sun, an error
> indeed that proceeds from the ruler: ⁶ Folly is set on
> great heights, and the rich sit in a low place. ⁷ I have
> seen slaves upon horses, and princes walking on foot
> like slaves.

Social order turned topsy-turvy

Qohelet offers staying calm and gentle as a practical course for dealing
with angry rulers. He next speaks of yet another evil he has seen, one
for which he holds the ruler responsible: a mix-up in roles that stands
social order on its head, with servants riding horses and princes having
to walk.

With our modern sensibilities we may chafe at the idea of a social
hierarchy, with servants and princes, but such a hierarchy was the norm
in the Israelite culture of Qohelet's time. Still, when Qohelet contrasts
the fools with the rich rather than the wise we may not share his sym-
pathies. Plumptre says, "The 'rich' here are those who by birth and station are looked on as the natural leaders of mankind." And here Qohelet
does seem to take that view.

The Vedic culture also involves a natural social order, but the Vedic
writings specify that the place one deserves in society should by understood not from one's birth or one's bank balance but from one's qualities and the work one actually does. If one's birth is matched by one's
talents, fine, but otherwise birth should be ignored.

The Vedic sages observe that because nature has endowed different
people with different qualities, each person will have a natural social
role in which best to live and best contribute to the welfare of the social
body. Therefore a "classless society" is foreign to the Vedic culture.

And so it is that in the Vedic culture the intellectuals are like the
head of the social body, providing thought and vision, and the military
and political leaders are the arms, providing protection and making sure
the state is properly run. Next, the farmers are the stomach, supplying

the strength of food, and the general workers are the legs, on whose labor the whole body stands. And every part of the body is valuable.

According to the Vedic view, society should be divided into these four classes. Or, rather, we should recognize that these divisions naturally exist, and we should organize society accordingly, in concert with nature's arrangement.

In the Bhagavad-gītā Krishna says that these four parts are found in every social body, anywhere in the world, because they are all created by him. In the Soviet Union's "classless society," built on the ideal of Communism, these four classes naturally persisted, some people teaching, some people managing, some farming, some still doing manual labor. Street sweepers don't make good professors, nor professors good street sweepers. (The notion that ordinary workers can master everything – should we call it utopian or just foolish?)

The Bhagavad-gītā recommends that instead of trying to pretend social divisions don't exist we recognize that sages will be sages, workers workers, respect each person's natural contribution, and see equality where it really lies, not in strength of muscle or in clarity of mind, where everyone surely differs, but in the spiritual force of life itself, in which everyone equally shares. Every one of us, Krishna says, is essentially a spiritual living being, a spiritual part of him, of the ultimate divinity, and therefore every one of us, by becoming conscious of him, can attain spiritual perfection while doing our own work. We need not change our work, only our consciousness, from material consciousness to spiritual consciousness, or consciousness of Krishna.

And so the duty of the ruler is to see that all the natural parts of the social body are in the right place and working well, in harmonious cooperation. When he does this, the society is in proper order; everyone plays their part, and everyone reaps the benefits.

Why should fools provide the vision, businessmen and thieves run the government to swell their own profits, brutal men with no feeling for the land torment and slaughter the animals and suck out the very life from the earth, and millions go unemployed?

When social roles are confused and reversed, Qohelet says, the error proceeds from the ruler. Under such circumstances, one suspects that the ruler himself is foolish or incompetent. In modern democracies, when the people themselves elect the leaders of their governments, the foolishness and incompetence of the leaders reflect the qualities of those who voted them in. By nature's way, the most intelligent are the most rare, the most foolish most abundant.

10:8–11: Danger at every step

[8] He who digs a pit may fall into it, and he who breaks through a wall may be bitten by a snake. [9] He who quarries stones may be hurt by them, and he who splits logs may be endangered by them. [10] If the iron is blunt and one does not whet the edge, then he must exert more strength; but wisdom helps one succeed. [11] If the snake bites before it is charmed, there is no advantage in a charmer.

Occupational hazards

The Śrīmad-Bhāgavatam says that this world is a place where there is "danger at every step." Even a routine task can spring upon us a calamity.

For the wall Qohelet mentions, Seow pictures a rural affair, a low fence built up of rough stones, perhaps with loose fill between them. Such a wall might surround an orchard, a garden or a vineyard, or mark the edge of a field. And when a man in the course of working breaks one down, from any of its crannies might emerge an unexpected snake, venomous and angry.

Dig a pit, quarry stones, split a log, fix a window, mow a lawn, cut a potato, walk down a set of stairs – at every step there is danger.

In Sanskrit a word for danger is *vipada*, and in recommending that the only source of safety is Krishna, the Bhāgavatam plays on the word.

samāśritā ye pada-pallava-plavaṁ
mahat-padaṁ puṇya-yaśo murāreḥ
bhavāmbudhir vatsa-padaṁ paraṁ padaṁ
padaṁ padaṁ yad vipadāṁ na teṣām

Krishna's feet (*pada*) are here compared in beauty to flower buds and are said to be the shelter (*padam*) of *mahat*, which can refer either to the entire cosmos or to the mahātmās, the great souls. Krishna's renown itself is pure and sacred. And for those who have completely taken shelter of the boat of the lotus feet of Krishna (for whom another name is Murāri), the vast ocean of material existence becomes like the water in the small hoofprint of a calf (*vatsa-padam*). The place for such devoted souls is not the material world, where there are dangers (*vipadām*) at every step (*padam padam*). Rather, the place for them is the supreme abode (*param padam*), the eternal abode of Krishna.

In this way the Bhāgavatam recommends that one not stay in the dangerous material world but return to the spiritual world by hearing about Krishna and taking shelter of him.

Of course, where the Bhāgavatam sees a spiritual world, Qohelet with his one-life viewpoint sees (as he has mentioned earlier) only the grave or a dim quasi-existence in Sheol. And when he looks at the present world, the world before him, he observes that everywhere danger may, unavoidably, be only a moment away.

Skill and wisdom and their limits

At the end of the book we'll hear it said that Qohelet taught people knowledge by "arranging many proverbs," and that is evident in this portion of the book.

For translators verse 10 poses linguistic difficulties that need not detain us here. Barton glosses the verse by saying that if the axe is not sharp one "must accomplish by brute strength what he might have done more easily by the exercise of intelligence."

Verse 11 can refer either to "a snake that cannot be charmed" or "a snake before it can be charmed." For a snake that cannot be charmed, obviously there is no use in a charmer. And so skill and wisdom have their limits. If a snake bites before it can be charmed, the moral can be drawn that skill and wisdom, to be useful, must be used timely. But Longman astutely observes that when a snake suddenly appears we're unlikely to have a charmer at hand. And then, when our life depends on it, the skill and wisdom, however impressive, are of no practical use. However we look at the verse, skill and wisdom have their limits. Whom time has marked for death, no charmer or doctor can save.

10:12–15: The talk and the labor of fools

[12] The words of a wise man's mouth win favor, but the lips of a fool will swallow him. [13] The words of his mouth begin in foolishness, and his talk ends in grievous madness. [14] A fool also multiplies words; yet a man does not know what will be, and who can tell him what will happen after him? [15] The labor of a fool wears him out, for he does not even know how to go to town.

Foolish talk

The wise man's words bring him favor. Or, an alternative meaning, they bring favor to those who hear him. But though the wise man's words benefit both speaker and hearer, the words of a fool benefit no one. One who speaks in error may have to eat his own words, but when a fool speaks, his words eat him – he is devoured by his own lips. His words go from bad to worse, beginning in foolishness and ending in insanity.

I am reminded of an incident, told in the Śrīmad-Bhāgavatam, concerning a king named Śiśupāla who lived while Lord Krishna, the Personality of Godhead, was performing pastimes on earth. At an august assembly on a sacred occasion at which Lord Krishna was personally present and was to be honored, Śiśupāla rose to insult him. The learned dignitaries who had assembled, he began, had all had their intelligence misled, and so they had chosen to honor such an unworthy person as Krishna, a disgrace to his family, someone no better than a crow, a mere cowherd with no good qualities. As Śiśupāla raged on, Lord Krishna simply sat tolerant, ignoring him. But as the diatribe grew to a crescendo of insults, warriors like the Pāṇḍavas finally jumped up and drew their swords to kill the frenzied king. Undaunted, Śiśupāla now began insulting *them*. Then Lord Krishna, seeing bloodshed imminent at this holy gathering, released his Sudarśana disc, a divine weapon, neatly beheading Śiśupāla (and without spilling a drop of blood).

Traditional commentators cleverly reinterpret the Sanskrit of Śiśupāla's insults in such a way as to see them all as praises. And the Bhāga-

vatam says that being killed by Krishna himself granted Śiśupāla liberation from material existence. Śiśupāla also did us the favor of serving
as an extreme model of a ranter whose words begin in foolishness and
end in wicked madness by which he himself is devoured. Though Śiśupāla multiplied his words, talking on and on, he did not know what
would happen. And who could have told him?

Foolish labor

The fool may wear himself out by his labors, but that's all he accomplishes because, blockhead that he is, he can't even do the most ordinary
thing, like find his way to town. He can stumble about and go first down
one wrong path, then another, but he can't get there.

From a philosophical point of view, the Vedic teachers say that
anyone simply working for a living, wearing himself out, but not trying to understand the ultimate destination in life and how to reach
it is a fool who lives for nothing. One must inquire about spiritual
realization.

Even then, the Śrīmad-Bhāgavatam deprecates the path of imperfectly speculating about what is what and instead commends as the
best means for spiritual realization the path of devotional service to
the Supreme, to Krishna, especially by hearing about him from self-
realized souls.

This, of course, is a path we don't trust. We *want* to speculate, to
figure things out for ourselves, by our own powers of discrimination.
But transcendence, or the ultimate reality, must lie beyond our speculative powers because the mind itself is material and therefore materially limited. On the other hand, the Bhāgavatam says, the path of devotional service enables one to achieve gradual spiritual enlightenment
because the process itself purifies the heart, freeing it from passion and
ignorance, so that in goodness one can gain a clear understanding of
the Supreme. One thus gradually realizes the Supreme first as the all-
pervading ultimate reality, then as the Supersoul within one's heart, and
ultimately as the Personality of Godhead. By this path of devotional
service – again, beginning with hearing from self-realized souls – one
realizes the Supreme by the grace of the Supreme. As a traveler might
find out the path to town by getting proper directions, one who is spiritually inquisitive finds his way by proper hearing.

If one rejects this path, the Bhāgavatam says, and instead tries to achieve knowledge merely by speculating, all one gains is one's own trouble, nothing else, like a foolish farmer at a rice harvest who, instead of beating the full husks to extract the grains, beats the empty husks. For all his labor, all he does is wear himself out.

10:16–17: The land in trouble and the happy land

¹⁶ Woe to you, O land, when your king is a lackey and your princes feast in the morning! ¹⁷ Happy are you, O land, when your king is a free man and your princes eat at the proper time, for strength and not for drunkenness!

When your king is a lackey
The king should be fully capable and fully in charge, so that he can properly administer the kingdom for the welfare of all the citizens. But sometimes, instead of being his own man, the king, president, or prime minister is merely a puppet of others – a mere lackey of a foreign state, or else a pawn of his nation's businessmen or of multinational corporate powers. His masters keep him in his post so that with his acquiescence they can loot the land and its resources or deploy it for their own geopolitical objectives. And he himself and those who surround him live in luxury, either because the hands that control him provide it or because they allow him some scope to plunder the land as well. How miserable such a land! In contrast, the king or head of state who is truly free can act in the best interests of his people.

The Hebrew word translated "lackey" can also mean "youth" – the King James Version says "a child" – in which case the land's misfortune is to have at its helm someone woefully immature and inexperienced. Such a leader can easily be fooled or manipulated. Several traditional commentators offer that he may be enslaved to his own youthful lusts. A common Sanskrit way of putting it would be to call him a "servant of his senses."

Alternatively, since the word translated "lackey" can also mean "servant," Qohelet may again be condemning a state of social chaos in which servants are posted as kings. According to the Vedic analysis, the men fit only to work as servants are those whose natures are predominated by the quality of ignorance. They tend to be lazy, foolish, whimsical, even mad, and if given the responsibility to govern they will act only as thieves and rogues and cause destruction and misery. The men who rule should be those mainly stirred by the quality of passion, who take pleasure in power but use it nobly, for the public benefit, and who take guidance from persons in the mode of goodness, those endowed with calm, practical wisdom and deep spiritual understanding.

The word translated "free man" can be more closely translated as "son of free men" or "son of nobles." Crenshaw comments that a land is blessed when its ruler "belongs to nobility by birth and thus is not consumed by a passion to abuse newfound power the way a slave might do who assumes control of the highest office in the land ... Because this freeborn king is fully in control, his princes exercise proper decorum and restraint, eating to keep up their strength and drinking in moderation."

As Qohelet said earlier, there is a time for everything – and the morning is the time for responsible duties, not the time for feasting. But irresponsible government officers – how many drinks before lunch? – are more concerned with enjoying their own senses than attending to their duties. Rashi comments that in the fortunate kingdom the princes "engage in the vigorous pursuit of wisdom and understanding rather than in drinking wine."

10:18–19: Sagging rafters, leaky house, and feasting, wine, and money

[18] Through laziness the rafters sag, and through idleness of the hands the house leaks. [19] A feast is made for laughter, and wine makes life glad, and money answers everything.

The mode of ignorance

Laziness and idleness are cardinal signs of *tamo-guṇa*, the material "mode," or quality, of darkness or ignorance. In the Bhagavad-gītā Lord Krishna says that this darkness born of ignorance is the delusion of all living beings and that it binds one by madness, idleness, and sleep. In this mode one doesn't want to do anything. One would rather put things off, close one's eyes, tune out the world. A few beers, or a few martinis, or some cannabis or what have you – all these support the "ignorance effect," dulling reality, or bending and distorting it, turning it dreamy or fantastic, blurring its edges. Ignorance makes one gross, stubborn, two-faced, lazy, morose, procrastinating, and expert only in the art of insulting others. This mode is just the opposite of the mode of goodness, which fosters knowledge, purity, and a natural sense of happiness.

The sagging rafters and leaking roof are signs that the man who is lazy and idle can't get up the energy even to maintain his own house.

Laughter, wine, and money

In verse 19, when Qohelet speaks about feasting, laughter, and wine, it's hard to know what spin he means to put on what he says.

Perhaps, as some commentators hold, he is offering a straightforward observation, with a mood of approval. When there are festive occasions like marriages, there must be feasting and wine and joy, and to provide these there must be money, which one must be industrious to earn, not lazy and idle as in the previous verse.

Alternatively, he is being cynical and critical. The dissolute princes who feast in the morning are drinking and laughing and having a merry time for themselves, all with money they have plucked from the hard-working citizens and are squandering for their own enjoyment.

The phrase "money answers everything" could indeed be sarcastic. The phrase is sometimes translated "money meets every need." Yet at the start of this book Qohelet told us that although he had plenty of money it did *not* meet his every need. On the contrary, despite his money, he felt empty and frustrated.

Using an example given by my spiritual master, I might tell the story of a woman who had a bird in a cage. The cage was quite a fine one, and she polished it every day, keeping it to a bright shine. But she never fed the bird, and so it starved to death. Similarly, my spiritual master said, we may diligently tend to all our external needs – the needs of our bodies – but this will not satisfy the needs of the self within the body. That spiritual self will not be satisfied with any amount of gratification of the outward material senses. It must have "spiritual food," spiritual nourishment, gained only by spiritual inquiry and realization – that is, realization of the self's eternal spiritual nature and ultimately of its relationship with the Supreme Self, or Krishna.

Laughter and gladness in forgetfulness of Krishna (or, for that matter, groaning and sorrow in forgetfulness of Krishna) are products of māyā, illusion. In the Vedic culture, therefore (or, for that matter, any God conscious culture), feasts are occasions for remembering Krishna, or God, and so the gladness and laughter, instead of being superficial expressions of joy over brief events of no ultimate conse-quence, have depth and meaning because they are connected to the ultimate reality, the ultimate source of meaning. To insist that there be no feasting, no laughter, is to insist that life be lifeless, that it be artificially harsh and stern. But to feast and laugh in forgetfulness of Krishna, as if enjoyment itself were the goal of life, is to be lifeless in another way, by superficiality.

Since the word translated "answers" can also mean "occupies," the last phrase in the verse can also be rendered "money occupies every-one" – that is, "money keeps everyone busy." The whole world is busy, preoccupied, with either gathering money or spending it. And so we forget that death is approaching, and we forget the importance of achieving spiritual realization before we die.

By the way, the Vedic culture looks upon the gladness that comes from wine as not only superficial but low. Wine dulls the mind. A dull mind may be a glad one, but it's not a clear one. A clear mind belongs to the mode of goodness, a dull one to ignorance. And ignorance is not recommended.

10:20: "A little bird told me"

[20] Do not curse the king, even in your thoughts, and do not curse the rich, even in your bedroom, for a bird of

the air may carry your voice, or some winged creature
may tell the matter.

"The walls have ears"

Because the king and the rich have power, speaking ill of them may
provoke reprisals. One could lose one's post, have one's home or possessions confiscated, be thrown into prison, or see cruel things done to
one's family. One could be tortured or put to death.

These are not merely ancient customs. During the Communist times
in the former Soviet Union, friends of mine, for being Hare Krishna
devotees, were thrown into mental hospitals, and "medicine" was used
to torture them. And the American public now understands, and largely
takes for granted, that its own government employs torture (verbally
prettified as "enhanced interrogation techniques") as part of its reper-
toire for getting little birds to sing. Assassinations and "suicides" can
be, and are, employed by operatives of democratic states. And the rich,
with or without government help, can employ coercion and reprisals as
well.

So Qohelet's advice is pragmatic: If you have a grievance against
the king or the rich, watch out what you say! Against the rich, don't
say anything, even in the privacy of your own sleeping chamber. And
against the king, don't even think anything. What you think, you may
come to mutter. And what you breathe to others in secret may come to
be known.

Since the most ancient times, kings have had their spies and informers. The saying "the walls have ears" goes back at least as far as the
Midrash (nine to fifteen centuries). "A little bird told me" often appears
in homey contexts (when I was a child, it was a favorite answer of my
mother's), but those little birds speak into the ears of the rich and
powerful as well.

In modern times, the walls and birds have gone digital. Your phone
calls, your mail, your bank transactions, what books you borrow
from the library – all this and more, your government may pry into.
If they want to monitor where you go, whom you meet, what you say,
that too has become pushbutton easy. "Winged creatures"? We might
think of government spy planes, but some of the drones now in use for

photographic and video surveillance – "microdrones," as they're called – are smaller than a sparrow or even a hummingbird.* And apart from high technology, the old ways of spies and informers are still among the simplest and best. So Qohelet's warning is as relevant as ever.

Yet it may be that in the previous verses Qohelet himself has been doing what he warns against. Those verses seem like generic proverbs, but if the lackey king, the drunkard princes, the lazy and negligent officials, the money lavished on wine, banquets, and laughter were all features of the regime under which Qohelet lived, he must have hoped the birds of the air and the winged creatures would hear only innocuous proverbs and miss their more pointed meaning.

With regard to discretion: In the tenth chapter of the Bhagavad-gītā Lord Krishna speaks of himself as the supreme source of all power, all beauty, and all splendor and says that to realize his presence everywhere one may meditate on him, the Personality of Godhead, as being present as the most outstanding example of whatever category there might be. For instance, "Of lights I am the radiant sun," "Of bodies of water I am the ocean," "Of seasons I am flower-bearing spring." And ... "Of secret things I am silence."

---

* I first heard this from a friend connected with the U.S. Department of Defense and later saw it confirmed in the *New York Times:* "Microdrones, Some as Small as Bugs, Are Poised to Alter War " (June 20, 2011).

11

11:1–2: Bread upon the waters

> [1] Cast your bread upon the waters, for you will find
> it after many days. [2] Give a portion to seven people –
> indeed, even to eight – for you do not know what evil
> will be upon the land.

You shall find it after many days

"Cast your bread upon the waters" is a well-known saying. Modern scholars generally hold that the word translated "cast" means "release" or "send out" rather than "throw." But that's a small point. The larger one is, What are these verses about? It seems clear that "bread" is a metaphor. If we were to release literal bread into the water, the most we could expect back after many days would be some awfully soggy bread. But what does the metaphor stand for?

According to one view, what Qohelet has in mind in the first verse is that in business one should be willing to take risks for the sake of an expected return. And in the second verse, in contrast, he counsels hedging against risk by investing in more than one venture. After all, who knows what evil, what calamity, might occur? Send out your goods, then, but not all in one ship.

The most prevalent traditional view (accepted also by modern scholars like Fox and Seow) is that here Qohelet is encouraging charity. One should give charity even to strangers one might never expect to see again, and one day the charity will be returned. Rashi says, "If you have shared your food and drink with seven people who need kindness, share further with eight who come after them, and do not cry 'Enough!' Perhaps someday you will need them all, and your charity will save you from disaster." Traditional commentaries cite examples in which acts of selfless generosity were later generously repaid.

In the Bhagavad-gītā it is said that charity purifies the giver's heart. But the Gītā says that people perform acts of charity, like so much else, in accordance with nature's three modes: goodness, passion, and ignorance. Charity in goodness is recommended. In goodness we give charity because we are convinced that giving charity is something a human being ought to do, and we give without expecting anything in return. We give timely, at a suitable place, to a person who deserves it, and especially to saintly people dedicated to a spiritual life. Future benefits we might gain may be uncertain, but that is not the point. "Charity is its own reward."

If we're in passion, however, we calculate, "What will I get out of this?" We think about how the person to whom we could give might repay the favor, or we think about what our gifts could do for our reputation. We want our name on that building, or on that plaque on the wall. If we're a corporation, perhaps our charity may serve as a cover for our rapaciousness: We advertise our concern about ecological "greenness" when the green we're really concerned about is money. Even doing "good karma" with the idea that the good may come back to us "after many days" is still tinged by passion; we still think, "What's in it for me?" And if we give grudgingly, because we are stuck and see no way out, that too is in the mode of passion.

Finally, in the third mode, ignorance, we are in the dark about what we are doing. So we give at the wrong time, to the wrong person, at the wrong place, for the wrong cause – for example, at night to a bum on the street so he can buy himself a drink.

Bums and drinks aside, we generally think we ought to give charity "to make this a better world." But as Qohelet has said from the start, this is never going to be a better world. It's always going to be the same world, a world of hard work for no discernible purpose, a world where enjoyment is only flickering, a world of birth and death, disease and old age, generation after generation, a world where nothing ever changes. We may think we can wipe out hunger, or rid the world of poverty, or make sure every kid has a chance for a healthy and happy life. But we are dreaming – and what we are dreaming will not come true. Hunger, poverty, disease, violence, and death have been with the world since the beginning, and they will stay with the world till the end. We may wipe out polio and tuberculosis, but nature will replace them with cancer and AIDS and whatever disease may come next. When I was a teenager President Johnson declared a "war on poverty." But poverty won – it is still with us – and Mr. Johnson wound up with the Vietnam War on his hands. There was a huge protest movement: "Stop the war!" At last the war stopped. And since then America has fought wars in Grenada, Libya, El Salvador, Nicaragua, Panama, Bosnia, Sudan, Yugoslavia, Afghanistan, and Kuwait; while I write it's fighting a war in Iraq; and later who knows?, but wars must continue.

It is the nature of the world to inflict miseries upon us, and this is not something we can change by any amount of charity or endeavor. Individually and collectively, we all have a background of karma that brings us a certain portion of happiness, a certain portion of distress, and no one can change this by any material means. A person for whom poverty is destined as a result of his own past acts will not escape poverty. A person destined for disease will not escape disease. Save a man from one disease, and he'll be afflicted by another. The world will not change. Charity workers will come, and charity workers will go, generation after generation, and the earth will stay the same till its last day.

This is not to say we shouldn't give charity. But the Bhagavad-gītā says we should give with a spiritual objective in mind, not a material one. We should give because that is something human beings are meant to do, for the satisfaction of the Supreme, without expecting to get something back. All of us give out of faith – faith that we'll make the bum happy, or faith that we'll enhance our reputation, or faith that we'll help uplift the poor or preserve the natural balance of the earth. But the Bhagavad-gītā says that if we want to give charity that goes beyond ignorance, passion, and limited material goodness, beyond the ultimate uselessness of material endeavors and entanglements, beyond trying to change what cannot be changed, we should give for the service of the Supreme, with faith in the Supreme, not for any other purpose. And so Krishna says in the Bhagavad-gītā, "Whatever charity you give, do that as an offering for me."

The greatest charity, my spiritual master taught, is to use whatever one has – one's life, wealth, intelligence, or words – to help others get free from material existence, from the endless cycle of birth and death, free by reviving their eternal relationship with the Supreme. Without faith in the Supreme, the Gītā says, whatever charity we give – or whatever else we do – will be useless, both for this life and for the next.

What if I have no faith in the Supreme? What if for me "the Supreme" is just an illusion people believe in because it makes them feel better? Then I'll stay a materialist and live out my useless life for nothing, for vanity. But better we seek out those who have greater spiritual understanding, give charity to them, however much or little, and hear from them. Those who are genuinely advanced in spiritual understanding are not trying to "make this a better world" for us to stay in. They're trying to get out of this material world, and help us get out, by reviving our eternal consciousness, or Krishna consciousness, our consciousness of our eternal relationship with the Supreme.

"Cast your bread upon the waters." Some commentators say that means "Go ahead and take a chance." All right, then: Take a chance by seeking out spiritual realization. "Cast your bread upon the waters, for you will find it after many days." As a young priest once told me, "Seek, and you shall find." The Bhagavad-gītā says: "In this endeavor there is no loss or diminution, and a little advancement on this path can protect one from the most fearful type of danger." We do not know what evil will be upon the land, what sort of calamities might befall us, because the world is full of calamities. But the greatest evil, the greatest calamity, is to spend one's life working hard for nothing, without spiritual inquiry or understanding, only to be reborn in some lower species, where spiritual inquiry is no longer possible. It is from such calamities that even slight progress on the path of spiritual advancement can save us.

I might say, "I don't think there is a next life." Or "I don't think one could possibly be born again into a lower species." All right. But I don't *know*, do I? And therefore the human life is meant for inquiry – not inquiry about how to eat better, sleep better, have better sex, and fight better. If that's all we inquire about, we're animals already, in this life, polished animals, because we have no aim higher than theirs. Human life is meant for inquiring about spiritual realization and finally for inquiring about the Supreme, the ultimate, the Absolute.

If one puts material prospects aside for the sake of the Supreme one loses nothing, because whatever one has put aside will be smashed and destroyed anyway in course of time. And one stands to gain everything because one may realize the Supreme, the ultimate source of all existence. But if for the sake of material prospects one puts aside inquiry about the Supreme, one loses everything – all material gains because time will smash them, and the Supreme because that is what one has left aside. And so the Vedānta-sūtras say that now, in this human life, one should inquire about the Supreme.

11:3–6: Certainty and uncertainty

> [3] If the clouds are full, they will empty rain upon the
> earth, and whether a tree falls to the south or to the
> north, in the place where the tree falls, there will it be.
> [4] He who watches the wind will not sow, and he who
> gazes at the clouds will not reap. [5] Just as you do not
> know what is the way of the wind, nor how the bones
> are formed in the mother's womb, so you do not know
> the work of God, who does all things. [6] In the morning
> sow your seed, and in the evening do not withhold your
> hand; for you do not know which will prosper, whether
> this or that, or whether both alike will be good.

Inevitable, but not always predictable

Full clouds will deliver rain, and a tree uprooted will fall wherever it falls. As Crenshaw comments, "Hidden laws make certain things inevitable. Regardless of human effort, some things occur without fail." Some events, however, are consistent and predictable, like the falling of rain from full clouds, and other events seem random, like which way a tree will fall. What is inevitable is not always within our power to know.

Since the word for "tree" can also mean "wood" or "stick," McNeile has suggested that the text can refer to the practice of divination in which, to be guided in one's actions, one throws a rod into the air and observes the direction in which it falls. No one can know or control which direction that might be.

Watching the wind and gazing at the clouds

One wants to start harvesting in dry weather, not when expecting rain. But if one watches the wind, what is one looking for – wind or its absence? Some commentators say that winds are good for sowing because they foretoken rain. Others say, on the contrary, that winds are bad because they will scatter the seeds unevenly or blow them away. I have to admit being so distant from a natural rural life that I had no idea which is right. To set myself straight, I checked with a Krishna devotee who's a farmer. He told me "the winds are bad" is right, for the reasons given: They can scatter or blow away your seeds. The thought, in any case, is that although the future may be uncertain, we must act nonetheless. If we wait to act until conditions are perfect, we'll never get anything accomplished. As Plumptre comments, "The very watching for opportunities may end in missing them." Uncertainty should not lead to paralysis.

We do not know

In verse 5 Qohelet turns to mysteries, though in the first half, because of the syntax of the Hebrew, we can't be sure whether one mystery or two. If two mysteries, we can't know which way the wind will blow, nor can we fully understand how the bones are formed in the mother's womb. If what Qohelet has in mind is one mystery, then the word translated "wind" (the word *ruah*, which we've encountered before) can be taken as life air, and what we don't know is the way the air of life, the breath of life, comes to a child's bones and forms them in the womb.

Bones can be read as an instance of synecdoche, that figure of speech by which a part may stand for the whole. For example, if we hear "Twenty swords followed him into battle," we know that *sword* means not only a sword but the man who holds it. And so, *bones* can stand for the entire bodily structure.

For Qohelet's ancient readers, how the child's body develops within the womb or how life comes to that body would be an obvious example of a mystery. Today, perhaps, that mystery may appear solved because science has illuminated the subject. We've all seen pictures of the fetus and how it develops. Yet although we know "how the bones are formed" – how the bodily structure takes shape – how life comes to that body is still a mystery.

This too we may think science has solved. As my biology teacher Dr. Hill explained, life simply arises from chemicals. But though this notion, as I've already discussed, may look good in a high-school text-book, when carefully examined it stumbles. The theory requires that a system of exquisite complexity arise from an origin of the barest simplicity; the jump has never been demonstrated (no one has ever taken chemicals and turned them into a living thing); and, at a technical level, no one has even come up with a tenable step-by-step for how this sup-posed transformation from lifeless chemicals to conscious living entity takes place. We might say that as science progresses this will all be forthcoming; it's "in the future." But as my spiritual master pointed out, this is a post-dated check, signed on an account that doesn't have the needed funds. My account is empty, but I promise I'll pay "in the future." My spiritual master liked to quote the proverb "Trust no fu-ture, however pleasant." How the breath of life comes to the bones is still a mystery, and the notion that it's a mystery solved is both a blun-der and a conceit. We don't really know, and yet we advertise that we do. As the Vedic literature says, among our faults in this world are the tendency to blunder and the tendency to cheat.

In Qohelet's verse, the everyday mysteries set before us by the wind or the development of life in the mother's womb introduce a simile: As these mysteries lie beyond what we understand, so too does the greater mystery of how God does all things. Reductionistic explanations that try to strip everything down to mechanical interactions of matter would have us believe that matter does all things on its own, automatically: On its own, matter forms itself into all the complexities of the universe. The great cosmic machinery just works, all by itself, with no need of any God to do anything. And life springs up automatically, through the mechanics of biochemical interactions. God, in this view, is a superfluous concept, an unnecessary accretion, an entity we invent to make us feel good, a needless holdover from prescientific thought.

But in our everyday experience, matter doesn't do things on its own. Cars don't drive themselves, without anyone's guidance. Computers don't work without personal intelligence behind them. Bricks and wood and glass and steel don't assemble themselves into houses and office buildings. There may be machines that run other machines, but finally at the end of the chain we'll find intelligent personal direction – an engineer at the controls, a programmer writing code, a man with his finger on the start button. In our everyday experience, behind the movements of material things we'll find consciousness, belonging to a conscious person. Why then should we think that the greatest material thing, the universe, just runs on its own? In our everyday experience, too, we never see life spontaneously springing forth from chemicals. Why should we think that "in the beginning" some inert chemical compounds self-organized into living beings?

In the Bhagavad-gītā the notion that the great cosmic machinery ultimately has no personal direction, no God in control, is condemned as ignorant, even demonic. The demonic promote ignorance as knowledge, godlessness as "rationality," a worldview that ultimately explains nothing as a worldview with the potential to explain everything. The Gītā describes those who hold to such views as "small in intelligence" and "spiritually lost." They may think that life arises from matter, all on its own. But their logic, according to the Vedic view, is like "the logic of the rice and the scorpions." From piles of rice some scorpions might crawl out, and a naive observer might reason that the rice must have produced the scorpions. In just such a way, people with a materialistic outlook see life emerging from nonlife – from biochemicals, from atoms – and not from the ultimate antecedent living being. But a thoughtful and humble person willing to listen will hear Qohelet say "You do not know ... You do not know ..." and will know that Qohelet is right.

Even amidst uncertainty, we must act

"In the morning sow your seed, and in the evening do not withhold your hand." Though we may not know which seeds will sprout, better than doing nothing is to plant twice so we'll have a better chance (and we may even succeed both times).

Qohelet's advice is again pragmatic. He is concerned with what will prosper – that is, with the success of work. He here gives no ultimate reason to work; the work is still the meaningless toil that dismays him earlier, a toil with no true profit. And yet we must work or perish. As Krishna says in the Bhagavad-gītā, "One cannot even maintain one's own body without work." The alternative, as Qohelet has said earlier – the alternative of fools – is to idly fold one's hands and "consume one's own flesh."

And Qohelet, it seems, would not just have us survive and subsist; he would have us prosper. But for what end, what purpose? To enjoy. In his dark moments he laments that we must toil away for nothing, and in his bright ones he proclaims we should enjoy. And as we'll see in upcoming verses, "enjoy" means "enjoy while you still can."

The Vedic sages see things differently. For them the purpose of work is not to enjoy work's fruits but rather to give enjoyment to the Supreme, to Krishna, by devotional service. By working for one's own enjoyment, the Gītā says, one becomes entangled and bound by one's work, but by working for the Supreme one becomes liberated. For the Krishna conscious person, the issue is not the success or failure of the work. The issue is to be engaged in Krishna's service. When one is engaged in Krishna's service, whether the work fails or succeeds it succeeds, for the success lies not in the result but in the endeavor. When one is devotedly engaged in Krishna's service, one thinks of Krishna and remembers him, and one acts according to one's eternal nature, as the hand acts according to its natural function when it serves the whole body. And this acting for Krishna makes one's entire life a success. As the hand that gives food to the body gets nourishment itself, the person who acts for Krishna's enjoyment automatically enjoys.

That enjoyment, however, does not depend on material circumstances, upon prosperity or want, success or failure; that happiness comes from within. As Krishna says in the Bhagavad-gītā, "One whose happiness is within, who is active and rejoices within, and whose aim is inward is actually the perfect mystic. Such a person, liberated in the Supreme, ultimately attains the Supreme." Both in the morning and in the evening of life, such persons engage in Krishna's service.

Therefore throughout life they enjoy the spiritual pleasure of Krishna consciousness, and at the end of life, absorbed in thoughts of Krishna, they transcend all material conditions and attain Krishna's eternal association.

11:7–8: Sweet is the light, and many are the days of darkness

> [7] Sweet is the light, and pleasant it is for the eyes to behold the sun. [8] Indeed, even if a man live many years, let him rejoice in them all, yet keep in mind the days of darkness, for they will be many. All that comes is vanity.

Just to be alive

To "behold the sun," a set phrase Qohelet has used earlier (in 6:5 and 7:11), means "to be alive." However deeply Qohelet has agonized over the miseries and injustices of life under the sun, however burdensome, frustrating, and profitless he has found it, however much he has despaired over life's absurdity, pain, and futility, even to the point of saying that he "hated life" and that never having been born would have been better, now he declares that just to be alive is pleasant and sweet.

At the New York World's Fair in 1964, my parents brought me to the Johnson's Wax pavilion to see a short film – the surprise hit of the fair – called *To Be Alive!*, an artistic and sensitive work (showing images, as I recall, on three different screens) that celebrated the joy of life as found in cultures throughout the world. Sweet is the light! How glorious to be alive!

In Sanskrit the root form of the verb "to live" is *jīv*, and so a living being is called a *jīva*. The jīva wants to go on living because that is its eternal nature. If we try to swat a mosquito it speeds away because it wants to stay alive. Having uppermost in one's life this desire to live represents one of five stages of consciousness, mentioned in the Taittirīya Upaniṣad. In the first stage, called *annamaya* (*anna* means "food," and

maya means "made of"), one is preoccupied with eating.* To eat becomes practically the goal of life. We see this in animals and other lower
creatures (and perhaps some people we know), who are busy all day
tracking down food or eating. Above *annamaya*, the next stage is *prāṇamaya*, in which what concerns us most is simply to stay alive. Again,
this preoccupies the lower creatures, who are always looking this way
and that, alert against attack. And for human beings too, simply to stay
alive may become the goal of life itself.

I had an aunt who in her eighties, obviously dwindling and failing,
was finally stricken with cancer and told she had less than a year to live.
Yet her doctors told her that by a surgical operation that would remove
most of her stomach (they'd do some plumbing to work around the loss)
she could perhaps extend her life a few months more. Such an operation would be expensive, and not everyone was eligible – one would
have to get on a short list of patients who could undergo it. And she
was *desperate* to get on that list. (She made it, and a few months later
she was dead.)

Above *prāṇamaya* comes *manomaya*, in which the focus of consciousness becomes one's thoughts and philosophical speculations – the
workings of the mind: philosophy, psychology, scientific theorizing,
literary musings, and so on. Above *manomaya* comes *vijñānamaya*, in
which one surpasses speculative theories and realizes – not just understands in theory but experiences in fact – that one is a spiritual living
being, distinct from the material body and mind. One then sees that
one's true self lies beyond ties to family, country, race, gender, religious
denomination, and so on, which come and go with the body, and even
above the subtle, ever-changing workings of the mind. And finally,
going beyond *vijñānamaya*, one comes to the stage of *ānandamaya*,
in which one realizes the eternal relationship between one's true self
and the Supreme Self, the ultimate source of all pleasure (*ānanda*), the
Personality of Godhead.

The first three stages – *annamaya* (life is for food), *prāṇamaya* (life
is for staying alive), and *manomaya* (life is for our creative headwork) –
are considered material because they pertain only to the physical body

---

* *Maya*, "made of," is distinct from *māyā*, the energy of illusion.

and the subtle material mind. Food, survival, and headwork are not the ultimate goal of life. They are meant to bring us to the higher stages, to serve the higher purposes of spiritual realization and realization of God. Yet "sweet is the light, and pleasant it is to behold the sun," and strong is the illusion that simply to go on living makes one's life a success.

The Śrīmad-Bhāgavatam tells of the last days of the blind King Dhṛtarāṣṭra. This was the king who had supported his evil son Duryodhana in conspiring to usurp the kingdom of Hastināpura from the legitimate heirs to the throne, the sons of Pāṇḍu, Dhṛtarāṣṭra's elder brother. The conflict between the sons of Pāṇḍu and those of Dhṛtarāṣṭra culminated in the Battle of Kurukṣetra, in which all of Dhṛtarāṣṭra's sons were killed. After the battle, the aged Dhṛtarāṣṭra, ruined and defeated, continued to live in the palace, where he was graciously honored and maintained by those against whom he had conspired. Finally, however, after many years, the palace was visited by Dhṛtarāṣṭra's younger brother, the sagacious Vidura, who had come to free Dhṛtarāṣṭra from his illusions and awaken him to spiritual realization.

Vidura told him, "Just see how fear has overtaken you! Death, frightful death, cannot be remedied by any person in this material world. My lord, it is the Supreme Personality of Godhead as eternal time that has approached us all. Whoever is under the sway of eternal time must surrender his most dear life, and what to speak of other things, such as wealth, honor, children, land, and home. Your father, brother, well-wishers, and sons are all dead. You yourself have expended most of your life. Your body is now overcome by invalidity, and you are living in the home of another. You were blind from your very birth, and lately you have become hard of hearing. Your memory is short, your intelligence disturbed, your teeth are loose, your liver has gone bad, and you are coughing up mucus. Alas, how powerful are the hopes of a living being to continue his life!"

As my spiritual master said, "Strong words are sometimes needed to awaken a sleeping man."

Dhṛtarāṣṭra, Vidura said, was "living just like a household dog," eating scraps of food thrown to him by Bhīma, the nephew who had slain Dhṛtarāṣṭra's favorite sons. Vidura told Dhṛtarāṣṭra, "There is no need to live a degraded life by subsisting on the charity of those whom you tried to kill by arson and poisoning, whose wife you insulted, and whose kingdom and wealth you tried to usurp." Death was surely approaching, and Dhṛtarāṣṭra, Vidura said, must free himself from the desire to go on living at any cost and must turn toward spiritual realization before death arrived. Vidura said, "Despite your unwillingness to die and your desire to live even at the cost of honor and prestige, your miserly body will certainly dwindle and wear out, like an old garment."

However sweet the light, however pleasant the sun for the eyes to behold, death is certain, and with it the end of light, sun, and the very eyes with which we see them. The Bhagavad-gītā says, "For one who is born, death is certain." And: "One who has died is certain to be born yet again." The Vedic culture therefore directs that before death comes we should fully use our years for spiritual realization because the next destination we achieve will depend on what our consciousness has come to by the time of death.

Rejoice in them all

There is of course no guarantee that a man may live many years. But suppose he does. Can he rejoice in them all? Longman translates "Let him enjoy all of them." And Fox: "He should take pleasure in them all." But how? The world is set up in such a way that the more we try to enjoy, the more we become frustrated. Qohelet himself, speaking of his own life, has testified to precisely that experience. And he has lamented "the tears of the oppressed" who have "no one to comfort them" and for whom enjoyment is out of the question.

How much we can enjoy lies beyond our control. Happiness and misery, by the workings of fate, come to us of their own accord, mixed in a proportion we can't set. Fate may give us a miserable childhood, or a youth full of pain. If fate makes us starve, or throws acid in our face, or sends us into enemy hands to be imprisoned and tortured, will we set about to have a merry time of it?

Old age, in particular, is unlikely to be a joyride. If a man lives many years, in his later years he can expect to be sorely afflicted – by bodily pains, by impotence, by loss of appetite, loss of teeth, hardness of hearing, dimming of vision, befuddlement of memory … by all the troubles

Vidura spelled out for Dhṛtarāṣṭra. In such years, is one supposed to take pleasure and enjoy? The project is hopeless.

In the Vedic culture, therefore, the later years of life are to be dedicated not to pathetic efforts to relish some last geriatric scraps of enjoyment but to freeing oneself from attachment to illusory pleasures so that one can realize the greater pleasure of spiritual realization. And ultimately one is meant to go beyond birth and death to enter the world where that pleasure is an eternal reality.

That is why the Vedic social system divides a man's life into four stages: student life, married life, retired life, and renounced life. After spiritual training as a student and after a life of spiritual culture in marriage, a man was not expected to remain at home forever. By the age of fifty, he would retire from work, business, sex, and family affairs, and he and his wife would concentrate their attention on spiritual advancement. And finally, by the age of seventy-five, a man would accept *sannyāsa*, the life of complete renunciation. Instead of being overcome by death, he would voluntarily "die" by giving up all material attachments, even attachment to his beloved wife.

In this way, in the Vedic culture, if a man were to live for many years, neither he nor his wife would waste them all in a false spirit of enjoyment. Keeping in mind the true problems of life – birth, death, disease, and old age – and seeing the need to solve them, to go beyond them, they would dedicate themselves to spiritual realization.

The days of darkness

What are the "days of darkness" Qohelet advises one to keep in mind? Seow regards them as "a time of gloom and misery," belonging especially to old age but able to appear at any time. On the other hand, Rashi and other scholars both traditional and modern say that the days of darkness are the endless days of death, the bleak, vacant eternity of Sheol. Longman and Murphy say both: old age and death.

In any case: Why, if one is to rejoice, should one keep those dark days in mind?

Rashi says one should remember them so that one will improve one's deeds and be saved from the dark fate of the wicked. Other commentators offer that Qohelet is prompting us to enjoy now, while still able. In

India people commonly sprinkle a bit of salt on fruit to make the fruit taste more sweet. So Qohelet, some say, would have us remember the darkness so that we may savor the light all the more. As both Barton and Plumptre mention, the Greek historian Herodotus tells us that at the end of banquets in Egypt a servant would carry around to the guests a coffin bearing within it a wooden image of a corpse, carved and painted to resemble nature as nearly as possible, and while showing it to each guest in turn would say, "Look at this, then drink and enjoy yourself, for when dead you will be like this." The purpose, Plumptre says, was "not to destroy or damp the joy, but to make it more lasting by making it more controlled."

Looking at Qohelet's words a different way, Longman and others accept that the text can mean that one *should* remember those days of darkness, but they offer the alternative translation "*will* remember." One will have to remember those days, whether one likes it or not.

In any case, what awaits us, Qohelet says, is nothing better than vanity. What will come at the end of our life will be meaningless, empty, futile, absurd. "Look at this, then drink and enjoy yourself, for when dead you will be like this."

Enjoy and remember

In text 8 Qohelet begins a motif of "enjoy and remember" that continues through 12:1 (and, implicitly, through 12:7).

But why "enjoy and remember"? The theme in the Bhagavad-gītā is different: serve and remember. Instead of "Enjoy!" Krishna advises us to perform our work with a spirit of detachment, to work simply as a matter of duty and not worry about whether the outcome brings us enjoyment. Enjoyment will come on its own – or not. The mission of human life is not to try to enjoy the illusions of this material world (and become entangled in them) but to become free from them and revive our spiritual nature.

A young man hardly needs a sage to urge him to enjoy; his own urges are enough. What the Vedic sages would advise him to do is master his urges, control his senses, and learn how to remember – to remember the transitory nature of the material world, to remember his own spiritual identity, and to remember the Supreme, or Krishna.

11:9–10: While young, rejoice! Rejoice! Vainly rejoice!

⁹ Rejoice, young man, while in your youth, and let your heart cheer you in the days of your youth. Follow the ways of your heart and the sight of your eyes. But know that for all these things God will bring you into judgment. ¹⁰ Therefore put away vexation from your heart, and turn away pain from your flesh; for youth and its black hair are vanity.

What sort of advice?

What at first seems like an unalloyed validation of youthful exuberance, a call to follow the promptings of the heart's desires and the visions that enchant the eyes, turns contradictory with the warning that for whatever a young man does to enjoy, God will judge him. And then, as if those words about judgment had never been spoken, we flip around again: Since you ought to enjoy, you should put aside anxiety and pain. And why? Because youth is finally no more than vapor!

What are we to make of such strange and equivocal advice?

Some traditional commentators, clearly not comfortable with the surface meaning of Qohelet's words, take the urging to enjoy as sarcastic. "Go ahead, put your hand in the fire!" Other scholars try to resolve the contradictions in Qohelet's advice by supposing that the righteous bit about God and judgment was inserted by some pious interpolator, keen to guard traditional norms. Knock out that intrusive insertion, and Qohelet is in fact urging gung-ho enjoyment. When the senses are strong, passions high, dreams within reach, new worlds to be explored, and the best parts of life right before you, why should you hold back? Youth comes but once, and soon it will be gone, so now, while it's yours, follow the promptings of your heart and the pleasures your eyes flash upon. Brush aside mental annoyances and physical stings and enjoy. In this view, Qohelet champions the very message a youth might most want to hear.

In support of this message, there's even another way to look at God's judgment: Whatever comes your way to enjoy is a gift from God, and he'll call you on the carpet for any enjoyment you turn down. As the Talmud says, "Everyone must give an account before God of all the good things he saw in life *and did not enjoy*" (emphasis added).

Or else the mention of divine judgment might merely be what Longman calls a "theological reflex," no more intended than an eyeblink. Earlier, Qohelet seems to have given up hope of fair judgment on earth, having seen instead that reward and punishment come at random, even perversely; and as for life after death, he says "Who knows?" Where then is the scope for divine judgment? The very mention of it might be no more than an automatic involuntary mumbling.

Alternatively, Qohelet mentions God's judgment as a reminder that enjoyment should be pursued, but only within limits, within the bounds of God's law. It seems unlikely that Qohelet – a sage, after all – would counsel all-out hedonistic indulgence. Suppose your heart fancies plundering the local bank vault or your eyes start to light upon a friend's wife. It's hard to picture Qohelet cheering, "Go for it!"

In this view, then, Qohelet is urging what the commentator Franz Delitzsch calls "an intelligent and responsible enjoyment of life." As Delitzsch says, "It is in the spirit of the whole book that, along with the call to earnest activity, there should be the call to the pleasant enjoyment of life: he who faithfully labors has a right to enjoy his life; and this joy of life, based on fidelity to one's calling, and consecrated by the fear of God, is the most real and the highest enjoyment here below."

To me this sounds like a sensible interpretation – perhaps a little too pat, as though Qohelet had now worked through his contradictions and arrived at a balanced and satisfying closure, pious, conventional, and tame, and as though the verses here were a tidy package, not a jumble, and also as though in counterpoint to "here below" Qohelet looks forward to a "there above," which he most certainly does not. But now Qohelet is in fact beginning his final advice, and a call for a life of pleasant, intelligent, responsible enjoyment, embraced with virtuous gusto, does seem to fit what he has in mind.

So let us look yet again, from the Vedic point of view, at the project for enjoyment.

From the viewpoint of the Śrīmad-Bhāgavatam, Qohelet's advice is second class. The same advice is found in the Vedic literature, but the

Bhāgavatam, from the very outset, rejects the path of righteous, intelligent, responsible enjoyment as "deceitful dharma."

Why? First of all, it doesn't work. In the beginning it may seem to, but finally it doesn't. And second – and this is *why* it doesn't work – "enjoyers of the world" is simply not what we are.

Let's look at the first point first: It doesn't work.

We can't actually have the enjoyment for which we hanker. Instead we get enjoyment and suffering mixed. And that amounts to suffering. To illustrate this point, my spiritual master sometimes gave an example concerning an Indian dish called *khīr*, a sweet pudding made with rice, sugar, and milk. Quite a tasty item. But suppose someone were to mix into it one spoonful – just one small spoonful – of sand. How would we like it then? Would we shrug and smile and say, "Well, you know – you've got to take the good with the bad"? However tasty the item, the sand grinding between our teeth would spoil the whole thing. And so: Enjoyment mixed with suffering amounts to suffering.

And the more we try to enjoy, the more we suffer. Qohelet has said, "In much wisdom there is much vexation." And he might as well have said also, "In much pleasure, much grief." The more I love you, the more pain I feel when you leave me or die. And as Qohelet found in his experiment with pleasure, the more we have, the more empty it will finally seem.

When we can't enjoy we get angry and frustrated. And we can't enjoy more than fate will let us. Moreover, if we really want to enjoy, we need to turn our eyes away from the darker context – we need to think as though we'll never die – because death sours our enjoyment and makes it seem like pointless nonsense. (Or else we need to tell ourselves that death makes life sweeter.) In other words, enjoyment is what we can rejoice in only by dulling our edge, by numbing our critical faculties, by saying, "Yes, I know, but anyway ..." – in essence, by holding our intelligence in abeyance. To enjoy, I have to make myself a fool.

The enjoyment of youth depends on the youthful material body, which will grow old and feeble and decrepit. And then I'll be left with a lifelong attachment to youthful pleasures I can yearn for and imagine but no longer have. So again, "enjoyment" leads to frustration.

And strong attachment to enjoyment puts spiritual realization out of reach because that enjoyment rivets us to the material body on which the supposed enjoyment depends.

So: "Enjoy, young man," but all these problems are like flies in the ointment. And as Qohelet has said, a fly in the ointment makes the perfume stink.

So now let us question the underlying assumption – that what we naturally are is beings meant to enjoy.

The Bhāgavatam tells us just the opposite: We are beings meant to *give* enjoyment. And where? To Krishna, the Supreme. We are parts, small parts, of the Supreme, the ultimate reality. And as parts we are meant to serve the whole. A hand cannot make itself happy by clenching food in its palm; the hand has to supply the food to the stomach, for the benefit of the whole body. Just so, we are meant not to try to enjoy independently but to give enjoyment to the Supreme, to Krishna. The real enjoyer is Krishna, and we are all Krishna's servants. And when we give enjoyment to Krishna, we also enjoy, just as the hand enjoys strength and nourishment when it gives food over to the stomach.

To serve Krishna, or the Supreme, is what my spiritual master used to refer to as our "constitutional position" – what we are meant for, our natural slot, our small place in harmony with the grand scheme of things. It is our dharma, the natural thing we are eternally meant to do.

That eternal dharma of service to Krishna is also known as bhakti, or pure devotional service. Such devotional service is described in the Bhagavad-gītā as ever joyful. Consciousness, the Gītā says, is joyful by nature. So when one realizes that one is not one's material body but an eternal spark of spiritual consciousness, one becomes joyful, free from longings and lamentations. And when one advances still further, from realization to action, one engages in bhakti, the spiritual activity of the soul – pure devotional service to Krishna. In bhakti, the small spark of consciousness is connected by service with the supreme reservoir of all consciousness, Krishna, the Supreme Personality of Godhead, and so tastes a joy beyond all material limitations.

This differs from the enjoyment Qohelet recommends. The ever-contradictory Qohelet would have us follow our hearts, pursue our desires, but remember God. In pure bhakti, in contrast, one puts material desires aside (thereby skipping the troubles they get us caught in) and simply engages in God's service. In this way the happiness one enjoys transcends the mind and its anxieties, the body and its pains, and youth and its limited days.

Enjoy for yourself

While young you should enjoy, Qohelet says. And we might naturally find this appealing. We like the message: The center of everything is me – me and my enjoyment.

Still, when I want to enjoy everything for myself (which I can only do at the expense of others) I am terribly selfish, and, whatever the outward show, at the core I will be frustrated and lonely. When I share with others – say with my family and friends – I will find greater satisfaction. I am still selfish, but now I have found the pleasure of "extended selfishness." By sharing enjoyment with others, I myself enjoy more.

If I go beyond family and friends and give myself to greater causes – to philanthropy, humanitarian efforts, ecological campaigns, and so on – if I give food to the poor, shelter to the homeless, relief to the oppressed, protection to endangered species, I can enjoy more deeply and profoundly, for now I have extended my open hand still further. As I give service to many others, I feel greater pleasure myself.

But the center is still my self: "my happiness" – or, extended, "our happiness." And at the end, what profit do I come away with? The generous man and the miser both wind up equally dead. If, as Qohelet says, I'm inevitably headed for oblivion, for Sheol, where "there is no work or thought or knowledge or wisdom," what's the use?

And even if I work for the welfare of others, what good will that ultimately do them? If the point of my empty and meaningless life on the way to the grave is to help others in their empty and meaningless lives on the way to the grave – what is the use?

The Śrīmad-Bhāgavatam tells us that attempts for selfish happiness, whether for me only or extended to include my family, my friends, my countrymen, or even my world, are pointless. One has to go beyond a false sense of I and mine and see that the real owner of everything, the rightful enjoyer of everything, and the true friend of all living beings is the origin of everything, the Personality of Godhead.

The notion that I should enjoy while acknowledging that all comes from God is progressive, the Bhāgavatam says – it's far better than all-out materialism – but it shows a mixture of God consciousness and material attachment. In Sanskrit terminology, this is called *karma-miśra-bhakti*, devotion to God mixed with devotion to my own project for enjoyment. What the Bhāgavatam recommends is pure devotional service, unmixed with selfish motives. In pure bhakti, the individual self strives only to give enjoyment to the Supreme Self, to Krishna, and though in this way the individual self incidentally enjoys to the greatest possible extent, that is beside the point. The point is to please Krishna. This might seem yet another form of "extended selfishness," but because it's extended to the ultimate, to the Supreme, to the absolute reality, it is transformed from utterly meaningless to absolutely real. By full dedication to the Supreme, to Krishna, one becomes both self-fulfilled and "selfless" in the true sense of the term.

The highest aim

Qohelet, in his final advice, does urge (in the next chapter) the importance of remembering our creator. And for commentators such as Rashbam, the essential distinction between the enjoyment Qohelet rejects and the enjoyment he accepts is a question not just of degree – "moderation" – but of recognizing that our modest enjoyment is what we have been allotted, that it has come from the hand of God.

In that case, we are accepting our portion and not trying for more. We are accepting for ourselves the rule of "satisfaction," of being content to enjoy what God has given, and not making efforts to push our enjoyment further. This attitude is approved in the Vedic literature, for example in the Īśopaniṣad. But the Śrīmad-Bhāgavatam cautions that such enjoyment is not the "ultimate good"; it is incidental. Our senses need a moderate degree of satisfaction – we need to eat, to sleep, to mate, and to defend ourselves – but we should keep these needs minimal and focus on the real purpose of life: inquiry about *jīvasya-tattva*, "the truth of the self," or "who we really are."

The Bhāgavatam advises us to be content with that which comes naturally of its own accord, as given by God, but not be complacent, thinking that enjoying whatever we naturally gain is the ultimate goal of life. Unless we aim higher, the Bhāgavatam says, our life is a failure. Our aim should be for pure bhakti, pure devotional service.

Prospects of heaven

Briefly, let's look at a prospect that might distract one from the path of pure bhakti, and that is the prospect of "going to heaven." When I was young, that's not a prospect that attracted me. The place seemed imaginary, unlikely to exist – and, to tell you the truth, downright boring. Someplace up in the clouds, you float piously about in a toga with a halo over your head and play a harp all day. Give me a break!

Of course, I don't suppose people who believe in heaven dream of literally going to a realm of clouds, but popular notions of heaven do seem, well, nebulous. It's someplace you go where God gives you some sort of "heavenly rewards."

From time to time I've received tracts which seem to say that some blessed and fortunate souls will be resurrected in the very same bodies they used to have on earth. From the pictures in the tracts it seems that in heaven one will live in a nice little cottage with one's family, maybe one's dog, and the sun shining pleasantly overhead, the whole picture the very image of suburban perfection: "Just another beautiful day in San Diego."

Other people, of course, have other ideas of heaven. But the general theme, at least in the popular imagination, is that it's a place where one eternally enjoys. In heaven, Qohelet's failed experiment in pleasure actually succeeds. There one can have the vineyards and gardens and parks and fruit trees, the herds and flocks, the treasures and perhaps, some might hope, the young sexual companions, and instead of feeling empty, by the grace of God one will feel eternally fulfilled.

In the view of the Śrīmad-Bhāgavatam, this is just another brand of "deceitful dharma" because it perpetuates, this time as if for all eternity, the idea of one's own self-centered enjoyment.

The Vedic literature too promises that as a reward for good deeds one may be promoted to "heaven," but the heaven described is but a more elevated realm within the material world. According to the Vedic writings, within the material world there are higher abodes – the "heavenly planets" – where those who live are blessed with a higher standard of sense gratification. Because of previous lives rich in performing "good karma," those granted entrance into those regions of paradise live for thousands of years, a seeming eternity, with beautiful bodily forms, with celestial strength and vitality, with heavenly surroundings full of lush gardens and waterfalls, with ambrosial food, heavenly sex – with everything material one might want. But because it's material, it's all temporary. Finally, from those higher planets one falls back down to a lifetime on earth and continues in the cycle of birth and death.

Therefore the Bhagavad-gītā says that those who aspire to live in such abodes have only "meager intelligence" because going there doesn't finally solve the problems of life – birth, death, old age, and disease. It only puts one in the "up" swing of a cycle whose next arc inevitably swings down – down to another life on earth. Since in the heavenly planets, even though one might have reverence for God, one is very much concerned with one's own enjoyment, those who live there are not in their "constitutional position," their natural slot of pure bhakti, pure devotional service. And therefore the prospect of enjoying there is finally only another illusion.

For Qohelet, of course, heaven is not in the picture. He earlier considered the prospect of some sort of elevation after death but left it aside with a dismissive "Who knows?" And by now he seems to have rejected it entirely because two chapters ago he said that after death one goes only to Sheol, that dark place where "there is no work or thought or knowledge or wisdom."

Nothingness and oneness
Apart from Sheol or heaven or reincarnation on earth, there's of course another theoretical alternative: nothingness. Taking a strictly materialistic view (or, for that matter, the view expounded by the Buddha), life is no more than an epiphenomenon of matter, a byproduct of matter's interactions. So you are just one small batch of chemicals brewing and bubbling in such a way as to give off the vapor we call "consciousness." When the bubbling is over, your life is over: The last whiff of conscious vapor vanishes once and for all. The chemical mixture has gone flat, and that you're dead means that "you" are now utterly nonexistent. Some people still alive – that is, some chemical mixtures still bubbling – can dispose of your body. They can burn it and let it turn to ashes, bury it and let it turn to earth, or throw it to the vultures and let it turn to the excrement of the raptors – vulture dung. Your self-reflective consciousness, with its thoughts, its feelings, its desires, has ceased to exist, and the biochemical stuff that once gave off the vapor of your life is trashed and recycled.

Till then: Enjoy?

Or let's take another approach. Forget biochemistry. Imagine we are all but small drops of one great spiritual ocean. From that ocean we emerge as individual drops, as living beings with names and forms and thoughts and feelings and a sense of who we are, with homes and families and our own personal histories and aspirations. And when our life is over – or perhaps after many lives – the drop will merge back into the ocean, into perfect oneness, no longer bound by the limits of who we now think we are, with our individuality and the differences between us. All that truly exists is that unlimited spiritual oneness, beyond names and forms, beyond words and descriptions, beyond even our power to conceive. That oneness is the only reality, and all else is illusion. All dualities – success or failure, fame or obscurity, joy or suffering, my very existence or nonexistence – are but illusions for me to leave behind as I, that spiritual drop, merge back into the oneness of that spiritual ocean.

This notion has some serious problems with it. If everything is ultimately one, how could varieties exist at all, or even seem to exist? And how could that individual drop ever arise from the ocean at all, or merge back into it, or even seem to? We might say that varieties and individuality only seem to exist because of illusion, but that still sends us back to the same problem: If everything is absolutely *one*, how could there possibly be this *second* thing called illusion? If from the very start we have two things – reality and illusion – that doesn't give us oneness. It gives us duality.

But for a moment let's put those problems aside and treat the notion of absolute oneness as if true. If nothing actually exists but absolute oneness, why should I try to enjoy, whether greatly or moderately? That would just perpetuate my false sense of being an individual self and thereby keep me stuck in duality. And besides, what could there be for me to enjoy? For in this view, all enjoyments are but illusions. And why should illusions be something for me to pursue? Would this not be a foolish and meaningless "chasing after wind"? Finally, whether we merge into a great spiritual oneness (as some Hindu philosophies say) or we dissolve our ego in favor of a great emptiness or void (as in some Buddhist doctrines), the same question still holds: How could illusions be something for the wise to enjoy?

One last, deeper look at enjoyment

As many commentators have observed, Qohelet's book is not merely a study in pessimism. The book clearly does have two strands: an overwhelming argument for the uselessness, emptiness, absurdity, and pain of human existence and, alongside this, a positive endorsement of full-hearted enjoyment.

Quite a number of commentators take the advice to enjoy as the conclusive finding, the essential message, of the book. In the words of Robert Gordis:

> The basic theme of the book is its insistence upon the enjoyment of life, of all the good things in the world. There is the love of woman – and the singular is noteworthy –
>
> > Enjoy life with the woman whom you love
> > Through all the vain days of your life,
> > Which God has given you under the sun,
>
> but the counterpoint of melancholy is never absent:
>
> > Throughout your brief days,
> > For that is your life's reward
> > For your toil under the sun. (9:9)
>
> With a moving sense of the transitoriness of life, he calls for the vigorous and full-blooded enjoyment of all it affords, food and drink, oil and fine clothes, beautiful homes and music:
>
> > Whatever you are able to do, do with all your might, for there is neither action nor thought nor knowledge nor wisdom in the grave toward which you are moving. (9:10)
>
> In practice, Koheleth advocates a moderate course, not very different from the attitude of the rabbis of the Talmud:
>
> > Three things bring a sense of ease and contentment to a man: a beautiful home, an attractive wife, and fine clothes. (Ber. 57b)

What set his standpoint apart from theirs was that his attitude stemmed not from a full-hearted acceptance of the world, as preached by religion, but from a sense of frustration and resignation, induced by his philosophy.

Morris Jastrow, another commentator, expresses a similar view:

But why, then, enjoyment as the best way of spending one's days on earth? Simply, because there is nothing else to do, certainly nothing better. Koheleth does not preach happiness as the goal of life, but as the only means of not being overwhelmed by the sadness of life, which must ensue if you have the courage to look at things as they are.

As Fox says, concisely, "Pleasure dulls the pain of consciousness, the same pain that wisdom exacerbates."

McNeile vividly portrays Qohelet and his plight:

He flings himself against fate in despair. Every fresh wrong or injustice or inequality which he meets in the world causes a new pang.... And each time that his heart is driven back wounded and sore, he cries "there is no good in life except present enjoyment!" It is not the *summum bonum* [highest good]; that is quite unattainable; he had made every possible attempt to reach it, and had failed (i. 12–ii. 11). It is simply a *minimum malum* [least bad], fortunately allowed to man by God, whereby "he shall not much remember the days of his life."

Qohelet returns to this minimum malum no fewer than seven times. It is what God has allotted us; there is nothing better; it will divert our hearts and keep us from brooding. By the time Qohelet reaches the eighth chapter, though, he goes so far as to positively "commend enjoyment," and by the ninth chapter and here again in the eleventh the advice to enjoy has become an imperative: "Rejoice!" But vanity and death are never far off. Each time he revisits enjoyment, it is infected with vanity and death; and finally, in vanity and death is where enjoyment ends.

Some commentators, though, would have Qohelet's call for enjoyment be something more, indeed a true way of finding God. In the words of the biblical scholar Thomas Kelly Cheyne:

> It is just in these enjoyments that man comes nearest to God:
> he meets God in them, feels his favour, and knows that in
> them God is 'responding to the joy of his heart' (5:20).

There is something to be said for seeing the presence of God within everything and acknowledging that God's favor is the source of all we might enjoy. But the notion that one comes nearest to God when one's senses are most gratified doesn't seem to follow. Are we supposed to think that at the apex of enjoyment – the moment of sexual climax – one attains the highest communion with divinity? Blessed then are the monkeys, for they get more of it.

As for finding God in sense gratification, the Bhāgavatam bluntly says, "Even though perhaps very learned and wise, one is mad if one does not understand that the endeavor for sense gratification is a useless waste of time. Forgetful of one's own interest, one tries to be happy in the material world, centering one's interests on one's home, which has its basis in sexual intercourse and which brings one all kinds of material miseries. In this way one is no better than a foolish animal."

A Vedic sage would not encourage one to live like a "two-legged animal." The Bhāgavatam says, "Like an experienced doctor, who never encourages a patient to eat food bad for his health even if the patient wants it, a person who has knowledge will never instruct one who doesn't know the goal of life to work for material enjoyment, let alone help him in such work." The enjoyment the Bhāgavatam recommends is the pleasure of bhakti, pure devotional service to Krishna.

The advice I received

Qohelet speaks as an elder to the young man. In Qohelet's time and culture, I would suppose, young people afforded great respect to the advice of their elders, as we find in some cultures even today. In India, though tradition is waning, such respect for elders still largely survives. But these days in the West it seems that young men hold the words of old men in low esteem or even contempt. Fair enough: Old men are so often fools. But then again, so too are the young.

This was true of me. I had little respect for my parents and teachers. What could they teach me? Could they answer with more than superficial platitudes the issues raised by Qohelet? (But then again, could I?)

I was fortunate, therefore, to hear from a certain priest "Seek, and you shall find; knock, and it shall be answered unto you." And I was even more fortunate, while still young, to meet my spiritual master and place myself under his guidance. I trusted his words and received the benefit of his wisdom, even in the most simple and practical matters of daily life. And – what matters the most – he guided me to that which fills life with ultimate meaning and purpose. He rescued me from an empty life.

12

12:1–7: The ending of life

[1] Remember your creator in the days of your youth, before the evil days come and the years draw near when you will say "I have no pleasure in them"; [2] before the sun and the light and the moon and the stars grow dark and the clouds return after the rain; [3] in the day when the keepers of the house tremble, and the strong men are bent, and the women who grind cease because they are few, and those that look out grow dark in the windows; [4] when the doors in the street are shut, and the sound of the grinding is low, and one starts up at the voice of a bird, and all the daughters of song are brought low; [5] when one is afraid of heights, and terrors are in the road; and the almond tree blossoms, and the locust drags itself along, and the caperberry fails; because a man goes to his eternal home, and the mourners go about the streets; [6] before the silver cord is snapped, and the golden bowl is shattered, and the pitcher is broken at the fountain, and the wheel falls shattered into the pit, [7] and the dust returns to the earth as it was, and the breath returns to God who gave it.

A dark poem

Qohelet ends his words with a dark poem, which speaks to us in vivid but strange and portentous images, telling its story obliquely, telling but not telling, or telling and more than telling, because much of its meaning reaches us by how the pictures make us feel.

The obscurity of the poem contributes to a feeling of tension, of dread, of terror. How much of the obscurity is intentional we can't know. Over the centuries, surely, meanings once certain have become ambiguous, old customs have been forgotten, and scribal errors or intrusions may have damaged the original text. To ancient readers the passage may have been more clear. But for them too it must have been suggestive and oblique, and they too must have equally felt its tension, chill, foreboding, and gloom, its melancholy and dread, built up through omens and images and ending in snap, shatter, and dust.

Remember your creator – but why?

The first verse, at least, is clear. The coming "days of trouble" – days and years – are surely those of old age, when the exuberance of youth is gone, the body is afflicted, and the senses have lost their power to enjoy.

Before those days come, Qohelet advises, remember your creator. But why? Qohelet gives no reason. If while young one should enjoy, how would remembering one's creator help? We can eat, drink, and enjoy without remembering him, thank you very much, and remembering him might even get in the way.

Presumably one should remember the creator while young so that one will remember him when old. But again: Why? What reason could there be? What benefit? If all go inevitably to Sheol, where there is neither punishment nor reward, where there is no life but only an inert, shadowy semblance of existence, why should one think of one's creator at death? What difference would it make?

Alternatively, if we follow the worldview of modern reductionistic science, in which life is no more than the bubbling of chemicals in complex patterns, ending at death when the bubbling stops and we no longer exist, again why think of one's creator, either in youth or at the end? (Besides, if we take the reductionistic route all the way, there is no creator to think of.)

Since the Hebrew word Qohelet uses for "creator" is an unusual one as a name for God, some commentators think the original word in the text was a similar word that means "grave." Or perhaps Qohelet wrote "creator" but intended to bring "grave" to mind too. But in any case, if all ends in Sheol or in nothingness, what benefit in remembering the grave, any more than the creator?

Some commentators would see yet another Hebrew word, meaning "health." But if we're all going to the grave, why think about our health?

As yet another alternative, some commentators suggest a Hebrew word that literally means "fountain" or "well" but metaphorically would mean "wife," one's wellspring of sensuous joy. But a young man, as I've mentioned, hardly needs a sage to urge him to think of getting down with his wife. And if this is the best advice the sage can offer us – to enjoy with our wife while we still can … How pathetic!

Most commentators agree on "creator." But again: Why remember him? If this one life is all, if "All go to one place; all are from the dust, and all turn to dust again," what matter what we think of, either while young or in old age?

What we think of at death …

In the Vedic worldview, as I've touched on before, what we think of at the time of death is crucial because what we think of at death determines our next lifetime. In the words of the Bhagavad-gītā, "Whatever state of being one remembers when quitting the body, that state one will attain without fail." Just as the air around us picks up different aromas – the scent of flowers, for example, or the stench of garbage – our mind picks up different things to think about, different conceptions of life. And according to what we think of – what fills our mind, what "state of being" – the mind at death carries us to the next lifetime.

The same process works even during our present life. First we think of going somewhere – to a friend's house, for example – and then we wind up going there. The thoughts of a person in the mode of goodness might lead to a library or to a meeting of philosophers, the thoughts of a person in passion to a love nest or into a war, the thoughts of a person in ignorance to a place to get drunk or take drugs. Similarly, one's thoughts when one's mind has turned toward God are likely to draw one to a spiritual place, a place where one can have the company of spiritually minded people and hear about God. The thoughts of the mind set the course for where we'll go.

In a similar way, the thoughts we have at the time we leave the body – the time of death – set the course for the state we'll attain next. If our minds are absorbed in thoughts in the mode of goodness, the Gītā says, we'll ascend to a higher material realm, a realm of higher enjoyment; if our thoughts are in the mode of passion, we'll be born once again among those who toil and struggle for flickering enjoyment in a frustrating human life; and if our thoughts are in the mode of ignorance, we risk being consigned to a birth as a dull-witted beast. The quality of our thoughts determines where we go.

And the Gītā says that when we rise above all these material qualities by thinking of the supreme transcendence – of God, or Krishna – we can go beyond all material destinations and attain his supreme abode. In the Bhagavad-gītā Krishna says, "Whoever, at the end of life, quits his body remembering me alone at once attains my nature. Of this there is no doubt."

Krishna's nature, the Gītā says, is transcendental, and because we are integral spiritual parts of Krishna we originally have the same nature. When we think of Krishna at death, we reattain this spiritual nature. Our thoughts then carry us to him, the supreme transcendence, and to his abode in the spiritual world, the realm of pure consciousness.

Therefore even while carrying out our work in the present world, Krishna says, throughout our life we should always think of him, always be "Krishna conscious," so that we will enjoy transcendental happiness even in this life and at the end of life return to our fully spiritual nature and live in eternal transcendence, in the company of Krishna himself.

This is possible, Krishna says, by constant practice. The Vedic literature recommends that in the present age the most suitable practice, the most effective, is the chanting of the mahā-mantra: Hare Krishna, Hare Krishna, Krishna Krishna, Hare Hare/ Hare Rāma, Hare Rāma, Rāma Rāma, Hare Hare. The Upaniṣads say that this sixteen-word mantra can free one from all the grime of the present age of quarrel and hypocrisy and that in all the Vedic literature there is no method higher. The chanting is transcendental sound, identical with Krishna himself, so one who chants this Hare Krishna mantra has the association of Krishna, even in the present life. The thoughts of such a person will naturally dwell with Krishna, and at the time of death this "Krishna consciousness" will carry one to Krishna.

The Vedic sages recommend that one take up this practice from one's youth – better yet, from childhood – so that throughout one's life one can be Krishna conscious and at the crucial time of death one can attain perfection.

What is happening?

Verses 6 and 7, in which the cord is snapped, the bowl is shattered, and the dust returns to earth, are certainly metaphorical descriptions of death. But what of verses 2 through 5? What do they describe? We cannot be sure. Again, the images are dark, obscure, shadowy.

The early interpreters of Ecclesiastes saw the poem as allegorically depicting old age through a series of images representing various parts of the body. So, for example, the grinders that have become few are the old man's few remaining teeth. "Those that look out" but now "grow dark in the windows" are the eyes, growing weak or blind. For some of the images, this approach works well. But trying to fit them all into this framework soon leads to matches that seem arbitrary and far-fetched. Are the "keepers of the house" the arms? the legs? the ribs? (All have been proposed.) Do the darkened sun, light, and moon symbolize (as Rashi would have it) the forehead, the nose, and the soul? Or (in line with other opinions) is the sun the spirit? the light the cheeks? the moon the forehead? Or is the sun the heart? When we try to read these verses strictly as an anatomical allegory, such are the problems.*

---

* Fox mentions that the "allegorical interpretation" points more to a series of figurative images than to an allegory in the proper sense of the term. Strictly speaking, an allegory is a prolonged, sustained metaphor, its figures usually pulling together in the form of a narrative, as, for example, in a fable. But the imprecise use of the term *allegory* is a small matter, as Fox acknowledges by using the term anyway. In any case, a proper allegory culminating in conquest by old age and death appears in the Fourth Canto of the Śrīmad-Bhāgavatam, chapters 25 through 29, in the story of King Purañjana, "the man of the city," a symbolically rich narrative in which the "city" – the physical body – is besieged and finally overwhelmed by 365 male and female soldiers (the days and nights of the years).

Fox has helpfully suggested that the text speaks to us on several levels – literal, symbolic, allegorical – but that before probing other levels we should first consider what story it tells us literally.

The literal story too, however, can be seen differently. Perhaps what we are seeing is the onset of a terrible cataclysmic storm, as signaled in verse 2. With the storm approaching, tension fills the air, and the people of the estate or village stop their work and shut their doors, in the face of the oncoming devastation. Or perhaps what we are seeing is a house – a large, aristocratic house, with guards, servants, and the like – falling into ruin under the sweep of time. Or else what we are seeing may be a funeral, with people gathered in communal mourning. All of these various story lines (and others) have been offered, and all have their own strengths and weaknesses.

One might suspect that the story of what is literally going on is elusive because the author has deliberately made it so. *Something* is happening, something terrible, but it's something strange, something we don't understand. We know something's happening, but we don't know what it is. And it's happening amidst a landscape full of symbols and figurative images.

Let us proceed.

The lights grow dark, the clouds return

In the beginning of the book, the world "under the sun" is full of activity. The sun rises and sets and rises again, marking the days and years of time; generations come and go; the rivers make their way to the sea; and the wind blows around in its circuits. True, all this activity may seem devoid of meaning. It may seem unspeakably wearisome and empty. But at least it's kinetic. The sun brings life, and "whoever is joined with the living has hope, for a living dog is better than a dead lion." But now even the dog is about to die, and time reach its end, for the sun will grow dark and lifeless. "Sweet is the light, and pleasant it is for the eyes to see the sun." But now the sun – and every other source of light – is about to give way to darkness.

And then there are the clouds, unnaturally returning after the rain, and surely not benevolent clouds but clouds that betoken destruction. (If the clouds return *with* the rain – a possible translation – yet again we would expect not a kindly shower but a fierce and terrible storm.)

In biblical imagery, such clouds and universal darkness mark the fearful day when the Lord strikes the world with judgment and retribution, when sinners are destroyed and the earth is made desolate, the day of cosmic annihilation – the end of the world.

People in fear and grief

We now see the picture of a house or estate or village overcome by fear and desolation. The guards tremble, and the Hebrew word indicates that they tremble not in weakness but in fear. The strong men are bent, and this is more than mere stooping; the Hebrew, though hard to pin down, seems to indicate that the men are either cowering in fear or convulsed, twisting, or writhing. Their forms are bent and distorted either by terror or by grief.

For women to grind grain into flour would be part of the daily routine of any household or village, but that work has now ceased because the grinders have become few. Scholars have puzzled over why their fewness has made the work stop. If the grinders are fewer, shouldn't they each have to work more? The various speculations are all uncertain. Have most of the women gone in mourning to join the funeral procession? Have they suddenly been wiped out? We don't know. But the picture is one of desolation; most of these women are gone.

Other women – "those who look through the windows" – now "grow dark," or else (another translation) they "see dimly." In traditional Middle Eastern culture, women of refinement would not subject themselves to public view. So, as Zlotowitz says, "Scripture often depicts women as modestly peering through windows." But now, as the clouds return and the men tremble, the women peering through the windows are deep in gloom, despondent. Perhaps they are hopeless over the impending disaster signaled by the clouds. Perhaps they are in mourning. Or perhaps, as Seow suggests, these may be wives and mothers waiting in vain for their loved ones to return. Again, we don't quite know what is happening. But wherever we turn we see fright or grief.

Commentators have noted the symmetries in verse 3. The first half of the verse tells of men; the second half, women. And the men and the women belong to both low station and high. The "keepers of the house" – in some translations they are "guards" – are servants of some sort, entrusted with watching over things. And the "strong men" – sometimes "valiant men" or "landowners" – are men of power, wealth, influence, position. Similarly, the grinding maids are servants engaged in ordinary menial work, whereas the women who peer through the windows are women of leisure and high station. The disaster affects everyone.

In verse 3 the figurative anatomical approach does seem to have something going for it. In the Hebrew the grinding maids are more literally "grinders" (and the word is feminine, and so "the women who grind"). But the same word can also literally mean the molar teeth.* And so we may be reminded here of the loss of teeth in old age. With similar ambiguity, the word for "those that look" (and again it's feminine) usually refers to the eyes, which of course may grow dim in old age. In old age, too, men's bodies tremble and bend.

More signs of disaster

The doors that are open in happy and active times are now being shut. The Hebrew grammar tells us these are double doors, as might befit a great house. Or, as Seow suggests, these might be the doors on a street bazaar, in which case a market usually bustling with life is now shutting down into silence. In the allegorical approach, these doors could be the two lips or two ears.

As the description continues, not only do we see signs of disaster, but ominous and tragic things are happening with what we hear. The everyday hum of grinding so familiar to a busy estate or village has faded low. "And one starts up at the sound of a bird," as an old man may be startled from sleep, or startled at any time, even by the slightest sound. These words may also be translated "The sound of the bird rises." In that case, as the grinding fades, we now hear in the eerie quiet the sound of a bird – and it may be a "bird of evil omen." As Seow comments, what we hear may be "birds hooting ominously" or scavengers like hawks and vultures "making a commotion when they sense death" or descend into a place of desolation.

The term "daughters of song" – a poetic phrase of uncertain meaning – might refer to either birds or women. If birds, perhaps those hawks

---

* In English, too, our word *molar* comes from the Latin *mola*, indicating a mill or millstone.

and vultures may be swooping down, keen to tear and pick and feed. Or else if these are sparrows or nightingales or other singing birds, their voices, instead of rising, have now been brought low – hushed. If instead of birds we have women, these may be professional mourners, singing songs of lament and bending low to express grief. If indeed these are hired mourners, the laments we hear are those of women bewailing the deceased only because paid to do so. As Gordis comments, "the vanity of life is climaxed by the vanity of death!"

The landscape

In verse 5, doubts about the meaning of several Hebrew words make the meaning of the images still more doubtful.

As we begin, the phrase "one is afraid of heights" – the usual translation – fits the traditional view of the poem as depicting old age. The old man fears heights, from which he might fall, and he fears to venture out because any sort of mishap might occur. Seow, who says this reading comes from an overinterpretation of the Hebrew, suggests that if in the previous verse the "daughters of song" are birds of prey, perhaps swooping low, then we may read "even from on high they see terror on the way." Fox, on the other hand, taking the daughters of song as professional mourners, says that they, or the members of the funeral procession they lead, "fear what is on high." That is, "they dread the power lurking over their heads," the terrifying power of God.

With the images of the almond tree, the locust, and the caperberry the poem gives us pictures from nature. (If what we were seeing was a disaster-stricken house, now we are looking at what's outside.) And what do we see?

If we take a figurative approach, we may see what happens to an old man's body, dwindling on the way to death. His hair turns white, like the almond tree in blossom. The bounce gone from his step, he drags himself along like an old or food-glutted grasshopper. And the caperberry, said to stimulate appetite or sexual passion, can do nothing for him. (As the King James Version has it, "desire fails.")

Or else, viewing the scene more directly as the text paints it: Perhaps spring is upon the land, so that the almond blooms, the locusts gorge themselves so heavily they can barely drag along (or else the locust tree becomes heavily laden with fruit), and the caperberries (rather than "fail") burst from the fullness of growth. In this view, nature moves on in her great cycles, unconcerned with an event so trivial as the death of a man, grieved by the mortals around him.

Metaphors of death

At the end of verse 5, whatever interpretations we have followed, now all meanings converge: A man must go to his "eternal home," the grave. And the mourners (who will eventually go to graves of their own) walk in the funeral procession.

Verse 6 presents four vivid pictures of destruction, and though we may not understand the metaphors precisely, we know that the pictures all finally stand for death. The silver cord and golden bowl are precious items, rendered useless when snapped and smashed. The bowl could be a vessel from which the wicks of a lamp draw their oil. With the snapping of the cord that holds the lamp, the bowl smashes, and the light of the lamp goes out. In the other two images, a broken jug and broken wheel can no longer be used to get water. So the ruined body, no longer able to drink of life's waters or to hold the glow of life, is all at once reduced from the form of a living man to a heap of broken and useless rubble. Soon, as Ibn Ezra comments, "Only the bones remain – and even they eventually disintegrate."

In Genesis, God formed Adam, the first man, of the dust of the ground and breathed life into him and later told him, "Dust you are, and unto dust shall you return." Now it happens: The man's body returns to dust, and God takes back the life-breath that once made the man alive.

In translations such as the King James Version, what here returns to God is the "spirit," and perhaps a reader will see a comforting image of a soul returning to heaven. This is foreign to Qohelet's thought. For him there is no separate "spirit." When the body dies, life is over. The word he uses here is the by now familiar *ruah* – in context the "life force," the breath of life. When God takes back that borrowed life-breath, a man is dead, and the dust returns to dust.

As Fox writes, "In the Hebrew conception, the person *is* the body, no less than the animal's body *is* the animal, and he *has* a life-spirit or breath." So when the life-spirit is withdrawn and the body dies, the person ceases to exist. This is a view Qohelet never examines or questions (except for a brief "who knows?") – and it is a view the Vedic sages, who *have* examined it, do not share.

Of course, the Vedic sages are close to Qohelet in what they say about the body and the life-breath. The Īśopaniṣad says, "Let the temporary body be burnt to ashes, and let the air of life be merged with the totality of air." In Vedic culture, at death the body is burned rather than buried, so it turns not to dust but to ashes. In any case, the basic elements of which the body is made rejoin the total supply of those elements in the universe, and the subtle (but still material) life air merges back into a similar universal pool. As the body was brought together and formed of such elements, now what was formed is undone, and those elements are dispersed.

But in the Vedic view, the person is *not* the body (any more than the animal's body is the animal). The Bhagavad-gītā says, "Those who are seers of the truth have concluded that matter [which makes up the body] has no permanent existence whereas consciousness never ceases to exist. Learned seers have concluded this by studying the ultimate nature of both."

The Vedic Sāṅkhya philosophy, as taught by the sage Kapiladeva, the son of the princess Devahūti, examines the gross and subtle characteristics of the primordial stuff of nature, matter's basic units. And it sees, finer than the subtlest elements of matter, a separate element that when joined to matter infuses it with consciousness. When the elements of the body are dismantled and dispersed, that element of consciousness, the ātmā, the spiritual self, continues to exist and moves on in its many-lives journey until ultimately freed from entanglement with matter and restored to its natural state. In that liberated state, that tiny spark of consciousness resumes its natural engagement in the service of the Supreme Consciousness and thus attains perfection. In other words, the soul is reunited with Krishna in eternal loving service.

The funeral

Among the several literal ways to see the elusive story line of these verses – we are seeing a village threatened by a cataclysmic storm, or seeing the destruction of a great house, or seeing a funeral and a village in mourning – this last interpretation is the one favored by Fox, who finds merit in the arguments given for it in the late 1800s by the scholar

Charles Taylor. Before we leave these verses, let us look at this interpretation a bit more.

In this view, in verse 1 the days in which we say we no longer have pleasure are the miserable days of old age. In verse 2 the sun, the moon, and every other source of light goes out on the day of death. Verses 3 through 5 paint a picture of a village in extreme mourning (with nature appearing in the background). And verses 6 and 7 give a final picture of death and disintegration.

Qohelet's poem leads us through a landscape of surreal strangeness and supernatural intensity, with storm clouds, trembling, desolation, and silence, with omens of disaster and cries of lamentation, into a darkened, pained, and terrified village mourning someone's death.

"For whom are they mourning so intensely?" Fox asks. And he answers: It is you. It is the you to whom Qohelet gives his final advice – at last, you who read these words. "Qohelet wants you to look upon your death and funeral from the outside. It is your fate that appalls the village. Your death is eclipsing their world, and you are present at the terrible scene."

By leading us to look upon our own death and funeral, Qohelet gives the final stroke for his argument that all is vanity. This is *why* life is vain, empty, meaningless, absurd – because this is what it finally comes to.

A text from the Śrīmad-Bhāgavatam, though with a different view of life, shares the image of a person witnessing his own destruction. The Bhāgavatam says:

yad arthena vināmuṣya   puṁsa ātma-viparyayaḥ
pratīyata upadraṣṭuḥ   sva-śiraś chedanādikaḥ

"A person who has misunderstood who he is, and who therefore lives in distress, a distress without purpose or meaning, is like a man who sees his own head cut off in a dream."

When I forget my spiritual nature and falsely identify with my body, the Bhāgavatam says, whatever happens to my body seems to be happening to me. When my body is diseased, *I* am diseased. When my body grows old, *I* am old. When my body dies, *I* die. In fact, however, none of this happens to me – it happens only to my body. I might surely be distressed to see my head cut off in a dream. But however terrible the sight, to see it I must still have my eyes, and therefore my head. While I dream, the illusion seems real; when I awaken, the dream disappears.

And so would it be if I were compelled to look upon my own funeral. As long as I identify with my body, I must admit that this most terrible of events – the very snuffing out of my life – will come for me and will be real. Even once I know I am not the body, the event will still come – the body will be shattered, the life-breath withdrawn, and the dust returned to dust – but the death and funeral will be only those of my body, not of my self.

The Vedic sages say that by the process of bhakti, by devotional service to the Personality of Godhead, this understanding comes about. One becomes gradually enlightened and detached, freed from the illusion of identifying the body with the self, and therefore liberated from the miseries the body must endure, liberated even from death. All this becomes possible through hearing and chanting of transcendental sound, as found, for example (in the path I took), in the narrations of the Bhagavad-gītā and Śrīmad-Bhāgavatam and in the form of the mahā-mantra: Hare Krishna, Hare Krishna, Krishna Krishna, Hare Hare / Hare Rāma, Hare Rāma, Rāma Rāma, Hare Hare.

12:8–10: The epilogue begins

> [8]Vanity of vanities, says Qohelet; all is vanity. [9]Still left to say is that Qohelet was wise and he also taught the people knowledge. Having listened and deliberated, he set in order many proverbs. [10]Qohelet sought to find pleasing words, and he wrote words of truth honestly.

The frame narrator returns

A switch from first person to third, from words spoken by Qohelet to words spoken about him, signals the return of the "frame narrator," who so briefly introduced Qohelet at the start of the book. And the last words the narrator has us hear from Qohelet are those with which Qohelet began: "Vanity of vanities; all is vanity." The argument is sealed.

The narrator now proceeds with a few words, a very few words, about Qohelet himself. Beyond being wise, Qohelet also taught others. As befits a sage, he heard and pondered and put many sayings in order. The Bhagavad-gītā says that words in the mode of goodness are truthful, pleasing, beneficial, and not agitating to others. Yet the Vedic sages placed truth above pleasantness, and as we've seen in the strong words spoken by Vidura to the blind King Dhṛtarāṣṭra, for the sake of someone's benefit a sage would sometimes speak words pointedly meant to agitate, to shake someone up. "Strong words are sometimes needed to awaken a sleeping man." Qohelet too, it seems, though he sought to find pleasing words, was intent on speaking words of truth, honestly and plainly.

12:11–12: The words of the wise, the weary endlessness of books

[11] The words of the wise are like goads, and like nails well fastened by a shepherd are the sayings of the masters of collections. [12] And furthermore, my son, of these be wary. Of making many books there is no end, and much study is a weariness of the flesh.

Book knowledge and realized knowledge

Sages in general, "the masters of collected sayings," speak words with a sting to them, the narrator says, like the sting of a goad or a nail-studded prod. And then the narrator, a teacher himself, warns his son or student: "Of these be wary." Though again what *these* refers to may seem hazy, the narrator appears to want his son or student to be wary even about the sayings of the wise, Qohelet included. As Longman observes, "In essence, he says to his son, 'Qohelet's thinking is dangerous material – be careful.' "

And then there's a warning about books and study. There's no end to books! Making them, acquiring them, poring through them. One can get completely caught up in books, burdened down with books – and go nowhere.

I love to read books. I'd be safer in a brothel than a library. But shortly the shelves of books overwhelm me. How much can one read? Then too (and this is something that struck me in my youth), what is the use of all those words? People write and write and write, and what does it amount to, all that writing?

Perhaps the books that schoolchildren are made to read are the worst. Full of dates and names and facts, all ultimately useless. But are books for adults any better? The Bhāgavatam says, "In human society, those who are materially engrossed, blind to matters of ultimate truth, have hundreds and thousands of topics to hear about." All of no consequence.

What is the meaning of life? What is life for? We will not find out from mundane books, however fascinating or well written. We will not find out from bestsellers, nor from classic novels, nor from books of merely academic excellence, nor from the endless speculations of great philosophers, to say nothing of the supposedly spiritual books dishing out platitudes about self-fulfillment and sharing "powerful techniques and secrets" for achieving our "full potential."

Even immersing ourselves in books of authentic spiritual wisdom will finally prove inadequate. Both the Gītā and the Bhāgavatam say that finally we must come in touch with a self-realized person, a person who has deeply understood those books and is "a seer of the truth." By reading books we may get "book knowledge," knowledge in theory, but by submissively hearing from such a self-realized soul and by serving him, we ourselves can gain a deep and practical understanding of what we have read. It then becomes "realized knowledge," knowledge in fact, knowledge that frees one from material illusions and entanglements and revives one's eternal relationship with the Absolute, with Krishna.

When I first came in touch with Krishna consciousness, I appreciated also that although books like the Bhagavad-gītā had so much to offer, at the same time one could come directly in touch with Krishna by the simple hearing and chanting of the Hare Krishna mantra. Since Krishna, the Vedic teachers said, was identical with his name, one could come directly in touch with Krishna simply by chanting and hearing the mahā-mantra: Hare Krishna, Hare Krishna, Krishna Krishna, Hare Hare / Hare Rāma, Hare Rāma, Rāma Rāma, Hare Hare.

12:13–14: Closing words

¹³ The end of the matter; all has been heard. Fear God,
and keep his commandments, for this is the whole of
man. ¹⁴ For God will bring every deed into judgment,
even every hidden thing, whether good or evil.

Going further

Enough! The report of Qohelet's words ended with verse 8. In four verses more the narrator has spoken about Qohelet's endeavors, about the words of sages, and about books and the weariness of study.

Now we are given just a few more final words. Whether these are the words of the frame narrator or, as some commentators suggest, have been added by a later hand, their effect is the same. We have heard Qohelet's arguments, his discourses with his heart, his expressions of despair, his advice that we enjoy what little pleasure God has given us. And we have heard, from beginning to end, that all is vanity. Now, leaving Qohelet's doubts and arguments and unorthodox thoughts behind, the final verses give us a mainstream religious message: Fear God and follow his commandments.

Even today these words, as when I first read them, strike me as a non sequitur, an add-on, a conclusion Qohelet's arguments don't lead to. Are they consistent with Qohelet's thoughts? Perhaps. Qohelet has never denied God or the standard teaching that one should fear him and obey him. Yet Qohelet never goes so far as to say, "This is it, the conclusion, the wrap-up. This is where my thoughts all lead."

It may be that the narrator or scribe has added these words so he can bring us Qohelet's unorthodox and even dangerous thoughts and yet accommodate them within the boundaries of accepted religious doctrine. An orthodox rabbi can read the book and approvingly say, "It concludes with the teachings of the Law."

In any case, the book does conclude with these two imperatives – fear God and keep his commandments – and gives two reasons. First: "This is the whole of man." That is, this is the substance of what a human being is meant for: to revere God and obey him. And second: God will judge everything we do.

Qohelet himself, always debating, searching, subjecting all ideas to cross-examination in the light of his experience, never lent either reason his unwavering support. The book endorses them; Qohelet never conclusively goes that far.

The Vedic sages go farther – beyond fear and reverence, beyond obedience, beyond judgment for good and evil deeds, beyond one birth and one death and what for me was a distant and unknowable God. And they give their own reasons, to me more satisfying, reasons I have somewhat explored in this book.

When I'd first heard from Qohelet, there I was, sitting as a boy in a classroom and suddenly seeing, with instant clearness, the absurd futility of the world – and seeing amidst that futility the uselessness of my own life. I knew that Qohelet's despairing cry that all was vanity was true. And the pious wrap-up from the narrator didn't reach me, didn't click. Living in fear of God (whether it be reverence or dread or nervous apprehension) and following ten commandments (or however many) could not be the whole of my life.

And so I entered a malaise.

I soon dropped out of the meaningless life of home and school into another meaningless life, a life not only meaningless but confused and risky, messing with my own mind, looking forward to a changed world in which a fresh, exuberant generation of turned-on youth would crash down the barriers erected by previous generations, stuck in their old ways, and we would have freedom. "Rejoice, young man, while in your youth, and let your heart cheer you in the days of your youth. Follow the ways of your heart and the sight of your eyes." I did that. Or tried, because mixed with the joy and exuberance, underlying it – spoiling it – were pain and loneliness, because after you got high you came down again, because crashing down barriers didn't mean you were up, because freedom didn't get you anywhere, because I was still who I was, lost in New York City ... because it didn't work. And still I imagined it would.

And then came a mantra, and the Bhagavad-gītā, and a philosophy that validated Qohelet's cries of emptiness and absurdity but didn't pretend that meaning could be found through exuberant "enjoyment" or being happy with one's measly little portion and didn't jump from vanity to fear and commandments.

Meaning could be had when we realized our spiritual nature, when we gave up on chasing after wind and realized that what would make us happy was not our pathetic little portion of love and coins and hamburgers but our eternal loving relationship with the unlimited, with Krishna, a relationship always there but waiting to be rediscovered, a relationship with a sweetness that could be tasted even from the very start.

The way in, it seemed, was through the philosophy and through the mantra, not a secret mantra but the one the Vedic writings openly recommend as the mahā-mantra, the "great mantra" to free the mind from illusions and bring us back to our spiritual nature:

Hare Krishna, Hare Krishna, Krishna Krishna, Hare Hare
Hare Rāma, Hare Rāma, Rāma Rāma, Hare Hare.

Something I didn't mention when I told my story at the start of this book is that while still living at home as a young boy in New Jersey, sometime after Qohelet and my bar mitzvah and my encounter with the priest at the World's Fair, I found in a record store an album of Śrīla Prabhupāda chanting that Hare Krishna mantra with his earliest students in New York. An endorsement from Allen Ginsberg said, "It brings a state of ecstasy!" and so I paid a few dollars and took the record home.

On one side Śrīla Prabhupāda led a fifteen-minute session of chanting Hare Krishna. And on the other side, along with a Sanskrit prayer, he gave a five-minute talk explaining the chanting and the philosophy behind it. His Bengali accent made some of what he said hard for me to catch, but I got the gist of it: The chanting was not, he said, "an artificial imposition on the mind." Rather, it was a "transcendental vibration" that "springs automatically from the spiritual platform" to revive our original nature. So one didn't even need to understand the language of the mantra. It would work.

I played the chanting session several times over. I tried to let the sound fill my mind. And there at home in our den, listening to the chanting on our stereo system (otherwise used for folk music, Broadway musicals, Tchaikovsky, and the like), I got my first taste of the Hare Krishna mantra. I even began to chant along.

It's not that the heavens opened up and light burst forth and symphonic music thundered in crescendo. But in contrast to the drizzly grey feeling of emptiness brought on when I'd first heard from Qohelet at Temple Sinai, the chanting was joyful and seemed to give a glimpse of a higher reality, vibrant and alive, surpassing, as Śrīla Prabhupāda had said, the sensual, the mental, and the intellectual.

It was a small breakthrough, but I didn't stick with it. "A wise man's heart is at his right hand, but a fool's heart at his left." I turned left.

But the chanting had been added to the mix. The mantra was there, it could purify the mind, and now and then in the times that followed, as I drifted about, seeking but not finding, lost in Pittsburgh and New York, at Carnegie Tech and on the Lower East Side, in my brighter moments I used to chant it.

But it didn't take hold until one Sunday in New York when I wandered down Second Avenue, and eyed Śrīla Prabhupāda's makeshift storefront ashram from the other side of the street, and then crossed the street and peered through the window, and then screwed up a little courage and walked in.

The place was quiet. No one was there but a young American woman in a sari, sitting on the floor near the back of the room and stuffing envelopes. Covering the floor was an Oriental rug, adorning the walls were some paintings of scenes and figures I didn't understand, and near the front, as I walked in, were some books on an improvised shelf.

I was welcomed. Yes, I could look through a book. So I sat and read for a while, and wondered about the ashram and the scenes and figures I saw in the paintings, and recalled what I had read about the spartan austerity of the place.

Soon people began wandering in, the room began filling up, some devotees with a drum and small hand cymbals began chanting Hare Krishna in a pattern of call and response, and I joined in the chanting again, this time not alone at home but in the company of the devotees. The tempo picked up, the "transcendental vibration" carried us along, and as we chanted, one part of me felt happily drawn to what seemed like a higher level of consciousness – "a state of ecstasy" – while in the background another part stayed on guard, wondering whether I was truly coming closer to a higher reality, to spiritual truth, or instead just getting sucked into something.

The chanting was followed by a talk from the Bhagavad-gītā. And then came a feast of "spiritual food" so varied and tasty that Ginsberg's endorsement – "It brings a state of ecstasy!" – could equally have applied. (And there was no "second part of me" wondering about it.)

I came back the next morning, and the morning after that, and kept coming. I chanted with the devotees, attended their classes, shared in their simple weekday meals, and bombarded the devotees with questions. "If A, why B?" "If B, how C?" I was still the skeptic, looking to punch holes in the philosophy, to find its contradictions and bad assumptions, to find reasons to reject it, as I had rejected so many others. But Krishna spoke a philosophy I couldn't punch holes in, and his mantra was pleasing to the mind and heart. "In much wisdom is much vexation," Qohelet had said, "and he that increases knowledge increases sorrow." But in Krishna's wisdom I found – instead of vexation and sorrow – a path to enlightenment and joy. And two months later, when Śrīla Prabhupāda came to New York and I first met him and attended his chanting sessions and classes, I knew I had found an extraordinary saintly person, authentic, joyful, philosophically grounded, deep in spiritual realization, a person I could feel confident to follow.

I've followed him now for forty-five years, chanting Hare Krishna, reading his books, editing and publishing them, and speaking from them, doing my best to pass his teachings on to others.

There is nothing new under the sun. But the teachings of Krishna and the chanting of Hare Krishna, though old beyond old, seem to me always new and fresh. Whenever I pick up the Bhagavad-gītā, Krishna has more for me to think about – new lights, new angles of vision – and whenever I chant Hare Krishna, Krishna is right there in the sound, as if dancing on my tongue, making himself available as much as I am keen to reach him.

"Seek, and you shall find," a young priest once told me. And at just about that time, thousands of miles away, in a little holy town in India, an elderly teacher was about to venture forth to spread the message of

Krishna in America, and I was soon to meet him. And so it is that, crossing cultures, I made my way from where I was to where I am, from one way of life to another, and from Qohelet to Krishna.

Appendices

Guide to Hebrew pronunciation

Modern Hebrew speakers hailing from different communities differ somewhat in how they pronounce the language. Precisely how Hebrew was pronounced in biblical days is a matter of speculation.

Vanity Karma uses only a few Hebrew words. This guide explains only the letters needed for the words in the book.

The letter *ḥ* represents a raspy sound, somewhat like the *ch* in Ba*ch* or the *j* in the Spanish word *jota*.

The letter *q* is pronounced like the *k* in *k*ite.

The letter *r* is pronounced with something of a roll in the back of the throat. You can pronounce it as in English.

You can treat the other consonants as in English.

Now for the vowel sounds:

> *a* as in b*a*rn
> *i* as in b*i*t or b*ee*t
> *e* as in b*e*d
> *o* as in g*o*
> *u* as in r*u*le

To hear the Hebrew words and names used in *Vanity Karma*, or hear the entire text of Ecclesiastes recited in Hebrew, you can go to www.vanitykarma.com/resources/audio.

Guide to Sanskrit pronunciation

This book spells Sanskrit words according to a scholarly system that uses our familiar roman type to represent each Sanskrit letter. Because each letter in Sanskrit is pronounced only one way, this method serves as a reliable guide to how to pronounce each word.

No letter is silent. Every letter is pronounced. Double letters are pronounced twice (so, for example, the *m*'s in *sammata* are pronounced as in *some man*).

Sanskrit has short vowels and long. The long ones (the ones with the long mark) are held roughly twice as long.

a as in b*u*dge
ā as in mir*a*ge
i as in b*i*t
ī as in b*ee*t
u as in p*u*t
ū as in p*oo*l

These vowels too are treated as long:

e as in th*ey*
ai as in *ai*sle
o as in g*o*
au as in th*ou*

The *ṛ* is a vowel. You can pronounce it like the *ri* in *ri*m. Likewise, the vowel *ḷ* is like the *li* in *li*p. (There are also a long *ṝ* and long *ḹ*.)

The *ṁ* is a nasal sound like the *n* in the French word bo*n*.

An *ḥ* at the end of a word gives the final vowel a bit of an echo, so *aḥ* sounds like *aha*, and *iḥ* like *ihi*. In the midst of a word the effect is slight, and you can pretty much ignore it.

Now for the consonants.

c as in *c*iao or DaVin*c*i
g is always hard, as in *g*o
ñ as in ca*ny*on
y is always pronounced as in *y*ou.

With the letters *ṭ*, *ḍ*, and *ṇ*, the dot below indicates a kind of letter unfamiliar to English speakers. If you touch your tongue to the roof of your mouth, towards the back, you'll notice that what touches the roof is the underside of your tongue. For these three letters, you put your tongue there and then come out with the letter – *t*, *d*, or *n*, but pronounced in that unfamiliar way.

If you really want to get your Sanskrit right, you can practice that. Otherwise, you can ignore the dot and still get by.

Sanskrit has some letters pronounced with an extra puff of breath, like the breath we might use to blow out a candle (but without pursing our lips). In the combinations that follow, an *h* indicates that extra puff: *kh, gh, ch, jh, th, dh, ṭh, ḍh, ph, bh*.

(The *c* in *ch* is still the soft Italian *c*, as in *ciao*, but with that extra breath. And *th* is *t* plus breath, never as in *thin*.)

Another way to get across roughly what these extra-breath letters are like is to say that *kh* is pronounced as in "ki*ck h*ard," *gh* as in "di*g h*ard," and so on.

When not in the combinations above, *h* is pronounced as in *h*ome.

The letter *ṅ* is pronounced as in si*ng*.

The letter *ṣ* is pronounced as in *sh*ine.

The letter *ś* is pronounced as in the German word *s*prechen. (Or you can get by quite well enough by pronouncing it too as in *sh*ine.)

And just two more combinations: *jña* is pronounced *gya*, and *jñā* is pronounced *gyā*.

To hear all these letters pronounced – and hear the Sanskrit words and names most often used in *Vanity Karma* – you can go to www.vanitykarma.com/resources/audio.

Traditional authorities cited: a brief guide

Throughout *Vanity Karma* I refer to various traditional authorities, Jewish, Christian, and Vedic. Here I briefly identify them.

Traditional Jewish authorities

TORAH ("The Law"). The Tanakh – the canonical Hebrew Bible – has three divisions: the Law (Torah), the Prophets (Nevi'im), and the Writings (Ketuvim). The Torah consists of the first five biblical books – Genesis and so on – although sometimes the term *Torah* is used more broadly to refer to the entire Tanakh. Ecclesiastes belongs to the Ketuvim.

TALMUD ("Teaching" or "Learning"). A compilation of oral law and rabbinical discussions written down in final form sometime before 700 CE. There are two Talmuds – the Jerusalem (also called Palestinian) and the Babylonian. The Babylonian is the one usually referred to.

MIDRASH ("Study" or "Exposition"). The midrashim, as they are known in the plural, are biblical commentaries formed of the collected opinions of distinguished rabbis. For Ecclesiastes most of the relevant midrashim were compiled in the ninth or tenth century CE in the Qohelet Midrash Rabbah.

SEPTUAGINT. The Greek translation of the Hebrew Bible, written for the benefit of Greek-speaking Jews and most likely completed sometime during the first century.

TARGUM. An ancient translation of the Hebrew Bible into Aramaic, a sister language. The Targum for Ecclesiastes takes the form of an elaborate paraphrase, often interpreting the text to reconcile it with traditionally accepted teachings.

SA'ADIA GAON (Sa'adia ben Yosef Gaon). 882–942,
Egypt, Palestine, Babylonia

TOVIAH (Toviah ben Eliezer). 1036–1108, Greece and Belgium

RASHI (R. Solomon ben Issac). 1040–1105, France

QARA (Yosef ben Simeon Qara). ca. 1060–1130, France

IBN EZRA (Abraham ibn Ezra). 1089–1164, mainly Spain

RASHBAM (R. Samuel ben Meir). twelfth century, France

DI TRANI (Isaiah ben Mali di Trani). ca. 1180 – ca. 1250, Italy

ALBO (Yosef Albo). ca. 1380 – ca. 1444, Spain

SFORNO (Obadiah ben Jacob Sforno). ca. 1470 – ca. 1550, Italy

IBN YAḤYA (Yosef ben David ibn Yaḥya). 1494–1534, Italy

ALSHEIKH (Moshe ben Ḥayyim Alsheikh). 1508–1601, Israel

ALTSCHULER (Yeḥiel Hillel ben David Altschuler).

Eighteenth century, Prague

"THE ḤIDAH" (Ḥayyim Yosef David Azulai). 1724–1806,
mainly Israel and Italy

Traditional Christian authorities

Of the various traditional Christian commentators, I mention only Martin Luther (1483–1546), Hugo Grotius (1583–1645), and Jerome (ca. 342–420). Jerome, apart from his commentary on Ecclesiastes and his other works, was the main author of the Vulgate, the Latin translation of the Bible

Traditional Vedic authorities

VEDAS. The four vast "books of knowledge," the original Sanskrit sacred texts. Traditionally they are held to have originated from God himself, from whom they are given to sages and passed down in an oral tradition until written down by the sage Vyāsa. Secular scholars say that the oldest of the Vedic hymns date back to 1500 BCE.

UPANIṢADS. The Sanskrit texts, traditionally considered part of the Vedas, that deal with the nature of the Absolute, the relationship of the Absolute with the universe and with the individual self, and how one can attain the Absolute.

MANU-SAṀHITĀ. "The laws of Manu." One of the *dharma-śāstras*, or books that set forth norms of conduct.

VEDĀNTA-SŪTRAS. A work that presents the conclusion (*anta*) of the Upaniṣads in 555 aphorisms (*sūtras*).

PURĀṆAS. "The ancient works." Eighteen supplements to the Vedas in the form of historical narrations.

MAHĀBHĀRATA. One of the two great *itihāsas*, or epic histories. At more than 75,000 verses, it is the longest poem in the world, roughly seven times as long as the Iliad and the Odyssey combined.

BHAGAVAD-GĪTĀ. The eighteen chapters of the Mahābhārata that impart spiritual wisdom in the form of a 700-verse dialogue between Śrī Krishna and Arjuna.

ŚRĪMAD-BHĀGAVATAM. The Bhāgavata Purāṇa, regarded in the Krishna tradition as the most important of the Purāṇas and as "the ripe fruit of the tree of Vedic knowledge."

CĀṆAKYA-NĪTI-ŚĀSTRA. A collection of moral aphorisms popularly attributed to the royal advisor Cāṇakya (370–283 BCE). It exists in various versions.

HITOPADEŚA. A Sanskrit book of fables giving moral precepts that most likely dates back to the twelfth century.

BRAHMA-SAṀHITĀ. A book in praise of Śrī Krishna of which a chapter was discovered in the sixteenth century by Śrī Caitanya (1486–1534).

BHAKTI-RASĀMṚTA-SINDHU. A Sanskrit work systematically explaining bhakti, devotional service to Krishna, written in roughly 1552 by Śrīla Rūpa Gosvāmī (1489–1564), a direct follower of Śrī Caitanya.

UPADEŚĀMṚTA. A brief guide to devotional service also written by Śrīla Rūpa Gosvāmī.

CAITANYA-CARITĀMṚTA. A biography of Śrī Caitanya Mahāprabhu written in Bengali by Kṛṣṇadāsa Kavirāja Gosvāmī (1496?–?) and completed in 1615. Apart from telling the events of Śrī Caitanya's life, it serves as a source for advanced spiritual teachings.

GOVINDA-BHĀṢYA. The commentary on the Vedānta-sūtras written by Śrīla Baladeva Vidyābhūṣaṇa (eighteenth century) in 1718.

About the Hebrew text and its English rendering

The Hebrew text

When I began my research for *Vanity Karma*, I naively assumed that the Hebrew text for Ecclesiastes was a long-settled affair. The King James Version and the version I first read as a boy follow the Masoretic text, the Hebrew version diligently compiled by rabbis sometime during the second century (or even earlier) and followed ever since. But scholars grappling with Ecclesiastes have often been at odds with one or another reading of the Masoretic text.

Many modern scholars, perhaps most, believe that at least one verse or another is an added extra, an interpolation. At least one scholar, back in the early twentieth century, declared that the interpolations add up to more than twenty-five percent and that to get to the "real" book we must lop them off. Other scholars have agreed that some verses have been sprinkled in, but have largely disagreed about which ones. One ingenious theory tries to persuade us that the original pages of the book were reshuffled and tries to show us what the true order should be.

More recent scholars tend to accept the integrity of the Hebrew text but disagree about finer points. In many places the grammar or meaning of the text is puzzling, often extremely so, and to resolve a puzzle a scholar may suggest that a scribe erred in copying, for example by mistaking one letter for another, or by mistakenly transposing or repeating letters, or by leaving something out that ought to have been kept in. Or now and again a scholar will suggest that a verse, or part of one, has had its position shifted.

And one special feature of Hebrew introduces further ambiguity. The ancient authors wrote only in consonants, leaving the reader to supply the vowels. Which vowels are to be supplied can sometimes be a question, and such were the questions the Masoretic rabbis tried to resolve. Thus the Masoretic text came to include the vowels. But are the vowels supplied the right ones? The vowels appear as "points" – dots and strokes – added to the consonants, and a scholar may suggest that for a proper reading a word here or there should be "repointed," so that we wind up with different vowels and so a different word.

All this considered, modern scholars generally agree that the Hebrew text for the book has come down to us in good shape.

The English rendering

This brings us, of course, to questions concerning translation. In a given verse, does *ruah*, for example, mean "breath," "wind," "appetite," or "throat"? Any of these may be possible, just as in English a *block* might mean a cube of wood for a child to play with, a barrier that keeps us from getting somewhere or remembering something, or the portion of a street on which we live.

Scholars, accordingly, have translated Ecclesiastes in various ways, sometimes vigorously debating the best way to read a given passage. But despite the best scholarly efforts, some passages remain almost hopelessly obscure, and translators have just had to render them obscurely or else give a best shot, guessing at a most probable meaning.

What of the version you find in *Vanity Karma*?

The English text of Ecclesiastes used in this book is my own updated version of the translation published in 1917 by the Jewish Publication Society. Sometimes I have picked up words that other translations use. Sometimes, taking note of matters clarified by modern scholarly discussions, I have switched to an alternative meaning preferred by one or another learned commentator. And I have made other small adjustments. In all cases, I made sure that whatever choices I made that affected meaning were supported by one or more respected mainstream scholars.

I have chunked the text into groups of verses for the sake of convenience. My groupings reflect no commitment to any theory about the structure of the book. The book's most obvious structural feature – its division into chapters – was first brought into it only during the Middle Ages, some thousand or more years after the book was written. Originally the book had no chapters; it was one continuous text.

With some commentaries I've read, I've felt bothered by not being able to find the English text of Ecclesiastes all in one place. So here you'll find it, in the pages that follow.

Ecclesiastes:
the full English text

1

¹The words of Qohelet, the son of David, king in Jerusalem.

²Vanity of vanities, says Qohelet. Vanity of vanities, all is vanity! ³What profit does a man have from all his labor at which he labors under the sun? ⁴One generation passes away, and another generation comes, and the earth abides forever. ⁵The sun also rises, and the sun goes down, and hastens to his place where he arises. ⁶The wind goes toward the south, and it circles to the north; round and round goes the wind, and on its circuits the wind returns. ⁷All the rivers run into the sea, yet the sea is not full; to the place where the rivers go, there they go again. ⁸All things toil to weariness, more than man can express; the eye is not satisfied with seeing, nor the ear filled with hearing. ⁹That which has been is that which will be, and that which has been done is that which will be done, and there is nothing new under the sun. ¹⁰Is there a thing of which it might be said, "See, this is new"? It has already been, in the ages before us. ¹¹There is no remembrance of the people of former times; nor of the people of times yet to come will there be any remembrance among those who come after.

¹²I, Qohelet, have been king over Israel in Jerusalem. ¹³And I set my heart to seek and to search out by wisdom all that is done under heaven. It is a sore task that God has given to men to be busy with. ¹⁴I have seen all the works that are done under the sun; and, indeed, all is vanity and a chasing after wind. ¹⁵That which is crooked cannot be made straight, and that which is wanting cannot be counted. ¹⁶I spoke with my heart, saying, "Just see, I have gotten great wisdom, more also than all who

were before me over Jerusalem." Indeed, my heart had great experience of wisdom and knowledge. [17] And I applied my heart to know wisdom, and to know madness and folly. I perceived that this also was a chasing after wind. [18] For in much wisdom is much vexation, and he that increases knowledge increases sorrow.

2

[1] I said in my heart, "Come now, let me make you try pleasure. Enjoy what is good!" And – just see! – this also was vanity. [2] I said of laughter "It is mad" and of pleasure "What does it accomplish?" [3] I searched in my heart how to ply my body with wine – my heart still guiding me with wisdom – and how to lay hold on folly, till I might see what is best for men to do under heaven the few days of their life.

[4] I made great works: I built myself houses; I planted myself vineyards. [5] I made myself gardens and parks, and I planted trees in them of all kinds of fruit. [6] I made myself pools from which to water the forests springing up with trees. [7] I bought men and women as servants, and had servants born in my house. I also had great possessions of herds and flocks, more than all who were before me in Jerusalem. [8] I also gathered myself silver and gold, and the treasures of kings and provinces. I got myself singers, both men and women, and many concubines, the delights of men.

[9] So I became great and flourished more than all who were before me in Jerusalem. And also my wisdom stood with me. [10] Nothing that my eyes desired did I keep from them, nor did I withhold my heart from any joy, for my heart had joy in all my labor and this was my portion from all my labor. [11] Then I turned to look upon all the works that my hands had done, and on the labor I had labored to do. And – just see! – all was vanity and a chasing after wind, and there was no profit under the sun.

[12] And I turned to look upon wisdom, and madness and folly. For what can the man do who comes after the king? Just that which has already been done. [13] Then I saw that wisdom excels folly as much as light excels darkness. [14] The wise man's eyes are in his head, but the fool walks in darkness. And I also perceived that one event happens to

them all. ¹⁵ Then I said in my heart, "As it happens to the fool, so will it happen even to me. And why then have I become so very wise?" Then I said in my heart that this also is vanity. ¹⁶ For there is no lasting remembrance of the wise man any more than of the fool; in the days to come, all will have long been forgotten. And how must the wise man die just like the fool!

¹⁷ So I hated life because the work that is done under the sun was grievous to me; for all is vanity and a chasing after wind. ¹⁸ And I hated the fruit of all my labor at which I had labored under the sun, because I must leave it to the man who will be after me. ¹⁹ And who knows whether he will be a wise man or a fool? Yet he will have power over all for which I have labored, and in which I have shown myself wise under the sun. This also is vanity.

²⁰ Therefore I turned my heart to despair over all the labor at which I had labored under the sun. ²¹ For there is a man whose labor is with wisdom, and with knowledge, and with skill, yet to a man who has not labored at it he must leave his portion. This also is vanity and a great evil. ²² For what does a man have from all his labor, and from the striving of his heart, at which he labors under the sun? ²³ For all his days are painful, and his occupation vexing; even at night his heart has no rest. This also is vanity.

²⁴ There is nothing better for a man than that he should eat and drink and let himself enjoy pleasure for his labor. This also, I saw, is from the hand of God. ²⁵ For who will eat, or who will enjoy, apart from him? ²⁶ For to the man who pleases him God gives wisdom and knowledge and joy, but to the one who is offensive he gives the task of gathering and heaping up, only to give to one who pleases God. This also is vanity and a chasing after wind.

3

¹ To every thing there is a season,
  and a time to every purpose under heaven:
² A time to be born, and a time to die;
  a time to plant, and a time to pluck up what is planted;
³ A time to kill, and a time to heal;

a time to break down, and a time to build up;

[4] A time to weep, and a time to laugh;

a time to mourn, and a time to dance;

[5] A time to cast away stones, and a time to gather stones together;

a time to embrace, and a time to refrain from embracing;

[6] A time to seek, and a time to lose;

a time to keep, and a time to cast away;

[7] A time to rend, and a time to sew;

a time to keep silence, and a time to speak;

[8] A time to love, and a time to hate;

a time for war, and a time for peace.

[9] What profit has he who works in that in which he labors? [10] I have seen the travail that God has given man to be busy with. [11] He has made everything fitting for its time. He has also set the world in their hearts, yet they cannot find out the work that God has done from the beginning to the end.

[12] I know that there is nothing better for them than to rejoice and to get pleasure so long as they live. [13] And also for any man to eat and drink and enjoy pleasure in all his labor – this is a gift of God.

[14] I know that whatever God does will be forever; nothing can be added to it, nor anything taken from it. And God has so made it so that men should fear him. [15] That which is has been long ago, and that which is to be has already been; and God seeks that which is pursued.

[16] And moreover I saw under the sun: There in the place of justice, wickedness! In the place of righteousness, wickedness there! [17] I said in my heart, "The righteous and the wicked, God will judge, for there is a time there for every purpose and for every work." [18] I said in my heart in regard to men, God is testing them so they may see that they are but beasts. [19] For what happens to men and what happens to beasts are the same. As the one dies, so dies the other; they all have one breath, and man has no advantage above the beast, for all is vanity. [20] All go to one place; all are from the dust, and to dust all return. [21] Who knows whether the spirit of man goes upward and the spirit of the beast goes downward to the earth? [22] And so I perceived that there is nothing better than that a man should rejoice in his works, for that is his portion. For who will bring him to see what will be after him?

4

[1] Then I turned and considered all the oppressions that are done under the sun. And oh, the tears of the oppressed, and they had no one to comfort them! And on the side of their oppressors there was power – and no one to comfort them. [2] So I declared that the dead, since already dead, are better off than the living who are still alive. [3] But better than both is he who has not yet been, who has not seen the evil work that is done under the sun.

[4] Again, I saw that all labor and all excelling in work arise from a man's rivalry with his neighbor. This also is vanity and a chasing after wind. [5] The fool folds his hands and eats his own flesh. [6] Better is a handful of quietness than both hands full of labor and a chasing after wind.

[7] Then I turned and saw another vanity under the sun. [8] There is one who is alone, and he has no one else; he has neither son nor brother. Yet there is no end to all his labor, nor is his eye satisfied with riches: "And for whom then do I labor and deprive myself of pleasure?" This also is vanity – a grievous business.

[9] Two are better than one because they have a good reward for their labor. [10] For if they fall, the one will lift up his fellow; but woe to him who is alone when he falls, and has no one to lift him up. [11] Again, if two lie together, then they have warmth; but how can one be warm alone? [12] And though an attacker might prevail against one man alone, two will withstand him. And a threefold cord is not quickly broken.

[13] Better a poor but wise youth than an old but foolish king who no longer knows how to receive advice. [14] For out of prison he [the youth] came forth to be king, though in his reign too a poor man was born. [15] I saw that all the living who walk under the sun were with the second youth, who was to succeed him. [16] There was no end to all the people, all those whom he led; yet those who come later will not rejoice in him. Surely this also is vanity and a chasing after wind.

5

[1] Watch your step when you go to the house of God. Drawing near to listen is better than offering the sacrifice of fools, for they do not know

that they do evil. [2] Do not be rash with your mouth, and let your heart not be hasty to utter a word before God, for God is in heaven and you are on earth. Therefore let your words be few. [3] For dreams come with many doings, and a fool's voice with many words. [4] When you make a vow to God, do not be slack to pay it, for he has no pleasure in fools. Pay what you vow. [5] Better for you not to vow than to vow and not pay. [6] Do not let your mouth bring you into sin, and do not say before the messenger that it was an error. Why should God be angry at your voice and destroy the work of your hands? [7] For through a multitude of dreams and vanities there are also many words; but fear God.

[8] If you see in the state the oppression of the poor and the perversion of justice and right, do not be astonished at the matter, for the high official is watched by one higher and there are still higher ones over them. [9] But the profit for a land in every way is a king who makes himself a servant to the field.

[10] He who loves silver will not be satisfied with silver, nor he who loves wealth, with gain. This also is vanity. [11] When goods increase, those who eat them increase, and what advantage has their owner but to see those goods with his eyes? [12] Sweet is the sleep of a laboring man, whether he eats little or much; but the overfullness of the rich man will not allow him to sleep.

[13] There is a grievous evil I have seen under the sun: riches are kept by their owner to his hurt, [14] and those riches perish by a bad venture; and though he has begotten a son, there is nothing in his hand. [15] As he came forth of his mother's womb, so again will he go, naked as he came, and will take nothing for his labor that he may carry away in his hand. [16] And this also is a grievous evil, that just as he came, so will he go; and what profit does he have that he should labor for the wind? [17] All his days also he eats in darkness, and he has much vexation and sickness and wrath.

[18] This is what I have seen to be good: It is fitting for one to eat and to drink and to enjoy pleasure for all his labor at which he labors under the sun all the few days of the life God has given him, for this is his portion. [19] Every man also to whom God has given riches and property and the power to enjoy them, and to take his portion and rejoice in his labor – this is a gift of God. [20] For he will scarcely mark the days of his life, for God keeps him occupied with the joy of his heart.

6

[1] There is an evil I have seen under the sun, and it lies heavy upon men: [2] a man to whom God gives riches, property, and honor, so that he lacks nothing for himself of all he may desire, yet God gives him no power to enjoy it, but a stranger enjoys it. This is vanity, and it is an evil disease. [3] If a man begets a hundred children and lives many years, so that the days of his years are many, but his desire to enjoy good things is not fulfilled and moreover he has no burial, I say that a stillborn child is better than he. [4] For it comes in vanity and departs into darkness and its name is covered with darkness; [5] moreover, it has not seen the sun nor known anything; yet it has more rest than he. [6] Indeed, though he live a thousand years twice told, if he enjoys no good – do not all go to one place? [7] All a man's labor is for his mouth, and yet his appetite is not satisfied. [8] For what advantage does the wise have over the fool? Or what advantage the poor man in knowing how to conduct himself before the living? [9] Better is the seeing of the eyes than the wandering of desire. This also is vanity and a chasing after wind.

[10] Whatever has come to be, its name was already given; and what man is, is foreknown; nor can man contend with him who is mightier than he. [11] The more words, the more vanity. How then is man the better? [12] For who knows what is good for man in his life, all the days of his vain life, which he spends like a shadow? For who can tell a man what will be after him under the sun?

7

[1] A good name is better than precious oil, and the day of death than the day of one's birth. [2] Better to go to the house of mourning than to go to the house of feasting, for that is the end of all men, and the living should take it to heart. [3] Vexation is better than laughter, for with a bad face the heart is made better. [4] The heart of the wise is in the house of mourning but the heart of fools in the house of mirth. [5] Better to hear the rebuke of a wise man than to hear the song of fools. [6] For as the crackling of thorns under a pot, so is the laughter of the fool. This also is vanity.

[7] Surely oppression turns a wise man into a fool, and a bribe corrupts the heart. [8] Better is the end of a thing than its beginning, and better the patient in spirit than the proud. [9] Do not be hasty in your spirit to be angry, for anger rests in the bosom of fools. [10] Do not say, "How was it that the former days were better than these?" for it is not out of wisdom that you ask this.

[11] Wisdom is good with an inheritance – indeed, a profit to those who see the sun. [12] For wisdom is a refuge, even as money is a refuge; but the advantage of knowledge is that wisdom preserves the life of him who has it.

[13] Consider the work of God, for who can make straight what he has made crooked? [14] In the day of prosperity be joyful, and in the day of adversity consider: God has made the one as well as the other, so that man should find out nothing that will come after him.

[15] Both I have seen in the vain days of my life: there is a righteous man who perishes in his righteousness, and there is a wicked man who prolongs his life in his evildoing.

[16] Do not be righteous overmuch, nor make yourself overwise; why should you ruin yourself? [17] Do not be overly wicked, nor be foolish; why should you die before your time? [18] It is good that you should take hold of the one while not letting go of the other, for he that fears God will succeed with both. [19] Wisdom gives strength to the wise more than ten mighty men who are in a city. [20] Surely there is not a righteous man on earth who does good and does not sin. [21] And do not give heed to all words that are spoken, lest you hear your servant revile you; [22] for your own heart knows that you yourself have likewise many times reviled others.

[23] All this have I tested by wisdom. I said, "I shall be wise," but it was far from me. [24] Far away is that which is, and deep, very deep. Who can find it out?

[25] I turned, I and my heart, to know and to search out and to seek wisdom and the sum of things, and to know the wickedness of folly and the foolishness of madness.

[26] And more bitter than death I found woman, whose heart is snares and nets, whose hands are chains. He with whom God is pleased will escape her, but he who goes wrong will be taken by her. [27] Just see, says Qohelet, this I have found, adding one thing to another to find the sum,

[28]which my soul sought again and again but I have not found. One man among a thousand I have found, but a woman among all those I have not found. [29]Only, see this that I have found, that God made man upright but they have sought out many inventions.

8

[1]Who is like the wise man? And who knows the interpretation of a thing? Wisdom makes a man's face shine, and the hardness of his face is changed.

[2]Keep the king's command, in the manner of an oath to God. [3]Do not be hasty to go out of his presence, and do not persist in an evil thing, for he does whatsoever pleases him. [4]For the king's word has power, and who may say to him, "What are you doing?"

[5]Whoever obeys the command will come to no harm, and a wise man's heart discerns the time and way. [6]For to every matter there is a time and a way. Truly the troubles of man are heavy upon him, [7]For he does not know what is to be, for who can tell him when it will be? [8]There is no man who has power over the wind to restrain the wind, nor power over the day of death, and there is no discharge from war, nor can wickedness save the one who has it. [9]All this I saw as I applied my heart to all that is done under the sun, when one man has power over another to the other's hurt.

[10]Then I saw the wicked buried, and they entered into their rest; but they who had done right went away from the holy place and were forgotten in the city. This also is vanity.

[11]Because a sentence against an evil deed is not executed speedily, the heart of man is fully set to do evil. [12]For a sinner does evil a hundred times and prolongs his days. And I also know that it will be well with those who fear God, who fear before him, [13]but it will not be well with the wicked man, nor will he prolong his days, which are like a shadow, because he does not fear before God.

[14]There is a vanity which takes place upon the earth: that there are righteous men to whom things happen that are fit for the acts of the wicked; again, there are wicked men to whom things happen that are fit for the acts of the righteous. I said that this also is vanity.

[15] So I commended enjoyment, for a man has no better thing under the sun than to eat and to drink and to be merry, for this should accompany him in his labor all the days of the life that God has given him under the sun.

[16] When I applied my heart to know wisdom, and to see the business that is done upon the earth – for neither day nor night do men's eyes see sleep – [17] then I saw all the work of God, that man cannot find out the work that is done under the sun. Though a man labor to seek it out, he will not find it. And even though a wise man claims to know, he will not be able to find it out.

9

[1] Indeed, all this I laid to my heart, and I examined all this: that the righteous and the wise and their works are in the hand of God. Whether it be love or hatred, man does not know; all is before them. [2] All things come alike to all; there is one event to the righteous and to the wicked, to the clean and to the unclean, to him who sacrifices and to him who does not; as it is for the good, so it is for the sinner, and for him who swears as for him who fears to swear. [3] This is an evil in all that is done under the sun, that there is one event for all. Moreover, the hearts of men are full of evil, and madness is in their hearts while they live, and after that – to the dead!

[4] For him who is joined to all the living there is hope, for a living dog is better off than a dead lion. [5] For the living know that they will die, but the dead do not know anything, nor do they any longer have any reward, and even the memory of them is forgotten. [6] Their love, their hatred, and their envy have already perished; nor do they have a portion any longer in anything done under the sun.

[7] Go your way, eat your bread with joy, and drink your wine with a merry heart, for God has already approved what you do. [8] Let your garments be always white, and let oil not be lacking for your head. [9] Live joyfully with the woman you love all the days of your life of vanity, which he has given you under the sun, all the days of your vanity; for that is your portion in life, and in your toil at which you labor under the sun. [10] Whatever your hand finds to do, do with your strength, for

there is no work, nor thought, nor knowledge, nor wisdom in Sheol, to which you are going. [11] I turned and saw under the sun that the race is not to the swift, nor the battle to the strong, nor yet bread to the wise, nor yet riches to men of understanding, nor yet favor to men of skill; but time and chance happen to them all. [12] Indeed, man does not know his time; like fish taken in an evil net, and like birds caught in a snare, even so are men snared in an evil time, when it falls suddenly upon them.

[13] This also have I seen as an example of wisdom under the sun, and it seemed great to me: [14] There was a little city, and few men within it; and there came a great king against it, and surrounded it, and built great siegeworks against it. [15] Now there was found in it a man poor but wise, and he by his wisdom delivered the city. Yet no one remembered that poor man. [16] Then I said, "Wisdom is better than strength; but the poor man's wisdom is despised, and his words are not heard."

[17] The quiet words of the wise are more to be heeded than the shouts of a ruler among fools. [18] Wisdom is better than weapons of war, but one bungler destroys much good.

10

[1] A dead fly makes the perfumer's ointment stink; so does a little folly outweigh wisdom and honor. [2] A wise man's heart is at his right hand, but a fool's heart at his left. [3] And even when a fool walks by the way, he lacks sense, and he says to everyone that he is a fool.

[4] If the anger of the ruler rises up against you, do not leave your place, for gentleness allays great offenses. [5] There is an evil I have seen under the sun, an error indeed that proceeds from the ruler: [6] Folly is set on great heights, and the rich sit in a low place. [7] I have seen slaves upon horses, and princes walking on foot like slaves.

[8] He who digs a pit may fall into it, and he who breaks through a wall may be bitten by a snake. [9] He who quarries stones may be hurt by them, and he who splits logs may be endangered by them. [10] If the iron is blunt and one does not whet the edge, then he must exert more strength; but wisdom helps one succeed. [11] If the snake bites before it is charmed, there is no advantage in a charmer.

¹²The words of a wise man's mouth win favor, but the lips of a fool will swallow him. ¹³The words of his mouth begin in foolishness, and his talk ends in grievous madness. ¹⁴A fool also multiplies words; yet a man does not know what will be, and who can tell him what will happen after him? ¹⁵The labor of a fool wears him out, for he does not even know how to go to town.

¹⁶Woe to you, O land, when your king is a lackey and your princes feast in the morning! ¹⁷Happy are you, O land, when your king is a free man and your princes eat at the proper time, for strength and not for drunkenness!

¹⁸Through laziness the rafters sag, and through idleness of the hands the house leaks. ¹⁹A feast is made for laughter, and wine makes life glad, and money answers everything.

²⁰Do not curse the king, even in your thoughts, and do not curse the rich, even in your bedroom, for a bird of the air may carry your voice, or some winged creature may tell the matter.

11

¹Cast your bread upon the waters, for you will find it after many days. ²Give a portion to seven people – indeed, even to eight – for you do not know what evil will be upon the land.

³If the clouds are full, they will empty rain upon the earth, and whether a tree falls to the south or to the north, in the place where the tree falls, there will it be. ⁴He who watches the wind will not sow, and he who gazes at the clouds will not reap. ⁵Just as you do not know what is the way of the wind, nor how the bones are formed in the mother's womb, so you do not know the work of God, who does all things. ⁶In the morning sow your seed, and in the evening do not withhold your hand; for you do not know which will prosper, whether this or that, or whether both alike will be good.

⁷Sweet is the light, and pleasant it is for the eyes to behold the sun. ⁸Indeed, even if a man live many years, let him rejoice in them all, yet keep in mind the days of darkness, for they will be many. All that comes is vanity.

⁹Rejoice, young man, while in your youth, and let your heart cheer

you in the days of your youth. Follow the ways of your heart and the sight of your eyes. But know that for all these things God will bring you into judgment. [10] Therefore put away vexation from your heart, and turn away pain from your flesh; for youth and its black hair are vanity.

12

[1] Remember your creator in the days of your youth, before the evil days come and the years draw near when you will say "I have no pleasure in them"; [2] before the sun and the light and the moon and the stars grow dark and the clouds return after the rain; [3] in the day when the keepers of the house tremble, and the strong men are bent, and the women who grind cease because they are few, and those that look out grow dark in the windows; [4] when the doors in the street are shut, and the sound of the grinding is low, and one starts up at the voice of a bird, and all the daughters of song are brought low; [5] when one is afraid of heights, and terrors are in the road; and the almond tree blossoms, and the locust drags itself along, and the caperberry fails; because a man goes to his eternal home, and the mourners go about the streets; [6] before the silver cord is snapped, and the golden bowl is shattered, and the pitcher is broken at the fountain, and the wheel falls shattered into the pit, [7] and the dust returns to the earth as it was, and the breath returns to God who gave it.

[8] Vanity of vanities, says Qohelet; all is vanity. [9] Still left to say is that Qohelet was wise and he also taught the people knowledge. Having listened and deliberated, he set in order many proverbs. [10] Qohelet sought to find pleasing words, and he wrote words of truth honestly.

[11] The words of the wise are like goads, and like nails well fastened by a shepherd are the sayings of the masters of collections. [12] And furthermore, my son, of these be wary. Of making many books there is no end, and much study is a weariness of the flesh.

[13] The end of the matter; all has been heard. Fear God, and keep his commandments, for this is the whole of man. [14] For God will bring every deed into judgment, even every hidden thing, whether good or evil.

Endnotes

*"He who cites a matter in the name of him who said it
brings redemption to the world."*

Rabbinic dictum, cited by Gordis (1968, *viii–ix*)

In these endnotes I mainly identify sources I have drawn upon, and to
which I am indebted. Where I cite multiple authorities, I do so for the
sake of additional confirmation or because I no longer recall which of
them I first relied on.

Apart from the works of Fox, I cite book-length commentaries by the
author's surname alone. *Fox* alone refers to Fox 2010. *OED* refers to the
Oxford English Dictionary, 2nd edition (CD-ROM, version 3.0). *MWD*
refers to the Monier-Williams Sanskrit-English Dictionary, *Strong* to
Strong's Hebrew Bible Dictionary (Sword module version 1.2).

Editions of the Bible are abbreviated thus: *JPS 1917*, Jewish Publication Society 1917 edition; *KJV*, King James Version; *NIV*, New
International Version; *NRSV*, New Revised Standard Version.

Gītā refers to the Bhagavad-gītā, *Bhāgavatam* to the Śrīmad-Bhāgavatam.
References to *Bhagavad-gītā As It Is* and to Gītā "purports" are to Bhaktivedanta Swami [1972] 1983. Because the *Cāṇakya-nīti-śāstra* exists in
many differing editions, for its verses I give the Sanskrit text rather
than verse numbers.

Introduction

A first encounter

"FOR IN MUCH KNOWLEDGE IS MUCH GRIEF." Eccl. 1:18 (KJV)

"LET US HEAR THE CONCLUSION." Eccl. 12:13

LYSOL A brand of disinfectant, like Dettol in Britain.

1964 WORLD'S FAIR. My memories were refreshed and corrected by a website dedicated to the fair: www.nywf64.com.

PROGRESSLAND: MAN, WIFE, AND DOG. Other family members may have been onstage as well, but man, wife, and dog are the ones I remember.

"SEEK, AND YOU SHALL FIND." Matthew 7:7 and Luke 11:9.

HUNDREDS OF THOUSANDS, PERHAPS MILLIONS, IN THE COUNTERCULTURE. Timothy Miller, an academic expert on the 1960s counterculture, says that his research indicates that hundreds of thousands is a conservative estimate and that the numbers "could well run into the millions." (Timothy Miller, personal communication, May 22, 2014)

Crossing cultures

A CROSS-CULTURAL COMMENTARY. Though I haven't seen any commentaries on Vedic writings from an explicitly Jewish perspective, several Christian authors have explored and commented on the Bhagavad-gītā. (For example, see Griffiths 1987 and Cornille 2006.) And Francis X. Clooney has published sensitive Christian readings of Indian devotional texts. Far more rarely, however, have followers of Eastern traditions ventured more than passing comments on a book of the Bible, and still more rarely on Ecclesiastes. Two scholarly articles I am aware of (Heard 1996 and Dobe 1997) bring Ecclesiastes into dialogue with the Tao Te Ching. Another (Jarick 2000) looks at passages in Ecclesiastes using concepts from the

I Ching. These articles, however, are relatively short excursions, and the authors are not dedicated followers of the Chinese texts they employ. A journal article by Seree Lorgunpai (1994) explores the common ground between Ecclesiastes and Thai Buddhism, and one by Daniel F. Polish (1998) offers the teachings of the Buddha as a lens for better understanding Qohelet. But again these two excursions are brief, and neither author is a Buddhist. Till now, no work I know of has read Ecclesiastes through the lens of the Bhagavad-gītā and related works from the tradition of Krishna bhakti.

In "Chinese Wisdom and Biblical Revelation" (an excursus in Ogden, 233–39), Graham Ogden offers a thoughtful discussion of how God makes truth known through the wisdom traditions of different cultures.

THE NEO-ROMANTIC 1960s. Camille Paglia (2003, 58, 62) has commented on neo-Romantic features of the era.

A LONG SUCCESSION OF TEACHERS. The succession is listed at the end of the introduction to Bhagavad-gītā As It Is.

ŚRĪ CAITANYA AND GAUḌĪYA VAIṢṆAVISM. Gupta 2014, xi; preface.

What right do I have?

A "CONFUSED WISE MAN." Longman, 184, 204, 207, 273.

Scope

WHAT CAN WE SAY ABOUT THE BOOK'S LITERARY STRUCTURE? Scholars, as usual, hold diverse opinions, from those who see the book as having virtually no plan, being rather a free-form mixture of thoughts, poetry, advice, and proverbs, to those who see as the very key to the book its deliberate structure, carefully elaborated with verses arranged in precise numerical patterns. Wright (1968, 314) summarizes the "no plan" view and lists various commentators who espouse it. He himself argues for a carefully elaborated plan and (in Wright 1980) precise numerical patterns. Scholars are also diverse in their proposals about how the text divides into "literary units."

Common questions

"THE WRITINGS." Gordis, 8–9

WISDOM BOOKS. Genung 1906, 3; Murphy, 132. Alter (xiii –xvii) offers an extended discussion.

QOHELET "A WISE MAN WHO TAUGHT PEOPLE KNOWLEDGE," etc. Eccl. 12:9–10.

QOHELET ETYMOLOGY. Plumptre, 15–16; Crenshaw, 32–34; Murphy, xx; Seow, 95–97.

POSSIBLE TRANSLATIONS OF QOHELET. Power (4) gives a sample list.

LATER BIBLICAL SCHOLARS RAISED DOUBTS ABOUT AUTHORSHIP. Many scholars have reported that the first to raise such doubts was Martin Luther (1483–1546). But Christianson (2007, 95–96) offers evidence that Luther's supposed expression of doubt was a misquote but that such doubts were strongly raised by Hugo Grotius in 1644 (and raised by others even centuries earlier).

NOT WRITTEN BY A KING, especially not *this* king. Longman, 4–6; Seow, 37.

ECCLESIASTES WRITTEN IN LATE BIBLICAL HEBREW. Kugel 2007, 513. But Fredericks (1988), against the scholarly consensus, argues for early biblical Hebrew.

QOHELET'S ROYAL PERSONA A LITERARY FICTION. Bartholomew (1999, 6) says, "Very few scholars defend Solomonic authorship nowadays." Longman (3) mentions "a small, but vocal, group of evangelical scholars" as an exception. Solomonic authorship is also accepted by a section of contemporary Jewish scholars, such as Leiman (1978) and Zlotowitz and Scherman (in Zlotowitz 1976).

HISTORY OF THE TITLE *ECCLESIASTES*. Plumptre, 15–16.

GREEK SIMILARLY OBSCURE. Gordis, 4.

MEANING OF *ECCLESIA*. OED.

EGYPT AND PHOENICIA PROPOSED. As mentioned by Crenshaw (49). PALESTINE MOST LIKELY: Seow, 37; Whybray, 13.

DATE FOR SOLOMON: 10th century BCE. Loader, 3.

DATE FOR THE BOOK. That fragments of Ecclesiastes have been found among the Dead Sea Scrolls at Qumran indicates that the book could not have been composed later than the mid second century BCE. Fredericks (1988, 1–2) writes, "Today the majority of scholars and commentators of all schools of thought consider the book to have been written during the Second Temple Period, the dates ranging from the fourth to the second century B.C." On linguistic grounds, however, he argues (262) for the minority view that the book "should not be dated any later than the exilic period [586–538 BCE]" and could possibly have been written earlier.

"THE IMMORTALS ARE ALWAYS OUR CONTEMPORARIES." Gordis 1945, 41.

CANONICITY THANKS TO SOLOMON AND EPILOGUE. Crenshaw (52) mentions the former and weighs in for the latter.

NOT COUNCILS BUT A HISTORICAL PROCESS. Fox 2004, xv.

"A NATIONAL LITERATURE UPON A RELIGIOUS FOUNDATION." A. B. Ehrlich, quoted by Gordis 1945, 28. Gordis elsewhere (1968, 357, footnote 1) gives the source as "A. B. Ehrlich, *Die Psalmen* (Berlin, 1905), p. vi."

A BOOK TO KEEP. Alter (343) mentions the likelihood that many ancient Hebrew readers would have wanted the book preserved as part of their nation's literary legacy.

SANCTITY DEBATED AFTER THE BOOK WAS IN THE CANON. Fox, 2.

Vedic sources

THE WORD *VEDIC*. MWD entries for *veda* and *vid*. OED for *wise*, a., and *wit*, v[1].

RIPE FRUIT OF THE DESIRE TREE. Bhāgavatam 1.1.3.

Gender neutrality

WOMEN IN CHAPTER 7. Eccl. 7:26–28.

Vanity of vanities

VANITY THIRTY-EIGHT TIMES. Machinist 2004, 1606; Ogden, 32. Various commentators give differing numbers.

THE MEANING OF *HEVEL*. Virtually every commentator deals with this topic. Among those who discuss the translation of *hevel* as *mataios* and *vanitas* is Anderson (1999). For *mataios* as denoting "the world of appearance as distinct from that of being" and as "what is against the norm," Anderson (64) quotes the entries on that word from the *Exegetical Dictionary of the New Testament* and the *Theological Dictionary of the New Testament*. Fox (27–42) critiques various English translations for *hevel* and gives his reasons for favoring "absurd."

Some translators render *hevel* according to its different contexts within the book, sometimes as "fleeting," sometimes "meaningless," and so on. In doing so, however, they sacrifice the rhetorical power of Qohelet's hammering away with the one word *hevel*, and lose along with it Qohelet's singular idea (whatever we might think it to be) that he means to get across.

Some translators prefer a term that gives the original concrete sense – "vapor" (Scott) or "merest breath" (Alter) – and leave to us the work of extracting meaning from metaphor.

VANITY DEFINED. OED.

"MULTIVALENT SYMBOL." Miller 2002.

"LOADED IMPLICATION OF ABSURDITY." Anderson 1999, 71.

THE BEST COURSE MAY BE TO LEAVE THE TERM *HEVEL* IN HEBREW. Anderson 1997 translates Ecclesiastes using this approach.

Chapter 1

1:1–11

What profit does a man have?

YITRON a commercial term. Kugel 1989, 32.

"Under the sun"

"UNDER THE SUN" (frequency of use). Seow, 104; Whybray, 37. The phrase in Hebrew is *taḥat hashemesh.*

WITH EVERY RISING AND SETTING, ANOTHER DAY LOST. Bhāgavatam 2.3.17.

THE SUN EXPOSES EMPTINESS. Fuerst, 103.

Generation after generation

THE ROOT FOR *GENERATIONS*. Strong, entry 1755. Also mentioned by Longman (67). Crenshaw (62) notes the ambiguity of the Hebrew word, *dor*, which can suggest generations either of natural phenomena or of people. He says the former is likely the primary sense. "But the other nuance must also be present, lending immense irony to the observation that the stage on which the human drama is played outlasts the actors themselves."

THE STEADY EARTH MOCKS OUR BRIEF LIVES. This point, made by Jerome, is repeated by Barton (70), from whom I have borrowed the term "workshop."

"THE WORLD" = ALL THE PEOPLE OF THE WORLD. Fox, 166. Hebrew: *ha'arets*.

All things are weary

"HASTENS." Literally, "pants." Longman, 69; Murphy, 6. The Hebrew word is *sho'ef.*

IMPLIES TIREDNESS: Seow, 107.

"THE ELEMENTAL INGREDIENTS OF NATURE." Mentioned by Ibn Ezra in his commentary on 1:4 and 1:7–8. Discussed by Gordis (203) and others.

"THE WHOLE UNIVERSE GROANS." Barton, 71.

"THINGS" / "WORDS" (Hebrew: *devarim*). Discussed by Plumptre (107), Fox (167) (who says "only words"), Loader (21, "only words"), Longman (71, "only things"), and others.

"WEARY, STALE, FLAT, AND UNPROFITABLE." *Hamlet*, act 1, scene 2.

Nothing is new
"AS THE WORLD IS NOW . . ." Bhāgavatam 3.10.13.

NEW THINGS AND EVENTS. Fox, 168.

"CHEWING THE CHEWED." Bhāgavatam 7.5.30.

No remembrance
PEOPLE, THINGS, OR EVENTS? Discussed by Crenshaw (68), Fox (169), Longman (75), Murphy (9), and others.

"THE WORLD OF NAMES." Bhāgavatam 2.2.3.

1:12–18
"I spoke with my heart"
QOHELET INTRODUCES HIMSELF. In Longman's view, only in verse 12 does the frame narrator leave off and Qohelet himself begin. (Longman notes similar patterns in other autobiographical works from the ancient Middle East.) Some others share this view.

SOLOMON AND DAVID. Seow (119, 145), Longman (76–77), and others.

HEART THE CENTER OF THE INTELLECT. Crenshaw, 72. Longman (78) says that the Hebrew word for "heart" (*lev*) "refers not to the emotions, as in English, but to the mind or will, or even the core of one's personality."

"SEARCH" AND "SEEK OUT" (Hebrew: *lidrosh* and *tur*) = search deeply and broadly. Barton, 78; Gordis, 209. But Longman (79) regards the supposed fine distinctions between the words as "tenuous and lacking semantic defense." Crenshaw (72), on the other hand, says that the first word "refers to the length and breadth of the search" and the second "adds the inner depth dimension, the penetration beyond the surface of reality."

"TO BE AFFLICTED" (Hebrew root: *'nh*). Crenshaw (72–73) mentions this possible translation. The Apostle's Bible and the New American Standard Bible use it.

GOD GIVING MAN TROUBLE, at first mention. Plumptre, 110.

ELOHIM, forty times and universal. Seow, 66.

ELOHIM AS IMPERSONAL. Discussed by Alter (341) and others.

Chasing after wind
"CHASING AFTER WIND" (Hebrew: *re'ut ruaḥ*). Among those who discuss the various possible meanings are Crenshaw (73), Plumptre (110), Fox (42–48), Longman (81–82), and Seow (121–22).

Chapter 2
2:1–11
"Come now, let me make you try pleasure"
ODYSSEUS AND THE SIRENS. The story appears in Book 12 of The Odyssey.

"POT IS FUN." An iconic photograph taken in March of 1964 by Benedict Fernandez – "Allen Ginsberg Outside Women's House of Detention, New York" – shows Ginsberg wearing a placard with this slogan.

AMERICA'S NATIONAL DRUG. Alcohol is not, of course, "the national drug" only of the United States.

"YOU HAVE TO GO OUT OF YOUR MIND TO USE YOUR HEAD." Timothy Leary used this as an opening line in a lecture at The Cooper Union in November 1964. Audio file at https://archive.org/details/PsychedeliaLa23-tl-at-cooper-union-1964.

"MANY CONCUBINES, THE DELIGHTS OF MEN" (Hebrew: *ta'anugot bene ha'adam shiddah weshiddot*). Seow (130–31) is among those who give an alternative translation.

SEVEN HUNDRED WIVES, THREE HUNDRED CONCUBINES. 1 Kings 11:3.

SEX THE FINAL ITEM. Stuart, 129–30.

The path of karma

VIKARMA. Bhāgavatam 5.5.5.

DESIRE / DEMAND (Hebrew: *sha'alu*). Strong, entry 7592; Stuart, 130.

THE MODES OF NATURE. See Gītā, 14.5–13. David B. Wolf, a psychologist and Krishna devotee, has published studies using empiric research to show the value of "the modes of nature" as a construct for a psychological model or map. See Wolf 1998 and 1999.

ḤELEQ. Fox (109–11) discusses the word at length. It appears in 2:10, 2:21, 3:22, 5:18–19, 9:6, 9:9, and 11:2.

2:12–16

For the fool and the wise, the same fate

"WHAT (OF) THE MAN WHO COMES AFTER THE KING?" Fuerst, 109–110.

"ONCE EVEN THE KING HIMSELF HAS TRIED . . ." Ibn Ezra.

"IN MUCH WISDOM IS MUCH VEXATION." Eccl. 1:18

"THE VERY WISDOM OF THE SEEKER . . ." Plumptre, 119.

2:17–23

Pleasure turns bitter

HAPPINESS IN THE MODE OF PASSION. Gītā 18.38

HAPPINESS IN IGNORANCE. Gītā 18.39

HAPPINESS IN GOODNESS. Gītā 18.37. Commenting on Eccl. 7:8, Ibn Ezra also says, "In fact one can observe that one who is wise takes a medicine that is bitter at the beginning so that it may be helpful at the end."

"WISDOM EXCELS FOLLY . . ." Eccl. 2:13.

DUAL MEANING OF LABOR (Hebrew: *'amal*). Seow (55), Fox (97–98), and others.

What is left but despair?

DESPAIR. OED, entry for "despair, *v.*"

"GIVE UP FOR LOST" (Hebrew: *yi'esh*). Fox 2004, 17.

"AN INTENSITY OF EXPRESSION NOT BEFORE EMPLOYED." Stuart, 138

"THE DESIRE OF HIS HEART." Hebrew: *ra'yon libbo*.

"HIS HEART'S THOUGHTS." Fox, 185

DESIRES "COMING FORTH FROM THE MIND." Gītā 2.55.

DESIRES "BORN OF SOME NOTION IN THE HEART." Gītā 6.24.

"ONE WHO DESIRES TO DESIRE." This can never lead to peace. Gītā 2.70.

2:24–26

Eat, drink, and enjoy

QOHELET'S "JOYOUS MESSAGE." See, for example, Whybray 1982 (though Whybray doesn't use precisely that phrase).

KĀMASYA NENDRIYA-PRĪTIR, Bhāgavatam 1.2.10.

NĀYAM DEHO, Bhāgavatam 5.5.1

Strange notions, but so what?

"WHO WILL FRET?" (Hebrew: *yaḥush*.) Fox, 185, 189.

A PIOUS INTERPOLATION. Fuerst (111) notes this view.

Qohelet in the modern world

MOSES STUART biographical information. Entry in *Encyclopædia Britannica*, 11th Edition, 1911.

"NOT A SINGLE GRAMMATICAL DIFFICULTY . . . UNTOUCHED." Stuart, vi.

"A STRUGGLING MIND . . . TRIUMPHANT AT LAST . . ." Stuart, 142.

STUART'S SUMMARY. Stuart, 140.

"Such is the conclusion . . . " and the following six quotations. Stuart, 140–41. In the original these quotations form one uninterrupted text.

The gross body and subtle body. Discussed, for example, in Bhāgavatam 4.29.60.

"In our day . . ." Stuart, 142

Worldly happiness compared with "the world to come" and "hope animated by a living faith," Stuart, 141.

"Nay, one cannot help the feeling . . ." Stuart, 142

Chapter 3
3:1–8

Qohelet's song

"Turn! Turn! Turn!" written in 1959. Seeger 2003 (a book for children) says "around 1961." I take 1959 from the record of the song's registration with the US Copyright Office.

"A time of peace" to even out a verse, and he sang the song around. Pete Seeger in a video posted on youtube.com but no longer online. He tells much the same story in the introduction to Seeger 2003.

Seeger recording in 1962. The song appeared on his album *The Bitter and the Sweet*, released by Columbia Records in that year.

Number-one song for three weeks. Bronson 2003, 188.

Why is there time at all?

Not time in the abstract. Fox, 195; Longman, 114; Crenshaw, 92. Fox (194–206) examines at length what Qohelet means by *time* (Hebrew: *'et*).

Śrī Krishna grants Arjuna spiritual eyes. Gītā 11.8. The universal form and its aspect as time are described in subsequent verses.

Time as the impersonal aspect of God. Bhāgavatam 12.4.36–37.

How much is predetermined, and how much are we free?

The Hebrew word for *season* (*zeman*) "is ordinarily used of predetermined or appointed time." Seow, 170.

"The text is not about moments that people choose." Seow, 49. So also Fox 1987, 192; Murphy, 33; Delitzsch, 254–55.

A matter of free choice. Fox (citing other parts of this poem) mellows from a strictly deterministic reading in 1987 to a reading in 2010 in which he sees times we cannot choose as well as times over which we have some degree of control.

Is Qohelet saying the time for everything is fixed or speaking of times we can choose? The scholar Stuart Weeks suggests, aptly, that this is not Qohelet's point. "The point, rather, is that individuals have no choice but to partake in something much greater than themselves" (Weeks 2013, 107). Qohelet, it seems, is "talking about human actions in relation to the divine will: whatever we do, whether we perceive it as creative or uncreative, good or bad, forms a part of the processes which characterize the world, and which are, in some sense, the responsibility of God. Even if each action might be evaluated differently when considered in the abstract, no action can be other than proper when it happens as part of such a divinely-approved plan or process" (Weeks 2013, 106–7).

Despite caring parents a child may die, etc. Bhāgavatam 7.9.19.

prakṛteḥ kriyamāṇāni. Gītā 3.27.

Goodness, passion, and ignorance. Gītā 14:6–13.

The living being is by nature pure. Bṛhad-āraṇyaka Upaniṣad 4.3.16 (*asaṅgo hy ayaṁ puruṣaḥ*), quoted in Caitanya-caritāmṛta, *Madhya* 20.118, purport. I heard the example of water colored by minerals from my spiritual master.

BY KNOWLEDGE ONE SEES EVERYTHING IN RELATIONSHIP WITH THE SUPREME TRUTH. Gītā 4.35.

NOTHING SO SUBLIME AND PURE AS TRANSCENDENTAL KNOWLEDGE. Gītā 4.38.

BALADEVA VIDYĀBHUṢAṆA: THE FREEDOM TO FOLLOW SUCH ADVICE. Commentary on the Vedānta-sūtras 2.3.31. (Vasu 1912, 369)

QOHELET GIVES ADVICE FOR A YOUNG MAN. Eccl. 11:9–10.

Suitable times

TRYING TO STAVE OFF SORROW AND BOOST OUR JOY. Bhāgavatam 1.5.18.

A FUNERAL IS NOT THE TIME TO LAUGH. Fox, 205.

CASTING OR GATHERING STONES TO MAKE A FIELD UNFIT OR FIT. Stuart, 144.

"CAST AWAY STONES" = HAVING SEXUAL INTERCOURSE. Midrash Rabbah.

THE SEXUAL CONGRESS OF MONKEYS. Bhāgavatam 5.14.30.

LORD KRISHNA IN ALL THAT IS BEAUTIFUL OR POWERFUL (Gītā 10.41), including sex not contrary to dharma (Gītā 7.11).

"CONQUERS THE LOWER SELF BY THE HIGHER SELF." Gītā 3.43.

"A TIME TO EMBRACE" may refer to friendly embracing or the embracing of parents and children: Crenshaw, 95. OR IT MAY REFER TO SEXUAL ACTIVITY: Longman, 116.

A time to seek and a time to lose

TAKING ON A NEW BODY THE WAY A PERSON PUTS ON NEW CLOTHES. Gītā 2.22.

A CAPTAIN THROWS MERCHANDISE OVERBOARD. Fox, 208, citing Midrash Rabbah.

A time to rend and a time to sew

RENDING GARMENTS IN MOURNING, SEWING LATER; silence in mourning, speaking later. Seow, 162.

A time for war and a time for peace

BHAGAVAD-GĪTĀ ON A TIME OF PEACE. Gītā 5.29.

3:9–11

"Times" in context. Alas!

"GOD'S IN HIS HEAVEN, ALL'S RIGHT WITH THE WORLD." The line appears in Browning's *Pippa Passes* at the end of the song sung by Pippa in the morning.

"HUMAN ACTIVITIES ARE LIMITED TO CERTAIN TIMES AND SEASONS . . ." Barton, 47.

WHAT GOD HAS PUT IN OUR HEARTS. Commentary on this is abundant. The Hebrew word is *'olam* (*ha'olam*). Ibn Ezra favors "eternity" and says, "'He has put eternity in their heart' means that men are busily engaged as though they were going to live eternally, and so, being thus engaged, they do not understand the work of God 'from the beginning to the end.'" Fox (210–11) critiques various approaches and favors the reading "toil" (*he'amal*). Gault 2008 surveys the options at length (and favors the reading "ignorance": *ha'elem*).

"I have seen"

QOHELET'S WAY OF GAINING UNDERSTANDING is summed up by Fox (2004, xi–xii).

THE FOUR DEFECTS are listed in Caitanya-caritāmṛta, *Ādi* 7.107, which draws on previous sources.

ACINTYĀḤ KHALU YE BHĀVĀ NA TĀṀS TARKEṆA YOJAYET. Mahābhārata, *Bhīṣma Parva* 5.22.

3:12–13

Nothing better?

"CHEWING THE CHEWED." Bhāgavatam 7.5.30.

"MANY CONCUBINES, THE DELIGHTS OF MEN."
Eccl. 2:8.

TOIL ('AMAL) LINKED WITH "EXTREMELY
NEGATIVE TERMS." Seow, 104.

HAPPINESS, LIKE DISTRESS, WILL COME OF ITS
OWN ACCORD. Bhāgavatam 7.6.3.

WORK ONLY FOR SPIRITUAL INQUIRY.
Bhāgavatam 1.2.10.

Here to enjoy
"SO ENTIRELY DEPENDENT ARE WE ON THE
DIVINE BEING . . ." Stuart, 150.

ĪSOPANISAD: ENJOY ONLY YOUR OWN PORTION.
Mantra 1.

"THOSE ENJOYMENTS . . . ARE THE VERY
SOURCES OF MISERY." Gītā 5.22.

THE BHĀGAVATAM REJECTS "FRAUDULENT
DHARMA" and invites us to discriminate.
Bhāgavatam 1.1.2.

3:14–15
Keeping us in fear
REMINISCENT OF A LEGAL DECREE.
Blenkinsopp 1995, 62.

QOHELET REALLY MEANS FEAR. Fox, 136–37;
Longman, 36, 123–24. The Hebrew verb
is yar'e.

"COSMIC BULLY." Longman, 132.

What is and what will be
"GOD SEEKS OUT . . . THAT WHICH HAS BEEN
DRIVEN INTO THE PAST." McNeile, 48, 63.

3:16–22
Justice where and justice when?
"THE PLACE OF RIGHTEOUS JUDGMENT." Fox,
214.

SYNTAX ABRUPT. Longman, 127.

THE HEBREW CAN MEAN THERE OR THEN.
Stuart, 152–53. (Stuart favors appointed.)
The Hebrew word is sham.

JUDGMENT FOR THE RIGHTEOUS AND THE
WICKED AN INTERPOLATION. Barton (108)
and others.

All have the same breath
"THE BREATH OF LIFE." GENESIS 2:7, 6:17, 7:15,
7:22.

"VITAL BREATH," NOT AN "IMMORTAL SOUL."
Fox, 215; Stuart, 158; Barton, 110.

ETYMOLOGY OF PRĀNA. MWD entry for prān.

THE ĀTMĀ RESTS ON FIVE KINDS OF PRĀNA.
Mundaka Upanisad 3.1.9. Quoted in
Bhagavad-gītā As It Is, purport to 2.17.

THE RIGORS OF YOGA. Gītā 6.11–14.

THE AIR OF LIFE MERGES WITH THE TOTALITY
OF AIR. Īsopanisad, mantra 17.

"EATING, SLEEPING, DEFENDING, AND SEX
– these the animals and human beings
hold in common." This proverb is often
attributed to the Hitopadeśa, but it
appears in only some versions of that
book. Halbfass 1998, 288.

The nature of the self
ESO 'NUR ĀTMĀ CETASĀ VEDITAVYAH. Mundaka
Upanisad 3.1.9. Quoted in Bhagavad-gītā
As It Is, purport to 2.17.

KNOWERS OF THE TRUTH HAVE STUDIED TWO
KINDS OF ENTITIES. Gītā 2.16.

WHAT ENDURES IS THE CONSCIOUSNESS THAT
PERVADES ONE'S BODY. Gītā 2.17.

THE BODY ENDS, BUT NOT THE CONSCIOUS
SELF. Gītā 2.18.

THE SELF NEVER COMES INTO BEING, etc. Gītā
2.20.

THE NOTION THAT CONSCIOUSNESS DEVELOPS
FROM MATTER WAS KNOWN BUT REJECTED.
Gītā 2.26. See also Śrīla Prabhupāda's
purport.

DEMONSTRATION BY INFORMATION THEORY.
Thompson later expounded these ideas in
chapter 5 of a more readily available book,
Mechanistic and Nonmechanistic Science
(Thompson 1981).

CONSCIOUSNESS PERSISTS through the bodies of childhood, youth, old age, and on to another body. Gītā 2.13.

LIKE PUTTING ASIDE OLD CLOTHES FOR NEW. Gītā 2.22.

THE ĀTMĀ CANNOT BE PIERCED BY WEAPONS, etc. Gītā 2.23.

"SOME SEE IT AS AMAZING," etc. Gītā 2.29.

The "cheery gospel of work"

QOHELET'S "CHEERY GOSPEL OF WORK." Genung 1906, 232–33

"A VERSE FAIRLY REPRESENTATIVE OF THE WHOLE BOOK." Genung 1901, 3.

Chapter 4

4:1–3

"No one to comfort them"

MISERIES GROUPED INTO THREE. See for example Bhāgavatam 1.1.2 and Śrīla Prabhupāda's purport.

"THE MOST PERNICIOUS RACE OF LITTLE ODIOUS VERMIN . . ." Swift, *Gulliver's Travels*. The words quoted conclude chapter 6.

OPPRESSORS PLURAL, COMFORTERS NOT EVEN ONE. Mott (1998, 39), citing Lavoie 1995.

"NO ONE TO COMFORT THEM!" Scholars cite this passage as evidence that Qohelet was not King Solomon. Had he been Solomon, he could have taken executive action.

THE SUFFERINGS OF OTHERS HE WILL FEEL LIKE HIS OWN. Gītā 16.2, 6.32.

EQUAL VISION. Gītā 5.18.

"ALL THE OPPRESSIONS." Seow (186) mentions that the *all* is hyperbolic.

THE BETTER OPTION IS NOT AN OPTION ONE CAN CHOOSE. Seow (187) points out this irony.

Qohelet and the Buddha

"THE SAME FEELING LIES AT THE ROOT OF BUDDHISM . . ." Plumptre, 139.

THE STORY OF BUDDHA'S LIFE is differently told in different traditional texts. I have largely relied on one of the accounts related in Harvey 1990, 16–23.

BUDDHA'S SERMON IN THE DEER PARK. For the basic teachings of Buddha, I have drawn upon Harvey (1990, 47–72) and other sources.

THE MISERIES OF BIRTH . . . Though the miseries of death, disease, and old age are quickly understood, sometimes we think of birth as quite a pleasant affair. We picture the embryo peacefully and contentedly floating in the womb, then sailing forth into life. But living for nine months in forced confinement, cramped in a little bag, surrounded by guts and the products of digestion, only to be laboriously expelled like a bowel movement and met with a smack – how pleasant is that?

And for the mother? My friend Dhīra Govinda Dāsa told me a story he heard from a rabbi while studying at Yeshiva Aish Hatorah in the Old City of Jerusalem, overlooking the Wailing Wall. After an Orthodox Jewish woman gave birth, she went to the Wailing Wall to beg forgiveness from God. Forgiveness for what? For breaking her promise to him. What promise? The promise she made just after giving birth the time before that she would never, ever go through this again.

The Buddha and the Gītā

PURUṢAḤ PRAKṚTI-STHO HI. Gītā 13.22

YE HI SAṀSPARŚA-JĀ BHOGĀ. Gītā 5.22

FOR BUDDHA THE SENSE OF "I" IS ILLUSORY, etc. Harvey 1990, 50–53.

GETTING FREE FROM SELF-EXISTENCE IS LIKE COMMITTING SUICIDE. I picked up this view from my spiritual master.

The oppressed and the Vedic way

ELSEWHERE THE BIBLE SPEAKS OF A GREAT COMFORTER. Mott (1998) cites Isaiah 40:1 and 52:9 and Psalms 71:20–21.

BOUND BY THE TRAITS OF HIS CLASS. Gordis, 29.

"WHAT IS CROOKED CANNOT BE MADE STRAIGHT." Eccl. 1:15.

QOHELET SEVERAL TIMES URGES, "SEIZE THE DAY." Eccl. 7:14, 9:7–9, 11:8–10.

BRĀHMAṆAS GUIDE, KṢATRIYAS PROTECT. See Bhāgavatam 3.22.4 and Śrīla Prabhupāda's purport.

4:4–6

Excelling for nothing

"ONE CANNOT EVEN MAINTAIN ONE'S OWN BODY WITHOUT WORK." Gītā 3.8.

WORKERS IN THE THREE MODES. Gītā 18.26–28.

4:7–8

"For whom do I labor?"

THE EYE AS THE ORGAN OF DESIRE. Barton, 115; Crenshaw,110; Zlotowitz, 100.

IN THAT LONELY MISER HE SEES HIMSELF. Longman (140) says this is the opinion of "most commentators."

4:9–12

Joint efforts

PALESTINIAN NIGHTS GET SHIVERING. Barton, 115.

BENEFITS OF FRIENDSHIP "CHEERLESS," emotional benefits not mentioned. Fox, 222. For a very few commentators, "If two lie together, then they have warmth" sends a signal that Qohelet was gay. For a well-reasoned refutation of an article floating this view, see Lyons 2006.

A threefold cord

A REFERENCE TO THE TRINITY. John Jarick, as quoted by Longman (143), mentions that Jerome sees this.

GUṆA AS MODE, QUALITY, AND ROPE. MWD.

THE THREE MATERIAL QUALITIES are described in the Gītā, chapter 14.

A MAN, A WOMAN, A KNOT OF ATTACHMENT, etc. Bhāgavatam 5.5.8.

"THE WHOLE WORLD IS BEWILDERED" and so fails to understand Krishna. Gītā 7.13.

THE MODES ARE SUPERNATURALLY POWERFUL, but one who surrenders to Krishna crosses beyond them. Gītā 7.14.

4:13–16

Taking advice

"TREES ON A RIVERBANK. . ." Cāṇakya-nīti-śāstra: nadī-tīre ca ye vṛkṣāḥ, pāra-geheṣu kāminī / mantri-hīnaś ca rājānaḥ, śīghraṁ naśyanty asaṁśayam.

"ALL WHO WALK UNDER THE SUN." Barton (120) notes the hyperbole.

ONE YOUTH, TWO, OR EVEN THREE. If three, the "second youth" would, rather, be the "next youth." For this reading see Fox, 224–27.

Chapter 5

5:1–7

The superiority of hearing

"DO NOT RUN TO THE PLACE . . ." Barton, 122.

SACRIFICING OF ANIMALS. Tucker 2001, 1448–9.

ANIMAL KILLED, OFFERING USED AS A MEAL. Eaton, 113.

THE PRIESTS MAY BE THE FOOLS, OR THE WORSHIPERS MAY BE. Jastrow, 153.

THE FOOLS DON'T KNOW THEY ARE DOING EVIL. How best to translate the Hebrew text (ki 'eynam yode 'im la'ashot ra') is a problem, discussed by Crenshaw (116), Fox (230–31), Longman (150–51), Seow (194–95), and others.

ANĀVṚTTIḤ ŚABDĀT. Vedānta-sūtras 4.4.22.

Do not be rash

WE SHOULD NOT TURN INTO A PRAYER OUR EVERY WISH. Plumptre, 146.

ONE SHOULD NOT MAKE RASH VOWS. Barton, 123.

PERHAPS QUOTING A PROVERB. Longman, 152.

DREAMS AS ILLUSIONS. Seow, 200.

Pay what you vow

A TIME WHEN VOWS ENTERED PERSONAL RELIGION. Plumptre, 147.

GOD'S ANGEL, PRIEST, OR MAN. Barton, 124. For angel, Zlotowitz (110–11) cites Ibn Ezra and Alshich (Moshe Alsheikh) and for the collector from the congregation cites the Midrash, Rashi, and Qara. The Hebrew word is *mal'ak*.

REPOSSESS YOUR PROPERTY. Instead of "destroy the work of your hands," Kugel (1989, 33–35) argues for the translation "distrain your possessions." Hebrew: *ḥibbel 'et ma a'sheh yadeka*.

Beyond fear of God

"THIS VERSE IS DIFFICULT . . ." Longman, 155.

"FOR WHEN DREAMS MULTIPLY . . ." Longman, 150.

"YES, IN A MULTITUDE OF DREAMS . . ." Crenshaw, 114.

"IN SPITE OF ALL DREAMS . . ." Zlotowitz, 111–13.

GOD'S MAJESTIC FEATURE AND SWEET FEATURE. Bhaktivinod 1896, 25.

GOD CAN EXPRESS HIS DIVINITY IN MORE THAN ONE ROLE, etc. For a summary of such roles, see Bhāgavatam, First Canto, chapter 3.

VADANTI TAT TATTVA-VIDAS. Bhāgavatam 1.2.11

KRISHNA THE PERSONALITY OF GODHEAD HIMSELF. Bhāgavatam 1.3.28.

THE EXAMPLE OF THE SUN. *Bhagavad-gītā As It Is* 2.2 purport and elsewhere.

KRISHNA'S PASTIMES are described in the Tenth Canto of Śrīmad-Bhāgavatam. Śrīla Prabhupāda has presented this canto in a summary study, *Kṛṣṇa, the Supreme Personality of Godhead.* In both the Tenth Canto and its summary, Krishna's pastime of stealing butter and being chased appears in chapter 9.

Why is God here at all?

"THE MODERN READER MIGHT EXPECT . . ." Gordis, 122.

MOZART BEGAN CREATING worthy music at five, etc. Encyclopædia Britannica, entry on Wolfgang Amadeus Mozart. http://www.britannica.com/EBchecked/topic/395455/Wolfgang-Amadeus-Mozart. British Library Online Gallery, http://www.bl.uk/onlinegallery/onlineex/musicmanu/mozart/.

"SPIRITUAL CREDIT" THAT NEVER DIMINISHES. Gītā 2.40, 6.41–45.

WE CAN BE FREED FROM DUALITY AND ILLUSION . . . Gītā 7.28.

"BOTH THE LOWEST OF FOOLS AND THE PERSON TRANSCENDENTAL TO INTELLIGENCE ENJOY HAPPINESS . . ." Bhāgavatam 3.7.17.

5:8–9

Hands of oppression and injustice

"ANYONE WHO HAS LIVED IN THE EAST . . ." I'm sure I've picked up this point from one well-traveled commentator, but try as I might I can no longer find the reference. My apologies.

THE HIGHER OFFICIALS FEED OFF THE LOWER ONES. The way the commentator Duane Garrett reads the verse (Garrett 1989, 165), the problem lies not in the hierarchy itself but in the sheer number of officials, each a hand likely to need grease. In such a corrupt state, with so many greedy hands, oppression is normal and justice not to be expected.

THE SUPERIOR WATCHES PROTECTIVELY.
Fox (234) provides evidence for this
interpretation, for which Longman (157)
provides some history.

AN OBLIQUE REFERENCE TO THE KING.
Barton, 127.

HEADS OF STATE HARDLY BETTER THAN
PLUNDERERS. Bhāgavatam 1.3.25.

LAW AND JUSTICE ONLY WITH THOSE WHO
WIELD POWER. Bhāgavatam 12.2.2.

A plowed field

"THE MEANING OF THIS VERSE IS TOTALLY
OBSCURE." Crenshaw, 119.

THE VERSE MAY BE INTERPRETED POSITIVELY
OR NEGATIVELY. Longman, 158–59.

"ALL LIVING BEINGS LIVE ON FOOD GRAINS."
Gītā 3.14.

A LAND FLOWING WITH HONEY AND WITH
MILK. Exodus 3:8, 3:17, 13:5, 33:3, Leviticus
20:24, etc.

5:10–11

The love of wealth

"THE MISER IS NEVER SATISFIED." Bhāgavatam
7.9.45.

COINS WERE OF SILVER. Stuart, 187. So *SILVER*
= "MONEY": Strong, entry 3701. Hebrew:
kesef.

WEALTH. Hebrew: *hamon.*

GAIN. Hebrew: *tvu'ah.*

A WIDE RANGE OF STUFF. Crenshaw, 121.

XENOPHON. *The Cryopedia* 8.3.40, quoted
by Barton, 127. Barton seems to have used
the 1855 translation by Rev. J. S. Watson.

AUSTRALIA AND CANADA USE BILLS
OF PLASTIC. Other countries also. In
December 2013 the Bank of England
announced its plan to join the switch to
plastic.

The rich can't sleep

INDIGESTION OR ANXIETY. Among those
who mention these two possible causes

are Seow (22) and Crenshaw (121), who
says that the ambiguity as to which one
"may be intentional."

"EVER THOROUGHLY DISTURBED ARE THE
THOUGHTS OF THOSE WHO GRASP AT THE
UNREAL." Bhāgavatam 7.5.5.

"IN MUCH WISDOM IS MUCH VEXATION."
Eccl. 1:18.

5:13–17

Lost wealth

THE EVIL IS PAINFUL RATHER THAN MORAL.
Ogden 1988, 424

"SICKENING EVIL." Longman, 166. Or "a sick
evil": Alter, 364. Hebrew: *ra'ah holah.*

AGAINST HURT. Ogden 1988, 425.

AMBIGUOUS PRONOUNS, scholars divided.
Ogden 1988, 423.

"EATING IN DARKNESS," possible
interpretations. Seow, 221–22.

5:18–20

What's good? Not much.

DAYS "NUMBERED." Strong 4557. Hebrew:
mispar.

QOHELET'S GOSPEL OF JOY. Though not
using the word *gospel*, Whybray (1982)
argues for this view. His predecessors in
this regard include Gordis (1968).

JOY AS GOD'S ANSWER. Instead of "God
keeps him occupied with the joy of his
heart," an alternative translation would
be "God answers [or "speaks" or "reveals
himself"] by the joy of the heart." Lohfink
(1990) proposes this interpretation and
mentions traditional commentators who
followed it. The Hebrew word is *ma'aneh*,
from the root *'nh.*

A WORLD FULL OF MISERIES, WHERE NOTHING
LASTS. Gītā 8.15.

CONDITIONING BY THE THREE QUALITIES.
Gītā 14.6–8.

THE QUALITIES MIX AND BLEND IN DIFFERENT
PROPORTIONS. Gītā 14.10.

INDRA BECOMES A PIG. My spiritual master several times told this story.

Chapter 6

6:1–6

Back to what's bad

"HEAVY" OR "FREQUENT." Longman (169) cites proponents for each. The Hebrew word is *rabbah.*

"EVIL DISEASE" OR "SICKENING EVIL." This is the same term used in 5:16.

"THE ATTEMPTS TO MITIGATE DIVINE RESPONSIBILITY . . ." Longman, 170.

FROM CHILDHOOD TO YOUTH TO OLD AGE AND ON TO ANOTHER LIFETIME. Gītā 2.13.

KARMA ARRANGED NOT DIRECTLY BY GOD BUT BY NATURE'S LAWS. See Gītā 5.15 and Śrīla Prabhupāda's purport.

GOD IS THE REMOTE CAUSE. Bhāgavatam 2.10.45.

THE CAUSE OF ALL CAUSES. Brahma-saṁhitā 5.1.

THE FORCES OF NATURE ARE HIS ENERGIES. Gītā 7.14.

GOD'S VARIOUS ENERGIES, WORKING AUTO-MATICALLY. God "has nothing he needs to do." Śvetāśvatara Upaniṣad 6.8. Quoted in *Bhagavad-gītā As It Is* 3.22, purport.

Better a moment of full awareness

MANY CHILDREN AND A LONG LIFE A BLESSING. Zlotowitz, 121.

"THE DIREST OF WOES." Plumptre, 155.

"ITS NAME IS COVERED WITH DARKNESS" = it has no name. Barton, 129; Delitzsch, 306.

MORE THAN TWICE THE AGE OF METHUSELAH. Zlotowitz, 123; Longman, 172.

"GRUNT AND SWEAT UNDER A WEARY LIFE." *Hamlet,* act 3, scene 1.

SANĀTANA GOSVĀMĪ ASKED "WHO AM I?" Caitanya-caritāmṛta, *Madhya* 20.102.

NEFESH TRANSLATED AS SOUL. E.g., in the KJV.

NEFESH not an "eternal soul." Fox 2004, 39.

NEFESH, various meanings. Van Leeuwen 2001, 33.

"SEERS OF THE TRUTH" have seen two categories. Gītā 2.16.

THE SELF IS JOYFUL BY NATURE. Vedānta-sūtras 1.1.12.

THE "SELF WITHIN HIMSELF." Gītā 4.38.

ONE WHO REALIZES THE SELF BECOMES JOYFUL and enters the world of bhakti. Gītā 18.54.

"I" AND "MINE." Bhāgavatam 5.5.8.

"GRIEVES FOR WHAT IS NOT WORTHY OF GRIEF." Gītā 2.11.

"I SAID OF LAUGHTER, 'IT IS MAD'" Eccl. 2:2.

"THIS IS WHAT I HAVE SEEN TO BE GOOD." Eccl. 5:18.

THE SELF IS TOO SUBTLE TO BE CUT, etc. Gītā 2.23.

BY SUICIDE ONE BECOMES A GHOST. Śrīla Prabhupāda mentions this in his commentary on Bhāgavatam 4.26.10. It is also implicit in Caitanya-caritāmṛta, *Āntya* 2.156.

"AND IF HE LIVED A THOUSAND YEARS AND THEN RELIVED HIS LIFE . . ." Zlotowitz (123) cites *Nahal Eshkol,* written by "the Ḥidah."

"OF WHAT USE IS A LONG LIFE THAT IS WASTED . . ." Bhāgavatam 2.1.12.

"PARĪKṢIT, CURSED TO DIE, WENT OFF TO INQUIRE FROM SAGES. This narrative appears in the First Canto of the Bhāgavatam, chapters 18 and 19.

6:7–9

Working for the mouth

"THE EYE IS NOT SATISFIED WITH SEEING . . ." Eccl. 1:8.

YAN MAITHUNĀDI . . . Bhāgavatam 7.9.45.

"A PERSON UNDISTURBED BY THE INCESSANT FLOW OF DESIRES . . ." Gītā 2.70.

BE SATISFIED WITH HAPPINESS THAT COMES OF ITS OWN ACCORD. Gītā 4.22.

ONE EXPERIENCES A HIGHER TASTE. Gītā 2.59.

UNLIMITED ENJOYMENT, IN TOUCH WITH THE SUPREME. Gītā 5.21, 6.28.

No advantage

PERHAPS THE VERSE IS A PROVERB. Fox, 245.

WISDOM SHOULD LEAD TO WEALTH. Longman, 165.

The wandering of desire

"MAN MAY LONG FOR CERTAIN GOALS . . ." Sforno, as paraphrased by Zlotowitz, 125.

YASYA YAD DAIVA-VIHITAM . . . Bhāgavatam 4.8.33.

6:10–12

Halfway

A NOTE BY THE MEDIEVAL SCHOLARS and "repeated emphasis on what people cannot know . . ." Seow, 240–41.

Known long before, determined long ago

NAME "ALREADY GIVEN." Literally, "Its name has already been called." Fox, 248; Barton, 146. Hebrew: kevar niqra' shemo.

"NAMED" = KNOWN, so nothing is new. Fox, 248.

"WHAT HAS COME TO BE" = "WHAT HAS HAPPENED." Fox, 247.

WHATEVER WAS TO HAPPEN WAS PREDETERMINED. Delitzsch (310–11) and others.

"FOR ONE WHO HAS BEEN BORN, DEATH IS CERTAIN." Gītā 2.27.

PRACTICALLY EVERYTHING IS CONTROLLED BY NATURE, but we think "I am making it happen." Gītā 3.27.

THE SUPREME MUST BE SUPREMELY INDEPENDENT. Bhāgavatam 1.1.1.

LIVING BEINGS ARE TINY PARTS OF THE SUPREME. Gītā 15.7. LIKE SPARKS OF A FIRE: Viṣṇu Purāṇa 1.22.56; Caitanya-caritāmṛta, Madhya 20.108–9.

"WHEN STANDING IN THE WORLD OF MATTER . . ." Gītā 13.22.

THE FORCES OF NATURE ARE INSURMOUNTABLE, but by surrender to Krishna one crosses beyond them. Gītā 7.14.

It is known what we are

"AND IT IS FOREKNOWN WHAT MAN IS." JPS 1917.

"AND IT IS KNOWN THAT HE IS BUT A MAN." Zlotowitz, 126, 127.

MAN, 'ADAM, 'ADAMAH. Crenshaw, 130; Plumptre, 158.

THE STRONGER ONE IS GOD. Barton, 136; Fox, 247; Longman, 177; Seow, 233, 241; Sforno, cited by Zlotowitz, 126.

THE STRONGER ONE IS THE ANGEL OF DEATH. Rashi.

KRISHNA THE WELL-WISHER OF ALL LIVING BEINGS. Gītā 5.29.

"I COME AS TIME . . ." Gītā 11.32

"AS DEATH, I TAKE AWAY ALL." Gītā 10.34.

A "SELF-DIRECTED IRONY." Fox, 247. More precisely, the irony Fox points out is that although man cannot say what is good to do, "Qohelet has done just that several times and is about to launch into a series of such statements."

THE APHORISM ON THE VANITY OF WORDS is adorned with fine alliteration. Crenshaw, 131.

REAL TALKING BEGINS when we inquire about the Absolute. Vedānta-sūtras 1.1.1.

THE ONE ABSOLUTE, REALIZED IN THREE PHASES. Bhāgavatam 1.2.11.

TWO VERSES DISTINGUISHING useless words from those with value. Bhāgavatam 1.5.10–11.

Who knows what is good?

THE HEBREW WORD EXPRESSES AN INDETERMINATE NUMBER. Strong, entry 4557. Hebrew: *mispar.*

THE SHADOW LENGTHENS UNTIL LOST. Crenshaw, 132.

"THE EFFECT IS PARTICULARLY TOUCHING . . ." Crenshaw 1986, 283.

PLUMPTRE (159) QUOTES SOPHOCLES (*Aias,* 127).

"MAN'S IGNORANCE OF THE FUTURE" is another element in the vanity, etc. Plumptre, 159.

"POWER, POSSESSIONS, SENSUAL ENJOYMENT, AND WISDOM have been shown to be vanity." Barton, 137.

THE CURSING OF KING PARĪKṢIT is described in the First Canto of Śrīmad-Bhāgavatam, chapter 18, and his meeting with Śukadeva Gosvāmī in chapter 19.

"WHAT IS IT THAT A MAN SHOULD DO IN THIS LIFE?" Bhāgavatam 1.19.24. The question is repeated in 1.19.37.

"YOUR QUESTION IS GLORIOUS . . ." Bhāgavatam 2.1.1.

"THOSE WHO STAY AT HOME MATERIALLY ENGROSSED . . ." Bhāgavatam 2.1.2–4.

"THEREFORE ONE WHO WANTS TO BE FREE OF FEAR . . ." Bhāgavatam 2.1.5.

"THE HIGHEST PERFECTION IS TO REMEMBER THE PERSONALITY OF GODHEAD AT THE END." Bhāgavatam 2.1.6.

ŚUKADEVA HAD BEEN MORE ATTRACTED TO THE SUPREME AS IMPERSONAL yet became attracted by Krishna. Bhāgavatam 1.7.9–11, 2.1.9.

FROM THE UNREAL TO THE REAL, from darkness to light, from death to immortality. Bṛhad-āraṇyaka Upaniṣad 1.3.28.

Chapter 7

7:1–6

Better is the day of death

MASHALS. Among those who discuss the *mashal* as a literary form are Genung (1906, 57–87) and Kugel (1999, 113).

A GOOD REPUTATION TRAVELS FARTHER. The *Sefer Ha'ikkarim* of Rabbi Yosef Albo, cited in Zlotowitz, 128.

A GOOD REPUTATION PRESERVES THE DEAD. Alshich (Moshe Alsheikh), cited in Zlotowitz, 128.

NO NAME AT BIRTH, an uncertain future, but a secure reputation at death. Kugel 2007, 512–13; Murphy, 63.

THE DAY OF DEATH IS SUPERIOR because one's miserable life is over. Longman, 182.

"AFTER MANY, MANY BIRTHS ONE ACHIEVES THIS RARE HUMAN FORM . . ." Bhāgavatam 11.9.29.

"AS THE EMBODIED SOUL CONTINUALLY PASSES . . ." Gītā 2.13.

"EVERY FUNERAL ANTICIPATES OUR OWN." Eaton, 125.

Better than laughter and song

THE SCOWLING FACE OF A PERSON WHO REBUKES AND INSTRUCTS US . . . Fox, 252.

THE HOUSE OF MOURNING IS ALWAYS WITHIN THEM. Ibn Ezra, as paraphrased by Zlotowitz, 131.

QOHELET'S USE OF THE SINGULAR AND THE PLURAL. Ogden, 112.

SOME TRANSLATIONS SAY "PRAISE." Crenshaw, 132, 135; Gordis, 174, 269. The Hebrew word is *shir.*

ARJUNA'S DEJECTION AND DESPAIR upon surveying the field at Kurukṣetra are described in the first chapter of the Bhagavad-gītā. His turning to Krishna for guidance is described in the beginning of chapter two.

"WHILE SPEAKING LEARNED WORDS, YOU ARE MOURNING FOR WHAT IS NOT WORTHY OF GRIEF." Gītā 2.11.

"STRONG WORDS ARE SOMETIMES NEEDED TO AWAKEN A SLEEPING MAN." I was present on one occasion when Śrīla Prabhupāda said this.

ARJUNA AFFIRMED THAT HIS ILLUSIONS HAD BEEN DISPELLED. Gītā 18.73.

EVEN BY THE BRIEFEST ASSOCIATION, ONE CAN ACHIEVE THE HIGHEST PERFECTION. Caitanya-caritāmṛta, *Madhya* 22.54.

GĪTĀ REFERS TO A POEM OR SONG. MWD.

BHAGAVĀN DEFINED. Viṣṇu Purāṇa 6.5.47, quoted in Bhaktivedanta Swami 1977 (in the article "Real Advancement Means Knowing God," part of section 1, "Learning the Science of the Soul").

FUEL AND THORNS IN THE MIDDLE EAST. Barton (140) and many others.

QOHELET PLAYS WITH SOUND TO HIS ADVANTAGE. Seow (236–37) is among those who discuss the wordplay.

"NETTLES UNDER KETTLES." Barton, 138, 140. Through Christian Ginsburg (372), Longman (185) leads us back to August Knoble's German rendering, "der Nettel unter dem Kettle."

THE FUTILITY OF LAUGHTER is hardly worth mentioning. Fox, 253.

DENYING THAT "THE WISE . . . CAN REALLY BE RELIED ON MORE THAN FOOLS." Seow, 247.

SPEAKING ABOUT HIS OWN THOUGHT PROCESS. Fuerst, 130.

7:7–10

Better patience than pride

CRENSHAW (136) QUOTES THE BIBLICAL PROVERB. I Kings 20:11.

THING / WORD. Japhet and Salters 1985, 154. Hebrew: *devar.*

WE CAN'T KNOW THE FULL VALUE OF WHAT SOMEONE HAS BEGUN TO SAY until he has finished speaking. Rashbam.

"BETTER LONG PATIENCE THAN SOARING PRIDE." Longman, 187.

FROM ANGER, BEWILDERMENT ARISES. Gītā 2.63.

"AS THE WORLD IS NOW, SO IT WAS IN THE PAST . . ." Bhāgavatam 3.10.13.

7:11–12

The ultimate refuge

WISDOM IS GOOD *WITH AN INHERITANCE.* Alshich (Moshe Alsheikh), cited in Zlotowitz, 135.

WISDOM IS GOOD WITH AN INHERITANCE. Rashbam.

WISDOM IS *AS GOOD AS* AN INHERITANCE. Seow (239, 249) advocates this reading, noted also by Crenshaw (138) and Longman (189–90).

WISDOM IS GOOD *AS AN INHERITANCE.* Midrash Rabbah, 7.11 §1.

"TRY TO LEARN THE TRUTH BY APPROACHING A SPIRITUAL MASTER." Gītā 4.34.

"I SPOKE THIS SCIENCE OF YOGA TO VIVASVĀN . . ." Gītā 4.1–2.

"THOSE WHO SEE THE SUN" = all on earth, all who benefit. Rashi. The Hebrew is *ro'e hashemesh.*

LITERALLY, SHADE, Fox, 256. (Hebrew: *tsel.*)

WITH WELCOME PROTECTION IN HOT CLIMATES: Stuart, 218.

THE MIDRASH GIVES EXAMPLES of how people have saved their lives. Zlotowitz, 136.

SHADOWS ARE BRIEF AND INSUBSTANTIAL. Seow, 249–250.

"DON'T THE TREES ALSO LIVE?" etc. Bhāgavatam 2.3.18.

BETTER ONE MOMENT OF FULL CONSCIOUSNESS, Bhāgavatam 2.1.12.

THE ULTIMATE REFUGE OF EVERYTHING. Bhāgavatam 2.10.1, as quoted in Caitanya-caritāmṛta, *Adi* 2.91–92.

THE SOURCE OF EVERYTHING IS NOT DEPENDENT ON ANYTHING ELSE. Bhāgavatam 1.1.1.

EVERYTHING AS ENERGY OF THE SUPREME. Viṣṇu Purāṇa 1.22.53, quoted in Caitanya-caritāmṛta, *Madhya* 20.110.

ALL ISSUES FORTH FROM THE SUPREME. Gītā 7.4–6.

THE ALL-PERVADING REALITY, THE SUPERSOUL, AND THE PERSONALITY OF GODHEAD. Bhāgavatam 1.2.11.

7:13–14

The crooked world

AN UPSIDE-DOWN BANYAN. Gītā 15.2–4.

Prosperity and adversity

"THE DAY OF GOOD," "THE DAY OF BAD." Seow, 240. (Hebrew: *beyom tovah / beyom ra'ah*.)

"BE IN GOOD" = "enjoy the good." Fox, 259.

ETERNAL PERFECTION, "THE GREATEST GOOD." Sforno, cited in Zlotowitz, 137.

NOT REJOICE WHEN ONE OBTAINS WHAT IS PLEASING, etc. Gītā 5.20–21.

"GOD HAS MADE THE ONE TO HAPPEN *NEXT TO* THE OTHER." Fox, 257.

"O KING, NO ONE CAN KNOW THE PLAN OF THE LORD." Bhāgavatam 1.9.16.

7:15–22

Virtue and wisdom

ŚRĪLA RŪPA GOSVĀMĪ ON *NIYAMĀGRAHA*, Upadeśāmṛta (Bhaktivedanta Swami 1975), text 2.

BEFORE ONE'S TEACHER, IT IS WISE TO THINK ONESELF A FOOL. Caitanya-caritāmṛta, *Ādi* 7.72, purport.

"DO NOT BE TOO UPRIGHT IN YOUR DEALINGS . . ." Cāṇakya-nīti-śāstra: *nā 'tyanta saralair bhāvyaṁ, gatvā paśya vanasthalīm / chidyante saralās tatra, kubjās tiṣṭhanti pādapāḥ.*

QARA ON "THE ONE" AND "THE OTHER." Cited in Zlotowitz, 140. Discussed by Shnider and Zalcman 2003, 435–39.

Proverbial truths

A HEART FREE FROM THE TENDENCY TO SPEAK ILL OF OTHERS is found at the highest level of God consciousness. Śrīla Rūpa Gosvāmī, Upadeśāmṛta (Bhaktivedanta Swami, 1975), text 5. (The most highly self-realized persons may criticize, but only as a matter of duty and out of genuine concern for the welfare of others.)

7:23–24

Wisdom: deep and distant

"I COULD NOT MASTER THE WISDOM TO SOLVE THE DEEPER PERPLEXITIES." Ibn Yahya, as paraphrased by Zlotowitz, 142.

THE "ASCENDING METHOD" AND "DESCENDING METHOD." See Bhāgavatam 10.13.57, purport.

HEARING FROM SELF-REALIZED SOULS and receiving guidance from within. Bhāgavatam 1.2.16–17.

"THE REALITY BELOW ALL CHANGING PHENOMENA." Barton, 146. (Hebrew: "That which is" = *mah shehayah*.)

"THE SUPREME TRUTH EXISTS OUTSIDE AND INSIDE," etc. Gītā 13.16.

NĀYAM ĀTMĀ PRAVACANENA LABHYO . . . Kaṭha Upaniṣad 1.2.23. Quoted in Bhāgavatam 10.13.54, purport.

"THE SUPREME . . . IS ATTAINABLE ONLY BY UNALLOYED SERVICE." Gītā 8.22.

7:26–29

More bitter than death

A SUBSET OF WOMEN – the loose, lusty, seductive ones. Among advocates of this view are Barton (147), Murphy (75, 76), Stuart (224), Zlotowitz (144), and, as cited by Cohen 1984 (78), the traditional commentators Sa'adia Gaon and Altschuler.

FOLLY PERSONIFIED. Farmer, 179. APOSTASY PERSONIFIED: Rashi. UNTIMELY DEATH PERSONIFIED: Ogden, 130–31.

OTHER WAYS TO LIGHTEN HIS REMARKS. Lohfink, 102; Fox, 267. I should acknowledge, however, that the way a commentator, such as Fox, chooses to interpret these verses may rest on reasonable hermeneutical concerns, not merely an inability to digest a harsh view of women.

"THE ATTRACTION BETWEEN MALE AND FEMALE . . ." Bhāgavatam 5.5.8.

HAPPINESS IN PASSION. Gītā 18.38.

HER MIND AND EMOTIONS (HER HEART), etc. Rudman 1997, 417. Rudman 2001, 105.

THE OLD INDIAN WAY TO TRAP AN ELEPHANT. I heard this from my spiritual master.

THE FORCEFULNESS OF QOHELET'S EXPRESSION suggests he speaks from experience. Jastrow, 162.

WHEN A MAN SETS OUT TO SEEK THE TRUTH, WOMAN SERVES TO DIVERT HIM. Rudman 1997, 420. Rudman 2001, 108.

"THERE IS NO STRONGER OBSTRUCTION . . ." Bhāgavatam 4.22.32.

"THE INFATUATION AND BONDAGE . . ." Bhāgavatam 3.31.35.

"JUST TRY TO UNDERSTAND THE MIGHTY STRENGTH OF MY ENERGY OF ILLUSION . . ." Bhāgavatam 3.31.38.

"AS A RESULT OF ATTACHMENT TO A WOMAN IN ONE'S PREVIOUS LIFE . . ." Bhāgavatam 3.31.41–42.

"MY MATERIAL ENERGY IS DIFFICULT TO OVERCOME . . ." Gītā 7.14.

ONE WITH WHOM GOD IS PLEASED / ONE WHO GOES WRONG. Fox comments (269), "Qohelet calls a man pleasing or offensive to God in accordance with his fate rather than his deeds." From the Vedic point of view, however, one's fate is but an outcome of one's deeds, as performed both in this life and in former ones. Nothing just happens; there is no random, impersonal fate. Whatever fate may befall us is but a consequence, good or bad, of what we have done before. From this point of view, one who has acted for the pleasure of God in a previous life may be favored by God in the present life. And as the Bhagavad-gītā says (2.40), "Even slight progress on this path may save one from the greatest danger."

"ONE WHO MISSES THE MARK." Gordis, 93–94, 310; Crenshaw, 146. The Hebrew word is *hote'*.

A "BUNGLER" OR "LOSER." Seow, 141.

Finding and not finding

"ONE TO ONE TO FIND THE SUM." Crenshaw, 147. Hebrew: *'ahat le'ahat limtso' heshbon*.

SUCH MEN RARE, SUCH WOMEN NONEXISTENT. The categories "rare" and "nonexistent" are used by both Barton (148) and Seow (273).

A ROUND NUMBER. Barton, 147. OR SEVEN HUNDRED WIVES AND THREE HUNDRED MISTRESSES: Ibn Ezra and Barton (who cites 1 Kings 11:3).

Many inventions

"MAN MAY NOT BE ABLE TO STRAIGHTEN WHAT GOD HAS TWISTED . . ." Fox, 272.

"TO THINK, TO CALCULATE" (Hebrew root: *hshv*). Longman, 207.

"QOHELET'S SEARCH FOR THE SUM . . ." Crenshaw, 148. I have simplified the Hebrew transliteration. Crenshaw uses the scholarly spellings *ḥešbôn* and *ḥiššᵉbōnôt*.

"A MAN BEARING A HEAVY BURDEN ON HIS HEAD . . ." Bhāgavatam 4.29.33.

"EVERYONE IN THE WORLD WORKS TO BECOME HAPPY . . ." Bhāgavatam 3.5.2.

Chapter 8

8:1

Known by his words of wisdom

"Who is so wise?" Fox, 265, 272–73. Among scholars who share this view are Stuart (229–30), Longman (209), and Seow (276, 277, 291).

Roland Murphy on intentional ambiguity. Murphy, 82.

A man's wisdom brightens his face. Rashi and others.

A wise man puts on a good face. Seow, 291. Fox (275–76) and Crenshaw (149) note both meanings and lean towards this one.

Wisdom arises from "the mode of goodness." Gītā 14.17.

Goodness is pure, healthy, etc. Gītā 14.6.

"A fool can dazzle us – until he speaks." Hitopadeśa, Introduction, text 40 (tāvac ca śobhate mūrkho, yāvat kiñcin na bhāṣate).

One should seek a person of genuine wisdom, etc. Gītā 4.34.

"There is nothing so sublime and pure . . ." Gītā 4.38.

Knowing the future

Interpretation refers to prognostication. Jones 2006, 214–15. (Hebrew: pesher.)

8:2–4

The power of the king

Not in rebellious conspiracy. Qara (as cited by Cohen 1984, 81), Waldman (1979, 407–8), and others.

King as referring to God. Seow (290) says that the Targum, the Midrash, and "various early interpreters" read the text this way. Rashi and Rashbam are among them.

"The despot stands, or thinks he stands, . . ." Plumptre, 176.

8:5–9

Knowing the time and way

The man for whom troubles are great may be the king himself. Plumptre, 177; Delitzsch, 343.

The limits of power

Alternative meanings for wind. Plumptre, 177; Crenshaw, 152. (Hebrew: ruaḥ.)

One might arrange for a proxy. Seow, 293.

"And the days of David drew near that he should die." I Kings 2:1.

Kingship ignored. Zlotowitz, 149.

"Time and judgment." KJV and others. (Hebrew: 'et umishpat.)

Rogues in command

Kings and heads of state as plunderers. Bhāgavatam 1.3.25.

The Bhāgavatam foresaw . . . Bhāgavatam 12.1.38–40.

They will flee to the mountains and forests. Bhāgavatam 12.2.8.

To his hurt

"To his own hurt" (alternative translation). Rashi; NIV; Crenshaw, 153. (Hebrew: lera' lo.)

8:10

A problematic text

The textual issues. My English text here follows, arbitrarily, the 1917 JPS version. Longman, Fox, Plumptre, and other translators discuss the perplexities. Journal articles include those of Serrano (1954) and Pinker (2008).

8:11–14

Justice delayed . . .

Justice. Qohelet's views on justice are extensively discussed by Fox (51–70).

Words put into his mouth, some commentators say. E.g., Barton (153–54).

Fox (19–20) critiques the patchwork of this approach.

"LIKE A SHADOW" (Hebrew: *tsel*) are either the wicked or their days. Crenshaw, 156.

THE GAP BETWEEN ACT AND OUTCOME. My thoughts about this gained much from a lively discussion with Graham Schweig.

"THIS DIVINELY EMPOWERED MĀYĀ . . ." Gītā 7.14.

THE GĪTĀ MOST RECOMMENDS SURRENDER. Gītā 18.66.

8:15

Recommending what doesn't work
"QOHELET IS RECOMMENDING PLEASURE AS A distraction . . ." Fox, 287.

8:16–17

No one can understand it
EYES THAT SEE NO SLEEP. Hebrew: *'enennu ro'eh*.

THE EYES MAY BE EVERYONE'S. JPS 1917; NRSV.

THE EYES MAY BE THOSE OF QOHELET HIMSELF. Fox, 287, 289.

Chapter 9
9:1–3

In the hand of God?
"IF I ESPECIALLY FAVOR SOMEONE . . ." Bhāgavatam 10.88.8–10.

"MY DEAR LORD, ONE WHO EARNESTLY WAITS . . ." Bhāgavatam 10.14.8.

"All is before them"
"ALL IS BEFORE THEM." Hebrew: *hakkol lifnehem*.

EVERYTHING LIES IN THE FUTURE. Crenshaw, 159.

BEFORE IN A SPATIAL SENSE. Crenshaw, 160.

"I KNOW ALL THAT HAS HAPPENED . . ." Gītā 7.26.

The same fate for all
"BREAKS OFF LIKE LIFE ITSELF." G. Wildeboer, *Der Prediger*, Tubingen 1898, quoted by Gordis, 301.

9:4–6

Death snuffs out everything
"AN EVIL IN ALL" (Hebrew: *ra' bekol*) expresses the superlative. Barton, 159; Fox, 292.

CERTITUDE. Seow, 300.

"NO LONGER EVEN DEATH TO LOOK FORWARD TO," etc. Plumptre, 187.

BIRTH NOT ONLY INTO HUMAN BODIES. Gītā 14.15.

WITHOUT INQUIRY, IGNORANCE BRINGS DEFEAT. Bhāgavatam 5.5.5.

THE WRONG BANK ACCOUNT. This story popularly told in the Hare Krishna movement is likely to have come from my spiritual master.

"ONE WHO LIVES TO SATISFY HIS SENSES LIVES IN VAIN." Gītā 3.16.

NEVER ANY LOSS. Gītā 2.40, 6.40–45.

9:7–10

Enjoyment already approved
NOT HEDONISTIC ABANDON. Ogden (166), Whybray (144), and others.

TO LIVE IN TEARS OR WITNESS SUCH EVILS. Eccl. 4:1–2.

A LIFE OF WEALTH AND PRIVILEGE, ALL USELESS. Eccl. 2:4–11.

BHOGA-TYĀGA. Śrīla Prabhupāda explains the term in his preface to *The Nectar of Devotion* (Bhaktivedanta Swami [1970] 1982).

NOT THE HAPPINESS IN WHICH THE WISE TAKE DELIGHT. Gītā 5.22.

"RENUNCIATION" NOT MERELY GIVING THINGS UP but dedicating everything to Krishna. *Bhakti-rasāmṛta-sindhu* 1.2.255–56, quoted in *Bhagavad-gītā As It Is* 6.10, purport.

ONE IS HAPPY WITHIN, ONE ENJOYS WITHIN, ONE'S AIM IS INWARD. Gītā 5.24.

ONE REALIZES ONE'S SPIRITUAL IDENTITY AND MAKES PROGRESS. Gītā 18.54.

"THE TRANSCENDENTALISTS DERIVE TRUE AND UNLIMITED PLEASURE . . ." Padma Purāṇa, quoted in Caitanya-caritāmṛta, *Madhya* 9.29.

ONE BEGINS BY "TRANSCENDENTAL HEARING." Bhāgavatam 1.2.17.

"BY SOUND ONE BECOMES LIBERATED." Vedānta-sūtras 4.4.22.

BY HEARING, ONE'S HEART BECOMES FREE, etc. Bhāgavatam 1.2.17–20.

White garments, fine oil

WHITE FOR FESTIVITY, OIL A PLEASURE. Fuerst, 140.

Enjoy with the woman you love

"THE WOMAN YOU LOVE." Before *woman* the Hebrew gives no article, neither *a* nor *the*, so *a* would also be a proper rendering. Fox (294) comments, "The point is that a man should marry a woman he loves, not, say, one who only brings a hefty dowry or family connections." And as Longman (231) says, even if a man were to spend his life with a woman he loved without marriage, Qohelet's point about vanity would still hold.

QOHELET'S THOUGHTS IN CHAPTER 7 (26–28).

"NOTHING BETTER." Eccl. 8:15.

"ALL LIVING BEINGS ARE ATTRACTED . . ." Manu-saṁhitā (5.56). *Pravṛttir eṣa bhutānām nivṛttis tu mahā-phalā.*

"THOSE WHO ARE FREE FROM ANGER . . ." Gītā 5.26.

DEVOTIONAL SERVICE TO GOD IN HIS PERSONAL FORM. The Gītā 12:1–7 compares the personal and impersonal paths.

BY DEVOTIONAL SERVICE, ONE QUICKLY ACQUIRES KNOWLEDGE AND DETACHMENT. Bhāgavatam 1.2.7.

TRANSCENDENTAL QUALITIES THAT ATTRACT EVEN LIBERATED SOULS. Bhāgavatam 1.7.10.

IMPERSONAL REALIZATION LIKE THE PUDDLE IN THE HOOFPRINT OF A CALF. *Hari-bhakti-sudhodaya* (of the Nāradīya Purāṇa) 14.36, quoted in Caitanya-caritāmṛta, *Adi* 7.98, *Madhya* 24.37, and *Antya* 3.197.

"BY THE ENJOYMENT FOUND IN DEVOTIONAL SERVICE . . ." Bhāgavatam 4.22.39.

ONE EXPERIENCES THIS HIGHER TASTE. Gītā 2.59.

A DANCING DOG. Bhāgavatam 3.31.34.

Not all the days of your life

THE STRONGEST MATERIAL ATTACHMENT THERE IS. Bhāgavatam 5.5.8.

JACQUES ELLUL, more than 50 books, nearly 1,000 articles. The International Jacques Ellul Society, "Bibliography of Jacques Ellul's Books." http://ellul.org/?page_id=133.

REASON FOR BEING his "last word." Ellul 1990, 4.

MRS. ELLUL'S DEATH. Hanks 1991.

HOW THE VEDIC CULTURE WOULD DIVIDE ONE HUNDRED YEARS. *Bhagavad-gītā As It Is* 16.1–3, purport.

TRAINED TO REGARD WOMEN WITH RESPECT, as for their own mothers. *Cāṇakya-nīti-śāstra: mātṛvat para-dāreṣu.*

Where you are going

"WHATEVER YOUR HAND FINDS TO DO." Murphy, 93; Crenshaw, 163. Hebrew: *kol 'asher timtsa' yadeka la'asot.*

DESCRIPTION OF SHEOL. Gordis, 307; Jastrow, 129–30; Izak J. J. Spangenberg, personal interview, Johannesburg, March 2, 2012.

THE BREATH OF LIFE RETURNS to God, etc. Fox, 331.

A FIGURATIVE REFERENCE TO THE GRAVE. Michael Eaton (146) thinks that here *Sheol*, though a place name, is "no more than the state of death pictured in visible terms." As a person asleep has "gone to slumberland," a person dead has "gone to Sheol" (personal interview, Nairobi, February 1, 2012). For one who has gone to Sheol – however we think of it – all that makes one a living person is gone.

THROUGHOUT THE BODILY CHANGES, the self continues to exist. Gītā 2.13.

THOUGHTS AT DEATH LEAD TO THE NEXT LIFE. Gītā 8.6.

9:11–12

Not to the swift

SUCCESS DEPENDS ON FIVE FACTORS. Gītā 18.14–16.

The evil time

"EVIL TIME" (Hebrew: *'et ra'ah*) = death. Fox, 297.

9:17–18

Quiet words of wisdom

LIKE THE JOINING OF A POTENT MAN WITH A FERTILE WOMAN. *The Nectar of Devotion* (Bhaktivedanta Swami [1970] 1982), chapter 12, under the item "Associating with Advanced Devotees."

KRISHNA AND ARJUNA, from friends to master and student. Gītā 2.7–8, 10–11, and purports.

APPROACH A SPIRITUAL MASTER, etc. Gītā 4.34.

THE LEADER OF FOOLS IS A FOOL HIMSELF. *Midrash Lekah Tov*, attributed to Rabbi Toviah ben Eliezer, paraphrased in Zlotowitz, 171.

Chapter 10

10:1–3

The way of the fool

"A FLY IN THE OINTMENT." OED, under *fly*, n., i.e.

THE WORD *HEART*. Barton, 166. (Hebrew: *lev*.)

RIGHT AND LEFT for good and bad, etc. Crenshaw, 169.

THE FOOL CALLS EVERYONE ELSE A FOOL. Seow, 313; Midrash Rabbah.

10:4–7

Social order turned topsy-turvy

"THE 'RICH' HERE ARE THOSE . . . LOOKED ON AS THE NATURAL LEADERS . . ." Plumptre, 195.

SOCIAL CLASS NOT BY BIRTH BUT BY QUALITIES AND WORK. Gītā 4.13.

BIRTH CONSIDERED ONLY IF MATCHED BY QUALIFICATIONS. Bhāgavatam 7.11.35.

THE SOCIAL BODY, with head, arms, etc. See Bhāgavatam 2.5.37 and 11.5.2.

SOCIETY SHOULD BE DIVIDED. Gītā 18.41.

FOUR PARTS IN EVERY SOCIAL BODY. Gītā 4.13.

EVERY ONE OF US IS A SPIRITUAL PART OF KRISHNA. Gītā 15.7.

EVERY ONE OF US CAN ATTAIN PERFECTION WHILE DOING OUR OWN WORK. Gītā 18.46.

WE NEED NOT CHANGE OUR WORK, ONLY OUR CONSCIOUSNESS. Bhāgavatam 10.14.3.

THE DUTY OF THE RULER is to see that all the parts are in the right place. Bhāgavatam 4.14.18. See also the purport.

10:8–11

Occupational hazards

OCCUPATIONAL HAZARDS. Seow (326) here applies the term.

"DANGER AT EVERY STEP." Bhāgavatam 10.14.58.

SEOW PICTURES A RURAL AFFAIR built up of rough stones. Seow, 316, 326.

SAMĀŚRITA YE PADA-PALLAVA-PLAVAM. Bhāgavatam 10.14.58.

Skill and wisdom and their limits

QOHELET TAUGHT BY "ARRANGING MANY PROVERBS." Eccl. 12:9.

Verse 10 poses linguistic difficulties, as mentioned by many commentators. Ginsburg (431–34) and Gordis (321–23) discuss a range of interpretations.

"Brute strength" instead of intelligence. Barton, 171. Qara makes a similar comment (Zlotowitz, 176).

A snake "before it can be charmed" or "that cannot be charmed." Seow, 318. (Hebrew: belo' laḥash.)

We're unlikely to have a charmer at hand. Longman, 245–46.

10:12–15

Foolish talk
His words bring favor to those who hear him. Rashi.

Śiśupāla. The incident is narrated in the Tenth Canto, chapter 74, of the Bhāgavatam.

Foolish labor
Anyone working but not trying to understand the ultimate destination ... Bhāgavatam 5.5.5.

The Bhāgavatam deprecates speculating and commends devotional service, especially by hearing. Bhāgavatam 10.14.3.

By devotional service one achieves gradual enlightenment, etc. Bhāgavatam 1.2.17–21.

One gradually realizes the Supreme in three features. Bhāgavatam 1.2.11.

Beating the empty husks. Bhāgavatam 10.14.4.

10:16–17

When your king is a lackey
"Lackey" or "youth." Seow, 329. (Hebrew: na'ar.)

Enslaved to youthful lusts, several commentators say. Zlotowitz, 179.

"Servant of his senses." The Sanskrit term is go-dāsa.

Condemning a social chaos in which servants are posted as kings. Fox, 309; Seow, 339.

Servants predominated by ignorance. Śrīdhara Svāmī, as cited in Bhāgavatam 11.5.2, purport.

Lazy, foolish, whimsical, etc. Gītā 14.8, 18.25, 18.28.

"Son of free men." Crenshaw, 176. "Son of nobles": KJV. (Hebrew: ben-ḥorim.)

A land is blessed when its ruler "belongs to nobility by birth." Crenshaw, 176.

10:18–19

The mode of ignorance
Darkness the delusion of all living beings, etc. Gītā 14.8.

Gross, stubborn, two-faced, etc. Gītā 18.28.

Goodness fosters knowledge, purity, happiness. Gītā 14.17, 14.6, 14.9.

Laughter, wine, and money
Verse 19 could be approving or critical. Murphy, 106; Zlotowitz, 181.

"Money meets every need." NRSV.

It did not meet his every need. Eccl. 2:1–11.

The bird in a cage. Śrīla Prabhupāda gives the example (though not the story) in Bhāgavatam 1.2.8, purport.

The word translated "answers." Hebrew: ya'aneh.

Money occupies everyone, or keeps everyone busy. Fox, 308, 310.

10:20

"The walls have ears"
Hare Krishna devotees thrown into Soviet mental hospitals and tortured with medicine. Autobiographical accounts appear in Buniatyan 2007 (147–64) and CFSHK 1987.

Assassinations are employed by
democratic states. Documents released
by the United States Central Intelligence
Agency on May 23, 1997, after years
of resistance, tell of assassinations the
Agency planned, and in some cases carried
out, for political objectives in Guatemala.
Included among the documents is "A
Study of Assassination," a professional
how-to manual. The documents have been
placed online by The National Security
Archive, the Gelman Library, George
Washington University. http://www.gwu.
edu/~nsarchiv/NSAEBB/NSAEBB4/index.
html.

"[Barack Obama] became the first
president to [publicly] authorize the
assassination of a United States citizen,
Anwar-al-Awlaki, who was born in New
Mexico and played an operational role in
Al Qaeda, and was killed in an American
drone strike in Yemen." Peter L. Bergen, in
the Opinion Pages of the Sunday Review
of the *New York Times*, April 28, 2012.

assassinations masked as suicides. The
assassination manual mentioned above
speaks of "contrived accidents," and
contrived suicide is not far off.

"The walls have ears." Midrash Rabbah.
10.20 §1.

What your government may pry into.
In America, governmental powers for
such prying have been broadly expanded
by an act of Congress, Public Law
107–56, formally titled "Uniting and
Strengthening America by Providing
Appropriate Tools Required to Intercept
and Obstruct Terrorism (USA PATRIOT
ACT) Act of 2001" [*sic*]. I wrote this
section of *Vanity Karma* before Edward
Snowden, a former employee of the
American intelligence establishment,
leaked documents showing how closely
America's National Security Agency can
monitor what we do and say and how
extensively it uses this capability.

If the lackey king, etc., were features of
the regime . . . Fox, 310–11; Seow, 240–41.

"Of lights . . ." Gītā 10.21. "Of bodies of
water . . ." 10.24. "Of seasons . . ." 10.35. "Of
secret things . . ." 10.38.

Chapter 11

11:1–2

You shall find it after many days

Not "cast" but "release" or "send":
Fox, 313–14; Longman, 254; Seow, 334–35.
(Hebrew: *shalaḥ*.)

What are the verses about? Barton
(181–82), Fox (311–13), and Seow (341–44)
are among those who discuss the various
possibilities.

Examples of selfless generosity.
Zlotowitz, 183–84.

Charity purifies the giver's heart.
Gītā 18.5.

Charity in the three modes.
Gītā 17.20–22.

This is never going to be a better world.
Eccl. 1:15.

Charity for the satisfaction of the
Supreme. Gītā 17.23–28.

"Whatever charity, do as an offering for
me." Gītā 9.27.

Use life, wealth, intelligence, words . . .
Bhāgavatam 10.22.35.

Without faith in the Supreme, whatever
we do will be useless. Gītā 17.28.

Go ahead and take a chance. Crenshaw,
178; Fuerst, 148; Jastrow, 167; Seow, 342.

"In this endeavor there is no loss or
diminution." Gītā 2.40.

Human life is meant for inquiring about
spiritual realization. Vedānta-sūtras 1.1.1,
Bhāgavatam 1.2.10.

If one puts material prospects aside for
the sake of the Supreme, etc. See.

Cāṇakya-nīti-śāstra: san-nimitte varaṁ tyāgo, vināśe niyate sati.

NOW ONE SHOULD INQUIRE. Vedānta-sūtras 1.1.1.

11:3–6

Inevitable, but not always predictable

"HIDDEN LAWS MAKE CERTAIN THINGS INEVITABLE . . ." Crenshaw, 179.

INEVITABILITY AND RANDOMNESS. Longman, 257; Whybray, 159.

THE WORD FOR "TREE." Hebrew: *'ets.*

DIVINATION. McNeile, 85.

Watching the wind and gazing at the clouds

WINDS ARE GOOD FOR SOWING (for various reasons). Rashbam; Murphy, 109; Fox, 314; Gordis, 331.

WINDS ARE BAD FOR SOWING. Di Trani (cited by Cohen 1984, 102); Longman, 257; Crenshaw, 180; Barton, 183; Seow, 345.

I CHECKED WITH A KRISHNA DEVOTEE WHO'S A FARMER. Thank you, Mādhava Ghosh.

"THE VERY WATCHING FOR OPPORTUNITIES may end in missing them." Plumptre, 206.

We do not know

ONE MYSTERY OR TWO? Among other commentators, Longman (254–55) discusses the issue and cites various authorities who have opted for one view or the other.

BONES CAN BE READ AS SYNECDOCHE. Longman, 254. Though not here, synecdoche can also work by having a whole stand for a part: "New York City shivered in the snowstorm" (the city stands for the people).

THE TENDENCY TO BLUNDER AND THE TENDENCY TO CHEAT. Caitanya-caritāmṛta, *Ādi* 7.107.

THE NOTION THAT THE COSMIC MACHINERY HAS NO PERSONAL DIRECTION is condemned. Gītā 16.8.

"SMALL IN INTELLIGENCE" AND "SPIRITUALLY LOST." Gītā 16.9.

THE LOGIC OF THE RICE AND THE SCORPIONS. This example is given by the eighteenth-century commentator Śrīla Baladeva Vidyābhūṣaṇa, as quoted by Śrīla Prabhu-pāda in his purport to Caitanya-caritāmṛta, *Ādi* 6.14–15. The example, however, may likely be older.

Even amidst uncertainty, we must act

"ONE CANNOT EVEN MAINTAIN ONE'S OWN BODY without work." Gītā 3.8.

FOLD ONE'S HANDS AND CONSUME ONE'S OWN FLESH. Eccl. 4:5.

BY WORKING FOR ONE'S OWN ENJOYMENT ONE BECOMES BOUND; by working for the Supreme, liberated. Gītā 3.9.

THE ISSUE IS NOT SUCCESS OR FAILURE. Gītā 2.38, 2.48, 18.26.

AS THE HAND THAT FEEDS THE BODY GETS NOURISHMENT ITSELF . . . Bhāgavatam 4.31.14.

"ONE WHOSE HAPPINESS IS WITHIN . . ." Gītā 5.24.

11:7–8

Just to be alive

"TO BEHOLD THE SUN" = to be alive. Seow, 347. The Hebrew here is *lir'ot 'et-hashamesh.*

HE "HATED LIFE." Eccl. 2:17.

JĪV, JĪVA. MWD.

THE FIVE STAGES OF CONSCIOUSNESS. Taittirīya Upaniṣad 2.5. Quoted and explained in *Bhagavad-gītā As It Is* 13.5, purport.

DHṚTARĀṢṬRA'S LAST DAYS and the instructions given him by Vidura are described in Śrīmad-Bhāgavatam, First Canto, chapter 13.

"JUST SEE HOW FEAR HAS OVERTAKEN YOU!" etc. Bhāgavatam 1.13.18–25.

"FOR ONE WHO IS BORN, DEATH IS CERTAIN . . ." Gītā 2.27.

THE NEXT DESTINATION WILL DEPEND on our consciousness at death. Gītā 8.6.

Rejoice in them all

"LET HIM REJOICE IN THEM ALL." Hebrew: *bekhullam yismaḥ.*

"THE TEARS OF THE OPPRESSED." Eccl. 4:1.

The days of darkness

"A TIME OF GLOOM AND MISERY." Seow, 348.

THE ENDLESS DAYS OF DEATH. Barton, 184; Delitzsch, 398–99; Fox, 317; Zlotowitz, 189–90.

BOTH OLD AGE AND DEATH. Longman, 259; Murphy, 116.

ENJOY NOW, WHILE STILL ABLE. Fox, 317; Delitzsch, 398; Seow, 368.

HERODOTUS. Mentioned by Barton (185) and Plumptre (208–9). For the paraphrase and the direct quotation (from *The History*, 2.78), I have drawn on Barton and on Rawlinson 1885.

"NOT TO DESTROY OR DAMP THE JOY . . ." Plumptre, 208–9.

ONE *WILL* REMEMBER. Longman, 259–60. (Though Longman says the text should read "he *will* remember," his translation says "should." This appears to be an editorial lapse.) Ibn Ezra's reading also assumes "will." Seow (348) mentions others who take the verb this way.

Enjoy and remember

A MOTIF OF "ENJOY AND REMEMBER." Ogden 1984, 29–30; Ogden, 207–8.

"SERVE AND REMEMBER." Gītā 8.7.

WORK WITH DETACHMENT, don't worry about the outcome. Gītā 2.47–48, 3.19

11:9–10

What sort of advice?

SOME COMMENTATORS TAKE THE ADVICE AS SARCASTIC. E.g., Rashi and Ibn Ezra.

WORDS INSERTED BY SOME PIOUS INTERPOLATOR. Barton (185), Crenshaw (184), McNeile

(26), Schoors 1985 (300), and, as Fox (318) says, "many."

"EVERYONE MUST GIVE AN ACCOUNT BEFORE GOD . . ." Talmud, *y. Qidd* 4:12, quoted by Seow, 371. (Gordis, 92, dates the passage to the 3rd century.)

"A THEOLOGICAL REFLEX." Longman, 261.

REWARD AND PUNISHMENT COME AT RANDOM, even perversely. Eccl. 7:15, 8:14.

"WHO KNOWS?" Eccl. 3:21.

"AN INTELLIGENT AND RESPONSIBLE ENJOYMENT." Delitzsch, 399.

"IT IS IN THE SPIRIT OF THE WHOLE BOOK . . ." Delitzsch, 397–98.

"DECEITFUL DHARMA" rejected. Bhāgavatam 1.1.2.

AN EXAMPLE CONCERNING *KHĪR*. Among other times, Śrīla Prabhupāda gave this example in a class in Los Angeles on June 16, 1972.

"IN MUCH KNOWLEDGE, MUCH VEXATION." Eccl. 1:18.

AS QOHELET FOUND IN HIS EXPERIMENT WITH PLEASURE . . . Eccl. 2:1–11.

STRONG ATTACHMENT TO ENJOYMENT puts spiritual realization out of reach. Gītā 2.44.

A FLY IN THE OINTMENT. Eccl. 10:1.

WE ARE PARTS OF THAT ULTIMATE REALITY. Gītā 15.7.

THE HAND AND THE STOMACH. Bhāgavatam 4.31.14.

SUCH DEVOTIONAL SERVICE IS EVER JOYFUL. Gītā 9.2.

WHEN ONE REALIZES ONE'S SPIRITUAL NATURE ONE BECOMES JOYFUL and engages in bhakti. Gītā 18.54.

Enjoy for yourself

"EXTENDED SELFISHNESS." See Bhāgavatam 1.2.8, purport.

In Sheol "no work or thought" etc. Eccl. 9:10.

Krishna the owner, enjoyer, and friend. Gītā 5.29.

Karma-miśra-bhakti and pure bhakti. Bhāgavatam 11.11.29–32, purport.

The highest aim

For Rashbam, not just "moderation." Japhet and Salters 1985, 65–66.

This attitude is approved in the Īśopaniṣad. Mantra 1.

Focus not on enjoyment but on the real purpose of life. Bhāgavatam 1.2.9–10.

Prospects of heaven

"Just another beautiful day in San Diego." For some time in the 1990s when I lived in southern California, commuters on the freeway could see the image of a man at leisure on an idyllic golf course, bathed in sunshine from a clear blue sky, on billboards bearing this slogan.

The enjoyment in the heavenly planets, vast but temporary. Gītā 9.20–21.

The "meager intelligence" of those who aspire for the heavenly planets is disparaged in the Gītā, 7.23 and 2.42–43.

"Who knows?" Eccl. 3:21.

After death, only Sheol, where there is "no work or thought" etc. Eccl. 9:10.

One last, deeper look at enjoyment

"The basic theme of the book is its insistence upon the enjoyment of life . . ." Gordis, 124. The Talmudic reference (Ber. 57b) is to the Babylonian Talmud, tractate Berachoth.

"But why, then, enjoyment . . ." Jastrow, 140.

"Pleasure dulls the pain of consciousness . . ." Fox, 239.

"He flings himself against fate in despair." McNeile, 52.

Qohelet returns to this minimum malum seven times. In 2:24–26, 3:12–13, 3.22, 5.18–20, 8:15, 9.7–10, and 11:7–11:10.

It is what God has allotted us. Eccl. 3:13, 3:22, 5:18–19, 9:9.

There is nothing better. Eccl. 2:24, 3:12, 3:22, 8:18.

It will divert our hearts and keep us from brooding. Eccl. 5:20.

He goes so far as to "commend enjoyment." Eccl. 8:15.

An imperative: "Rejoice!" Eccl. 8:7–9, 11:9.

"It is just in these enjoyments . . ." Cheyne 1901. (Under "6. Practical Philosophy.")

"Even though perhaps very learned and wise . . ." Bhāgavatam 5.5.7.

"Like an experienced doctor . . ." Bhāgavatam 6.9.50.

Chapter 12

12:1–7

A dark poem

Meanings ambiguous, customs forgotten, damage from scribal errors or intrusions. Fox 1988, 59.

The word used for "creator" is unusual as a name for God. Plumptre, 212.

Alternatives to *creator* are discussed by Crenshaw (184–85), Gordis (340), Longman (267), Seow (351–52), and others.

The Hebrew words. "Your creator" = *bore'eka.* "Your grave" = *boreka.* "Health" = *beru'eka.* "Your well" = *be'ereka.*

What we think of at death . . .

"Whatever state of being one remembers . . ." Gītā 8.6.

As the air picks up different aromas, we pick up different conceptions of life. Gītā 15.8.

The quality of our thoughts determines where we go. Gītā 14.18.

"WHOEVER, AT THE END OF LIFE, QUITS HIS BODY REMEMBERING ME . . ." Gītā 8.5.

EVEN WHILE WORKING IN THE PRESENT WORLD one should think of him, etc. Gītā 8.7.

THIS IS POSSIBLE BY CONSTANT PRACTICE. Gītā 8.8.

FOR THE PRESENT AGE THE VEDIC LITERATURE RECOMMENDS THE MAHĀ-MANTRA. Bṛhannāradīya Purāṇa 38.126, quoted in Caitanya-caritāmṛta, Ādi 17.21.

THIS SIXTEEN-WORD MANTRA CAN FREE ONE, and there is no method higher. Kali-santaraṇa Upaniṣad 5, quoted in Caitanya-caritāmṛta, Ādi 3.40, purport.

ONE SHOULD TAKE UP THIS PRACTICE FROM YOUTH OR CHILDHOOD. Bhāgavatam 7.6.1.

What is happening?

THE EARLIEST INTERPRETERS SAW AN ALLEGORY OF OLD AGE. Fox (344), Longman (262), Seow (372), variously citing the Midrash, the Talmud, and the Targum.

A SERIES OF IMAGES. Power (123–26) gives a tabular list of various meanings assigned to the images in this passage.

NOT AN ALLEGORY in the proper sense of the term. Fox 1988, 68–69; Fox 1987, 294–95.

LITERAL, SYMBOLIC, ALLEGORICAL. Fox, 333.

A CATACLYSMIC STORM, THE RUIN OF A HOUSE, A FUNERAL. Summarized by Fox (334–35) and Seow (372–74).

THE LITERAL STORY DELIBERATELY MADE ELUSIVE. Fox, 344.

The lights grow dark, the clouds return

"WHOEVER IS JOINED WITH THE LIVING HAS HOPE." Eccl. 9:4.

"SWEET IS THE LIGHT." Eccl. 11:7.

IN THE BEGINNING OF THE BOOK, in contrast to the end. Fox, 320.

THE CLOUDS RETURN WITH THE RAIN. Seow, 353–354.

THE END OF THE WORLD. Seow, 353, 376.

People in fear and grief

THEY TREMBLE NOT IN WEAKNESS BUT IN FEAR. Seow, 355; Taylor 1874, 7–8. Hebrew: *yazu'u.*

COWERING OR CONVULSED. Seow, 355. TWISTING AND WRITHING: Fox, 323. Hebrew: *wehit'awwetu.*

SCHOLARS HAVE PUZZLED OVER WHY THEIR FEWNESS MAKES THE WORK LESS. As mentioned by Seow (355–56) and seen in many other commentaries.

"SEE DIMLY." NRSV. Hebrew: *hasheku.*

"SCRIPTURE OFTEN DEPICTS WOMEN AS MODESTLY PEERING through the windows." Zlotowitz, 194.

"WIVES AND MOTHERS WAITING IN VAIN FOR THEIR LOVED ONES TO RETURN." Seow writes (378), "The motif of women who look out of the window is a literary convention used to depict the dashed hopes of mothers, wives, and lovers."

THE SYMMETRIES IN VERSE 3. Sawyer 1976 (525) and others.

"GUARDS." NRSV. Hebrew: *shomere habbayit.*

"VALIANT MEN." Crenshaw, 181; Seow, 347, 355. "LANDOWNERS": Longman, 264, 265. Hebrew: *'anshe heḥayil.*

GRINDERS feminine and = *molars.* Delitzsch (1891, 407) and others. Hebrew: *hattoḥanot.*

ETYMOLOGY OF *MOLAR.* OED. Plumptre (215) alludes to this similarity between the English and Hebrew words.

"THOSE THAT LOOK" is feminine and = "eyes." Seow, 356. Hebrew: *haro'ot.*

More signs of disaster

"DOORS" DUAL AND *BEING* SHUT. Fox, 325.

DOORS ON A STREET BAZAAR. Seow, 356–57, 378.

LIPS OR EARS. Crenshaw, 186; Longman, 271.

AN OLD MAN STARTLED FROM SLEEP. Rashi.

STARTLED AT ANY TIME. Power, 127.

"THE SOUND OF THE BIRD RISES." Seow, 347. Hebrew: *veyaqum leqol hatsippor.*

"BIRD OF EVIL OMEN." Taylor 1874, 20, 21.

"BIRDS HOOTING OMINOUSLY" etc. Seow, 358.

BIRDS OR WOMEN. Plumptre, 216

BIRDS SWOOPING DOWN. Seow, 360, 379.

SPARROWS HUSHED. Revised English Bible.

OR OTHER SINGING BIRDS. Plumptre, 216.

PROFESSIONAL MOURNERS. Fox, 326.

"THE VANITY OF LIFE IS CLIMAXED BY THE VANITY OF DEATH!" Gordis, 347.

The landscape

AN OVERINTERPRETATION OF THE HEBREW. Seow, 360. Hebrew: *miggavoah yira'u.*

"EVEN FROM ON HIGH they see terror on the way." Seow, 347 (reading *yir'u*).

THEY "FEAR WHAT IS ON HIGH." Fox, 319 (reading *miggovahh*).

"THEY DREAD THE POWER lurking over their heads." Fox, 327.

HIS HAIR TURNS WHITE. Ibn Ezra.

FOOD-GLUTTED GRASSHOPPER. Gordis (who disagrees) cites (346) Hertzberg and Galling.

CAPERBERRY FOR APPETITE OR SEXUAL PASSION. Stuart (281) and others.

PERHAPS SPRING IS UPON THE LAND. Crenshaw (187) summarizes this view.

NATURE IS UNCONCERNED. Sawyer 1976, 524.

Metaphors of death

PRECIOUS ITEMS RENDERED USELESS. Longman, 272.

GOD FORMED ADAM AND BREATHED LIFE INTO HIM. Genesis 2:7.

"DUST YOU ARE . . ." Genesis 3:19.

"IN THE HEBREW CONCEPTION, THE PERSON *IS* THE BODY . . ." Fox, 331.

"LET THE TEMPORARY BODY BE BURNT TO ASHES . . ." Īsopaniṣad, mantra 17.

"Those who are seers of the truth have concluded . . ." Gītā 2.16.

THE SĀṄKHYA PHILOSOPHY TAUGHT BY KAPILADEVA. See Bhāgavatam, Third Canto, chapters 26-27.

The funeral

THE LITERAL INTERPRETATION MOST FAVORED BY FOX (335-38). Fox also explores symbolic and allegorical meanings.

"FOR WHOM ARE THEY MOURNING SO intensely? . . . Qohelet wants you to look . . ." Fox, 338.

YAD ARTHENA VINĀMUṢYA. Bhāgavatam 3.7.10.

BY BHAKTI, LIBERATION. Bhāgavatam 3.7.12.

ALL POSSIBLE THROUGH HEARING AND CHANTING. Bhāgavatam 3.7.14.

12:8-10

The frame narrator returns

WORDS IN GOODNESS ARE TRUTHFUL, etc. Gītā 17.15.

12:11-12

Book knowledge and realized knowledge

"DANGEROUS MATERIAL – BE CAREFUL." Longman, 281.

"HUNDREDS AND THOUSANDS OF TOPICS TO HEAR ABOUT." Bhāgavatam 2.1.2.

WE MUST COME IN TOUCH WITH A SELF-REALIZED PERSON. Gītā 4.34; Bhāgavatam 11.3.21.

12:13-14

Going further

ADDED BY A LATER HAND. Shead (1997, 67) offers a quotation from O. Kaiser as typifying this view.

"IT CONCLUDES WITH THE TEACHINGS OF THE LAW." Indeed, the Talmud (*Shabbat* 30b) records that Rabbi Jehuda ben Samuel cited this as a reason why earlier sages did not declare this self-contradictory book apocryphal. Ginsburg, 14-15; Fox 1998, 225.

Traditional authorities cited

For information about the traditional
Jewish authorities, I have largely relied
on Fox 2004, xxii–xxiv, and Zlotowitz,
205–224.

About the Hebrew text
and its English rendering

THE MASORETIC TEXT. Driver 1970, xv.

INTERPOLATIONS MORE THAN TWENTY-FIVE
PERCENT. This view is expressed by Jastrow
(10).

ORIGINAL PAGES RESHUFFLED. Barton (25)
says this idea "was put forward by the
late Professor [Gustav] Bickell of Vienna
in 1884 in his little book, *Der Prediger
über den Wert des Daseins*" (Innsbruck:
Wagner'sche Universitäts-Buchhandlung).

THE HEBREW IN GOOD SHAPE. Crenshaw, 53;
Gordis, 138; Longman, 25.

SOME PASSAGES ALMOST HOPELESSLY OBSCURE.
E.g. 5:9 and 8:10.

CHAPTER DIVISIONS INTRODUCED IN THE
MIDDLE AGES. Gordis 1945, 40, and
Zlotowitz, 66.

References

Alter, Robert. 2010. *The Wisdom Books: Job, Proverbs, and Ecclesiastes.*
New York: Norton.

Anderson, William H. U. 1997. *Qoheleth and Its Pessimistic Theology:
Hermeneutical Struggles in Wisdom Literature.* Mellen Biblical Press
Series 54. Lewiston, New York: Mellen.

——. 1999. "The Semantic Implications of *Hevel* and *Re'ut Ruah* in
the Hebrew Bible and for Qoheleth." *Journal of Northwest Semitic
Languages* 25 (2): 59–73.

Bartholomew, Craig. 1999. "Qoheleth in the Canon? Current Trends in
the Interpretation of Ecclesiastes." *Themelios* 24: 4–20.

Barton, George Aaron. 1908. *A Critical and Exegetical Commentary on
the Book of Ecclesiastes.* International Critical Commentary. New
York: Charles Scribner's Sons.

Bhaktisiddhānta Sarasvatī Gosvāmī, trans. and commentator.
(1932) 1985. *Brahma-samhitā.* Madras: Shree Gaudiya Math.
https://archive.org/details/brahmasamhita. Reprint, Los Angeles:
Bhaktivedanta Book Trust.

* Bhaktivedanta Swami Prabhupāda, A. C., trans. and commentator.
(1969) 1993. *Śrī Īśopaniṣad: The knowledge that brings one closer to
the Supreme Personality of Godhead, Kṛṣṇa.* 3rd ed. Los Angeles:
Bhaktivedanta Book Trust.

——. (1970) 1982. *The Nectar of Devotion: A summary study of Śrīla
Rūpa Gosvāmī's "Bhakti-rasāmṛta-sindhu."* 2nd ed. Los Angeles:
Bhaktivedanta Book Trust.

——. (1970-71) 1996. *Kṛṣṇa: The Supreme Personality of Godhead:
A summary study of Śrīla Vyāsadeva's "Śrīmad-Bhāgavatam," Tenth
Canto.* 2nd ed. Los Angeles: Bhaktivedanta Book Trust.

---

* For the works of authors marked by an asterisk, I have relied on the Bhaktivedanta
VedaBase 2014 (Sandy Ridge, NC: Bhaktivedanta Archives).

——, trans. and commentator. 1970–80. *Śrīmad-Bhāgavatam*. Multiple volumes. Cantos 1–9 and chapters 1–13 of canto 10. Los Angeles: Bhaktivedanta Book Trust.

——, trans. and commentator. (1972) 1983. *Bhagavad-gītā As It Is*. 2nd ed. Los Angeles: Bhaktivedanta Book Trust.

——, trans. and commentator. (1974–75). 1996. *Śrī Caitanya-caritāmṛta of Kṛṣṇadāsa Kavirāja Gosvāmī*. Multiple volumes. 2nd ed. Los Angeles: Bhaktivedanta Book Trust.

——, trans. and commentator. 1975. *The Nectar of Instruction: An authorized English presentation of Śrīla Rūpa Gosvāmī's "Upadeśāmṛta."* Los Angeles: Bhaktivedanta Book Trust.

——. 1977. *The Science of Self-Realization*. Los Angeles: Bhaktivedanta Book Trust.

* Bhaktivedanta Swami Prabhupāda, A. C., disciples of (Hridayānanda dāsa Goswami, Gopīparāṇadhana dāsa Adhikārī, and Draviḍa dāsa Brahmacārī), trans., ed., and commentators. 1985–1989. *Śrīmad-Bhāgavatam*. Multiple volumes. Cantos 11 and 12 and completing canto 10. Los Angeles: Bhaktivedanta Book Trust.

Bhaktivinod, Kedarnath Dutt. 1896. *Srimad-Gourangalila-Smaranamangal Stotram; or, Sri Chaitanya Mahaprabhu: His Life and Precepts*. Calcutta: K. P. Dutt. https://archive.org/details/srigourangasmaraoodutt.

Blenkinsopp, Joseph. 1995. "Ecclesiastes 3:1–15: Another Interpretation." *Journal for the Study of the Old Testament* 66: 55–64.

Bronson, Fred. 2003. *The Billboard Book of Number One Hits*. 5th ed. New York: Billboard Books.

Browning, Robert. (1901) 2010. *Pippa Passes*. Reprint, Whitefish, MO: Kessinger.

Buniatyan, Sarkis. 2007. *Salted Bread*. Badger, CA: Torchlight.

CFSHK (Committee to Free Soviet Hare Krishnas). 1987. *Psychiatric Abuse of Hare Krishna Devotees in the U.S.S.R.* Almviks Gård, Sweden: CFSHK. http://www.hkussr.com/hkdoco2pi.htm.

Cheyne, Thomas Kelly. 1901. "Ecclesiastes." In *Encyclopædia Biblica*. New York: Macmillan.

Christianson, Eric S. 2007. *Ecclesiastes through the Centuries*. Blackwell Bible Commentaries. Malden, MA: Blackwell.

Cohen, A., trans. 1977. "Ecclesiastes." In *The Midrash Rabbah*, edited by

H. Freedman and Maurice Simon. New compact ed. Vol. 4. London: Soncino.

———. 1984. *The Five Megilloth: Hebrew Text & English Translation.* Revised and expanded by A. J. Rosenberg. Vol. 2. London: Soncino.

Cornille, Catherine, ed. 2006. *Song Divine: Christian Commentaries on the Bhagavad Gītā.* Leuven: Peeters.

Crenshaw, James L. 1986. "The Expression *Mî Yôdēaʻ* in the Hebrew Bible." *Vetus Testamentum* 36: 274–88.

———. 1987. *Ecclesiastes: A Commentary.* Old Testament Library. Philadelphia: Westminster.

Davis, Miles (Patita Pavana dasa), ed. 1981. *Sri Chanakya Niti-Sastra.* Lucknow: Ram Kumar Press.

Delitzsch, Franz. 1891. *Commentary on the Song of Songs and Ecclesiastes.* Translated by James Martin. Edinburgh: T. & T. Clark. (German edition, Leipzig 1875.)

Dobe, Timothy S. 1997. "*Qoheleth* and the *Lao Tzu:* An Experiment with Wisdom." *Ching Feng* 40 (2): 129–48.

Driver, G. R. 1970. "Introduction to the Old Testament." In *The New English Bible with the Apocrypha.* Oxford: Oxford University Press, Cambridge: Cambridge University Press.

Eaton, Michael A. 1983. *Ecclesiastes: An Introduction and Commentary.* Tyndale Old Testament Commentaries 16. Leicester: InterVarsity.

Ellul, Jacques. 1990. *The Reason for Being: A Meditation on Ecclesiastes.* Grand Rapids, MI: Eerdmans.

Farmer, Kathleen Anne. 1991. *Who Knows What Is Good?: A Commentary on the Books of Proverbs and Ecclesiastes.* Grand Rapids, MI: Eerdmans.

Fox, Michael V. 1987. *Qohelet and His Contradictions.* Journal for the Study of the Old Testament Supplement 18. Sheffield: Almond. (Reprint 1989.)

———. 1988. "Aging and Death in Qohelet 12." *Journal for the Study of the Old Testament* 42: 55–77.

———. 1998. "The Innerstructure of Qohelet's Thought." In *Qohelet in the Context of Wisdom*, edited by Antoon Schoors, 225–38. Leuven: Leuven University Press.

———. 2004. *Ecclesiastes.* JPS Bible Commentary. Philadelphia: Jewish Publication Society.

———. 2010. *A Time to Tear Down and a Time to Build Up*. Grand Rapids, MI: Eerdmans.

Fredericks, Daniel C. 1988. *Qoheleth's Language: Re-Evaluating Its Nature and Date*. Ancient Near Eastern Texts and Studies. Lewiston, NY: Mellen.

Fuerst, Wesley J. 1975. *The Books of Ruth, Esther, Ecclesiastes, the Song of Songs, Lamentations: The Five Scrolls*. Cambridge Bible Commentary. Cambridge: Cambridge University Press.

Garrett, Duane A. 1989. "Qoheleth on the Use and Abuse of Political Power." *Trinity Journal* 8 (2): 159–77.

Gault, Brian P. 2008. "A Reexamination of 'Eternity' in Ecclesiastes 3:11." *Bibliotheca Sacra* 165 (January–March): 39–57.

Genung, John Franklin. (1901) 2005. *Ecclesiastes and Omar Khayyám: A Note for the Spiritual Temper of Our Time*. Reprint, Whitefish, MO: Kessinger.

———. 1906. *The Hebrew Literature of Wisdom in the Light of To-Day*. Boston: Houghton Mifflin.

Ginsburg, Christian D. 1861. *The Song of Songs and Coheleth, Commonly Called the Book of Ecclesiastes*. London: Longman.

Gordis, Robert. 1945. *The Wisdom of Ecclesiastes*. New York: Behrman House.

———. 1968. *Koheleth – The Man and His World*. 3rd ed. New York: Schocken.

Griffiths, Bede. 1987. *River of Compassion: A Christian Commentary on the Bhagavad Gita*. Warwick, NY: Amity House.

Gupta, Ravi M., ed. 2014. *Caitanya Vaiṣṇava Philosophy: Tradition, Reason and Devotion*. Burlington, VT: Ashgate.

Halbfass, Wilhelm. 1998. *Tradition and Reflection: Explorations in Indian Thought*. Albany: State University of New York Press.

Hanks, Joyce. 1991. "In Memory of Mme Yvette Ellul." In *Ellul Studies Forum*, no. 7 (July): 1. http://ellul.org/ELLUL%20FORUM%20 ARTICLES/EF_07_Jul91.pdf.

Harvey, Peter. 1990. *An Introduction to Buddhism: Teachings, History and Practices*. Cambridge: Cambridge University Press.

Heard, R. Christopher. 1996. "The *Dao* of Qoheleth: An Intertextual Reading of the *Daode Jing* and the Book of Ecclesiastes." Pepperdine

University, *Religion Division Faculty Scholarship.* Paper 1. http://
digitalcommons.pepperdine.edu/religionworks/1.

Ibn Ezra, Abraham. 1994. *El Comentario de Abraham Ibn Ezra Al Libro
Del Eclesiastés: Introducción, Traducción y Edición Crítica.* Translated
and edited by Mariano Gómez Aranda. Textos y Estudios "Cardenal
Cisneros" de La Biblia Políglota Matritense 56. Madrid: Instituto de
Filología del CSIC, Departamento de Filología Bíblica y de Oriente
Antiguo. (Ibn Ezra completed his commentary in 1140.)

Japhet, Sara, and Robert B Salters. 1985. *The Commentary of R. Samuel
Ben Meir (Rashbam) on Qoheleth.* Jerusalem: Brill.

Jarick, John. 2000. "The Hebrew Book of Changes: Reflections on
Hakkōl Hebel and *Lakkōl Z'mān* in Ecclesiastes." *Journal for the Study
of the Old Testament* 90: 79–99.

Jastrow, Morris, Jr. 1919. *A Gentle Cynic.* Philadelphia: Lippincott.

Jones, Scott C. 2006. "Qohelet's Courtly Wisdom: Ecclesiastes 8:1–9."
Catholic Biblical Quarterly 68 (2): 211–28.

Kugel, James L. 1989. "Qohelet and Money." *Catholic Biblical Quarterly*
51 (1): 32–49.

———. 1999. *The Great Poems of the Bible.* New York: Free Press.

———. 2007. *How to Read the Bible: A Guide to Scripture, Then and Now.*
New York: Free Press.

Lavoie, Jean-Jacques. 1995. "De l'inconvénient d'être né. Étude de
Qohélet 4,1–3." *Studies in Religion/Sciences Religieuses* 24 (3):
297–308.

Leiman, Harold I. 1980. *Koheleth, Life and Its Meaning: A Modern
Translation and Interpretation of the Book of Ecclesiastes.* English ed.
Jerusalem: Feldheim.

Lindau, S. T., L. P. Schumm, E. O. Laumann, W. Levinson, C. A.
O'Muircheartaigh, and L. J. Waite. 2007. "A Study of Sexuality and
Health among Older Adults in the United States." *New England
Journal of Medicine* 357 (8): 762–74.

Loader, J. A. 1986. *Ecclesiastes: A Practical Commentary.* Translated from
the Dutch by John Vriend. Grand Rapids, MI: Eerdmans.

Lohfink, Norbert. 1990. "Qoheleth 5:17–19 – Revelation by Joy."
Catholic Biblical Quarterly 52 (4): 625–35.

———. 2003. *Qoheleth: A Continental Commentary.* Translated by Sean

McEvenue. Minneapolis: Fortress. (German edition, Würzberg: Echter, 1980.)

Longman, Tremper, III. 1998. *The Book of Ecclesiastes*. New International Commentary on the Old Testament. Grand Rapids, MI: Eerdmans.

Lorgunpai, Seree. 1994. "The Books [sic] of Ecclesiastes and Thai Buddhism." *Asia Journal of Theology* 8 (1): 155–62.

Lyons, William John. 2006. "'Outing' Qoheleth: On the Search for Homosexuality in the Wisdom Tradition." *Theology & Sexuality* 12 (2): 181–202.

Machinist, Peter. 2004. "Ecclesiastes." In *The Jewish Study Bible*, edited by Adele Berlin, Marc Zvi Brettler, and Michael A Fishbane. Oxford: Oxford University Press.

McNeile, A. H. 1904. *An Introduction to Ecclesiastes*. Cambridge: Cambridge University Press.

Miller, Douglas B. 2002. *Symbol and Rhetoric in Ecclesiastes: The Place of Hebel in Qohelet's Work*. Atlanta: Society of Biblical Literature.

Monier-Williams, Monier, Ernst Leumann, Carl Cappeller, et al. 1899. *A Sanskrit-English Dictionary*. Oxford: Oxford University Press (Searchable Digital Facsimile Edition, Bhaktivedanta Book Trust, 2002).

Mott, Stephen Charles. 1998. "When There Is No Comforting Power." *Christian Social Action* 11: 39.

Müller, Max, ed. 1864. *The First Book of the Hitopadeśa*. Max Müller's Handbooks for the Study of Sanskrit. London: Longman, Green, Longman, Roberts & Green.

Murphy, Roland E. 1992. *Ecclesiastes*. Dallas: Word Books.

Ogden, Graham S. 1984. "Qoheleth XI 7 – XII 8: Qoheleth's Summons to Enjoyment and Reflection." *Vetus Testamentum* 34 (1): 27–38.

———. 1988. "Translation Problems in Ecclesiastes 5:13–17." *Practical Papers for the Bible Translator* 39 (4): 423–28.

———. 2007. *Qoheleth*. 2nd ed. Sheffield: Sheffield Phoenix.

Paglia, Camille. 2003. "Cults and Cosmic Consciousness: Religious Vision in the American 1960s." *Arion* 10 (3): 57–111.

Pinker, Aron. 2008. "The Doings of the Wicked in Qohelet 8:10." *Journal of Hebrew Scriptures* 8. http://ejournals.library.ualberta.ca/index.php/jhs/article/view/6204.

Plumptre, E. H. 1881. *Ecclesiastes*. Cambridge: Cambridge University Press.

Polish, Daniel F. 2008. "The Buddha as a Lens for Reading Koheleth / Ecclesiastes." *Journal of Ecumenical Studies* 43 (3): 370–82.

Power, A. D. 1952. *Ecclesiastes; Or, The Preacher*. London: Longmans, Green.

Rashi. *Commentary on Qohelet*. Translated by Abraham Joseph Rosenberg. *The Complete Jewish Bible, with Rashi Commentary*. Chabad.org. http://onlinebooks.library.upenn.edu/webbin/book/lookupid?key=olbp51235.

Rawlinson, George, trans. 1885. *The History of Herodotus*. Vol. 2. New York: Appleton. http://ebooks.adelaide.edu.au/h/herodotus/h4/book2.html.

Rudman, Dominic. 1997. "Woman as Divine Agent in Ecclesiastes." *Journal of Biblical Literature* 116 (3): 411–27.

———. 2001. *Determinism in the Book of Ecclesiastes*. Journal for the Study of the Old Testament Supplement 316. Sheffield: Sheffield Academic.

Sawyer, John F. A. 1976. "The Ruined House in Ecclesiastes 12: A Reconstruction of the Original Parable." *Journal of Biblical Literature* 94: 519–31.

Schoors, Antoon. 1985. "Koheleth: A Perspective of Life after Death?" *Ephemerides Theologicae Lovanienses* 61 (4): 295–303.

Scott, R. B. Y. 1965. *Proverbs. Ecclesiastes*. Anchor Bible 18. Garden City, NY: Doubleday.

Seeger, Pete. 2003. *Turn! Turn! Turn!* Book and CD-ROM. New York: Simon & Schuster Children's Publishing.

Seow, C. L. 1997. *Ecclesiastes*. Anchor Bible. New York: Doubleday.

Serrano, J. J. 1954. "I Saw the Wicked Buried (Eccl 8,10)." *Catholic Biblical Quarterly* 16: 168–70.

Shead, Andrew G. 1997. "Reading Ecclesiastes 'Epilogically.'" *Tyndale Bulletin* 48: 67–92.

Shnider, Steven, and Lawrence Zalcman. 2003. "The Righteous Sage: Pleonasm or Oxymoron? (Kohelet 7, 16–18)." *Zeitschrift Für Die Alttestamentliche Wissenschaft* 115 (3): 435–39.

Stuart, Moses. 1851. *A Commentary on Ecclesiastes*. New York: Putnam.

Taylor, C. 1874. *The Dirge of Coheleth in Ecclesiastes XII.* London:
Williams & Norgate.

Thompson, Richard L. 1977. *Demonstration by Information Theory that
Life Cannot Arise from Matter.* Bhaktivedanta Institute Monograph
Series 2. Boston: Bhaktivedanta Institute.

———. 1981. *Mechanistic and Nonmechanistic Science.* Los Angeles:
Bhaktivedanta Book Trust.

Tucker, Gordon. 2001. "Sacrifices." In *Etz Hayim "Torah and
Commentary,"* edited by David L. Lieber and Jules Harlow, 1446–50.
New York: Jewish Publication Society.

Van Leeuwen, Raymond C. 2001. "We Really Do Need Another Bible
Translation." *Christianity Today* 45 (13) (October 22): 28–35.

Vasu, Śrīśa Chandra, trans. 1912. *The Vedānta-Sūtras of Bādarāyaṇa:
With the Commentary of Baladeva.* Bahadurganj: Pāṇini Office,
Bhuvaneśwarī Āśrama.

Waldman, Nahum M. 1979. "The *Dābār Raʻ* of Eccl 8:3." *Journal of
Biblical Literature* 98 (3): 407–8.

Weeks, Stuart. 2013. "'Fear God and Keep His Commandments': Could
Qohelet Have Said This?" In *Wisdom and Torah: The Reception of
"Torah" in the Wisdom Literature of the Second Temple Period*, edited by
Bernd U. Schipper and D. Andrew Teeter, 101–18. Supplements to
the Journal for the Study of Judaism 163. Leiden: Brill.

Whybray, R. Norman. 1982. "Qoheleth, Preacher of Joy." *Journal for the
Study of the Old Testament* 23: 87–98.

———. 1989. *Ecclesiastes.* New Century Bible Commentary. Grand
Rapids, MI: Eerdmans.

Wolf, David B. 1998. "The Vedic Personality Inventory – A Study of the
Gunas." *Journal of Indian Psychology* 16 (1): 26–43.

———. 1999. "A Psychometric Analysis of the Three Gunas."
Psychological Reports 84: 1379–90.

Wright, Addison G. 1968. "The Riddle of the Sphinx." *Catholic Biblical
Quarterly* 30 (3): 313–34.

———. 1980. "The Riddle of the Sphinx Revisited: Numerical Patterns in
the Book of Qoheleth." *Catholic Biblical Quarterly* 42 (1): 38–51.

Zlotowitz, Meir, and Nosson Scherman. 1994. *Ecclesiastes.* New York:
Mesorah.

Index

Page numbers in **bold** refer to the text of Ecclesiastes.
The letter *a* or *b* after a number indicates an endnote
in the first or second column.